Praise for the First Edition of
Corporate Governance Matters

"No board of directors ought to be without Larcker and Tayan's *Corporate Governance Matters*. In today's increasingly regulated environment, this comprehensive book is not only an important reference manual, but also an interesting read and a valuable roadmap."

—**Joel Peterson**, Chairman, JetBlue Airways,
and former Lead Director, Franklin Covey

"An outstanding work of unique breadth and depth providing practical advice supported by detailed research. This should be required reading for all board members and everyone who serves as an advisor to boards."

—**Alan Crain, Jr.**, Senior Vice President and General Counsel,
Baker Hughes Incorporated

"*Corporate Governance Matters* is by far and away the most useful, fact-based book on corporate governance available. It is essential reading for all current and prospective board members, anyone interested in how boards work, and for students of corporate governance. Its chapters on executive and equity pay, in particular, shine a bright light on a topic too often discussed without substance and context."

—**Mark H. Edwards**, Chairman and CEO, Compensia

"The complexity of corporate governance often lies in its propensity to become highly subjective. David and Brian's objective and unbiased approach to this important subject is very refreshing. This book reflects the meticulous and thorough manner in which the authors have approached corporate governance systems. They have an eye for detail and present every statement and observation with a firm factual foundation. Extensively researched, with highly relevant insights, this book serves as an ideal and practical reference for corporate executives and students of business administration."

—**Narayana N.R. Murthy**, Infosys Technologies Limited

"*Corporate Governance Matters* should be on the reading list for any public or private company director. The authors present comprehensive coverage of current topics using both research and real-world examples to drive home the issues and uncover the best practices. I found their survey of foreign practices and cultural differences to be particularly fascinating and helpful as I work with one of my companies on an offshore partnership. Fascinating, engaging, and full of useful information—a must-read!"

—**Heidi Roizen**, Founder, CEO and Chief Lyrical Officer, Skinny Songs

"A tour de force. David Larcker and Brian Tayan have written an easy-to-read, crucial-to-know overview of corporate governance today. Powerfully blending real-world cases with the newest scientific research, *Corporate Governance Matters* identifies fundamental governance concerns that every board and shareholder needs to know about. The book also provides a valuable, real-world discussion of succession planning and the labor market for executives. If you really want to know about corporate governance (as opposed to following media pundits and governance rating firms), you must read this book!"

—**Stephen A. Miles**, Founder and CEO, The Miles Group

"They did it! Larcker and Tayan have cracked the code on the connections between corporate governance and corporate performance. Debunking lots of myths along the way, they give practical advice on what works and what doesn't. Their chapters on board composition and executive pay capture the challenge to directors to manage corporations in the best interests of shareholders. This is a must-read for anyone who is interested in improving the performance of corporations."

—**Ira Kay**, Managing Partner, Pay Governance

"When it comes to corporate governance, it seems that everyone has an opinion. David Larcker and Brian Tayan, however, have the facts. This refreshing, hard-headed review describes what we do and don't know about corporate governance.
It lays bare assumptions about governance that simply aren't correct and is destined to become a central reference for anyone interested in how corporate America governs itself."

—**Professor Joseph A. Grundfest**, The William A. Franke Professor of Law and Business,
Senior Faculty, Rock Center on Corporate Governance,
Stanford Law School

Corporate Governance Matters

Second Edition

Corporate Governance Matters

A Closer Look at Organizational Choices and Their Consequences

Second Edition

David Larcker
Brian Tayan

Publisher: Paul Boger
Editor-in-Chief: Amy Neidlinger
Executive Editor: Jeanne Levine
Cover Designer: Chuti Prasertsith
Managing Editor: Kristy Hart
Senior Project Editor: Lori Lyons
Copy Editor: Kitty Wilson
Proofreader: Paula Lowell
Indexer: Erika Millen
Senior Compositor: Gloria Schurick
Manufacturing Buyer: Dan Uhrig

This book is sold with the understanding that neither the author nor the publisher is engaged in rendering legal, accounting, or other professional services or advice by publishing this book. Each individual situation is unique. Thus, if legal or financial advice or other expert assistance is required in a specific situation, the services of a competent professional should be sought to ensure that the situation has been evaluated carefully and appropriately. The author and the publisher disclaim any liability, loss, or risk resulting directly or indirectly, from the use or application of any of the contents of this book.

For information about buying this title in bulk quantities, or for special sales opportunities (which may include electronic versions; custom cover designs; and content particular to your business, training goals, marketing focus, or branding interests), please contact our corporate sales department at corpsales@pearsoned.com or (800) 382-3419.

For government sales inquiries, please contact governmentsales@pearsoned.com.

For questions about sales outside the U.S., please contact international@pearsoned.com.

Company and product names mentioned herein are the trademarks or registered trademarks of their respective owners.

Printed in the United States of America

Second Printing February 2016

ISBN-10: 0-13-403156-3
ISBN-13: 978-0-13-403156-9

Pearson Education LTD.
Pearson Education Australia PTY, Limited.
Pearson Education Singapore, Pte. Ltd.
Pearson Education Asia, Ltd.
Pearson Education Canada, Ltd.
Pearson Educación de Mexico, S.A. de C.V.
Pearson Education—Japan
Pearson Education Malaysia, Pte. Ltd.

Library of Congress Control Number: 2015939612

To Sally, Sarah, and Daniel,
Jack, Louise, and Brad

Contents-at-a-Glance

Contents

Acknowledgments

First and foremost, we would like to thank Michelle E. Gutman of the Stanford Graduate School of Business, without whom this book would not have been possible. Michelle provided incredible support throughout this project and was instrumental at each step of the way, from concept and outline, to research, editing, and production. Her incredible work ethic and positive attitude are a model that researchers should strive to emulate, and our work and lives have been greatly enhanced because of her.

We would also like to thank the many experts who provided insight, commentary, and feedback to this work. In particular, we would like to thank Michael Klausner (Stanford Law School), who was invaluable in clarifying legal constructs—particularly those described in Chapter 3, "Board of Directors: Duties and Liability," and Chapter 11, "The Market for Corporate Control." Priya Cherian Huskins (Woodruff-Sawyer & Co) was similarly invaluable in clarifying indemnifications and D&O insurance. Stephen Miles (The Miles Group), and Thomas Friel (Heidrick & Struggles) provided real-world insight into CEO succession planning, the executive recruitment process, and the labor market for directors. Ira Kay (Proxy Governance) provided important contextual understanding of executive compensation. Abe Friedman (CamberView Partners) helped us understand proxy voting from an institutional investor perspective.

The factual depth of this book would not have been possible without the generous resources made available to us by Stanford University. We would like to extend a special thank you to Arthur and Toni Rembi Rock for their generous funding of governance research through the Rock Center for Corporate Governance at Stanford University. We have been greatly enriched through the collaboration this center has allowed, particularly with our colleagues Robert Daines, Joseph Grundfest, Daniel Siciliano, and Evan Epstein. Thank you also to Dean Garth Saloner of Stanford Graduate School of Business for his support of the Corporate Governance Research Initiative. We appreciate the resources and collaboration provided by Wendy York-Fess and our colleagues in the Centers and Initiatives for Research, Curriculum & Learning Experiences (CIRLCE) at Stanford Graduate School of Business. We would also like to thank David Chun and Aaron Boyd (Equilar) for providing some of the compensation data used in the book.

We are grateful to Christopher Armstrong, Maria Correia, Ian Gow, Allan McCall, Gaizka Ormazabal, Daniel Taylor, Youfei Xiao, Anastasia Zakolyukina, and Christina Zhu for their excellent assistance and thoughtful conversations about corporate governance. They also tolerated the idiosyncrasies of the lead author, for which he is particularly thankful.

Thank you to Sally Larcker for her rigorous and methodical editing of this work as we approached publication, and to Jeannine Williams for her diligent assistance throughout this project.

We are grateful to the high-quality support provided by Jeanne Levine, Lori Lyons, Kitty Wilson, Paula Lowell, and others at Pearson. We would like to thank Stephen Kobrin for encouraging us to write this book.

Finally, thank you to our families—Sally, Sarah, Dan, Amy, and Alexa—who love and support us each day.

About the Authors

David Larcker is James Irvin Miller Professor of Accounting at Stanford Graduate School of Business; Director of the Corporate Governance Research Initiative; and Senior Faculty, Arthur and Toni Rembe Rock Center for Corporate Governance. David's research focuses on executive compensation, corporate governance, and managerial accounting. He has published many research papers and is frequently quoted in both the popular and business press.

He received his BS and MS in engineering from the University of Missouri–Rolla and his PhD in business from the University of Kansas. He previously was on the faculty of the Kellogg Graduate School of Management at Northwestern University and The Wharton School at the University of Pennsylvania. Professor Larcker presently serves on the Board of Trustees for the Wells Fargo Advantage Funds.

Brian Tayan is a member of the Corporate Governance Research Initiative at Stanford Graduate School of Business. He has written broadly on the subject of corporate governance, including studies and other materials on boards of directors, succession planning, executive compensation, financial accounting, and shareholder relations.

Previously, Brian worked as a financial analyst at Stanford University's Office of the CEO and as an investment associate at UBS Private Wealth Management. He received his MBA from the Stanford Graduate School of Business and his BA from Princeton University.

Additional resources and supporting material for this book are available at:

Stanford Graduate School of Business
The Corporate Governance Research Initiative
www.gsb.stanford.edu/cgri-research

Preface

This is a book about corporate governance, written from an organizational perspective. It is intended for practitioners and aspiring practitioners who are interested in improving governance systems in their organizations. Unlike many other books on governance, this book is *not* written primarily from a legal perspective. Although we describe the legal obligations of selected organizational participants, our objective is not to rehash legal constructs. Books written by trained lawyers are much better for that purpose, and many fine works explain these obligations for the practitioner. Instead, our purpose is to examine the choices that organizations can make in designing governance systems and the impact those choices have on executive decision making and the organization's performance. This book is therefore relevant to corporate directors, executives, institutional investors, lawyers, and regulators who make organizational decisions.

Corporate governance is a topic that suffers from considerable rhetoric. In writing this book, we have attempted to correct many misconceptions. Rather than write a book that is based on opinion, we use the knowledge contained in the extensive body of professional and scholarly research to guide our discussion and justify our conclusions. This approach does not always lead to simple recommendations, but it has the advantage of being grounded in factual evidence. As you will see, not every governance question has been the subject of rigorous empirical study, nor is every question amenable to a simple solution. There are gaps in our knowledge that will need to be addressed by further study. Still, we hope this book provides a framework that enables practitioners to make sound decisions that are well supported by careful research.

In each chapter, we focus on a particular governance feature, describe its potential benefits and costs, review the research evidence, and then draw conclusions. Although the book is written so that it can be read from cover to cover, each chapter also stands on its own; readers can select the chapters that are most relevant to their interests (board structure, CEO succession planning, executive compensation, and so on). This book—along with our set of associated case studies and teaching materials—is also suitable for undergraduate and graduate university courses and executive education programs.

We believe it is important for organizations to take a deliberate approach in designing governance systems. We believe this book provides the information that allows them to do so.

1

Introduction to Corporate Governance

Corporate governance has become a well-discussed and controversial topic in both the popular press and business press. Newspapers produce detailed accounts of corporate fraud, accounting scandals, insider trading, excessive compensation, and other perceived organizational failures—many of which culminate in lawsuits, resignations, and bankruptcy. The stories have run the gamut from the shocking and instructive (epitomized by Enron and the elaborate use of special-purpose entities and aggressive accounting to distort its financial condition) to the shocking and outrageous (epitomized by Tyco partially funding a $2.1 million birthday party in 2002 for the wife of Chief Executive Officer [CEO] Dennis Kozlowski that included a vodka-dispensing replica of the statue *David*). Central to these stories is the assumption that somehow *corporate governance* is to blame—that is, the system of checks and balances meant to prevent abuse by executives failed (see the following sidebar).[1]

A Breakdown in Corporate Governance: HealthSouth

Consider HealthSouth Corp., the once high-flying healthcare service provider based in Birmingham, Alabama.[2]

- CEO Richard Scrushy and other corporate officers were accused of overstating earnings by at least $1.4 billion between 1999 and 2002 to meet analyst expectations.[3]

- The CEO was paid a salary of $4.0 million, awarded a cash bonus of $6.5 million, and granted 1.2 million stock options during fiscal 2001, the year before the manipulation was uncovered.[4]

- The CEO sold back 2.5 million shares to the company—94 percent of his total holdings—just weeks before the firm revealed that regulatory changes would significantly hurt earnings, causing the company's share price to plummet.[5]

- Former Chief Financial Officer (CFO) Weston L. Smith and other senior executives pleaded guilty to a scheme to artificially inflate financial results.[6]

- The CEO was found guilty of civil charges brought by shareholders in a derivative lawsuit and ordered to pay the company $2.88 billion in restitution.[7]

What was the board of directors doing during this period?

- The compensation committee met only *once* during 2001.[8]
- *Forbes* wrote that the CEO has "provided subpar returns to shareholders while earning huge sums for [himself]. Still, the board doesn't toss [him] out."[9]

What was the external auditor (Ernst & Young) doing?

- The audit committee met only *once* during 2001.[10]
- The president and CFO both previously were employed as auditors for Ernst & Young.
- The company paid Ernst & Young $2.5 million in consulting and other fees while also paying $1.2 million for auditing services.[11]

What were the analysts doing?

- A UBS analyst had a "strong buy" recommendation on HealthSouth.
- UBS earned $7 million in investment banking fees for services provided to the company.[12]

Perhaps not surprisingly, the CEO also received backdated stock options during his tenure—stock options whose grant dates were retroactively changed to coincide with low points in the company's stock price (see Figure 1.1).

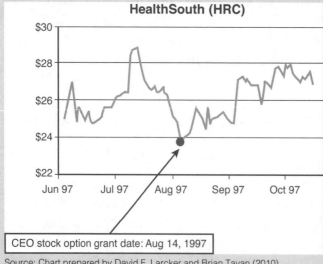

Source: Chart prepared by David F. Larcker and Brian Tayan (2010).

Figure 1.1   HealthSouth: CEO stock option grant date.

Interestingly, Scrushy was not convicted of accounting manipulations in a criminal trial brought by the U.S. Justice Department. However, he was ordered to pay $2.9 billion in a civil suit and, separately, was sentenced to seven years in prison for bribing a former Alabama governor.

As the case of HealthSouth illustrates, the system of checks and balances meant to prevent abuse by senior executives does not always function properly. Unfortunately, governance failures are not isolated instances. In recent years, several corporations have collapsed in prominent fashion, including American International Group, Bear Stearns, Countrywide Financial, Enron, Fannie Mae, Freddie Mac, General Motors, Lehman Brothers, MF Global, and WorldCom. This list does not even include the dozens of lesser-known companies that did not make the front page of the *Wall Street Journal* or *Financial Times* but whose owners also suffered. Furthermore, this problem is not limited to U.S. corporations. Major international companies such as Olympus, Parmalat, Petrobras, Royal Bank of Scotland, Royal Dutch Shell, Satyam, and Siemens have all been plagued by scandals involving breakdowns of management oversight. Foreign companies listed on U.S. exchanges are as likely to restate their financial results as domestic companies, indicating that governance is a global issue (see the following sidebar).

A Breakdown in International Corporate Governance: Olympus

In October 2011, Michael Woodford was fired as CEO of Olympus Corporation of Japan, after only two weeks in the position. Woodford uncovered evidence of fraud while investigating the legitimacy of a $687 million "advisory fee" made in association with a recent acquisition. When he confronted the board of directors, he was dismissed and replaced by former CEO Tsuyoshi Kikukawa. An independent investigation eventually exposed the details of a massive, long-running scheme to hide more than $1.5 billion in investment losses dating back to the 1980s.[13] Members of the board, current and former executives, auditors, and bankers were implicated. Kikukawa was arrested and sentenced to three years in prison.

Self-Interested Executives

What is the root cause of these failures? Reports suggest that these companies suffered from a "breakdown in corporate governance." What does that mean? What is corporate governance, and what is it expected to prevent?

In theory, the need for corporate governance rests on the idea that when separation exists between the ownership of a company and its management, self-interested executives have the opportunity to take actions that benefit themselves, with shareholders and stakeholders bearing the cost of these actions.[14] This scenario is typically referred to as the **agency problem**, with the costs resulting from this problem described as **agency costs**. Executives make investment, financing, and operating decisions that better themselves at the expense of other parties related to the firm.[15] To lessen agency costs, some type of control or monitoring system is put in place in the organization. That system of checks and balances is called **corporate governance**.

Behavioral psychology and other social sciences have provided evidence that individuals are self-interested. In *The Economic Approach to Human Behavior,* Gary Becker (1976) applies a theory of "rational self-interest" to economics to explain human tendencies, including one to commit crime or fraud.[16] He demonstrates that, in a wide variety of settings, individuals can take actions to benefit themselves without detection and, therefore, avoid the cost of punishment. Control mechanisms are put in place in society to deter such behavior by increasing the probability of detection and shifting the risk–reward balance so that the expected payoff from crime is decreased.

Before we rely on this theory too heavily, it is important to highlight that individuals are not always uniformly and completely self-interested. Many people exhibit self-restraint on moral grounds that have little to do with economic rewards. Not all employees who are unobserved in front of an open cash box will steal from it, and not all executives knowingly make decisions that better themselves at the expense of shareholders. This is known as **moral salience**, the knowledge that certain actions are inherently wrong even if they are undetected and left unpunished. Individuals exhibit varying degrees of moral salience, depending on their personality, religious convictions, and personal and financial circumstances. Moral salience also depends on the company involved, the country of business, and the cultural norms.[17]

The need for a governance control mechanism to discourage costly, self-interested behavior therefore depends on the size of the potential agency costs, the ability of the control mechanism to mitigate agency costs, and the cost of implementing the control mechanism (see the following sidebar).

Evidence of Self-Interested Behavior

How prevalent are agency problems? Are they outlier events or an epidemic affecting the broad population? How severe are agency costs? Are they chronic and frictional or terminal and catastrophic?

To gain some insight into these questions, it is useful to consider the frequency of negative corporate events that, in whole or in part, are correlated with agency problems. However, before looking at the statistics, we also need to highlight that not all bad outcomes are caused by self-seeking behavior. A bad outcome might well occur even though the managerial decision was appropriate (that is, other management might have made the same decision when provided with the same information). With that important caveat, consider the following descriptive statistics:

- **Bankruptcy**—Between 2004 and 2013, 1,118 publicly traded companies filed for Chapter 11 bankruptcy protection in the United States.[18] Of these, approximately 10 percent were subject to a Securities and Exchange Commission (SEC) enforcement action for violating SEC or federal rules, implying that some form of fraud played a part in the bankruptcy.[19] Bankruptcies linked to fraud are a severe case of agency problems, usually resulting in a complete loss of capital for shareholders and a significant loss for creditors.

- **Financial restatement**—Between 2005 and 2012, publicly traded companies in the United States issued 8,657 financial restatements. Although some financial restatements result from honest procedural errors in applying accounting standards, financial restatements also can occur when senior management manipulates reported earnings for personal gain. According to the Center for Audit Quality, approximately half of the restatements announced during this period were "serious," meaning that the company's previously published financial reports were no longer reliable.[20]

- **Class action lawsuits**—Between 2004 and 2013, almost 200 class action lawsuits were filed annually against corporate officers and directors for securities fraud. No doubt some of this litigation was frivolous. However, market capitalization losses for defendant firms totaled approximately $110 billion each year (measured as the change in market capitalization during the class period). This somewhat crude approximation averages $640 million per company (see Figure 1.2).

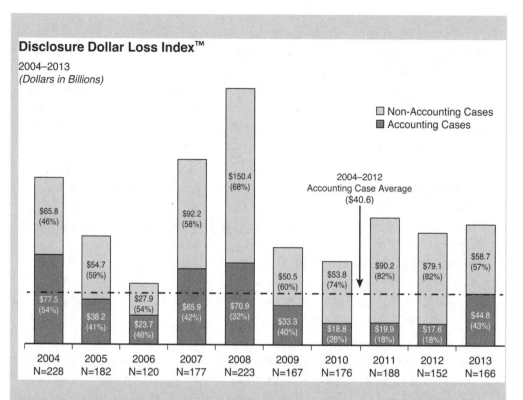

Disclosure Dollar Loss Index™

2004–2013
(Dollars in Billions)

Source: Cornerstone Research, Stanford Law School, Securities Class Action Clearinghouse, "Security Class Action Filings: 2013 Year In Review."

Figure 1.2 Annual number of class action filings and stock market loss following disclosure of lawsuit (2004–2013).

- **Foreign Corrupt Practices Act violations**—The Foreign Corrupt Practices Act (FCPA) of 1977 makes it illegal for a company to offer payments to foreign officials for the purpose of obtaining or retaining business, to fail to keep accurate records of transactions, or to fail to maintain effective controls to detect potential violations of the FCPA. Between 2004 and 2013, the SEC and the U.S. Department of Justice filed approximately 30 enforcement actions per year against U.S. listed corporations for alleged FCPA violations. Notably, this figure has trended upward. Violations are settled through a disgorgement of profits and other penalties. In 2013, the average settlement amount came to $80 million per violation.[21]

- **"Massaging" earnings**—Senior executives are under considerable pressure from the investment community to forecast future earnings and then to deliver on those targets. In a survey of senior financial executives, Graham,

Harvey, and Rajgopal (2006) found that a majority are willing to massage the company's earnings to meet quarterly forecasts.[22] For example, 55 percent state that they would delay starting a new project, even if the project is expected to create long-term value. Separately, respondents were given a scenario in which initiating a new project would cause earnings per share in the current quarter to come in $0.10 lower. The respondents reported an 80 percent probability that they would accept the project if doing so enabled them to still meet their earnings target but only a 60 percent probability if the project caused them to miss their earnings target.

These statistics suggest that agency problems caused by self-interested executives are likely to be quite prevalent, and the cost of managerial self-interest can be substantial. Dyck, Morse, and Zingales (2013) estimate a 14.5 percent probability that an average company engages in fraud in a given year and that, when uncovered, fraud costs investors 22 percent of the firm's enterprise value.[23]

Certain behavior attributes are known by the Association of Certified Fraud Examiners to be "red flags" displayed by fraudulent agents. These include living beyond one's means (44 percent of fraud cases), financial difficulties (33 percent), unusually close association with vendors (22 percent), control issues and a lack of willingness to share duties (21 percent), a "wheeler dealer" attitude (18 percent), divorce or family problems (17 percent), irritability or suspiciousness (15 percent), and addiction problems (12 percent). Other red flags include complaints about inadequate pay; previous employment problems; refusal to take vacations; excessive organizational pressure; social isolation; and other financial, legal, or personal stresses.[24]

Defining Corporate Governance

We define **corporate governance** as the collection of control mechanisms that an organization adopts to prevent or dissuade potentially self-interested managers from engaging in activities detrimental to the welfare of shareholders and stakeholders. At a minimum, the monitoring system consists of a board of directors to oversee management and an external auditor to express an opinion on the reliability of financial statements. In most cases, however, governance systems are influenced by a much broader group of constituents, including owners of the firm, creditors, labor unions, customers, suppliers, investment analysts, the media, and regulators (see Figure 1.3).

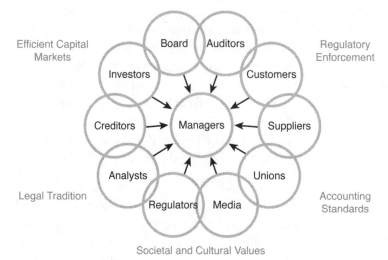

Societal and Cultural Values

Source: Chart prepared by David F. Larcker and Brian Tayan (2011).

Figure 1.3   Selected determinants and participants in corporate governance systems.

For a governance system to be economically efficient, it should decrease agency costs more than the costs of implementation. However, because implementation costs are greater than zero, even the best corporate governance system will not make the cost of the agency problem disappear completely.

The structure of the governance system also depends on the fundamental orientation of the firm and the role that the firm plays in society. From a **shareholder perspective** (the viewpoint that the primary obligation of the organization is to maximize shareholder value), effective corporate governance should increase the value of equity holders by better aligning incentives between management and shareholders. From a **stakeholder perspective** (the viewpoint that the organization has a societal obligation beyond increasing shareholder value), effective governance should support policies that produce stable and safe employment, provide an acceptable standard of living to workers, mitigate risk for debt holders, and improve the community and environment.[25] Obviously, the governance system that maximizes shareholder value might not be the same as the one that maximizes stakeholder value.

A broad set of external forces that vary across nations also influence the structure of the governance system. These include the efficiency of local capital markets, legal tradition, reliability of accounting standards, regulatory enforcement, and societal and cultural values. These forces serve as an external disciplining mechanism on managerial behavior. Their relative effectiveness determines the extent to which additional monitoring mechanisms are required.

Finally, any system of corporate governance involves third parties that are linked with the company but do not have a direct ownership stake. These include regulators (such as the SEC), politicians, the external auditor, security analysts, external legal counsel, employees and unions, proxy advisory firms, customers, suppliers, and other similar participants. Third parties might be subject to their own agency issues that compromise their ability to work solely in the interest of the company. For example, the external auditor is employed by an accounting firm that seeks to improve its own financial condition; when the accounting firm also provides nonaudit services, the auditor *might* be confronted with conflicting objectives. Likewise, security analysts are employed by investment firms that serve both institutional and retail clients; when the analyst covers a company that is also a client of the investment firm, the analyst might face added pressure by his firm to publish positive comments about the company that are misleading to shareholders. These types of conflicts can contribute to a breakdown in oversight of management activity.

Corporate Governance Standards

There are no universally agreed-upon standards that determine good governance. Still, this has not stopped blue-ribbon panels from recommending uniform standards to market participants. For example, in December 1992, the Cadbury Committee— commissioned by the accountancy profession and London Stock Exchange "to help raise the standards of corporate governance and the level of confidence in financial reporting and auditing"—issued a *Code of Best Practices* that, in many ways, provided a benchmark set of recommendations on governance.[26] Key recommendations included separating the chairman of the board and chief executive officer titles, appointing independent directors, reducing conflicts of interest at the board level because of business or other relationships, convening an independent audit committee, and reviewing the effectiveness of the company's internal controls. These standards set the basis for listing requirements on the London Stock Exchange and were largely adopted by the New York Stock Exchange (NYSE). However, compliance with these standards has not always translated into effective governance. For example, Enron was compliant with NYSE requirements, including requirements to have a majority of independent directors and fully independent audit and compensation committees, yet it still failed along many legal and ethical dimensions.

Over time, a series of formal regulations and informal guidelines has been proposed to address perceived shortcomings in governance systems as they are exposed. One of the most important pieces of formal legislation relating to governance is the Sarbanes– Oxley Act of 2002 (SOX). Primarily a reaction to the failures of Enron and others, SOX mandated a series of requirements to improve corporate controls and reduce conflicts of interest. Importantly, CEOs and CFOs found to have made material misrepresentations in the financial statements are now subject to criminal penalties. Despite these efforts, corporate failures stemming from deficient governance systems continue. In 2005, Refco, a large U.S.-based foreign exchange and commodity broker, filed for bankruptcy after revealing that it had hidden $430 million in loans made to its CEO.[27] The disclosure came just two months after the firm raised $583 million in an initial public offering. That same year, mortgage guarantor Fannie Mae announced that it had overstated earnings by $6.3 billion because it had misapplied more than 20 accounting standards relating to loans, investment securities, and derivatives. Insufficient capital levels eventually led the company to seek conservatorship by the U.S. government.[28]

In 2009, Sen. Charles Schumer of New York proposed additional federal legislation to stem the tide of governance collapses. Known as the Shareholder's Bill of Rights, the proposal stipulated that companies adopt procedural changes designed to give shareholders greater influence over director elections and executive compensation. Requirements included a shift toward annual elections for all directors (thereby disallowing staggered or classified boards), a standard of majority voting for director elections (instead of plurality voting) in which directors in uncontested elections must resign if they do not receive a majority vote, the right for certain institutional shareholders to directly nominate board candidates on the company proxy (proxy access), the separation of the chairman and CEO roles, and the right for shareholders to have an advisory vote on executive compensation (say-on-pay). The 2010 Dodd–Frank Wall Street Reform and Consumer Protection Act subsequently adopted several of these recommendations, including say-on-pay. The interesting question is whether this legislation was a product of political expediency or based on rigorous theory and empirical research.[29]

Several third-party organizations, such as GMI Ratings and Institutional Shareholder Services (ISS), attempt to protect investors from inadequate corporate governance by publishing governance ratings on individual companies. These rating agencies use alphanumeric or numeric systems that rank companies according to a set of criteria that they believe measure governance effectiveness. Companies with high ratings are considered less risky and most likely to grow shareholder value. Companies with low ratings are considered more risky and have the highest potential for failure or fraud. However, the accuracy and predictive power of these ratings have not been demonstrated. Critics allege that ratings encourage a "check-the-box" approach to governance that overlooks important context. The potential shortcomings of these ratings were spotlighted in the case of HealthSouth. Before evidence of earnings manipulation was brought to light, the company had an ISS rating that placed it in the top 35 percent of Standard & Poor's 500 companies and the top 8 percent of its industry peers.[30]

Changes in the business environment further complicate attempts to identify uniform standards of governance. Some recent trends include the increased prominence of activist investors, private equity firms, and proxy advisory firms in the governance space:

- **Activist investors**—Institutional investors, hedge funds, and pension funds have become considerably more active in attempting to influence management and the board through public campaigns and the annual proxy voting process. Are the interests of these parties consistent with those of individual shareholders? Does public debate between these parties reflect a movement toward improved dialogue about corporate objectives and strategy? Or does it constitute an unnecessary intrusion by activists who have their own self-interested agendas?

- **Private equity firms**—Private equity firms implement governance systems that are considerably different from those at most public companies. Publicly owned companies must demonstrate independence at the board level, but private equity–owned companies operate with very low levels of independence (almost everyone on the board has a relationship to the company and has a vested interest in its operations). Private equity companies also offer extremely high compensation to senior executives, a practice that is criticized among public companies but that is strictly tied to the creation of economic value. Should public companies adopt certain aspects from the private equity model of governance? Would this produce more or less shareholder value?

- **Proxy advisory firms**—Recent SEC rules require that mutual funds disclose how they vote their annual proxies.[31] These rules have coincided with increased media attention on the voting process, which was previously considered a formality of little interest. Has the disclosure of voting improved corporate governance? At the same time, these rules have stimulated demand for commercial firms—such as ISS and Glass Lewis—to provide recommendations on how to vote on proxy proposals. What is the impact of shareholders relying on third parties to inform their voting decisions? Are the recommendations of these firms consistent with good governance?[32]

Best Practice or Best Practices? Does "One Size Fit All"?

It is highly unlikely that a single set of best practices exists for all firms, despite the attempts of some to impose uniform standards. Governance is a complex and dynamic system that involves the interaction of a diverse set of constituents, all of whom play roles in monitoring executive behavior. Because of this complexity, assessing the impact of a single component is difficult. Focusing an analysis on one or two mechanisms without considering the broader context can be a prescription for failure. For example, is it sufficient to insist that a company separate the chairman and CEO positions without considering who the CEO is and other structural, cultural, and governance features of the company?

Applying a "one-size-fits-all" approach to governance can lead to incorrect conclusions and is unlikely to substantially improve corporate performance. The standards most often associated with good governance might appear to be good ideas, but when applied universally, they can result in failure as often as in success. For example, consider the idea of board independence. Is a board consisting primarily of independent directors superior to a board composed entirely of internal directors? How should individual attributes such as business acumen, professional background, ethical standards of responsibility, level of engagement, relationship with the CEO, and reliance on director fees to maintain their standard of living factor into our analysis?[33] Personal attributes might influence independence of perspective more than predetermined standards.[34] However, these elements are rarely captured in regulatory requirements.[35]

In governance, context matters. A set of governance mechanisms that works well in one setting might prove disastrous in another. This situation becomes apparent when considering international governance systems. For example, Germany requires labor union representation on many corporate boards. How effective would such a system be in the United States? Japanese boards have few outside directors, and many of those who are outside directors come from banks that provide capital to the firm or key customers and suppliers. What would be the impact on Japanese companies if they were required to adopt the independence standards of the United States? These are difficult questions, but investors must consider them when deciding where to allocate their investment dollars.

Relationship between Corporate Governance and Firm Performance

According to a survey by McKinsey & Company, nearly 80 percent of institutional investors responded that they would pay a premium for a well-governed company. The size of the premium varied by market, ranging from 11 percent for a company in Canada to around 40 percent for a company in Morocco, Egypt, or Russia (see Figure 1.4).[36]

Premium for Good Governance

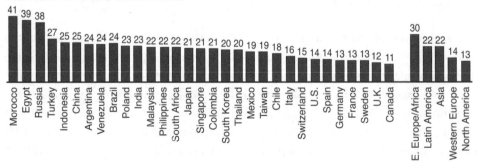

Source: Paul Coombes and Mark Watson, "Global Investor Opinion Survey 2002: Key Findings" McKinsey & Company (2002).

Figure 1.4   Indicated premiums for good corporate governance, by country.

These results imply that investors *perceive* well-governed companies to be better investments than poorly governed companies.[37] However, the extent to which this is true is not entirely clear.

As we will see throughout this book, many studies link measures of corporate governance with firm operating and stock price performance. Perhaps the most widely cited study was done by Gompers, Ishii, and Metrick (2003).[38] They found that companies that employ "shareholder-friendly" governance features significantly outperform companies that employ "shareholder unfriendly" governance features. This is an important research study, but as we will see in Chapter 13, "Corporate Governance Ratings," these results are not definitive. Currently, neither professionals nor researchers have produced a reliable litmus test that measures overall governance quality using a simple common tool.

The purpose of this book is to provide a basis for constructive debate among executives, directors, investors, regulators, and other constituents that have an important stake in the success of corporations. This book focuses on corporate governance from an *organizational* instead of purely *legal* perspective, with an emphasis on exploring the relationships between control mechanisms and their impact on mitigating agency costs and improving shareholder and stakeholder outcomes.

Each chapter examines a specific component of corporate governance and summarizes what is known and what remains unknown about the topic. We have taken an agnostic approach, with no agenda other than to "get the story straight." In each chapter, we provide an overview of the specific topic, a synthesis of the relevant research, and concrete examples that illustrate key points.[39] Sometimes the evidence is inconclusive (see the following sidebar). We hope that the combination of materials will help you arrive at intelligent insights. In particular, we hope to benefit the individuals who participate in corporate governance processes so that they can make informed decisions that benefit the organizations they serve.

Interpreting Empirical Research

Oliver Williamson, winner of the 2009 Nobel Prize in Economics, observed the following:

"I have no doubt that the economics of governance is influential in significant measure because it does speak to real-world phenomena and invites *empirical testing*. . . . All feasible forms of organizations are flawed, and . . . we need to understand the trade-offs that are going on, the factors that are responsible for using one form of governance rather than another, and the strengths and weaknesses that are associated with each of them."[40]

Still, the interpretation of empirical tests (academic or other) requires some understanding of their limitations:

1. The results cited in **empirical tests** are typically average results generated from the statistical analysis of large samples of firms. Large samples enable a researcher to identify trends that are generally prevalent across companies. However, they do not tell us what we can expect to find at a specific company. Case or field studies can help answer firm-specific questions, but their results are difficult to generalize because they are based on only a handful of firms that may not be typical of the general population of firms.

2. Empirical tests can identify associations or correlations between variables, but they do not generally demonstrate causality. This is a recurring problem in nonexperimental social science. If we observe a negative stock price return when a company adopts a governance change, it does not tell us that the change caused the stock price decline. It is possible that another (exogenous) factor might have been the cause. Ideally, we would control for this by observing what would have happened had another action been taken (the counterfactual outcome); however, this is impossible to observe. In corporate governance, we do not have the luxury of controlled samples. Still, competently generated empirical results are superior to guesswork or intuition.

3. The performance metrics that governance researchers typically use fall into two broad categories: operating metrics and stock price metrics. Operating metrics (such as return on assets and operating cash flow) are somewhat backward looking but are generally considered to provide insight into value changes within the firm. Stock price metrics are typically based on **abnormal** or **excess** returns (the so-called **alpha**, calculated as observed stock price returns minus the expected returns, given the risk of the stock). Assuming reasonably efficient markets, excess returns provide a measure of change in economic value for shareholders. The researcher must determine which metric is better for evaluating the question at hand. Presumably, studies based on stock price returns and operating performance should provide similar results.

4. Another metric that is commonly used in governance research is the market-to-book ratio (sometimes referred to as **Tobin's Q** or simply **Q**). Q is based on the theory that a firm with superior performance will trade in the market at a valuation that is higher than the accounting value of its net assets. While this may be somewhat true, we view Q to be an ambiguous measure of firm

performance and inferior to traditional operating metrics and excess stock price returns.[41]

5. We sometimes refer to **event studies**. Event studies measure the stock market's reaction to news or events. These studies have validity only to the extent that the reader believes that markets are at least partly efficient. Even if so, event studies cannot easily control for confounding events (such as other news released by the company during the measurement period). Moreover, event studies require the researcher to make important risk adjustments when computing excess stock returns. Although several risk adjustments have become "accepted," their computation is complex, and it is difficult to know whether the researcher made them properly.

Endnotes

1. Some material in this chapter is adapted from David F. Larcker and Brian Tayan, "Models of Corporate Governance: Who's the Fairest of Them All?" Stanford GSB Case No. CG 11, January 15, 2008. Accessed April 24, 2015. See http://www.gsb.stanford.edu/faculty-research/case-studies/models-corporate-governance-whos-fairest-them-all.

2. See Aaron Beam and Chris Warner, *HealthSouth: The Wagon to Disaster* (Fairhope, AL: Wagon Publishing, 2009).

3. Lisa Fingeret Roth, "HealthSouth CFO Admits Fraud Charges," FT.com (March 26, 2003).

4. HealthSouth Corporation, Form DEF 14A, filed with the Securities and Exchange Commission May 16, 2002.

5. *In re: HealthSouth Corporation Bondholder Litigation*. United States District Court Northern District of Alabama Southern Division. Master File No. CV-03-BE-1500-S.

6. Chad Terhune and Carrick Mollenkamp, "HealthSouth Officials May Sign Plea Agreements—Moves by Finance Executives Would Likely Help Build Criminal Case against CEO," *Wall Street Journal* (March 26, 2003, Eastern edition): A.14.

7. Carrick Mollenkamp, "Some of Scrushy's Lawyers Ask Others on Team for Money Back," *Wall Street Journal* (December 17, 2003, Eastern edition): A.16.

8. HealthSouth Corporation, Form DEF 14A.

9. Dan Ackman, "CEO Compensation for Life?" Forbes.com (April 25, 2002). Accessed November 16, 2010. www.forbes.com/2002/04/25/0425ceotenure.html.

10. HealthSouth Corporation, Form DEF 14A. See also Jonathan Weil and Cassell Bryan-Low, "Questioning the Books: Audit Committee Met Only Once During 2001," *Wall Street Journal* (March 21, 2003, Eastern edition): A.2.

11. HealthSouth Corporation, Form DEF 14A.

12. Ken Brown and Robert Frank, "Analyst's Bullishness on HealthSouth's Stock Didn't Waver," *Wall Street Journal* (April 4, 2003, Eastern edition): C.1.

13. Olympus Corporation, "Investigation Report, Third Party Committee" (December 6, 2011). Accessed April 24, 2015. See http://www.olympus-global.com/en/common/pdf/if111206corpe_2.pdf.

14. This issue was the basis of the classic discussion in Adolph Berle and Gardiner Means, *The Modern Corporation and Private Property* (New York: Harcourt, Brace, and World, 1932).

15. The phrase **rent extraction** is another commonly used term for agency costs and refers to economic costs taken out of the system without any corresponding contribution in productivity.

16. Gary Becker, *The Economic Approach to Human Behavior* (Chicago: University of Chicago Press, 1976).

17. For example, a study by Boivie, Lange, McDonald, and Westphal found that CEOs who strongly identify with their company are less likely to accept expensive perquisites or make other decisions that are at odds with shareholder interests. See Steven Boivie, Donald Lange, Michael L. McDonald, and James D. Westphal, "Me or We: The Effects of CEO Organizational Identification of Agency Costs," *Academy of Management Proceedings* (2009): 1–6.

18. Bankruptcydata.com, "2013 Public Company Bankruptcy Filings Annual Report," New Generation Research, Inc. (2013). Accessed April 24, 2015. See http://www.bankruptcydata.com/bankruptcyyearinreview_form.htm.

19. Enforcement actions are measured as the number of Accounting and Auditing Enforcement Releases (AAER) by the SEC. The SEC issues an AAER for alleged violations of SEC and federal rules. Academic researchers have used AAER as a proxy for severe fraud because most companies that commit financial statement fraud receive SEC enforcement actions. Deloitte, "Ten Things about Bankruptcy and Fraud: A Review of Bankruptcy Filings," (2008). Accessed April 24, 2015. See http://bankruptcyfraud.typepad.com/Deloitte_Report.pdf.

20. Susan Scholz, "Financial Restatement Trends in the United States: 2003–2012," Center for Audit Quality. Accessed April 24, 2015. See http://www.thecaq.org/docs/reports-and-publications/financial-restatement-trends-in-the-united-states-2003-2012.pdf?sfvrsn=2/financial-restatement-trends-in-the-united-states-2003-2012.

21. Gibson Dunn, "2013 Year-End FCPA Update," (2013). Accessed April 24, 2015. See www.gibsondunn.com/publications/pages/2013-Year-End-FCPA-Update.aspx.

22. John Graham, Campbell Harvey, and Shiva Rajgopal, "Value Destruction and Financial Reporting Decisions," *Financial Analysts Journal* 62 (2006): 27–39.

23. I. J. Alexander Dyck, Adair Morse, and Luigi Zingales, "How Pervasive Is Corporate Fraud?" Rotman School of Management Working Paper No. 2222608, *Social Science Research Network* (2013). Accessed April 24, 2015. See http://ssrn.com/abstract=2222608.

24. Association of Certified Fraud Examiners, "Report to the Nations on Occupational Fraud and Abuse: 2014 Global Fraud Survey" (2014). Accessed March 25, 2015. See http://www.acfe.com/rttn-red-flags.aspx.

25. The cost–benefit assessment of a governance system also depends on whether the company operates under a shareholder-centric or stakeholder-centric model. The fundamentally different orientations of these models makes it difficult for an outside observer to compare their effectiveness. For example, a decision to maximize shareholder value might come at the cost of the

employee and environmental objectives of stakeholders, but comparing these costs is not easy. We discuss this more in Chapter 2, "International Corporate Governance."

26. Cadbury Committee, *Report of the Committee on the Financial Aspects of Corporate Governance* (London: Gee, 1992).

27. Deborah Solomon, Carrick Mollenkamp, Peter A. McKay, and Jonathan Weil, "Refco's Debts Started with Several Clients; Bennett Secretly Intervened to Assume Some Obligations; Return of Victor Niederhoffer," *Wall Street Journal* (October 21, 2005, Eastern edition): C.1.

28. James R. Hagerty, "Politics & Economics: Fannie Mae Moves toward Resolution with Restatement," *Wall Street Journal* (December 7, 2006, Eastern edition) A.4. Damian Paletta, "Fannie Sues KPMG for $2 Billion over Costs of Accounting Issues," *Wall Street Journal* (December 13, 2006, Eastern edition): A.16.

29. A study by Larcker, Ormazabal, and Taylor found that the legislative provisions in Schumer and Dodd–Frank are associated with negative stock price returns for affected companies. These results seemed to have little impact on the congressional debate. Similarly, the legislators who drafted the Sarbanes–Oxley Act of 2002 did not take into account research literature. See David F. Larcker, Gaizka Ormazabal, and Daniel J. Taylor, "The Market Reaction to Corporate Governance Regulation," *Journal of Financial Economics* 101 (2011): 431–448; and Roberta Romano, "The Sarbanes–Oxley Act and the Making of Quack Corporate Governance," *Yale Law Journal* 114 (2005): 1521–1612.

30. Cited in Jeffrey Sonnenfeld, "Good Governance and the Misleading Myths of Bad Metrics," *Academy of Management Executive* 18 (2004): 108–113.

31. Legal Information Institute, "17 CFR 270.30b1-4 - Report of proxy voting record," Cornell University Law School. Accessed April 24, 2015. See https://www.law.cornell.edu/cfr/text/17/270.30b1-4. See also "Report of Proxy Voting, Record Disclosure of Proxy Voting Policies, and Proxy Voting Records by Registered Management Investment Companies," Securities and Exchange Commission: 17 CFR Parts 239, 249, 270, and 274 Release Nos. 33-8188, 34-47304, IC-25922; File No. S7-36-02. Accessed April 24, 2015. See http://www.sec.gov/rules/final/33-8188.htm.

32. See David F. Larcker and Allan L. McCall, "Proxy Advisers Don't Help Shareholders," *Wall Street Journal* (December 9, 2013, Eastern edition), A.17.

33. The NYSE acknowledges this risk. See Chapters 3, "Board of Directors: Duties and Liability," and 5, "Board of Directors: Structure and Consequences," for more detailed discussion of board independence.

34. Sonnenfeld (2004) wrote, "At least as important are the human dynamics of boards as social systems where leadership character, individual values, decision-making processes, conflict management, and strategic thinking will truly differentiate a firm's governance."

35. Milton Harris and Artur Ravi, "A Theory of Board Control and Size," *Review of Financial Studies* 21 (2008): 1797–1831.

36. Paul Coombes and Mark Watson, "Global Investor Opinion Survey 2002: Key Findings," McKinsey & Co. (2002). Accessed April 2, 2015. See http://www.eiod.org/uploads/Publications/Pdf/II-Rp-4-1.pdf.

37. This is what investors said they would do when asked in a formal survey. However, this study does not provide evidence that investors actually pay this premium when making investment decisions.

38. Paul Gompers, Joy Ishii, and Andrew Metrick, "Corporate Governance and Equity Prices," *Quarterly Journal of Economics* 118 (2003): 107–156.

39. We are not attempting to provide a complete and comprehensive review of the research literature. Our goal is to select specific papers that provide a fair reflection of general research results.

40. Emphasis added. Nobel Prize Organization, "Oliver E. Williamson—Interview" (2009). Accessed April 24, 2015. See http://nobelprize.org/nobel_prizes/economics/laureates/2009/williamson-telephone.html.

41. For a discussion of the limitations of Tobin's Q as a measure of firm performance, see Philip H. Dybvig and Mitch Warachka, "Tobin's Q Does Not Measure Firm Performance: Theory, Empirics, and Alternative Measures," *Social Science Research Network* (March 2015). Accessed April 24, 2015. See http://ssrn.com/abstract=1562444.

2

International Corporate Governance

In Chapter 1, "Introduction to Corporate Governance," we defined *corporate governance* as the collection of control mechanisms that an organization adopts to prevent or dissuade potentially self-interested managers from engaging in activities detrimental to the welfare of shareholders and stakeholders. The governance system that a company adopts is not independent of its environment. A variety of factors inherent to the business setting shape the governance system. These factors include the following:

- Efficiency of local capital markets
- Extent to which the legal system provides protection to all shareholders
- Reliability of accounting standards
- Enforcement of regulations
- Societal and cultural values

Differences in these factors have important implications for the prevalence and severity of agency problems and the type of governance mechanisms required to monitor and control managerial self-interested behavior.

In this chapter, we evaluate the research evidence on these factors and consider how they give rise to the governance systems observed in different countries. We then illustrate these principles by providing an overview of governance systems in selected countries. You will see that although globalization has tended to standardize certain features (such as an independence standard for the board of directors), international governance systems as a whole remain broadly diverse. This diversity reflects the unique combination of economic, legal, cultural, and other forces that have developed over time. Therefore, the national context is important to understanding how governance systems work to shape managerial behavior.

Capital Market Efficiency

Markets set the prices for labor, natural resources, and capital. When **capital markets** are efficient, these prices are expected to be correct based on the information available to both parties in a transaction. Accurate pricing is necessary for firms to make rational decisions about allocating capital to its most efficient uses. Owners of the firm are rewarded for rational decision making through an increase in shareholder value. When capital markets are inefficient, prices are subject to distortion, and corporate decision making suffers.

Efficient capital markets also act as a disciplining mechanism on corporations. Companies are held to a "market standard" of performance, and those that fail to meet the standard are punished with a decrease in share price. Companies that do not perform well over time risk going out of business or becoming an acquisition target. (We discuss this more in Chapter 11, "The Market for Corporate Control.") If the market is not reasonably efficient, shareholders cannot rely on the market for corporate control to punish management for making poor capital allocation decisions that decrease shareholder value.

Rajan and Zingales (1998) demonstrated the importance of capital markets by measuring the relationship between capital market efficiency and economic growth across countries. They found that industries that require external financing grow faster in countries with efficient capital markets. They concluded that a well-developed financial market is a source of competitive advantage for firms that rely on external capital for growth.[1]

If a country does not have efficient capital markets, its companies must instead rely on alternative sources of financing for growth, such as influential wealthy families, large banking institutions, other companies, or governments. As providers of capital, these parties also discipline corporate behavior because they actively monitor their investments. However, because their objectives might differ from the pure financial returns that the investing public seeks, their capacity to act as a disciplining mechanism might not align with the interests of shareholders or stakeholders. For example, a wealthy family might be satisfied with below-market returns if it can use a position of control over the organization to extract other benefits—such as corporate perquisites, social prestige, or political influence.

Masulis, Pham, and Zein (2011) demonstrate that family-controlled business groups are more prevalent in countries with weak capital markets and serve as an important source of financing in these countries. Across a broad sample of nations, they found that 19 percent of publicly listed companies belong to a family-controlled group. The figures are lowest (less than 5 percent) in developed economies such as Switzerland, the United Kingdom, and the United States, and highest (more than 40 percent) in emerging markets such as Chile, Israel, and Turkey (see Figure 2.1). The authors also found that pyramidal family groups are an important source of capital for "high-risk, capital intensive firms that could otherwise find it difficult to attract external funding, especially in weak capital markets."[2]

Family-controlled business groups bring increased risk to the economy when they operate with minimal external oversight and when their objectives are to extract rents at the expense of shareholders or stakeholders. For example, Black (2001) concluded that poor accounting disclosure and weak oversight enabled family-controlled business groups in Korea to mask operating problems and prop up weak subsidiaries with financial guarantees that were not disclosed to creditors. Such practices were not sustainable and eventually contributed to the Asian financial crisis of 1997.[3] As such, family control can lead to serious agency problems that retard economic growth.[4]

To this end, Leuz, Lins, and Warnock (2009) found that foreigners invest less money in companies that insiders control and that reside in countries with weak investor protections and lower transparency. They concluded that "firms with problematic governance structures, particularly those with high levels of insider control and from countries with weak institutions, are likely to be more taxing to foreign investors in terms of their information and monitoring costs, which in turn could explain why foreigners shy away from these firms."[5]

Finally, efficient capital markets can also serve as a disciplining mechanism on managerial behavior when they are appropriately used in compensation contracts. By offering equity-based incentives such as stock options, the firm can align the interests of management and shareholders. This discourages management from taking self-interested actions that reduce firm value. The absence of an efficient market essentially limits the effectiveness of these types of incentives. In such a setting, agency problems might be best addressed by requiring managers to hold direct and substantial equity positions, by active regulation, or by other governance features that do not rely on efficient capital markets. (We discuss equity incentives in greater detail in Chapters 8, "Executive Compensation and Incentives," and 9, "Executive Equity Ownership.")

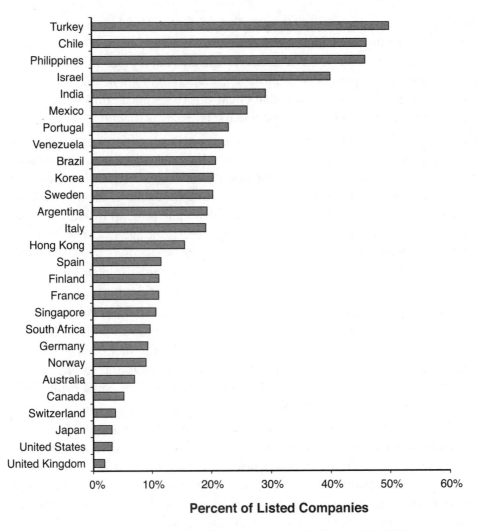

Source: Adapted by David F. Larcker and Brian Tayan. Data from: Masulis, Pham, and Zein (2011).

Figure 2.1   Family-controlled business groups in selected countries.

Legal Tradition

A country's legal tradition has important implications on the rights afforded to business owners and minority shareholders. Business owners are particularly concerned with the protection of their property against expropriation, the predictability of how claims will be resolved under the law, the enforceability of contracts, and the efficiency and honesty of the judiciary. Minority shareholders are concerned with how the legal system protects their ownership rights and discourages abuse by controlling owners.

A system that provides strong protection can be an important factor in mitigating the prevalence and severity of agency problems because penalties can be imposed on self-interested managers or insiders. However, if the legal system is corrupt or cannot be relied upon to provide appropriate protections, this disciplining device will not constrain agency problems.

La Porta, Lopez-de-Silanes, Shleifer, and Vishny (1998) found that countries whose legal systems are based on a tradition of common law afford more rights to shareholders than countries whose legal systems are based on civil law (or code law).[6] The authors also found that creditors are afforded greater protection in common-law countries. They concluded that governance systems are more effective in countries that combine common-law tradition with a reliable enforcement mechanism (discussed in the later section "Enforcement of Regulations"). In a separate study, La Porta, Lopez-de-Silanes, Shleifer, and Vishny (2002) found that companies operating in countries whose legal systems protect minority interests have higher stock market valuations than companies operating in countries with lesser protections.[7]

Similarly, studies have shown that political corruption has a negative impact on economic development. According to the World Bank, corruption "undermines development by distorting the rule of law and weakening the institutional foundation on which economic growth depends."[8] Mauro (1995) found that higher levels of corruption are associated with lower economic growth and lower private investment.[9] He explained that a corrupt government provides worse protection of property rights and that bureaucratic delay in granting licenses can deter investment in technological advancement. Finally, Pantzalis, Park, and Sutton (2008) found that political corruption is associated with lower corporate valuations.[10]

If the legal system is corrupt, unpredictable, or ineffective, alternative disciplining mechanisms are necessary in the governance process. For example, if contracts are not enforced through traditional legal channels, they could be "enforced" by the threat of not engaging in future business with the other party. Firms could place directors on the boards of companies that are important suppliers or customers to monitor management and to ensure that contracts are honored. These mechanisms would enable the firms to bypass the legal system and to ensure that shareholder and stakeholder interests are protected.

Accounting Standards

Reliable and sensible accounting standards are critical in ensuring that financial statements convey accurate information to shareholders. Investors rely on this information to evaluate investment risk and reward. Inaccurate information and low levels of transparency can lead to poor decision making and reduce the efficiency of capital markets. The practice of hiring an external auditor to review the application of accounting principles improves investor confidence in financial reporting.

Reliable accounting standards also are critical in ensuring the proper oversight of management. Shareholders and stakeholders use this information to measure performance and detect agency problems. The board of directors uses this information to structure appropriate compensation incentives and to award bonuses. If accounting standards lack transparency or if management manipulates their application, financial reporting will suffer, compensation incentives will be distorted, and shareholders and stakeholders will be less effective in providing oversight.

To improve the integrity of financial reporting, regulators have devised standards that are based on the expert opinions of economists, academics, auditors, and practitioners. In some countries, such as the United States and Japan, accounting systems are **rules-based**—that is, they prescribe detailed rules for how accounting standards should be applied to various business activities. In other countries, such as many European nations, accounting systems are **principles-based**—they outline general accounting concepts but do not always dictate the specific application of these concepts to business activities (see the following sidebar).

Harmonization of Accounting Standards

Country-specific accounting standards make it difficult for investors to compare corporate performance across nations. To improve this situation, the ***International Accounting Standards Board (IASB)*** was formed in 2001. The organization, which superseded the International Accounting Standards Committee, was established to develop reliable accounting standards that could be used worldwide. The IASB expects that a single set of accounting standards will support the efficiency of global capital markets through improved disclosure and transparency.

The IASB issued its first International Financial Reporting Standard (IFRS) in 2003. By 2014, more than 120 countries worldwide were either required or allowed to use IFRS. These countries included the European Union members, the United Kingdom, Australia, New Zealand, and South Africa, among others. In the United States, regulators have signaled an intention to convert from U.S. Generally Accepted Accounting Principles (GAAP) to IFRS. However, many practical considerations make harmonization a challenge in the United States, including differences in the treatment of certain principles; political pressure; and investor, managerial, and auditor education.

Despite the move toward harmonization, considerable differences in accounting quality among individual companies will likely remain. This is because the board of directors and management still retain discretion over the application of accounting principles and the level of transparency in reporting. Furthermore, external audit quality also varies across countries in the extent to which accounting problems are detected and enforcement is applied. (We discuss issues of accounting and audit quality in Chapter 10, "Financial Reporting and External Audit.")

Academic research demonstrates the importance of reliable accounting standards. Barth, Landsman, and Lang (2008) found, among a sample of companies in 21 countries, that firms that adopted international accounting standards exhibited less earnings management, more timely recognition of losses, and higher-quality measurements of net income and equity book value compared to companies that used domestic accounting standards.[11] Similarly, Ernstberger and Vogler (2008) found that German companies that adopted international accounting standards had a lower cost of capital than companies that continued to use German GAAP, which they attributed to an "accounting premium" that comes through improved earnings quality and disclosure.[12] Francis, Huang, Khurana, and Pereira (2009) found that transparency in financial disclosure contributed to higher national economic growth rates through efficient resource allocation.[13]

However, the adoption of reliable accounting standards does not guarantee the integrity of financial reporting. Benston, Bromwich, and Wagenhofer (2006) warned that principles-based accounting systems have potential shortcomings because they provide less-strict guidance and are subject to management interpretation. They cited a 2002 review by accounting regulators in the United States that questioned whether the adoption of a concept-based system "could lead to situations in which professional judgments, made in good faith, result in different interpretations for similar transactions and events, raising concerns about comparability."[14] Price, Román, and Rountree (2011) found that compliance with accounting codes does not necessarily lead to increased transparency or better corporate performance. They concluded that institutional features of the business environment—including ownership characteristics, board attributes, and protection of minority rights by the legal system—are also important contributors to effective governance.[15]

If accounting rules are unreliable or external auditors cannot be trusted to verify their proper application, countries will require a substitute mechanism to discourage agency problems. These might include severe legal penalties for abuse and vigilant enforcement mechanisms. Investors, customers, and suppliers might circumvent financial reporting information and only rely on companies trusted over time through long interaction or family relationships.

Enforcement of Regulations

Legal and regulatory mechanisms alone cannot protect the interests of minority shareholders. Government officials must be willing to enforce the rules in a fair and consistent manner. Regulatory enforcement mitigates agency problems by dissuading executives from engaging in behaviors such as insider trading, misleading disclosure, self-dealing, and fraud because they acknowledge a real risk of punishment.

Hail and Leuz (2006) found that countries with developed securities regulations and legal enforcement mechanisms have a lower cost of capital than those that lack these characteristics. Controlling for macroeconomic and firm-specific factors, the authors found that differences in securities regulation and legal systems explain about 60 percent of country-level differences in implied equity cost of capital. The importance of regulatory enforcement is greater in countries whose economies are not integrated into international capital markets (such as Brazil, India, and the Philippines) than in those whose economies are integrated (such as Belgium, Hong Kong, and the United Kingdom). When a country's economy is integrated into international capital markets, the efficiency of those markets can partially make up for deficiencies in the country-specific securities regulation and legal system.[16]

Regulatory enforcement also contributes to investor confidence that management will be monitored and property rights will be protected. Bushman and Piotroski (2006) found that companies apply more conservative accounting in countries where public enforcement of securities regulation is strong. Because regulators are more likely to be penalized if the companies they monitor overstate accounting results, they will be more rigorous in their enforcement. Knowing this, companies recognize bad news in their financial reports more quickly to avoid regulatory infractions.[17] Similarly, researchers have found that participation in equity markets increases when countries adopt insider trading laws because the laws put outside investors on more even footing with insiders who have access to nonpublic information.[18]

If regulatory enforcement is weak or inconsistent, shareholders cannot expect to have their interests protected by official channels. Therefore, they have to take a more direct role in governance oversight, either through greater rights afforded through the bylaws and charters or through direct representation on the board. Without these tools, they will demand higher returns on capital to compensate for the greater risk of investing their money.

Societal and Cultural Values

The society in which a company operates also strongly influences managerial behavior. Activities that might be deemed acceptable in some societies are considered inappropriate in others (such as conspicuous personal consumption). This impacts the types of activities that executives are willing to participate in and the likelihood of self-serving behavior. Cultural values also influence the relationship between the company and its shareholders and stakeholders. Although complex and difficult to quantify, these forces play a significant role in shaping governance systems.

For example, corporations in Korea have a responsibility to society as a whole, beyond maximizing shareholder profits. Executives who take actions that benefit themselves at the expense of others are seen as betraying the social trust and bringing disgrace on the corporation and its employees. This cultural norm—the concept of shame, or "lost face"—becomes a disciplining mechanism that deters self-interested behavior, similar to the threat of legal penalties in other nations. By contrast, in Russia, personal displays of wealth are tolerated, and corruption is widely seen as an inevitable aspect of the business process. Executives there might be more likely to take self-interested actions because they do not risk the same level of scorn as executives in Korea. In this case, cultural norms do not act as a successful deterrent, and explicit government regulation and enforcement are likely (see the following sidebar).

The Hofstede Model of Cultural Dimensions

Many systems categorize cultural values. One that has received considerable attention is a model developed by Geert Hofstede. The Hofstede model is based on survey data of employee values in more than 70 countries. It consolidates these values into six indices that are broadly used to characterize cultural attributes:

- **Power distance**—The extent to which members of society accept that power is distributed unequally

- **Individualism**—The extent to which members of society feel a responsibility to look after only themselves and their families rather than others in society

- **Masculinity**—The extent to which members of society are assertive or competitive

- **Uncertainty avoidance**—The extent to which members of society feel uncomfortable in unstructured situations

- **Long-term orientation**—The extent to which members of society tend toward thrift and perseverance

- **Indulgence**—The extent to which members of society tolerate personal gratification[19]

Although these measures are perhaps crude or stereotypical, they are indicative of a system that attempts to quantify differences across cultures. If properly developed, such a system might serve as an indicator of the likelihood that executives will engage in self-interested behavior and the extent to which a country's governance system requires rigorous controls. For example, the Hofstede system gives Korea a low score (18) for individualism and a high score (85) for uncertainty avoidance. This suggests that Korea has a cooperative business culture built around structured processes and is subject to a lower degree of agency risk.[20]

Although countries vary on many levels, one of the most important social attitudes that shapes governance systems is the role of the corporation in society. As mentioned in Chapter 1, some countries tend toward a **shareholder-centric** view, which holds that the primary responsibility of the corporation is to maximize shareholder wealth. Actions such as improving labor conditions, reducing environmental impact, and treating suppliers fairly are seen as desirable only to the extent that they are consistent with improving the long-term financial performance of the firm. Other countries tend toward a **stakeholder-centric** view, which holds that obligations toward constituents such as employees, suppliers, customers, and local communities should be held in equal importance to shareholder returns.

The United States and the United Kingdom are two countries that predominantly embrace the shareholder-centric view. The laws of these countries stipulate that boards and executives have a fiduciary responsibility to protect the interest of shareholders. If the board of directors of a U.S. company were to reject an unsolicited takeover bid on the premise that it would lead to widespread layoffs, it would likely face lawsuits filed by its investors for not maximizing shareholder value. However, all members of society in these countries might not uniformly adopt the shareholder-centric view. For example, union pension funds advocate stakeholder-friendly objectives, such as fair labor laws, and environmental groups encourage corporations to embrace sustainability goals even if they might increase the company's cost of production. Many corporations embrace these objectives as well, even as their primary focus remains on long-term value creation.

In other societies, the stakeholder-centric view dominates. For example, German law is based on a philosophy of **codetermination**, in which the interests of shareholders and employees are expected to be balanced in strategic considerations.

Germanic legal code enforces this approach by mandating that employees have either one-third or one-half representation on the supervisory board of German companies (depending on the size of the company). In this way, labor is given a real vote on corporate direction. (We consider the impact of employee board representation in Chapter 5, "Board of Directors: Structure and Consequences.") The Swedish government encourages full employment through consequences that make it difficult to carry out large-scale layoffs, even though such a policy runs the risk of decreasing firm profitability. In Asia, the Japanese are known for job protection and rewarding employees for tenure. In one survey of international executives, only 3 percent of respondents from Japan agreed that a company should lay off workers to maintain its dividend during difficult economic times. In the United States and the United Kingdom, 89 percent of respondents believed that maintaining the dividend was more important.[21]

Individual National Governance Structures

To get a better sense of how economic, legal, and cultural realities contribute to the governance systems in specific markets, we will consider and compare the United States, the United Kingdom, Germany, Japan, South Korea, China, India, Brazil, and Russia.

United States

The United States has the largest and most liquid capital markets in the world. U.S. publicly listed companies had an aggregate market value of $22 trillion, representing approximately 35 percent of the total value of equity worldwide, in 2014.[22] The U.S. market is the largest by trading volume, by value of public equity offerings, and by corporate and securitized debt outstanding.[23]

The most important governance regulatory body in the United States is the **Securities and Exchange Commission (SEC)**. Congress created the SEC through the Securities and Exchange Act of 1934 to oversee the proper functioning of primary and secondary financial markets, with an emphasis on the protection of security holder rights and the prevention of corporate fraud. Among its various powers, the SEC has the authority to regulate securities exchanges (such as the New York Stock Exchange [NYSE], the NASDAQ, and the Chicago Mercantile Exchange), bring civil enforcement actions against companies or executives who violate securities laws (through false disclosures, insider trading, or fraud), ensure the quality of accounting standards and financial reporting, and oversee the proxy solicitation and annual voting process.

Although the SEC bears ultimate responsibility for the quality of accounting standards, it has delegated the process of drafting them to the **Financial Accounting Standards Board (FASB)**. Founded in 1973, the FASB is a nonprofit organization composed of accounting experts from academia, industry, audit firms, and the investing public. These individuals draft accounting provisions based on accounting and economic principles, taking into consideration the perspective of practitioners. Then they release draft rules for public comment and update the rules as necessary before adoption. After these rules are adopted, they become part of U.S. GAAP. As mentioned earlier, U.S. regulators have signaled an intention to transition from U.S. GAAP to IFRS to increase comparability of financial reporting between the United States and other countries.

Approximately 27 percent of all publicly traded companies in the United States are incorporated in their state of origin, 63 percent in the state of Delaware, and 10 percent in a state other than these.[24] Delaware has the most developed body of case law, which gives companies clarity on how corporate matters might be decided if they come to trial. Furthermore, trials over corporate matters in Delaware are heard by a judge instead of a jury, a process that some companies prefer because they believe it reduces their liability risk.[25]

Companies are required to comply with the listing requirements of the exchanges on which their securities trade. The largest exchange in the United States is the **New York Stock Exchange (NYSE)**. The NYSE requires that a listed company have at least 400 shareholders, maintain a minimum market value and trading volume in its securities, and demonstrate compliance with the following governance standards:

- The listed company's board is required to have a majority of independent directors.
- Nonexecutive directors must meet independently from executive directors on a scheduled basis.
- The compensation committee of the board must consist entirely of independent directors.
- The audit committee must have a minimum of three members, all of whom are "financially literate" and at least one of whom is a "financial expert."
- The company must have an internal audit function.
- The chief executive officer (CEO) must certify annually that the company is in compliance with NYSE requirements.

The NYSE Corporate Governance Rules provide a detailed definition of board member independence, which the NYSE defines as the director having "no material relationship with the listed company."[26] However, each company is allowed a degree of discretion in determining whether a board member meets certain of these criteria.

Likewise, the NYSE affords flexibility to companies in establishing guidelines for director qualifications, director responsibilities, access to management and independent advisors, compensation, management succession, and self-review. (Legal and regulatory issues are discussed more fully in Chapter 3, "Board of Directors: Duties and Liability.")

One important piece of federal legislation related to U.S. governance is the **Sarbanes–Oxley Act of 2002**. Important provisions of Sarbanes–Oxley include the following:

- The requirement that the CEO and chief financial officer (CFO) certify financial results (with misrepresentations subject to criminal penalties)
- An attestation by executives and auditors to the sufficiency of internal controls
- Independence of the audit committee of the board of directors (as incorporated in the listing standards of the NYSE)
- A limitation of the types of nonaudit work an auditor can perform for a company
- A ban on most personal loans to executives or directors

A second important piece of legislation relating to U.S. governance is the **Dodd–Frank Wall Street Reform Act of 2010**. Some of the important provisions include the following:

- **Say-on-pay**—Shareholders are given a nonbinding vote on executive compensation.
- **Disclosure**—Companies must provide expanded disclosure on executive compensation, pay ratios, hedging of company equity by executives and directors, clawback policies, and golden parachute severance payments due upon a change in control.[27]

The U.S. governance system is shareholder-centric. Directors have a legal obligation to act "in the interest of the corporation," which the courts have defined to mean "in the interest of shareholders." With rare exceptions, employees are not represented on boards of directors. Although shareholders have submitted proxy proposals to further goals of social responsibility—such as environmentalism, fair labor practices, and internal pay equity—few have succeeded. An active market for corporate control and the threat of litigation for companies that do not satisfy shareholder demands serve as effective controls on company behavior. (The market for corporate control and shareholder activism are discussed in Chapters 11, "The Market for Corporate Control," and 12, "Institutional Shareholders and Activist Investors.")

Executive compensation is higher in the United States than in most other countries. Fernandes, Ferreira, Matos, and Murphy (2012) found that average total compensation for CEOs in the United States is more than twice what CEOs outside the United States earn ($5.5 million versus $2.3 million).[28] Most cross-country differences are explained by pay structure: CEOs who are more highly paid receive a larger percentage of their pay in the form of equity incentives, with U.S. CEOs falling at the high end of the spectrum. It is unknown why CEOs in the United States are paid higher than global averages, but cultural, tax, accounting, political, and other determinants likely are all contributing factors. (Compensation issues are discussed more fully in Chapters 8 and 9.)

United Kingdom

The British model of governance shares many similarities with that of the U.S. model. This likely results from the commonalities between these two countries in terms of capital markets structure, legal tradition, regulatory approach, and societal values. Like the U.S. model, the British model is shareholder-centric, with a single board of directors, management participation on the board (particularly for the CEO), and an emphasis on transparency and disclosure through audited financial reports. This model is generally referred to as the **Anglo-Saxon model**.

Instead of legislative bodies passing detailed statutes, the British model relies on market mechanisms to determine governance standards. Historically, British Parliament has taken a hands-off approach to regulation. For example, the Companies Act 1985, which consolidates seven Companies Acts passed by Parliament between 1948 and 1983, imposes few governance requirements on companies. The Companies Act 1985 states quite simply that companies are required to have a board (with at least two directors for publicly traded companies) and that the board is responsible for certain administrative functions, including the production of annual financial reports. The Act does not specify a required structure for boards, nor does it mandate procedures for conducting business. The company's shareholders determine such rules through the articles of association. As a result, U.K. tradition provides flexibility to the corporate body in developing governance standards.

Despite this hands-off approach to regulation, the U.K. has been a leader in governance reform, promoting the following standards of best practices based on the recommendation of expert panels:

- **The Cadbury Report (1992)**—The accountancy profession and London Stock Exchange commissioned the Cadbury Committee in the early 1990s to provide a benchmark set of recommendations on governance. The committee recommended a set of voluntary guidelines known as the Code of Best Practices. These included the separation of the chairman and CEO titles, the appointment of independent directors to the board, reduced conflicts of interest at the board level because of business or other relationships, the creation of an independent audit committee, and a review of the effectiveness of the company's internal controls. The recommendations of the Cadbury Committee set the basis for the standards for the London Stock Exchange and have influenced governance standards in the U.S. and several other countries. (See the sidebar that follows.)[29]

- **The Greenbury Report (1995)**—The Greenbury Committee was commissioned to review the executive compensation process. The committee recommended establishing an independent remuneration committee entirely comprised of nonexecutive directors.[30]

- **The Hampel Report (1998)**—The Hampel Committee was established to review the effectiveness of the Cadbury and Greenbury reports. The committee recommended no substantive changes and consolidated the Cadbury and Greenbury reports into the Combined Code of Best Practices, which the London Stock Exchange subsequently adopted.[31]

- **The Turnbull Report (1999)**—The Turnbull Committee was commissioned to provide recommendations on ways to improve corporate internal controls. The committee recommended that companies review the nature of risks facing their organization, establish processes by which these risks are identified and remedied, and perform an annual review of internal controls to assess their effectiveness. The report was updated in 2005.[32]

- **The Higgs Report (2003)**—The British government asked Sir Derek Higgs to evaluate the role, quality, and effectiveness of nonexecutive directors.[33] Higgs recommended structural changes to the board, including the standards that at least half of the board be nonexecutive directors, that the board appoint a lead independent director to serve as a liaison with shareholders, that the nomination committee be headed by a nonexecutive director, and that executive directors not serve more than six years on the board. The Higgs Report also advised an annual board evaluation.[34] The recommendations of the Higgs Report were combined with those of the Turnbull Report and the Combined Code to create the Revised Combined Code of Best Practices. The recommendations of the Higgs Report were replaced in 2011.[35]

- **The Walker Review (2009)**—David Walker was asked to review corporate governance practices among U.K. banks to reduce their risk to the economy. Walker recommended structural changes, particularly to executive compensation. These included the standard that at least half of bank employee remuneration be in the form of long-term incentives and that two-thirds of cash bonuses be deferred.[36]

- **Guidance on Board Effectiveness (2011)**—The Institute of Chartered Secretaries and Administrators (ICSA) was commissioned to review the recommendations of the Higgs Report. The ISCA recommended that the Higgs Report be withdrawn and replaced with updated guidance that place greater emphasis on the roles and behaviors of directors. These include standards that emphasize ethical leadership, clearly defined responsibilities, productive boardroom dynamics, and the timely sharing of information. These recommendations were incorporated into the Revised Combined Code, which is now known as the U.K. Corporate Governance Code.[37]

Together, these reports have shaped the board of directors into a monitoring and control body in addition to a strategy-setting body.[38]

Cadbury Committee on Corporate Governance: Code of Best Practices (1992)

The Cadbury Committee provided these original recommendations in 1992:

Relating to the board of directors:

- The board should meet regularly, retain full and effective control over the company, and monitor the executive management.
- A clearly accepted division of responsibilities should exist at the head of a company, to ensure a balance of power and authority so that no individual has unfettered decision-making powers. Companies in which the chairman is also the chief executive should have a strong and independent board with a recognized senior member.
- The board should include nonexecutive directors whose views carry significant weight in the board's decisions.
- The board should meet according to a formal schedule to ensure that the direction and control of the company rests firmly in its hands.
- Directors should follow an agreed-upon procedure in performing their duties and should consult independent professional advice, if necessary, at the company's expense.
- All directors should have access to the advice and services of the company secretary, who is responsible for ensuring that board procedures are followed and that applicable rules and regulations are complied with. The entire board must address the issue of removing the company secretary.

Relating to nonexecutive directors:

- Nonexecutive directors should pass an independent judgment on issues of strategy, performance, and resources, including key appointments and standards of conduct.

- The majority of nonexecutive directors should not have any business or other relationship that could prevent them from exercising independent judgment, apart from their fees and shareholding. Their fees should reflect the time they commit to the company.

- Nonexecutive directors should be appointed for specified terms, without automatic reappointment.

- The board should select nonexecutive directors through a formal process.

For the executive directors:

- Directors' service contracts should not exceed three years without shareholders' approval.

- Total compensation of the executive directors, the chairman, and the highest-paid U.K. directors should be disclosed, including pension contributions and stock options. Separate figures should be given for salary and performance-related elements, and documentation should explain the basis on which performance is measured.

- The executive directors' pay should be subject to the recommendations of a remunerations committee made up of nonexecutive directors.

On reporting and controls:

- The board should present a balanced and understandable assessment of the company's position.

- The board should maintain an objective and professional relationship with the auditors.

- The board should establish an audit committee of at least three nonexecutive directors, with clearly written terms regarding its authority and duties.

- The directors should explain their responsibility for preparing the accounts, and the auditors should prepare a statement about their reporting responsibilities.

- The directors should report on the effectiveness of the company's system of internal control.

- The directors should report that the business is a "going concern."

Publicly traded companies in the United Kingdom are not legally required to adopt the standards of the U.K. Corporate Governance Code. Instead, the London Stock Exchange requires that they issue an annual statement to shareholders, explaining whether they are in compliance with the Code and, if not, stating their reasons for noncompliance. This practice, known as **comply or explain**, puts the burden on public shareholders to monitor whether the company's explanation for noncompliance is acceptable. As a result, the Code advocates a flexible standard that grants a company, its board, and its shareholders discretion in devising appropriate governance processes.

It is widely accepted that the Code has improved governance standards in the U.K. and the countries that have adopted its key provisions. Still, sparse academic evidence supports this claim. Shabbir and Padgett (2008) found only weak evidence that compliance with Code provisions is correlated with stock price performance, and they found no evidence that compliance is correlated with operating performance.[39] This is not to say that the Code has not contributed to governance quality but simply that any improvements are difficult to detect. (We examine the evidence for specific provisions, such as independence, lead directors, and the separation of the chairman and CEO positions, in Chapter 5.)

Economics aside, the comply-or-explain system enables us to observe which governance provisions are deemed useful from the board's perspective. Surprisingly, a recent study by accounting firm Grant Thornton found that 43 percent of the largest 350 companies on the London Stock Exchange were not fully compliant. The most frequent areas of noncompliance were an insufficient number of independent directors (13 percent), failure to have a remuneration committee with at least three independent directors (7 percent), and failure to separate the roles of chairman and CEO (6 percent).[40] Such information might help explain why studies have not found a correlation between compliance levels and operating performance: perhaps companies are prudently rejecting recommended best practices that are inappropriate for their specific situation. Alternatively, it may be the case that the reported governance provisions are not generally important for mitigating agency problems and increasing shareholder value.

The U.K. has also been a leader in compensation reform. In 2002, Parliament passed the Directors' Remuneration Report Regulations, which require that shareholders be granted an advisory vote on director and executive compensation (say-on-pay). In 2012, Parliament approved legislation making the results of say-on-pay binding. Say-on-pay policies have been adopted in varying form by Australia, the Netherlands, Sweden, Norway, India, and the United States. However, as we discuss in Chapter 8, say-on-pay has had a mixed impact on the rate of compensation increases in countries that have adopted this practice.

Germany

Legal tradition in Germany is based on civil code instead of the common-law tradition of the United Kingdom and the United States. A civil-code tradition means that legislation mandates more aspects of governance, and German corporations are afforded less discretion to determine their own structures and processes. For example, German law stipulates that corporations have a two-tiered board structure (instead of the unitary structure practiced in the Anglo-Saxon model). One board is the **management board** *(Vorstand)*, which is responsible for making decisions on such matters as strategy, product development, manufacturing, finance, marketing, distribution, and supply chain. The second board is the **supervisory board** *(Aufischtsrat)*, which oversees the management board. The supervisory board is responsible for appointing members to the management board; approving financial statements; and making decisions regarding major capital investment, mergers and acquisitions, and the payment of dividends. No managers are allowed to sit on the supervisory board. Members of the supervisory board are elected annually by shareholders at the general meeting.[41]

The law requires the supervisory board to have employee representation. Under the German Corporate Governance Code, a company that has at least 500 employees must allocate one-third of its supervisory board seats to labor representatives; a company with at least 2,000 employees must allocate half to labor. These representation requirements are legal obligations that cannot be amended through bylaw changes. As a result, the German system implicitly places greater emphasis on the preservation of jobs, in contrast to the Anglo-Saxon emphasis on shareholder returns. As mentioned earlier, a system that balances employee and shareholder interest is commonly referred to as codetermination. (Employee board representation is discussed in more detail in Chapter 5.)

German corporate governance also has a tradition of significant ownership and influence from founding family members and German financial institutions. Historically, German corporations have relied heavily on banks instead of capital markets for financing. These relationships grew out of the post–World War II era in which German finance organizations provided loans to hard-hit businesses and received portions of the companies' ownership as collateral. In return, bank officials were given a seat on the supervisory board. This structure gave German corporations stability through the rebuilding process by ensuring a reliable source of capital for expansion and a major investor with a long-term outlook.[42] Even as late as the 1990s, a sample of 158 large German corporations showed that more than half had a shareholder holding more than 50 percent of the equity.[43]

Given the large representation by labor and financial institutions, German shareholders traditionally have had far less influence over board matters than shareholders in the U.K. and U.S. This structure poses a risk to minority shareholders because they have to rely on other stakeholders to protect their interests. However, increased liberalization of capital markets in recent years and a gradual shift from bank financing to financing through securities markets are beginning to undo several features of this system. German financial institutions have divested many of their block ownership stakes in public corporations. By 2014, none of the 30 companies comprising the DAX Index had a shareholder with more than 50 percent of the equity; the average ownership stake of the largest blockholder decreased from 31 percent in 2001 to 15 percent in 2014.[44]

The German corporate governance system faces several serious challenges from globalization. Although German citizens might prefer a system of codetermination, the international investment community demands financial returns. This has created conflicts as German corporations balance the needs of employees and shareholders. A second challenge is dealing with a rising level of executive compensation. As corporations grow in size and compete with foreign multinationals for executive talent, compensation levels have risen. For example, politicians and the media criticized Volkswagen CEO Martin Winterkorn for accepting €17.5 million ($23 million) in compensation in 2011 and €20 million in 2012, the highest among companies in the DAX Index.[45] Although payments of this magnitude are more common in the United States, it is considered unacceptable by the cultural standards of Europe, which place greater emphasis on social equality. Conflicts over the role of the corporation and executive compensation levels will likely continue in future years.

Japan

As in Germany, the Japanese system of governance has its roots in post–World War II reconstruction. At the end of the war, Allied forces banned the Japanese *zaibatsu*, the powerful industrial and financial conglomerates that accounted for much of the country's pre-war economic strength. The Japanese responded by developing a loose system of interrelations between companies, called the **keiretsu**. Under the *keiretsu*, companies maintain small but not insignificant ownership positions among suppliers, customers, and other business affiliates. These ownership positions cement business relations along the supply chain and encourage firms to work together toward an objective of shared financial success. As in Germany, bank financiers own minority stakes in industrial firms and are key partners in the *keiretsu*. Their investments indicate that capital for financing is available as needed.

The culture in Japan is highly stakeholder-centric, and companies view themselves as having a responsibility to contribute to the prosperity of the nation. One of the most important objectives of Japanese management is to encourage the success of the entire supply chain, including industrial and financial partners. Another objective is to maintain healthy levels of employment and preserve wages and benefits. Proponents believe that the Japanese system, unlike Western styles of capitalism, encourages a long-term perspective, builds internal commitment to organizational success, and shares the benefits of success more equitably among constituents. Critics of the Japanese system believe it to be insular and overly resistant to change. (See the following sidebar.)

Toyota Board of Directors

Japanese boards have few outside directors. For example, Toyota Motor Corp. had a 16-member board of directors in 2013, 13 of whom were executives and insiders. Each inside board member had extensive experience working within the company. Toyota explained its rationale for appointing a large number of insiders to the board:

"With respect to our system regarding directors, we believe that it is important to elect individuals that comprehend and engage in strengths, including commitment to manufacturing, with an emphasis on frontline operations and problem solving based on actual on-site situation (*genchi genbutsu*)."[46]

To protect against insider abuse, Toyota developed a system of adjunct committees that provide advisory or monitoring services to the board.[47] Toyota convenes an International Advisory Board (IAB) that includes external advisors with backgrounds in politics, economics, environmental issues, and business. The IAB provides an outside viewpoint on issues that are critical to the company's long-term strategy. Toyota also relies on the advice of several other committees, including those on labor, philanthropy, the environment, ethics, and stock options. Toyota maintains a seven-member corporate auditor board (comprising of three Toyota executives and four external auditors), which is responsible for reviewing accounting methods and auditing financial results. As a result, the Toyota corporate governance system seeks to compensate for potential deficiencies that might come from having a board that is dominated by executive directors, without compromising the traditional structure that has contributed to the company's success (see Figure 2.2).

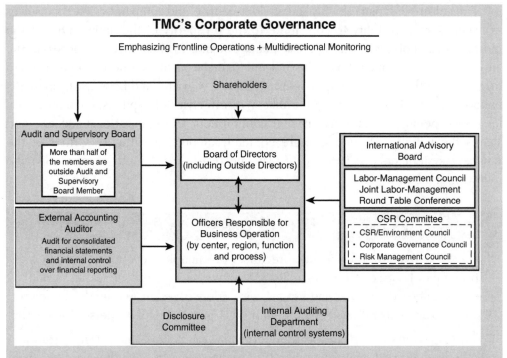

Source: Toyota Motor Corporation Annual Report (2014).

Figure 2.2 Toyota Corporation's corporate governance structure.

Not all Japanese companies have retained traditional Japanese board structures. In the late 1990s, Sony Corporation reduced the size of its board from 38 to 10, added outside board members, and created both nominating and compensation committees. It made these moves to improve policy and decision making. Subsequently, several other Japanese companies followed suit. Miyajima and Nitta (2007) found that out of a sample of 581 nonfinancial corporations, 64 percent reduced the size of their board and 22 percent increased the number of outside directors between 1997 and 2004. Average board size decreased from 17.7 members to 10.4 members over this period.[48]

In 2002, the Japanese Ministry of Justice modified its laws to encourage the adoption of Western-style systems of governance. The revised code enabled Japanese companies to choose between a *keiretsu* board structure and one with majority-independent audit, nomination, and compensation committees. It also granted board members new authority to delegate broad powers to senior management, including discretion to access public markets for debt and equity. The code revisions enhanced shareholder rights as well, such as the right to appoint or dismiss certain directors and the external auditor. Companies were also allowed more freedom to issue employee stock options. These revisions were intended to improve governance quality, facilitate access to global capital markets, and increase transparency and accountability.[49] Evidence shows that it was only moderately successful. Eberhart (2012) found that companies that adopted these governance changes experienced a subsequent increase in their market-to-book ratio. However, he did not find an improvement in operating performance.[50]

In addition, Japanese companies are facing many of the same pressures from globalization as German companies. As Japanese companies access global capital markets, international institutional shareholders have somewhat replaced the influence of major banks.[51] For the first time, Japanese companies find themselves faced with shareholder activists that emphasize operational efficiency and shareholder value over stable employment and conservative management. To shield themselves, companies have adopted defense mechanisms such as "poison pills" (discussed further in Chapter 11). Although shareholder activists are critical of these measures, traditionalists believe that the measures are necessary to preserve the prevailing culture of respect and cooperation between the company and its stakeholders.

Recent events, including a major accounting scandal at Olympus Corporation and renewed emphasis on economic revitalization, have given new momentum to governance reform. In 2014, the Japanese Financial Services Authority adopted a Stewardship Code to encourage dialogue between Japanese corporations and institutional investors. The Stewardship Code calls on shareholders to engage with corporations to enhance medium- and long-term investment returns and disclose how the fund votes at the annual meeting.[52] The Japanese government has also taken additional steps to encourage independent oversight of management. In 2014, Parliament enacted a law requiring companies to appoint at least one independent director or, if not, disclose the reason for not doing so. Separately, the prime minister announced the country's first effort to develop a national corporate governance code based on international principles to improve governance standards in the country. Major provisions included expanded shareholder rights, enhanced disclosure on cross-holdings and related-party transactions, and board-level reforms.[53] The changes were intended to attract foreign investors and improve economic returns.

South Korea

Korean economic activity is dominated by conglomerate organizations known as the **chaebol**, which means "financial house." *Chaebol* are not single corporations but groups of affiliated companies that operate under the strategic and financial direction of a central headquarters. A powerful group chairman, who holds ultimate decision-making authority on all investments, leads headquarters.

The *chaebol* structure was formed following the Korean War. During reconstruction, business leaders worked with government officials to develop a plan for economic growth. Together they identified industries that were deemed critical for the country's long-term success. These included everything from shipbuilding and construction, to textiles, to financial services. The government offered subsidized loans to business leaders to encourage new investment, and business leaders used these loans to expand aggressively. Although investments were managed as separate enterprises, they shared a common affiliation. The plan was highly successful: the Korean economy grew at an almost unprecedented rate. With economic prosperity came great wealth for the *chaebol*. In 1995, the 30 largest *chaebol* accounted for 41 percent of total domestic sales in South Korea.[54]

However, deficiencies in the *chaebol* structure came to light in the Asian financial crisis of 1997. First, they were overly insulated from the market forces that compel efficiency. Founding families had unequal voting rights in proportion to their economic interest (two-thirds voting interest compared with 25 percent economic rights), so their decision making was unchallenged. Second, *chaebol* did not rely on public capital markets for financing, instead relying on internal sources, bank loans, and government subsidies. Therefore, the *chaebol* were not subject to the disciplining force of institutional shareholders.

Over time, these factors led to deterioration in the financial strength of the *chaebol*. Despite their size, they were not very profitable. By the mid-1990s, most were publicly traded at a market-to-book ratio of less than 1, indicating that the financial value of their assets was less than historical investment cost. Furthermore, they were highly leveraged. A debt-to-equity ratio of 5 to 1 was not uncommon.[55] In addition, group affiliates were tied together by financial guarantees. This created interconnections that made affiliates more vulnerable to financial distress than was initially apparent. Because the groups were not required under accounting rules to disclose these obligations, their true financial condition was apparently unknown to regulators, investors, and creditors. However, the Asian financial crisis brought these troubles into public view. When the Korean currency collapsed, the *chaebol* were unable to repay their debts, many of which were denominated in U.S. dollars. Eight *chaebol* went bankrupt in 1997 alone.

To bring stability to the Korean economy and boost investor confidence, the government issued a series of reforms. First, the practice of transferring funds between *chaebol* affiliates was eliminated. Group companies were forced to become financially self-sufficient, although they could still operate under the strategic direction of group headquarters. Regulators also passed governance reforms that boosted board independence, eliminated intergroup guarantees, and afforded greater rights to minority shareholders. These standards applied only to large corporations with assets greater than 2 trillion won (approximately $2 billion); small companies were exempted.[56]

Black and Kim (2012) examined the impact of these reforms and found superior stock price performance for the companies that adopted them.[57]

China

The Chinese model of corporate governance reflects a partial transition from a communist regime to a capitalist economic system. The Chinese government owns a full or controlling interest in many of the country's largest corporations. Although the government seeks to improve the efficiency of its enterprises, it balances these objectives against stakeholder concerns. These include maintaining high levels of employment and ensuring that critical industries—such as banking, telecommunications, energy, and real estate—are protected from excessive foreign investment and influence.

Chinese companies issue three types of shares: those held by the state, those held by founders and employees, and those held by the public. Shares held by the public fall into three categories: A-shares, B-shares, and H-shares. **A-shares** trade on the Shanghai Stock Exchange and the Shenzhen Stock Exchange on mainland China. Ownership is restricted to domestic investors, and shares are denominated in renminbi. **B-shares** also trade on the Shanghai and Shenzhen markets but are denominated in foreign currencies. **H-shares** trade on the Hong Kong Stock Exchange and are available to foreign investors. H-shares are denominated in Hong Kong dollars. The ownership restrictions placed on these markets have created vastly different liquidity levels, and it is not uncommon for A-shares and H-shares to trade at divergent valuations (with A-shares trading at a significant premium). In addition, limited float and ownership restrictions limit the influence of public shareholders in China.

The Company Law of the People's Republic of China (revised in 2005) outlines the governance requirements for publicly traded companies.[58] Chinese companies are required to have a two-tiered board structure, consisting of a board of directors and a board of supervisors. The board of directors has between 5 and 19 members and usually includes a significant number of company executives. The board of directors is permitted (but not required) to have employee representation. In contrast, the board of supervisors is required to have three or more members, at least one-third of whom are employee representatives. No members of the board of directors or executives are allowed to serve on the board of supervisors.[59] Companies are not required to have audit or compensation committees unless they choose to list their shares on foreign exchanges that require them (such as the NYSE).

The Chinese government maintains significant influence over publicly traded companies. The government selects the companies that are eligible for public listing. It is also often a significant shareholder and has representatives serving on the board of supervisors. For example, PetroChina was a publicly traded company with shares listed on the NYSE (American depository shares, or ADSs), the Hong Kong Stock Exchange (H-shares), and the Shanghai Stock Exchange (A-shares) in 2014. However, only 14 percent of the company's shares were freely traded by the public in these three markets; the remaining 86 percent of its shares were held by China National Petroleum Corp. (CNPC), which was itself 100 percent owned by the Chinese government.[60]

Research suggests that governance quality might be lower among state-controlled entities. Conyon and He (2011) found that Chinese-listed companies with fewer independent directors were less likely to terminate an underperforming CEO. These companies were also less likely to grant equity-based compensation linking pay with performance.[61]

India

Following India's independence from British rule in 1947, the country pursued a socialist economic agenda. Public policy was intended to encourage economic development in a variety of manufacturing industries, but burdensome regulatory requirements led to low productivity, poor-quality products, and marginal profitability. National banks, which provided financing to private companies, often evaluated loans on the size of capital required and the number of jobs created instead of the companies' return on investment.[62] As a result, private companies had little incentive to deploy capital efficiently, and a weak system of corporate governance evolved.

By 1991, the economic situation in the country had deteriorated to such an extent that the Indian government passed a series of major reforms to liberalize the economy and encourage a competitive financial system. With these reforms came pressure to improve governance standards. As a first step, the Confederation of Indian Industries (CII) created a voluntary Corporate Governance Code in 1998. Large companies were encouraged, although not required, to adopt the standards of the Code. One year later, the Securities and Exchange Board of India (SEBI) commissioned the Kumar Mangalam Birla Committee to propose standards of corporate governance that would apply to companies listed on the Indian stock exchange. These reforms were incorporated in **Clause 49** and applied to all publicly traded companies. In 2004, a second panel, chaired by N. R. Narayana Murthy, chairman of Infosys, made additional recommendations to revise and further update Clause 49.

Clause 49 requires a majority of nonexecutive directors on the board. If the chairman is an executive of the company, at least half of the directors must be independent; if the chairman is a nonexecutive, the requirement for independent directors is reduced to one-third. Board members are limited to serving on no more than 10 committees across all boards to which they are elected. Companies are required to have an audit committee consisting of at least three members, two of whom must be independent directors. The CEO and CFO must certify financial statements. Clause 49 also includes extensive disclosure requirements for related-party transactions, board of directors' compensation and shareholdings in the company, and any financial relationships that might lead to board member conflicts. Companies are required to include a section in the annual report explaining whether they are in compliance with these standards.[63]

Although India has made significant regulatory reforms in recent years, several challenges remain. One is that capital markets are largely inefficient. Foreign individual investors are restricted in their ability to directly invest in companies listed on the Bombay Stock Exchange and the National Stock Exchange of India.[64] These restrictions reduce capital flows and remove an important disciplining mechanism on managerial behavior. The country's bond markets are also relatively undeveloped. In 2010, the corporate bond market in India had notional value of only $25 billion, less than 2 percent of gross domestic product (GDP). By comparison, the corporate bond market in the United States was $2.9 trillion notional and 20 percent of GDP.[65] With public financing less available, corporations must turn to private sources, which often come with their own agency problems and are less effective monitors.

Another challenge to governance reform is the outsized role that wealthy Indian families continue to play in most major corporations. Family-run companies continue to dominate the Indian economy. For example, Tata Group—which has subsidiaries in the auto manufacturing, agricultural chemicals, hospitality, telecommunications, and consulting sectors—accounts for more than 5 percent of the country's GDP.[66] In aggregate, company insiders and their families own approximately 45 percent of the equity value of all Indian companies.[67] When insiders own concentrated levels of a company's equity, corporate assets could be diverted for the personal benefits of these individuals (such as through excessive salary and perquisites), with minority shareholders bearing the cost of these abuses.

Brazil

As in many other emerging economies, corporate governance in Brazil is characterized by excessive influence by insiders and controlling shareholders and by low levels of disclosure. Brazilian law dictates that only one-third of board members must be nonexecutive. As a result, Brazilian boards tend to have a majority of executive directors. Furthermore, no independence standards exist for nonexecutive directors. Therefore, nonexecutive directors tend to be representatives of a controlling shareholder group or former executives. According to a survey by Black, de Carvalho, and Sampaio (2014), 15 percent of Brazilian companies did not have a single independent director, half had fewer than 30 percent independent directors, and only 20 percent had a majority of independent directors.[68] Disclosure rules provide further disincentive to add independent directors to the board: Brazilian companies are not required to disclose the independence status of board members, nor are they required to disclose biographical information that would enable a shareholder to infer this information.

Brazilian firms issue two classes of shares: common shares with voting rights and preferred shares that carry no voting rights. Preferred shares do not pay a fixed dividend. Almost all Brazilian companies have a controlling shareholder or a group that owns a majority of the voting shares. These shareholders hold considerable influence in nominating and electing directors, so the board essentially represents their interests. Minority common shareholders and preferred shareholders have much less influence over board selection and can elect only one director by majority vote.

Traditionally, Brazil has had highly regulated capital markets. In the early 1900s, the government ran public exchanges and set transaction fees. Brokers were employees of the state and could pass their positions on to their children. Liberalization began in the 1960s, and by the 1970s, brokerages were transitioned from government control to private ownership. By the 1980s, the largest trading market became the São Paulo Stock Exchange (Bovespa). To stimulate demand for listing on its exchange, Bovespa created three markets for listing based on a company's governance features. Nivel 1 has the least stringent governance requirements, Nivel 2 has more stringent requirements, and the Novo Mercado has the most stringent requirements. To satisfy the listing requirements of the **Novo Mercado**, a company must do the following:

- Issue only voting shares
- Maintain a minimum free float equivalent to 25 percent of capital
- Establish a two-year unified mandate for the entire board, which must have at least five members and at least 20 percent independent members
- Publish financial reports in accordance with either U.S. GAAP or IFRS
- Grant minority shareholders the rights to dispose of shares on the same terms as majority shareholders (known as **tag-along rights**)

These requirements are intended to provide the greatest level of protection for minority shareholders against expropriation by insiders.[69]

In 2001, the first year the new system was operational, 18 companies transferred their listing to Nivel 1 from the regular exchange. Novo Mercado did not receive its first listing until the following year and did not gain widespread traction until 2004, when Natura, Brazil's leading cosmetics company, transferred its listing there. Since that point, the number of listed companies on all three of these new exchanges has grown significantly (see Figure 2.3).

Novo Mercado and the Levels of Corporate Governance

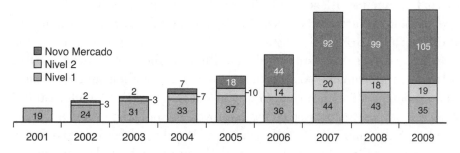

Source: Adapted by David F. Larcker and Brian Tayan. Data from: 9th European Corporate Governance Conference (June 28, 2010).

Figure 2.3   Number of companies listed on the Bovespa.

de Carvalho and Pennacchi (2012) found a positive impact on stock prices, trading volume, and liquidity for Brazilian companies that migrate their listing to these new exchanges. They concluded that shareholders positively view the governance changes associated with the new listing requirements.[70] Black, de Carvalho, and Sampaio (2014) also found that adoption of Novo Mercado and Level II listing standards was associated with higher market-to-book values.[71]

Russia

Corporate governance in Russia is characterized by concentrated ownership of shares, insider control, weak legal protection for minority shareholders, modest disclosure, inefficient capital markets, and heavy government involvement in private enterprise. Executives are often controlling shareholders or are closely affiliated with the controlling shareholder, whose interests they tend to serve. A disproportionate number of board members are insiders. In an examination of the boards of directors of the largest 132 public Russian companies in 2012, Deloitte found that an average of two-thirds are executive directors. Among state-controlled entities, insider representation is even higher: 80 percent.[72] The vast majority of board members do not represent minority investors.

Controlling shareholders use their influence to increase their claim on corporate assets, sometimes using illegal methods to do so. These methods include forcing solvent companies into bankruptcy to seize assets from minority shareholders, bribing the registrar to lose records of ownership by certain shareholders, manipulating transfer pricing to siphon money to an affiliated company that is wholly owned by the controlling shareholder, and forcing dilution of minority shareholders through a private offering to the controlling shareholder.[73] Because legal protections are weak, minority shareholders have limited ability to prevent these actions or seek compensation. For example, BP accused a Russian investor group in 2008 of trying to seize control of joint-venture assets (TNK–BP) by forcing the resignation of the BP-appointed CEO. The chairman of BP stated that the move was "just a return to the corporate raiding activities that were prevalent in Russia in the 1990s [after the fall of the Soviet Union]. Unfortunately, our partners continue to use them and the leaders of the country seem unwilling or unable to step in and stop them."[74] An international investor agreed: "Corporate governance has improved . . . but when someone really wants to break the rules, unfortunately, they can do it. It's a big concern, as it is causing real losses and damaging investor confidence in this country." He cited as an example his firm's investment in a Russian energy company in which "millions of dollars were transferred out of the company in exchange for assets of questionable value."[75]

The Russian government is another source of potential abuse for shareholders. The government has shown a tendency to intervene in business to promote its own interests. A primary method involves making dubious claims of unpaid taxes, which are then used as justification for seizing assets. This method was used in 2006 to transfer the assets from privately held Yukos to Gazprom—Russia's largest oil company, which the Russian government controls. Government corruption also occurs at the regional level, as regional governors accept bribes from local employers in exchange for protection from foreign competition. The government also interferes to maintain employment levels and prevent mass layoffs.

Finally, lack of transparency restricts the influence of shareholders. Disclosure requirements are weak, obscuring the nature of interparty transactions. A state-controlled media also contributes to a lack of transparency.

Black, Love, and Rachinsky (2006) examined the relationship between governance quality and share price in Russia. They found some evidence that firms with better governance features trade at higher market valuations than those with lesser protections.[76]

Endnotes

1. Raghuram G. Rajan and Luigi Zingales, "Financial Dependence and Growth," *American Economic Review* 88 (1998): 559–586.

2. Pyramidal family groups are two or more firms under a common controlling shareholder. See Ronald W. Masulis, Peter Kien Pham, and Jason Zein, "Family Business Groups around the World: Financing Advantages, Control Motivations, and Organizational Choices" *Review of Financial Studies* 24 (2011): 3556–3600.

3. Bernard Black, "Corporate Governance in Korea at the Millennium: Enhancing International Competitiveness," *Journal of Corporation Law* 26 (2001): 537.

4. That said, Kanna and Palepu (1999) warn that family-controlled business groups cannot be safely dismantled unless a so-called "soft infrastructure" is in place, including well-functioning markets for capital, management, labor, and information technology. Tarun Khanna and Krishna Palepu, "The Right Way to Restructure Conglomerates in Emerging Markets," *Harvard Business Review* 77 (1999): 125–134.

5. Christian Leuz, Karl V. Lins, and Francis E. Warnock, "Do Foreigners Invest Less in Poorly Governed Firms?" *The Review of Financial Studies* 22 (2009): 3245–3285.

6. Under common law, judicial precedent shapes the interpretation and application of laws. Judges consider previous court rulings on similar matters and use that information as the basis for settling current claims. By contrast, civil law (or code law) relies on comprehensive legal codes or statutes written by legislative bodies. The judiciary must base its decisions on strict interpretation of the law instead of legal precedent. Examples of common law countries include the United States, England, India, and Canada. Civil law countries include China, Japan, Germany, France, and Spain. See Rafael La Porta, Florencio Lopez-de-Silanes, Andrei Shleifer, and Robert W. Vishny, "Law and Finance," *Journal of Political Economy* 106 (1998): 1113–1155.

7. The results in these two La Porta, Lopez-de-Silanes, Shleifer, and Vishny papers have been examined in subsequent research. For example, Spamann (2010) constructs a new "antidirector rights index" using local lawyers and finds that many of the prior results in these papers become statistically insignificant. Thus, these results might be fragile. See Rafael La Porta, Florencio Lopez-de-Silanes, Andrei Shleifer, and Robert W. Vishny, "Investor Protection and Corporate Valuation," *Journal of Finance* 57 (2002): 1147–1170; and Holger Spamann, "The 'Antidirector Rights Index' Revisited," *Review of Financial Studies* 23 (2010): 467–486.

8. Cited in Jacob de Haan and Harry Seldadyo, "The Determinants of Corruption: A Literature Survey and New Evidence," paper presented at the Annual Conference of the European Public Choice Society, Turku (April 24, 2006).

9. Paulo Mauro, "Corruption and Growth," *Quarterly Journal of Economics* 110 (1995): 681–712.

10. Christos Pantzalis, Jung Chul Park, and Ninon Sutton, "Corruption and Valuation of Multinational Corporations," *Journal of Empirical Finance* 15 (2008): 387–417.

11. Mary E. Barth, Wayne R. Landsman, and Mark H. Lang, "International Accounting Standards and Accounting Quality," *Journal of Accounting Research* 46 (2008): 467–498.

12. Jürgen Ernstberger and Oliver Vogler, "Analyzing the German Accounting Triad—'Accounting Premium' for IAS/IFRS and U.S. GAAP vis-á-vis German GAAP?" *International Journal of Accounting* 43 (2008): 339–386.

13. Jere R. Francis, Shawn Huang, Inder K. Khurana, and Raynolde Pereira, "Does Corporate Transparency Contribute to Efficient Resource Allocation?" *Journal of Accounting Research* 47 (2009): 943–989.

14. George J. Benston, Michael Bromwich, and Alfred Wagenhofer, "Principles- Versus Rules-Based Accounting Standards: The FASB's Standard Setting Strategy," *Abacus* 42 (2006): 165–188.

15. Richard Price, Francisco J. Román, and Brian Rountree, "The Impact of Governance Reform on Performance and Transparency," *Journal of Financial Economics* 99 (2011): 76–96.

16. Luzi Hail and Christian Leuz, "International Differences in the Cost of Equity Capital: Do Legal Institutions and Securities Regulation Matter?" *Journal of Accounting Research* 44 (2006): 485–531.

17. Robert M. Bushman and Joseph D. Piotroski, "Financial Reporting Incentives for Conservative Accounting: The Influence of Legal and Political Institutions," *Journal of Accounting and Economics* 42 (2006): 107–148.

18. Victor Brudney, "Insiders, Outsiders, and Informational Advantages under the Federal Securities Laws," *Harvard Law Review* 93 (1979): 322. See Lawrence M. Ausubel, "Insider Trading in a Rational Expectations Economy," *American Economic Review* 80 (1990): 1022–1041. Hayne E. Leland, "Insider Trading: Should It Be Prohibited?" *Journal of Political Economy* 100 (1992): 859–887.

19. Geert Hofstede, "Cultural Dimensions," Itim Focus (2015). Accessed March 24, 2015. See http://geert-hofstede.com/national-culture.html.

20. The Hofstede research has been the subject of considerable criticism. We discuss it here as representative of a system for describing cultural attributes without commentary on its accuracy. See Nigel J. Holden, *Cross-Cultural Management: A Knowledge Management Perspective* (London: FT Prentice Hall, 2002). And Brendan McSweeney, "Hofstede's Model of National Cultural Differences and Their Consequences: A Triumph of Faith—A Failure of Analysis," *Human Relations* 55 (2002): 89–118.

21. Anonymous, "Whose Company Is It? New Insights on the Debate Over Shareholders vs. Stakeholders," *Knowledge@Wharton* (2007). Accessed July 7, 2008. See http://knowledge.wharton.upenn.edu/article.cfm?articleid=1826.

22. Despite the impression that diffuse ownership of U.S. securities exists, the ownership of U.S. firms is similar to and, by some measures, more concentrated than the ownership of firms in other countries. See World Federation of Exchanges, "2014 WFE Market Highlights," *WFE Statistics Database.* Accessed April 25, 2015. See http://www.world-exchanges.org/insight/reports/2014-WFE-market-highlights. And Clifford G. Holderness, "The Myth of Diffuse Ownership in the United States," *Review of Financial Studies* 22 (2009): 1377–1408.

23. However, U.S. markets have been losing their share in several of these categories during recent years. See Committee on Capital Markets Regulation, "The Competitive Position of the U.S. Public Equity Market," (2007). Accessed June 19, 2014. See http://capmktsreg.org/press/the-competitiveness-position-of-the-u-s-public-equity-market.

24. Computed using 2014 data for 1,871 companies in the Russell 2000 Index covered by SharkRepellent, FactSet Research Systems Inc.

25. Daines (2001) finds that companies incorporated in Delaware are worth approximately 5 percent more than firms incorporated in other states. Debate exists over whether this is because of increased governance quality, greater clarity on shareholder rights, or higher likelihood of receiving a takeover bid from another firm. See Robert M. Daines, "Does Delaware Law Improve Firm Value?" *Journal of Financial Economics* 62 (2001): 525–558.

26. See Chapter 5 for a discussion of NYSE independence standards. Source: "Corporate Governance Standards, Listed Company Manual Section 303A.02, Independence Tests," NYSE (2015). Accessed April 9, 2015. See http://nysemanual.nyse.com/LCMTools/PlatformViewer.asp ?selectednode=chp_1_4_3_3&manual=%2Flcm%2Fsections%2Flcm-sections%2F.

27. See Weil, Gotshal & Manges, LLP, "Financial Regulatory Reform: An Overview of the Dodd–Frank Wall Street Reform and Consumer Protection Act" (2010). Accessed November 2, 2010. See http://www.weil.com/~/media/files/pdfs/ny%20mailing%2010%20frr%2020100721%20weil_dodd_frank_overview_2010_07_21.pdf.

28. Nuno G. Fernandes, Miguel A. Ferreira, Pedro P. Matos, and Kevin J. Murphy, "Are US CEOs Paid More? New International Evidence?" EFA 2009 Bergen Meetings Paper; AFA 2011 Denver Meetings Paper; ECGI—Finance Working Paper No. 255/2009, *Social Science Research Network* (2012). Accessed April 9, 2014. See http://ssrn.com/abstract=1341639.

29. Adrian Cadbury, "The Financial Aspects of Corporate Governance; Report of the Committee on the Financial Aspects of Corporate Governance" (London: Gee & Co, 1992). Accessed November 3, 2010. See www.ecgi.org/codes/documents/cadbury.pdf.

30. Richard Greenbury, "Directors' Remuneration: Report of a Study Group Chaired by Sir Richard Greenbury" (London: Gee Publishing, 1995). Accessed November 3, 2010. See www.ecgi.org/codes/documents/greenbury.pdf.

31. Ronnie Hampel, "Committee on Corporate Governance: Final Report" (London: Gee Publishing 1998). Accessed November 3, 2010. See www.ecgi.org/codes/documents/hampel.pdf.

32. Nigel Turnbull, et al., "Internal Control: Guidance for Directors on the Combined Code" (1999). Accessed June 19, 2014. http://www.ecgi.org/codes/documents/turnbul.pdf.

33. Dechert, LLP, "The Higgs Report on Non-Executive Directors: Summary Recommendations" (2003). Last accessed December 5, 2007. See www.dechert. com/library/Summary%20of%20Recommendations1.pdf.

34. Cited in Rob Goffee, "Feedback Helps Boards to Focus on Their Roles," *Financial Times* (June 10, 2005): 32.

35. Martin Dickson, "Higgs and the History of Corporate Protest," *Financial Times* (February 18, 2003): 25. The Higgs Report was subsequently revised in June 2006 and in May 2010. See www.ecgi. org/codes/documents/frc_combined_code_june2006.pdf. Accessed October 30, 2010. Also see www.frc.org.uk/images/uploaded/documents/May%202010%20report%20on%20Code%20consultation.pdf. Accessed October 30, 2010.

36. David Walker, "A Review of Corporate Governance in UK Banks and Other Financial Industry Entities: Final Recommendations" (November 26, 2009). See http://webarchive.nationalarchives.gov.uk/20130129110402/http://www.hm-treasury.gov.uk/d/walker_review_261109.pdf.

37. Financial Reporting Council, "Guidance on Board Effectiveness," FRC (2011). Accessed July 15, 2014. See https://www.frc.org.uk/Our-Work/Publications/Corporate-Governance/Guidance-on-Board-Effectiveness.pdf.

38. Paul L. Davies, "Board Structure in the United Kingdom and Germany: Convergence or Continuing Divergence?" *Social Science Research Network* (2001): 1–24. Accessed October 30, 2010. See http://ssrn.com/abstract=262959.

39. Amama Shabbir and Carol Padgett, "The UK Code of Corporate Governance: Link between Compliance and Firm Performance," RP 2/08. Cranfield University School of Management (2008). Accessed March 24, 2015. See https://dspace.lib.cranfield.ac.uk/handle/1826/3931.

40. Grant Thornton UK, LLP, FTSE 350 Corporate Governance Review (2013). Accessed July 10, 2014. See http://www.grant-thornton.co.uk/Documents/FTSE-350-Corporate-Governance-Review-2013.pdf.

41. Commission of the German Corporate Governance Code, "German Corporate Governance—Code" (May 26, 2010). Accessed April 9, 2015. See http://www.ecgi.org/codes/code.php?code_id=308.

42. Christopher Rhoads and Vanessa Fuhrmans, "Trouble Brewing: Corporate Germany Braces for a Big Shift from Postwar Stability—Layoffs, Predators, Gadflies Loom with Unwinding of Cross-Shareholdings—Dry Times for Beer Workers," *Wall Street Journal* (June 21, 2001, Eastern edition): A1.

43. Jeremy Edwards and Marcus Nibler, "Corporate Governance in Germany: The Role of Banks and Ownership Concentration," *Economic Policy* 32 (2000) 239–268.

44. Wolf-Georg Ringe, "Changing Law and Ownership Patterns in Germany: Corporate Governance and the Erosion of Deutschland AG," Oxford Legal Studies Research Paper No. 42/2014, (2014); *American Journal of Comparative Law*, forthcoming.

45. Andreas Cremer, "Volkswagen CEO's Pay Nearly Doubles to 17.5 mln Euros," Thomson Reuters (March 12, 2012); Anonymous, "Interview with Volkswagen CEO: 'European Auto Crisis Is an Endurance Test,'" Spiegel Online International (February 13, 2013).

46. Toyota Motor Corporation, Form 6-K, filed with the Securities and Exchange Commission June 29, 2007. One of the guiding precepts of the Toyota Production System, *genchi genbutsu*, means "go and see for yourself."

47. Toyota Motor Corporation, "2006 Annual Report," Accessed June 23, 2008. See http://www.toyota-global.com/investors/ir_library/annual/pdf/2006/, "Toyota Governance." Accessed November 2, 2010. See http://www.toyota-industries.com/corporateinfo/governance/.

48. Hideaki Miyajima and Keisuku Nitta, "Diverse Evolution of the Traditional Board of Directors: Its Causes and Effects on Performance," in *Corporate Governance—Diversification and Prospects, Kinzai* (in Japanese) (2007).

49. TMI Associates and Simmons & Simmons, "Amendments to the Japanese Commercial Code." Amendment enacted in May 2002, in force as of April 1, 2003 (2003). Accessed April 3, 2015. See www.tmi.gr.jp/english/topic/2003/index.html.

50. Robert Eberhart, "Corporate Governance Systems and Firm Value: Empirical Evidence from Japan's Natural Experiment," *Journal of Asia Business Studies* 6 (2012): 176–196.

51. In the late 1980s, Japanese banks owned almost 50 percent of total tradable public equity. By 2006, they held around 20 percent. See Masahiko Aoki, "Conclusion: Whither Japan's Corporate Governance?" *Corporate Governance in Japan: Institutional Change and Organizational Diversity*, edited by Masahiko Aoki, Gregory Jackson, and Hideaki Miyajima (New York: Oxford University Press, 2007).

52. FSA.Gov, "Principles for Responsible Institutional Investors, Japan's Stewardship Code," The Council of Experts Concerning the Japanese Version of the Stewardship Code (2014). Accessed July 21, 2014. See http://www.fsa.go.jp/en/refer/councils/stewardship/20140407.html.

53. The Council of Experts Concerning the Corporate Governance Code, "Japan's Corporate Governance Code [Final Proposal]: Seeking Sustainable Corporate Growth and Increased Corporate Value over the Mid- to Long-Term," (March 5, 2015). Accessed April 15, 2015. See http://www.fsa.go.jp/en/refer/councils/corporategovernance/20150306-1/01.pdf.

54. Barry Metzger, Bernard S. Black, Timothy O'Brien, and Young Moo Shin, "Corporate Governance in Korea at the Millennium: Enhancing International Competitiveness," *Journal of Corporation Law* 26 (2001): 537–608.

55. Ibid.

56. Ibid.

57. Bernard Black and Woochan Kim, "The Effect of Board Structure on Firm Value: A Multiple Identification Strategies Approach Using Korean Data," *Journal of Financial Economics* 104 (April 2012): 203–226.

58. Sean Liu, "Corporate Governance and Development: The Case of China," *Managerial and Decision Economics* 26 (2005): 445–449.

59. Standing Committee of the NPC, Law Bridge, "The Company Law of the People's Republic of China (Revised in 2005)." Accessed April 24, 2015. See www.law-bridge.net/english/LAW/20064/0221042566163-5.html.

60. PetroChina Company Limited, Form 20-F, filed with the Securities and Exchange Commission April 25, 2014.

61. Martin J. Conyon and Lerong He, "Executive Compensation and Corporate Governance in China," *Journal of Corporate Finance* 17 (September 2011): 1158–1175.

62. Bernard Black and Vikramaditya Khanna, "Can Corporate Governance Reforms Increase Firms' Market Values? Evidence from India," *American Law & Economics Association Papers* 40 (2007): 1–38.

63. Securities and Exchange Board of India (SEBI), "Corporate Governance in Listed Companies: Clause 49 of the Listing Agreement" (2004). Accessed December 5, 2007. See http://www.sebi.gov.in/cms/sebi_data/attachdocs/1397734478112.pdf.

64. India Mart, "India Finance and Investment Mart: Foreign Institutional Investor" (2010). Last accessed November 3, 2010. See http://finance.indiamart.com/india_business_information/sebi_foreign_institutional_investor.html.

65. Development Research Group, "A Study of Corporate Bond Market in India: Theoretical and Policy Implications," Reserve Bank of India Study No. 40. Accessed July 25, 2014. See http://rbi.org.in/scripts/PublicationsView.aspx?id=15725.

66. Ravi Velloor, "Jewel of Corporate India," *The Straits Times* (March 17, 2013).

67. Nandini Rajagopalan and Yan Zhang, "Corporate Governance Reforms in China and India: Challenges and Opportunities," *Business Horizons* 51 (2008): 55–64.

68. In the study, independent directors are defined as "persons who are not officers or former officers and are independent of the controlling shareholder, controlling shareholder group, or controlling family." Bernard S. Black, Antonio Gledson de Carvalho, and Joelson Oliveira Sampaio, "The Evolution of Corporate Governance in Brazil," *Emerging Markets Review* 20 (2014): 176–195.

69. Nivel 2 primarily differs from the Novo Mercado in that companies are allowed to issue nonvoting shares. Nivel 1 does not require tag-along rights for minority shareholders and also does not have a 20 percent requirement for board independence. See Érica Gorga, "Changing the Paradigm of Stock Ownership from Concentrated Towards Dispersed Ownership? Evidence from Brazil and Consequences for Emerging Countries," *Northwestern Journal of International Law & Business* 29 (2009): 439–554.

70. Antonio Gledson de Carvalho and George G. Pennacchi, "Can a Stock Exchange Improve Corporate Behavior? Evidence from Firms' Migration to Premium Listings in Brazil," *Journal of Corporate Finance* 18 (2012): 883–903.

71. Black, de Carvalho, and Sampaio (2014).

72. Deloitte, "Corporate Governance Structures of Public Russian Companies Survey," Deloitte CIS Centre for Corporate Governance (2012). Accessed July 25, 2014. See http://www2.deloitte.com/kz/en/pages/finance/articles/survey-of-corporate-governance-structures.html.

73. Bernard S. Black, Inessa Love, and Andrei Rachinsky, "Corporate Governance Indices and Firms' Market Values: Time Series Evidence from Russia," *Emerging Markets Review* 7 (2006): 361–379.

74. Robert Anderson, Catherine Belton, and Ed Crooks, "BP Accuses Russian Partners in TNK–BP of 'Corporate Raiding,'" *Financial Times* (June 13, 2008): 13.

75. John Bowker, "Russia Held Back by Corporate Governance Weakness: Fund," *Reuters* (September 10, 2010). Accessed April 24, 2015. See www.reuters.com/article/idUS-TRE6893BO20100910.

76. Black, Love, and Rachinsky (2006).

Interlude

The board of directors plays a central role in the corporate governance system. All countries require that publicly listed companies have a board. The attributes of boards vary across nations (in terms of their mandated structure, independence levels, stakeholder representation, and other compositional features), but they universally share two fundamental responsibilities: to advise management and oversee its activities.

In the next few chapters, we take a critical look at the board of directors. We start by examining the basic operations of the board and the duties that come with directorship (in Chapter 3, "Board of Directors: Duties and Liability"). Then we discuss the process by which directors are selected, compensated, and replaced (in Chapter 4, "Board of Directors: Selection, Compensation, and Removal"). Finally, we review the scientific evidence on how the structure of the board does (and does not) impact firm performance and governance quality (in Chapter 5, "Board of Directors: Structure and Consequences").

These chapters are intended to help you think critically about board effectiveness and make concrete decisions about how a board should be structured.

3

Board of Directors: Duties and Liability

In this chapter, we examine the duties and liabilities that come with directorship. We start with an overview of the role of the board and the requirement for independence. We then review the basic operations of the board. This includes evaluating the process by which topics are selected, deliberated, and decided. Next, we review the process by which directors are elected and removed. Finally, we examine the legal responsibilities that come with directorship and consider the potential liability directors face when they fail to uphold their duties. While we focus on boards of U.S. corporations, the broad principles apply to boards in all countries.

Board Responsibilities

In a document called Principles of Corporate Governance, the Organisation for Economic Co-operation and Development (OECD) lays out a vision of the responsibilities of the board:

> The corporate governance framework should ensure the strategic guidance of the company, the effective monitoring of management by the board, and the board's accountability to the company and the shareholders.[1]

That is, the board is expected to provide both advisory and oversight functions. Although these responsibilities are linked in many ways, they have fundamentally different focuses. In an **advisory** capacity, the board consults with management regarding the strategic and operational direction of the company. Attention is paid to decisions that balance risk and reward. Board members are selected based on the skill and expertise they offer for this purpose, including previous experience in a relevant industry or function.

In its **oversight** capacity, the board is expected to monitor management and ensure that it is acting diligently in the interests of shareholders. The board hires and fires the chief executive officer, measures corporate performance, evaluates management contribution to performance, and awards compensation. It also oversees legal and regulatory compliance, including the audit process, reporting requirements for publicly traded companies, and industry-specific regulations. In fulfilling these responsibilities, the board often relies on the advice of legal counsel and other paid professionals, such as external auditors, executive recruiters, compensation consultants, investment bankers, and tax advisors. Effective board members are individuals that can capably complete both advisory and oversight responsibilities.

The responsibilities of directors are separate and distinct from those of management. Directors are expected to advise on corporate strategy but do not develop the strategy. They are expected to ensure the integrity of the financial statements but do not prepare the statements themselves. The board is not an extension of management. The board is a governing body elected to represent the interests of shareholders.

Survey data suggests that board members understand the role they are expected to serve. When asked to describe what areas directors should pay most attention to, directors list strategic planning, merger opportunities, and CEO succession as their top three priorities. Other areas of focus include international expansion, information technology, and the development of human capital.[2] Still, some evidence indicates that directors prefer the advisory function to the monitoring function. When asked what issues they would like to spend more time discussing, directors list strategic planning, competition, and succession planning among their top responses. By contrast, most want to spend the same or less time on executive compensation, monitoring performance, and compliance and regulatory issues.[3]

Board Independence

To be effective in an advisory and oversight capacity, board members are expected to exhibit independence. From a regulatory standpoint, independence is evaluated by the degree to which a director is free from conflicts of interest that might compromise his or her ability to act solely in the interest of the firm. Independence is critical in that it ensures that directors are able to take positions in opposition to those of management when necessary. In the United States, the New York Stock Exchange (NYSE) requires that listed companies have a majority of independent directors. It also requires solely independent audit, compensation, and nominating and governance committees.

However, regulatory standards are not necessarily the same as true independence. Board members who have worked with management over a long period of time may well form ties that will challenge a truly independent perspective. Independence may also be compromised by individual factors, such as a board member's background, education, experience, values, and personal relation to management. There are many examples of boards comprised of highly capable directors who went along with management decisions that later proved disastrous. For example, the board of Enron failed to rein in management actions that were later held to be criminal. Similarly, the board of the Walt

Disney Company acquiesced to management in the hiring and firing of Michael Ovitz as president, which later drew harsh criticism from shareholders.

Anecdotal evidence suggests that board members do not necessarily believe that formal independence standards are correlated with true independence. An informal study conducted by professors at Harvard Business School found that relevant experience is a more important indicator of director quality than regulatory requirements. According to one respondent, "I don't think independence is anywhere near as important as people thought it was. . . . It was a red herring."[4] Nevertheless, most directors believe that they are capable of maintaining independence. In a survey by *Corporate Board Member* magazine, 90 percent of directors responded that they and their fellow board members effectively challenged management when necessary.[5] (We discuss independence in more detail in Chapter 5, "Board of Directors: Structure and Consequences.")

The Operations of the Board

A chairman presides over meetings of the board of directors. The chairman is responsible for setting the agenda, scheduling meetings, and coordinating actions of board committees. As such, the chairman holds considerable sway over the governance process by determining the content and timing of matters brought before the board.

Traditionally, the CEO has served as the chairman of the board in most U.S. corporations. In recent years, however, it has become more common for a nonexecutive director to serve as chair. Given the advising and oversight responsibilities of the board, several obvious conflicts could arise from a dual chairman/CEO. Chief among them are the commingling of responsibilities that are afforded separately to management and the board, and the potential for weakened oversight in the areas of performance evaluation, compensation, succession planning, and recruitment of independent directors. At the same time, a dual chairman/CEO offers potential benefits regarding singular leadership within the organization and clear, efficient decision making. (We examine the evidence on independent chairmen in Chapter 5.)

In the debate over the Sarbanes–Oxley Act of 2002 (SOX), Congress considered but ultimately rejected calls to require an independent director to serve as chairman. Instead, SOX required that companies designate an independent director as "lead director" for each board meeting. The lead director may be named to serve on a meeting-by-meeting basis or may be appointed to serve continuously until replaced. The role of the lead director is to represent the independent directors in conversations with the CEO. This structure is intended to fortify an independent review of management among companies with a dual chairman/CEO. (We discuss the role of the lead director in more detail in Chapter 5.)

Board actions take place either at board meetings or by written consent. At a board meeting, resolutions are presented to the board and voted upon. An action is complete when it receives a majority of votes in support. When the board acts by **written consent**, a written resolution is circulated among board members for their signatures. The action is complete when a majority of the directors have signed the document. Because board actions by written consent do not require advance notice, they can occur more quickly than actions taken at board meetings.

In addition to attending meetings of the full board, independent directors meet at least once a year in **executive session**, in which executive directors are not present. This practice was mandated by SOX. Although no formal actions are taken at these meetings, executive sessions give outside directors an opportunity to discuss candidly the performance of management, operating results, internal controls, and succession planning. The lead independent director presides over these meetings.

Directors report spending approximately 20 hours per month on board matters. According to the National Association of Corporate Directors (NACD), the full board of directors convenes eight times per year either in person or over the phone, and a typical meeting lasts 7 hours.[6] Increased regulatory requirements in recent years have done much to lengthen board meetings. Still, most directors believe that the agenda is structured to make efficient use of their time and that 20 hours per month is sufficient to satisfy their duties.[7]

To inform its decisions, the board relies on materials provided by management. Survey data indicates that the quality of this information might not be adequate. For example, a study by the NACD reported that 17 percent of directors are not satisfied with the quality of information they receive from management about the company's strategy, 18 percent about nonfinancial risk, and 27 percent about information technology.[8] Nonexecutive directors can address these deficiencies by requesting that management improve reporting on nonfinancial as well as financial strategic performance measures. Directors may also benefit through direct contact with management. According to one director, "There is no substitute for time spent meeting with management of the different divisions or sectors that are the next level down the corporate ladder, having them present directly to the board, [and] visiting operations."[9] (We examine these issues in greater detail in Chapter 6, "Strategy, Performance Measurement, and Risk Management.")

Board Committees

Not all corporate matters are deliberated by the full board of directors. Some are delegated to committees. These committees can be standing or *ad hoc*, depending on the nature of the topic. Directors are assigned to committees based on their qualifications. On important matters, such as the design and approval of executive compensation contracts, recommendations of the committee are brought before the full board for a vote.

Historically, the creation of committees was left largely to the discretion of the board. The only committee that the Securities and Exchange Commission (SEC) required was an audit committee, which was mandated for all publicly listed companies in 1977. In 2002, the Sarbanes–Oxley Act required additional committees, including a compensation committee, a governance committee, and a nominating committee. The act stipulated that these committees and the audit committee consist entirely of independent directors.

The **audit committee** is responsible for overseeing the company's external audit and is the primary contact between the auditor and the company. This reporting relationship is intended to prevent management manipulation of the audit. Under SOX, the audit committee must have at least three members, all of whom are financially literate; the chair also must be a financial expert. The audit committee maintains a written charter that outlines its duties to the full board, including these obligations:

1. Overseeing the financial reporting and disclosure process
2. Monitoring the choice of accounting policies and principles
3. Overseeing the hiring, performance, and independence of the external auditor
4. Overseeing regulatory compliance, ethics, and whistleblower hotlines
5. Monitoring internal control processes
6. Overseeing the performance of the internal audit function
7. Discussing risk-management policies and practices with management[10]

According to the NACD, audit committees meet an average of eight times per year either in person or over the phone, and a typical meeting lasts 2.7 hours.[11] Ninety-seven percent of directors believe that the audit committee is effective in its oversight of the financial reporting process.[12] (We explore the duties of the audit committee in greater detail in Chapter 10, "Financial Reporting and External Audit.")

The **compensation committee** is responsible for setting the compensation of the CEO and for advising the CEO on the compensation of other senior executives. Sarbanes–Oxley established no minimum committee size. The obligations of the compensation committee include the following:

1. Setting the compensation of the CEO
2. Setting and reviewing performance-related goals for the CEO
3. Determining an appropriate compensation structure for the CEO, given these performance expectations
4. Monitoring CEO performance relative to targets
5. Setting or advising the CEO on other officers' compensation
6. Advising the CEO on and overseeing compensation of nonexecutive employees
7. Setting board compensation
8. Hiring consultants to assist in the compensation process, as appropriate[13]

Compensation committees meet an average of six times per year for 2.7 hours.[14] Eighty-nine percent of directors believe the compensation committee can properly manage CEO compensation.[15] (We explore compensation in greater detail in Chapters 8, "Executive Compensation and Incentives," and 9, "Executive Equity Ownership.")

The **governance committee** is responsible for evaluating the company's governance structure and processes and recommending improvements, when appropriate. The **nominating committee** is responsible for identifying, evaluating, and nominating new directors when board seats need to be filled. The **nominating committee** is also typically in charge of leading the CEO succession-planning process. In most companies, the nominating and governance committees are combined into a single committee with these responsibilities:

1. Identifying qualified individuals to serve on the board
2. Selecting nominees to be put before a shareholder vote at the annual meeting
3. Hiring consultants to assist in the director recruitment process, as appropriate
4. Determining governance standards for the corporation
5. Managing the board evaluation process
6. Managing the CEO evaluation process[16]

The nominating and governance committee meets an average of eight times per year for 1.8 hours.[17] Despite the independence of this committee, the CEO often has significant input into the choice of directors nominated to the board. This is true whether or not the CEO holds the dual role of chairman. (We explore director recruitment in Chapter 4, "Board of Directors: Selection, Compensation, and Removal," and CEO succession in Chapter 7, "Labor Market for Executives and CEO Succession Planning.")

Boards are free to establish additional committees beyond those required by listing exchanges. These committees generally monitor functional areas that the board believes to hold strategic importance for the firm, thus meriting additional oversight (**specialized committees**). According to Spencer Stuart, 31 percent of companies have a committee dedicated to finance, 11 percent to public policy or social and corporate responsibility, 8 percent to science and technology, 8 percent to the environment or health and safety, 8 percent to risk, and 6 percent to legal matters or compliance.[18] These committees oversee and advise these functions; they do not directly manage them, which is the purview of management (see the following sidebar).

Specialized Board Committees

The board of Merck & Co. convenes a Research Committee to monitor its drug discovery and development process:

"The purpose of the Research Committee is to assist the Board in its oversight of matters pertaining to the Company's strategies and operations for the research and development of pharmaceutical products and vaccines by:

- Identifying areas and activities that are critical to the success of Merck's drug and vaccine discovery, development and licensing efforts;

- Evaluating the effectiveness of Merck's drug and vaccine discovery, development and licensing strategies and operations;

- Keeping the Board apprised of this evaluation process and findings; and

- Making appropriate recommendations to the President of Merck Research Laboratories, the CEO and to the Board on modifications of strategies and operations."[19]

Fifth Third Bancorp has a Risk and Compliance Committee that monitors financial, credit, and regulatory risk:

"The Committee oversees management's compliance with all of the Company's regulatory obligations arising under applicable federal and state banking laws, rules and regulations, including any terms and conditions required from time to time by any action, formal or informal, of any federal or state banking regulatory agency or authority and any responses of management to any inquiries from any applicable banking regulator, and oversees management's implementation and enforcement of the Company's risk management policies and processes."[20]

The board of Cisco Systems has a Finance Committee that monitors a broad range of financial activities:

"The Finance Committee reviews and approves Cisco's global investment policy; reviews minority investments, fixed income assets, insurance risk management policies and programs, and tax programs; oversees Cisco's stock repurchase programs; and also reviews Cisco's currency, interest rate, and equity risk management policies. This committee is also authorized to approve the issuance of debt securities, certain real estate acquisitions and leases, and charitable contributions made on behalf of Cisco."[21]

General Mills has a Public Responsibility Committee that has these functions:

- Reviews public policy and social trends affecting General Mills;

- Monitors our corporate citizenship activities and sustainability programs;

- Evaluates our policies in the context of emerging corporate social responsibility issues; and

- Reviews our policies governing political contributions and our record of contributions.[22]

Duration of Director Terms

Traditionally, directors are elected annually to one-year terms. In some companies, directors are elected to two- or three-year terms, with a subset of directors standing for reelection each year. Companies that follow this protocol are referred to as having **staggered** (or **classified**) boards. Under a typical staggered board, directors are elected to three-year terms, with one-third of the board standing for reelection every three years. As a result, it is not possible for the board to be ousted in a single year; two election cycles are needed for a majority of the board to turn over. As we discuss in Chapter 11, "The Market for Corporate Control," staggered boards can be an effective antitakeover protection.

Largely in response to the increased incidence of hostile takeovers in the 1980s, firms began adopting staggered boards. For example, from 1994 to 1999, the percentage of firms that adopted staggered boards at the time they went public increased from 43 percent to 82 percent in the United States.[23] In recent years, however, the trend has reversed. Companies have come under fire from shareholder activists and proxy advisory firms who believe that staggered board elections insulate directors from shareholder influence. Institutional investors, particularly public pension plans, often have policies of opposing staggered boards. Some public companies have responded to shareholder pressure by destaggering their boards. In 2014, about 53 percent of publicly traded companies had staggered boards, down from 63 percent in 2002.[24]

Director Elections

In most companies, the board of directors is elected by shareholders on a one-share, one-vote basis. For example, if there are nine seats on a board, a shareholder with 100 shares can cast 100 votes for each of the nine people nominated. Shareholders who do not want to vote for one or all of the nominees can withhold votes for selected individuals. Directors win an election by obtaining a **plurality** of votes, meaning that the directors who receive the most votes win, regardless of whether they receive a majority of votes. In an uncontested election, a director is elected as long as he or she receives at least one vote.

Three main alternatives to this system of voting exist: dual-class stock, majority voting, and cumulative voting. A company with **dual-class shares** has more than one class of common stock. In general, each class has equal economic interest in the company but unequal voting rights. For example, Class A shares might be afforded one vote per share, whereas Class B shares might have ten votes per share. Typically, an insider, a founding family member, or another shareholder friendly to management holds the class of shares with preferential voting rights, which gives that person significant (if not outright) influence over board elections. Dual-class stock thus tends to weaken the influence of public shareholders. Approximately 10 percent of publicly traded corporations in the United States have some form of dual-class structure.[25] Berkshire Hathaway, Facebook, Google, the New York Times Co., and Hershey all have dual-class shares.

The second variation in voting procedures is **majority voting**. Majority voting differs from plurality voting in that a director is required to receive a majority of votes to be elected. This means that even in an uncontested election, a director can fail to win a board seat if over half of all outstanding votes are withheld from him or her. The specific procedures of majority voting systems vary. In some companies, candidates who receive more withhold votes than votes in favor are strictly refused a seat on the board. More commonly, the director is required to submit a letter of resignation, and the rest of the board has discretion over whether to accept it. Other companies require resignation, but only after a replacement director is appointed. Majority voting gives shareholders more power to control the composition of the board, even in the absence of an alternative slate of directors. In 2014, more than 85 percent of companies in the S&P 500 had adopted majority voting for director elections—a percentage that has been increasing in recent years. However, majority voting remains less common among small and midsized companies, with only 23 percent of companies in the Russell 2000 Index using this standard of voting.[26]

The third variation is **cumulative voting**. Cumulative voting allows a shareholder to concentrate votes on a single board candidate instead of requiring one vote for each candidate. A shareholder is given a number of votes equal to the product of the number of shares owned times the number of seats the company has on its board. For example, a shareholder with 100 shares in a company with a board of nine directors has 900 votes. The shareholder can allocate those votes among board candidates as he or she chooses. To increase the chances of electing a specific director, the shareholder might concentrate more votes toward a single candidate or a subset of candidates. Cumulative voting is relatively rare. Fewer than 5 percent of companies in the S&P 500 have adopted cumulative voting.[27]

In the ordinary course, board elections are uncontested. The company puts up a slate of directors for election, and the shareholders are expected to elect the slate. **Contested elections** occur in two circumstances. First, in the case of a hostile takeover battle, the bidding firm puts up a full slate of directors that is sympathetic to the acquisition. If the target shareholders elect the bidder's slate, those directors will remove impediments to the takeover (such as a poison pill) and vote in favor of the deal. The second context in which contested elections take place involves an activist investor who is dissatisfied with management and wants to gain influence over the company. In this situation, the shareholder might put up a "short slate" of directors—a limited number of directors who, if elected, would constitute a minority of the board. These directors would then serve as a vehicle through which the activist investor could participate in board-level decisions. Historically, the cost of nominating a dissident slate was borne entirely by the hostile bidder or activist. For this reason, proxy contests unrelated to takeovers have been quite rare. According to Institutional Shareholder Services, only 24 proxy contests occurred in 2013.[28]

The Dodd–Frank Wall Street Reform Act, as originally enacted, allowed investor groups that own at least 3 percent of a company's shares continuously for three years to nominate up to 25 percent of the board. However, this right—known as proxy access—was struck down by a federal court in 2011. Subsequently, the SEC issued a private ordering that allows companies to adopt proxy access on a voluntary basis. According to Sullivan & Cromwell, nine shareholder-sponsored proposals for proxy access were voted on in 2013; of these, only two received majority support, at CenturyLink and Verizon, both of which adopted bylaw changes to this effect the following year.[29]

Removal of Directors

Once elected, directors generally serve their full term—one year for annually elected boards and three years for staggered boards. Shareholders may be able to prevent directors from being reelected at the next election by withholding votes. Their ability to do so, however, depends on the voting procedures in place. They can also replace directors at the next election if a competing slate of nominees is put up for election. Finally, unless a company's certificate of incorporation provides otherwise, shareholders may vote to "remove" a director between meetings. That said, shareholder power to remove a director is generally limited. (We discuss director removal in greater detail in the next chapter.)

Legal Obligations of Directors

In the United States, state corporate law and federal securities law set forth the legal duties of the board. The state law applicable to a corporation is the law of the state in which the company is incorporated. A company may incorporate in any state, regardless of where its headquarters is located or where it does business. As we discussed in the previous chapter, Delaware is by far the most common state of incorporation. Delaware has the most developed body of case law, which gives companies greater clarity on how corporate governance and liability matters might be decided.

Under state corporate law, the primary duties of the board are embodied in the broad principle of **fiduciary duty**. Under federal securities law, the directors' duties stem from the corporation's obligation to disclose material information to the public.

Fiduciary Duty

Under state corporate law, the board of directors has a legal obligation to act in the "interest of the corporation."[30] In legal terminology, this is referred to as a fiduciary duty to the corporation. Although somewhat ambiguous—since a corporation is simply a legal construct that cannot have its own interests—the courts have interpreted this phrase to mean that a director is expected to act in the interest of shareholders. Indeed, court decisions often refer to a fiduciary duty to "the corporation and the shareholders" or even just to the shareholders.

The fiduciary duty of the board includes three components:

- A duty of care
- A duty of loyalty
- A duty of candor

The **duty of care** requires that a director make decisions with due deliberation. In the United States, courts enforce the duty of care through the rubric of the "business judgment rule." This rule provides that the judgment of a board will not be overridden by a court unless a plaintiff can show that the board failed to inform itself regarding the decision at issue or that the board was infected with a conflict of interest, in which case there may have been a violation of the duty of loyalty. Courts have rarely ruled against a board for a violation of the duty of care. Even if a board decision was clearly wrong, if the board can show that it engaged in some consideration of information related to the decision, the courts will adopt a hands-off posture. The business judgment rule is most protective of outside directors. In the absence of "red flags" regarding what management is telling them, outside directors are permitted to rely on what they hear from management to inform their decision. Moreover, companies are permitted to include exculpatory provisions in the charters that protect an outside director from suits for monetary damages for breach of the duty of care, so long as the director has not acted intentionally or in bad faith.

The **duty of loyalty** addresses conflicts of interest. For example, if management is considering a transaction with a company in which a director has a significant financial interest, the duty of loyalty requires that the terms of the transaction promote the interests of the shareholders over those of the director. As another example, if a director discovers a business opportunity in the course of his or her service to the company, the duty of loyalty requires that the director refrain from taking the opportunity before first determining whether the company will take it. The law lays out procedures for a board to follow in situations when a potential conflict of interest may exist.

The **duty of candor** requires that management and the board inform shareholders of all information that is important to their evaluation of the company and its management. The company's management is required in the first instance to provide accurate and timely information to shareholders, and the board is expected to oversee this process. In the absence of direct knowledge of wrongdoing, the board is permitted to rely on management assurances that the information is complete and accurate.

As a practical matter for publicly held companies, disclosure requirements mandated by federal securities law are more relevant than the duty of candor (discussed in the next section, "Disclosure Obligations under Securities Laws"). Like the duty of candor, federal securities laws require a company and its management to disclose material information to shareholders and that they do so in great detail. Consequently, public company shareholders are more likely to assert disclosure violations under securities laws than under the duty of candor. The duty of candor is important, however, for nonpublic companies.

Because the courts have interpreted the board's obligation to serve "in the interest of the corporation" to mean "in the interest of shareholders," corporate governance in the United States is said to be shareholder-centric. Survey data indicates that directors accept a shareholder-centric view of their responsibilities. When asked to identify in order of importance the constituents they serve, directors ranked "all shareholders" first, followed by institutional investors, customers, and creditors. They ranked other constituents such as employees and the community lower (see Table 3.1).[31]

Table 3.1 Constituents Directors Serve

Given that directors serve multiple constituencies, which are most important? (*Listed in order, according to director responses*)
All shareholders
Institutional investors
Customers
Creditors
Management
Employees
Analysts and Wall Street
Activist shareholders
The community

Source: *Corporate Board Member* and PricewaterhouseCoopers, LLP (2007).

In the 1990s, the legislatures of many states enacted statutes that allow the board to consider nonshareholder interests. These statutes are referred to as "nonshareholder constituency" or "expanded constituency" provisions. They allow the board to consider the impact of their actions on stakeholders such as workers, customers, suppliers, and the surrounding community. The primary application of these statutes is in the evaluation of a takeover bid. These statutes purportedly allow management and the board to reject a takeover offer that is in the interest of shareholders if the takeover would harm other constituents. Still, courts generally have not allowed these statutes to be used to the disadvantage of shareholders.

Ohio and Pennsylvania have gone further and *require* that the board consider nonshareholder interests. In 2010, Maryland became the first state to allow entrepreneurs to incorporate as a "benefit corporation" (or B Corp). A benefit corporation is formed for a "general public benefit"—such as the environment or community involvement—which is identified in its charter. The annual report to owners includes an assessment of its performance against this objective. Some states require periodic third-party verification of the company's activities. The enactment of benefit corporation legislation is intended to provide indemnity to corporate directors who take nonshareholder concerns into account in making decisions. Currently, more than 40 states have passed or proposed legislation recognizing benefit corporations (see the following sidebar).[32]

Statutes that provide for nonshareholder considerations have been litigated only to a limited extent. As a result, their meaning is still uncertain. To date, courts have interpreted them to mean that boards should take into account nonshareholder interests only to the extent that shareholder interests are not compromised. Thus, even the board of a corporation that is governed by one of these statutes has a duty to promote the interests of shareholders.

Stakeholder Interests

In the United Kingdom, the Companies Act 2006 allows for the consideration of nonshareholder interests in boardroom decisions. A director is required to "act in the way he considers, in good faith, would be most likely to promote the success of the company for the benefit of its members as a whole."[33] The act specifies that this includes employees, customers, suppliers, community members, the environment, creditors, and others.

In South Africa, governance standards are outlined in the King Report (1994), King Report II (2001), and King Report III (2009). These require that the board of directors identify all stakeholders and define the methods according to which the company promises to serve their interests. The company is expected to report financial, environmental, and social results (the so-called **triple-bottom line**), and the board of directors is expected to communicate progress against all three measures in a report to stakeholders.[34]

In the United States, Etsy filed to become one of the first B corporations listed for public trading on the NASDAQ. It is not clear how the company, which operates a crafts marketplace for independent vendors, will balance market pressures for financial performance with its obligations as a B corp. In filings with the SEC, Etsy cautioned that the company did not plan to issue quarterly or annual earnings guidance, stating "Quantitative earnings guidance is misaligned with Etsy's mission. For example, the pressure to hit a quarterly financial target could incent us too heavily to seek near-term gains, which could diminish our ability to fulfill our larger mission over the long-term."[35]

Disclosure Obligations under Securities Laws

Directors have legal obligations under federal securities laws as well as state corporate laws. Federal securities laws require companies to disclose information to the public through filings with the SEC. (As we discussed in Chapter 2, "International Corporate Governance," financial transparency improves the efficiency of capital markets by facilitating the flow of information needed for rational decision making.) SEC filings fall into three categories: filings made when a company issues securities; annual and quarterly filings; and filings upon the occurrence of transactions or events, such as a merger, a change in auditor, or the hiring of a CEO. SEC regulations specify in considerable detail the information that each of these filings must disclose. For example, the annual Form 10-K must contain a description of the company's business, risk factors, financial results by management, audited financial statements and footnotes, and compensation practices. In each filing, the company is required to include all **material information**, which is defined as information that an investor would consider important to an investment decision.

A failure to comply with these rules—by misstating material information or by omitting information and thereby making the information provided materially incorrect—exposes the company, its managers, and its directors to liability. Directors are expected to question management regarding the rationale for its disclosure decisions but, absent any red flags, they are not expected to verify information on their own.

Legal Enforcement of State Corporate Law (Fiduciary Duties)

Fiduciary duties under state corporate law are enforced through two types of judicial intervention. First, a court can issue an **injunction**, an order that the company take or refrain from taking a specified action. For example, the injunction might order that the company refrain from consummating a pending merger and allow other parties to bid. A judge might make this ruling if he or she believes that management and the board did not take all steps necessary to obtain the best deal for shareholders. Second, a court can require management and/or the directors to pay **damages** for losses sustained as a result of violating their duties.

When shareholders file suits alleging that directors have taken an action that violated their fiduciary duties, courts use different standards to review the action, depending on the nature of the alleged violation. As explained earlier, when a violation of the duty of care is involved, the courts apply the **business judgment rule**, which is most deferential to the board's decision. Under the business judgment rule, a court will not second guess a board's decision—even if, in retrospect, it was proved to be seriously deficient—if the board followed a reasonable process by which it informed itself of key, relevant facts and then made the decision in good faith. (**Good faith** requires that the board act without conflicting interests and that it not turn a blind eye to issues within its responsibility.) If the board can demonstrate that it satisfied these criteria, the courts will not intervene.

The *Disney* case is a recent high-water (or perhaps *low-water*) mark for nonintervention by the Delaware courts. In 2005, shareholders filed a derivative lawsuit against the Walt Disney Company in which they claimed that the directors did not sufficiently review the appointment of Michael Ovitz as president of the company in 1995 or his no-fault termination 14 months later. They sought to void his original employment agreement or, alternatively, to change his termination to "with cause," which under the agreement would mean the return of nearly $140 million in severance payments. Although the court agreed with the plaintiffs that the board's handling of the matter was seriously deficient, it nonetheless ruled that the business judgment rule protected the board's conduct and declined to intervene.

On the other hand, if a plaintiff successfully shows that a director has violated the duty of loyalty by virtue of a conflict of interest, the courts will not hesitate to intervene. The courts will apply a strict standard of review under which they make their own judgment whether the director has placed his or her own interest above the interests of shareholders. In such a case, the burden shifts to directors to demonstrate the fairness of their decision.

A board's decision to sell a company also receives a higher level of scrutiny by the courts. Because management self-interest may taint its decision to sell the company and, if so, to whom, the courts spend more time ensuring that the sale and process by which it was conducted were in the best interest of shareholders.

Legal Enforcement of Federal Securities Laws

As stated, a securities law violation stems from a material misstatement or omission of information to the public. Unless a public offering is involved, management or the directors will be held liable only if they acted intentionally or with a degree of recklessness that approaches intentionality. Importantly, the court must find that the misstatement was the cause of the investors' loss. Securities laws are stricter when a misstatement occurs in the context of a public offering. In this context, an individual can be held liable based on negligence.

Securities laws are enforced through both private lawsuits and SEC enforcement actions. Private lawsuits take the form of class actions by investors who bought (or sold) a security during the period in which its price was artificially high (or low) as a result of a material misstatement. Because it is difficult for investors to coordinate their efforts, the law allows lawyers to sue in the name of a class of investors who have suffered from a common alleged violation. Although U.S. Congress enacted reforms to the securities class action system in 1996 to facilitate a degree of oversight by institutional investors and lessen the influence of plaintiffs' lawyers, plaintiffs' lawyers remain largely in control of these lawsuits.

In a securities class action lawsuit, the plaintiff's lawyers typically name the company and its CEO as defendants. In cases involving financial misstatements, the CFO is typically named as well. Outside board members are named much less frequently. Brochet and Srinivasan (2014) found that, among a sample of securities class action lawsuits filed between 1996 and 2010, independent directors were named 11 percent of the time. The likelihood of being named is greater for audit committee members and directors who sell stock during the class period.[36]

In an SEC enforcement action, the SEC targets members of management who were responsible for a violation. Managers are subject to monetary penalties and can be barred from serving as officers or directors of a public company, either for a specified number of years or permanently. The SEC occasionally imposes monetary penalties on companies as well. It is very unusual, however, for the SEC to target outside directors.

Director Indemnification and D&O Insurance

State corporate law and federal securities laws create some risk of liability for board members, but two mechanisms reduce the actual danger of directors making out-of-pocket payments: indemnification agreements and the purchase of directors and officers liability insurance.

A company may indemnify directors for costs associated with securities class actions and some fiduciary duty cases. Indemnification generally is available to an individual director for any expense incurred in connection with litigation, including legal fees, settlements, and judgments against the director. Indemnification is only permitted, however, if the director has acted in good faith. Indemnification agreements have been widely adopted by most public companies. According to one study, 98 percent of a sample of Fortune 500 companies have indemnification arrangements for the benefit of their directors.[37]

Corporations also protect directors by purchasing **director and officer liability insurance (or D&O insurance)**. These policies cover litigation expenses, settlement payments, and, in rare cases, amounts paid in damages (up to a limit specified in the policy). A D&O insurance policy has three parts, referred to as Side A, Side B, and Side C. **Side A** protects the directors when indemnification is not available—for example, if the company becomes insolvent. **Side B** reimburses a corporation for its indemnification obligations to its directors. **Side C** insurance reimburses a corporation for its own litigation expenses and amounts it pays in settlement. As the name implies, D&O insurance covers both a company's directors and officers.

D&O insurance contracts are written broadly and are intended to apply when directors are sued in private action for violating securities fraud. However, as with all other insurance policies, D&O insurance has limits. First, these contracts contain dollar limits on the coverage they provide. Amounts owed in excess of coverage limits must be paid by the company. Second, they contain exclusions. The most important of these arises when the director has committed "deliberate fraud" or otherwise illegally enriched him- or herself. Third, although D&O insurance covers litigation expenses and some costs of responding to an SEC investigation that precedes litigation, it does not cover civil fines levied by the SEC (see the following sidebar).

D&O Claims and Payments

Most public attention is on high-level liabilities, such as securities violations. However, according to data from Towers Watson, a significant number of D&O claims are for other infractions, such as discrimination, wrongful termination, and contract disputes (see Table 3.2).

Table 3.2 D&O Claims and Payments

Source of Claim	Example of Allegations	% of All Claims	Average Payment	Average Defense Cost
Employees	Wrongful termination, discrimination, wage disputes	33%	$146,078	$158,698
Competitors, suppliers, and contractors	Contract disputes, business interference, copyright infringement	8%	$87,000	$420,026
Customers	Contract disputes, false advertising, deceptive trade practices	3%	—	$809,701

| Government, agencies, and other third parties | Breach of fiduciary duty, false advertising, dishonesty, antitrust | 16% | $13,818,125 | $3,768,747 |
| Shareholders | Inadequate disclosure, breach of fiduciary duty, stock offerings | 40% | $26,456,948 | $3,042,159 |

Source: Towers Watson, "Directors and Officers Liability: 2007 Survey of Insurance Purchasing and Claim Trends" (2007).

Despite the protections afforded to directors through indemnifications and D&O insurance, most directors believe they are at legal risk by serving on the board. When polled, more than two-thirds believe that the liability risk of serving on boards has increased in recent years. Almost 15 percent have thought seriously about resigning due to concerns about personal liability.[38] Notwithstanding this perception, the actual risk of out-of-pocket payment is quite low. Black, Cheffens, and Klausner (2006) found that between 1980 and 2005, outside directors made out-of-pocket payments—meaning unindemnified and uninsured—in only 12 cases.[39] This figure includes cases where directors only incurred out-of-pocket litigation expenses and did not incur settlement costs (see Table 3.3).

Table 3.3   Settlements in Which Outside Directors Made Out-of-Pocket Payments (1980–2005)

	Settlement Payment	Litigation Expenses	Payment and Expenses	Total
Securities suits under Section 10	—	2	—	2
Securities suits that included Section 11 Claims	4	1	1	6
SEC enforcement actions	1	—	—	1
Corporate law suits	3	—	—	3
Total	**8**	**3**	**1**	**12**

Source: Black, Cheffens, and Klausner (2006).

Although indemnification and D&O insurance afford directors considerable financial protection, they do not reimburse directors for the emotional cost of the litigation process, the time involved, and the adverse impact the lawsuits might have on their reputations.[40]

Endnotes

1. Organisation for Economic Co-operation and Development, "OECD Principles of Corporate Governance. Directorate for Financial and Enterprise Affairs" (2004). Accessed June 20, 2014. See http://www.oecd.org/daf/ca/corporategovernanceprinciples/31557724.pdf.

2. NYSE Corporate Governance Services, *Corporate Board Member*, and Spencer Stuart, "What Directors Think 2014: Annual Board of Directors Survey" (2014). Accessed July 16, 2014. See https://www.nyse.com/publicdocs/nyse/listing/What_Directors_Think_2014.pdf.

3. Corporate Board Member & PricewaterhouseCoopers LLP, "What Directors Think 2008: The Corporate Board Member/PricewaterhouseCoopers LLP Survey," *Corporate Board Member* (2008). Accessed May 5, 2015. See https://www.pwc.com/en_US/us/corporate-governance/assets/what-directors-think-2008.pdf.

4. Jay W. Lorsch, Joseph L. Bower, Clayton S. Rose, and Suraj Srinivasan, "Perspectives from the Boardroom—2009," *Harvard Business School Working Knowledge* (September 9, 2009): 1–20. Accessed January 21, 2010. See http://hbswk.hbs.edu/item/6281.html.

5. NYSE Corporate Governance Services, *Corporate Board Member*, and Spencer Stuart (2014).

6. National Association of Corporate Directors, "2013–2014 NACD Public Company Governance Survey" (Washington, D.C.: National Association of Corporate Directors, 2014).

7. Ibid.

8. Ibid.

9. Lorsch, Bower, Rose, and Srinivasan (2009).

10. AICPA, *The AICPA Audit Committee Toolkit, 3rd edition* (New York: American Institute of Certified Public Accountants, 2014).

11. National Association of Corporate Directors (2014).

12. NYSE Corporate Governance Services, *Corporate Board Member*, and Spencer Stuart (2014).

13. New York Stock Exchange, NYSE Listed Company Manual §303A.00, "Corporate Governance Standards." Accessed April 25, 2015. See http://nysemanual.nyse.com/LCMTools/PlatformViewer.asp?selectednode=chp_1_4_3&manual=%2Flcm%2Fsections%2Flcm-sections%2F.

14. National Association of Corporate Directors (2014).

15. NYSE Corporate Governance Services, *Corporate Board Member*, and Spencer Stuart (2014).

16. New York Stock Exchange, "Corporate Governance Standards."

17. National Association of Corporate Directors (2014).

18. Spencer Stuart, "Spencer Stuart U.S. Board Index 2013" (2013). Last accessed July 11, 2014. See https://www.spencerstuart.com/research-and-insight/spencer-stuart-us-board-index-2013.

19. Merck & Co., Inc., "Merck Research Committee Charter." Accessed July 11, 2014. http://www.merck.com/about/leadership/board-of-directors/charter_research.pdf.

20. Fifth Third Bancorp, Form DEF 14A, filed with the Securities and Exchange Commission March 6, 2014.

21. Cisco Systems, Inc., Form DEF 14A, filed with the Securities and Exchange Commission September 30, 2013.

22. General Mills, Inc., Form DEF 14A, filed with the Securities and Exchange Commission August 12, 2013.

23. Robert M. Daines and Michael Klausner "Do IPO Charters Maximize Firm Value? Antitakeover Protection in IPOs," *Journal of Law, Economics & Organization* 17 (2001): 83–120. John C. Coates, "Explaining Variation in Takeover Defenses: Blame the Lawyers," *California Law Review* 89 (2001): 1301.

24. These descriptive statistics were generated from data supplied by SharkRepellent, FactSet Research Systems, Inc. The sample used 1,871 firms in 2014 and 2,849 firms in 2002.

25. Ibid.

26. Ibid.

27. Ibid.

28. Institutional Shareholder Services, "2013 Proxy Season Review United States." Accessed December 12, 2014. See http://www.issgovernance.com/library/united-states-2013-proxy-season-review/.

29. Sullivan & Cromwell, "2013 Proxy Season Review." Accessed August 8, 2014. See http://www.sullcrom.com/siteFiles/Publications/SC_Publication_2013_Proxy_Season_Review.pdf.

30. See Joseph Hinsey IV, "Business Judgment and the American Law Institute's Corporate Governance Project: The Rule, the Doctrine, and the Reality," *George Washington Law Review* 52 (1984): 609–610.

31. Interestingly enough, directors apparently do not view "activist shareholders" as included in the group "all shareholders," given their disparate rankings. This implies that directors do not see themselves as serving all shareholders equally. Corporate Board Member & PricewaterhouseCoopers LLP, "What Directors Think 2007: The Corporate Board Member/PricewaterhouseCoopers LLP Survey," *Corporate Board Member* (2007). Accessed May 5, 2015. See http://www.pwc.com/en_US/us/corporate-governance/assets/what-directors-think-2007.pdf.

32. Smith Moore Leatherwood LLP, "Informed: FAQ about 'B Corps.'" Accessed April 3, 2015. See http://www.smithmoorelaw.com/bcorpfaq.

33. U.K. Companies Act of 2006 (c. 46), Part 10—A Company's Directors Chapter 2—General Duties of Directors Section 172 (1).

34. Institute of Directors Southern Africa, "King Report on Corporate Governance in SA." Accessed March 25, 2015. See http://www.iodsa.co.za/?kingiii.

35. Etsy Inc., Form S-1, filed with the Securities and Exchange Commission March 4, 2015.

36. Francois Brochet and Suraj Srinivasan, "Accountability of Independent Directors: Evidence from Firms Subject to Securities Litigation," *Journal of Financial Economics* 111 (2014): 430–449.

37. Lawrence A. Hamermesh, "Why I Do Not Teach Van Gorkom," *Georgia Law Review* 34 (2000): 477–490.

38. Corporate Board Member and PricewaterhouseCoopers LLP, "What Directors Think 2009: Annual Board of Directors Survey. A Corporate Board Member/PricewaterhouseCoopers LLP Research Study. Special Supplement," *Corporate Board Member* (2009): 1–16. Accessed January 21, 2010. See http://www.pwc.com/us/en/corporate-governance/publications/corporate-board-member-study-what-directors-think.jhtml.

39. Three of the cases are quite well known: Enron ($13 million for misleading statements and $1.5 million for violating ERISA), WorldCom ($24.75 million for misleading statements), and Tyco ($22.5 million from an SEC enforcement action). The fact that these high-profile cases resulted in out-of-pocket payments no doubt contributes to the perception that a director's risk of liability has increased. See Bernard S. Black, Brian R. Cheffens, and Michael Klausner, "Outside Director Liability," *Stanford Law Review* 58 (2006): 1055–1159.

40. Helland (2006) finds that board member reputation generally does not suffer following allegations of fraud and that the majority of directors named in such lawsuits do not experience a decrease in board seats. An exception arises for directors named in SEC-initiated cases and those named in class actions that end in large settlements. In these cases, director reputation does suffer. Fich and Shivdasani (2007) also found that outside directors named in class-action lawsuits experience a decrease in board seats. See Eric A. Helland, "Reputational Penalties and the Merits of Class Action Securities Litigation," *Journal of Law and Economics* 49 (October 2006): 365–395. Eliezer M. Fich and Anil Shivdasani, "Financial Fraud, Director Reputation, and Shareholder Wealth," *Journal of Financial Economics* 86 (2007): 306–336.

4

Board of Directors: Selection, Compensation, and Removal

In this chapter, we examine how companies select, compensate, and remove board members. We start by examining the size of the market for directors and the qualifications of board members. Next, we discuss how companies identify gaps in the board's capabilities and recruit individuals to fill those gaps. We then evaluate director compensation and equity ownership guidelines. Finally, we consider the resignation and removal of directors.

Market for Directors

The United States has approximately 40,000 directors of large private and publicly traded corporations (see Table 4.1). The average director stays on a corporate board for seven years. Among companies that establish an age limit for serving on a board, the average mandatory retirement age is about 72 years. Although survey data from the National Association of Corporate Directors (NACD) indicates that board members are replaced through a combination of director evaluations and age limits, general observation suggests that board members tend to retire voluntarily.[1] According to Audit Analytics, only about 2 percent of directors who leave the board are dismissed or not reelected.[2]

Table 4.1 Number of Directors in the United States

	2009	2010	2011	2012
Number of firms	4,650	4,972	4,624	4,249
Number of directors	42,642	45,242	42,557	39,547

Source: Based on data collected by Equilar and computations by the authors.

The typical board consists of a mix of professionals with managerial, functional, and other specialized backgrounds. Approximately half of newly elected directors have current or former experience as senior management (CEO, president, COO, chairman, or vice chairman). Twenty percent have experience in an operational or other functional position. The rest come from diverse backgrounds, including finance, consulting, law, academia, and nonprofits (see Figure 4.1).[3]

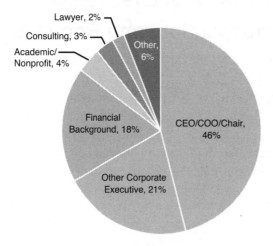

Note: "CEO/COO/Chair" also includes president and vice chair. "Other corporate executive" includes division heads and senior/executive vice presidents. "Financial background" includes CFO and treasurer, bankers, investment managers/investors, and accountants.

Source: Adapted from Spencer Stuart, "Spencer Stuart U.S. Board Index" (2013).

Figure 4.1 Background of new independent directors.

The most important qualification for directorship is relevant industry experience. According to the NACD, 83 percent of directors believe that industry experience is critical or important for recruiting new board candidates. Furthermore, directors have a strong preference to recruit executives with senior-level experience. Current and former CEOs, chief financial officers (CFOs), and chief operating officers (COOs) are the most sought after candidates to serve on the board in terms of function background. (Figure 4.2 illustrates this more completely.)

Criteria for Director Recruitment

CEOs within a company's industry are the most heavily recruited for director-ships. These results have remained mostly unchanged since 2006, demonstrating the importance of a director's industry knowledge and management experience.

Importance of Professional Experience as Criteria for Recruiting Board Candidates

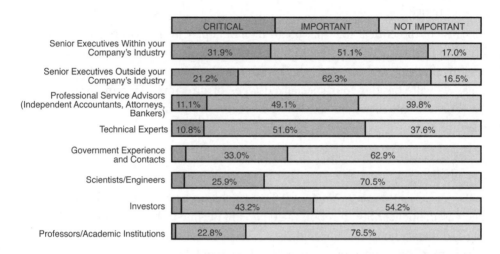

Importance of Functional Experience for Recruiting Board Candidates

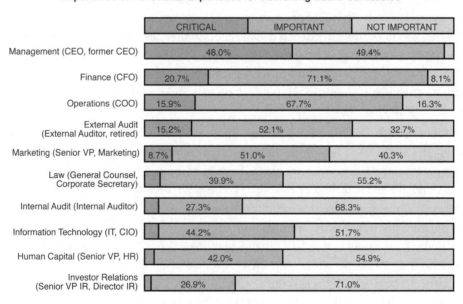

National Association of Corporate Directors (NACD) and The Center for Board Leadership, "2009 NACD Public Company Governance Survey" (2009).

Figure 4.2   Criteria for director recruitment.

Companies look for a diverse mix of personal and professional backgrounds beyond these qualifications. According to Spencer Stuart, directors most in demand as board candidates are those with ethnically diverse backgrounds (56 percent) and women (54 percent). Highly sought after professional qualifications include financial, international, risk management, information technology, marketing, regulatory, and digital or social media experience.[4]

Because of the critical role that board members play in the governance process, the quality of individuals who are elected to the board should have a direct correlation with the quality of advice and oversight the board provides to management. In the following sections, we will consider four specialized types of directors: directors who are active CEOs, directors with international experience, directors with specialized knowledge, and diverse directors.

Active CEOs

Active CEOs sit on an average of 0.6 external boards. In recent years, this number has decreased. Spencer Stuart reports a 40 percent decline in the number of active CEOs serving as directors between 2003 and 2013. The reasons cited for this trend are increased workload from active positions, too much time spent traveling for directorships, and limits placed on the number of outside directorships by current employers. More than three-quarters of all S&P 500 companies now limit outside directorships for CEOs, a policy that was not widely in effect a decade ago. Companies have responded to this trend by recruiting new directors who are executives below the CEO level or who are retired CEOs. According to Spencer Stuart, retired CEOs comprise 23 percent, and lower-level corporate executives comprise 21 percent of new independent directors, up from 12 percent each 10 years ago.[5]

Directors with CEO-level experience offer a useful mix of managerial, industry, and functional knowledge. These individuals can contribute to multiple areas of oversight, including strategy, risk management, succession planning, performance measurement, and shareholder and stakeholder relations. To this end, investors generally react favorably to the appointment of directors with CEO-level experience. Fich (2005) found that the stock market reaction to the appointment of a new outside director is more positive when that director is an active CEO than when he or she is not.[6] However, this does not necessarily mean that directors with CEO-level experience are better board members than directors with other backgrounds. Fahlenbrach, Low, and Stulz (2010) found no evidence that the appointment of an outside CEO to a board positively contributes to future operating performance, decision making, or the monitoring of management.[7]

Survey data also suggests that active CEOs might not be the best board members. According to a study by Heidrick & Struggles and the Rock Center for Corporate

Governance at Stanford University, nearly 80 percent of corporate directors believed that active CEOs are no better than non-CEO board members. Although respondents valued the strategic and operating expertise of CEO directors, when asked about their undesirable attributes, a full 87 percent responded that active CEOs are too busy with their own companies to be effective board members. Respondents also criticized active CEOs for being unable to serve on time-consuming committees, for being unable to participate in meetings on short notice, and for being too bossy, for being poor collaborators, and for not being good listeners.[8]

Finally, the research suggests that the appointment of active CEOs as directors might lead to increased CEO compensation. O'Reilly, Main, and Crystal (1988) found a strong association between CEO compensation levels and the compensation levels of outside directors, particularly members of the compensation committee. They argue that, consistent with social comparison theory, committee members refer in part to their own compensation levels as a benchmark for reasonable pay, leading to a distorted view of "fair market value" when approving CEO pay packages.[9] Faleye (2011) also found that the appointment of active CEO directors is associated with higher CEO compensation levels.[10]

International Experience

As companies expand into international markets, it is important that the board understand how the company might be impacted from strategic, operating, financial, risk, and regulatory perspectives. For this reason, directors with knowledge of local market conditions are highly valued. These directors have contacts with key government decision makers and business executives who can help with supply chain development, manufacturing, customer development, and distribution. This network should help a company enter or expand into a new market by minimizing risk and lowering the cost of executing an international strategy. To this end, Masulis, Wang, and Xie (2012) found that the presence of foreign independent directors on a board is associated with better cross-border acquisitions when the target company is from the foreign director's home country.[11]

Boards are becoming more international. According to Spencer Stuart, 29 percent of newly elected directors have international work experience, and 9 percent are of foreign birth. Larger corporations in particular are more likely to have international directors; 55 percent of the largest 200 companies in the S&P 500 have at least one non-U.S. director, compared with 47 percent five years ago.[12] The trend of recruiting international directors is not limited to the United States. A study by Egon Zehnder found that, across Europe, the proportion of foreign board members rose from 23 percent in 2006 to 32 percent in 2012.[13]

Some evidence suggests that the demand for international knowledge exceeds the available supply. In a separate report, Egon Zehnder compared the percentage of revenues that a company earns outside the United States to the percentage of directors with international experience (the logic being that if a company derives half of its revenue from outside the United States, roughly half of the board should have some international experience). They found that international revenue (37 percent) exceeds international board representation among S&P 500 firms when representation is measured by citizenship (7 percent) or work experience (14 percent).[14] This suggests that boards might have insufficient international experience, a potential competitive obstacle as U.S. firms expand into new markets.

Special Expertise

Companies also have demand for directors with special expertise that matches the functional or situational needs of the firm. For example, a technological firm needs directors who are experts in the industry to advise on research, development, and production (academics in engineering, computer science, medicine, and natural sciences are commonly used in this capacity). These directors might not have the background to oversee certain business or compliance functions, but their presence is critical for the commercial success of the firm. For example, defense contractor Lockheed Martin counts among its directors a former strategic commander for the U.S. Navy and a former deputy secretary for Homeland Security. Both of these individuals serve on a standing committee to oversee "classified business activities and the security of personnel, data, and facilities."[15] Similarly, companies in dire financial or operating condition might benefit from directors with experience in a corporate turnaround or financial restructuring. Specialized experience can also help companies that face regulatory or legal challenges and companies that regularly engage in mergers, acquisitions, or divestitures.

Given the increasingly important role that information technology plays in supply chain management and customer interaction through the Internet, social media, and mobile technology, more companies are recruiting directors with experience in these areas (known as "digital directors"). Russell Reynolds found that among a sample of large corporations in 2013, 19 percent of newly appointed directors in the United States and 8 percent of newly appointed directors in Europe had digital backgrounds, up sharply from 12 percent and 2 percent, respectively, two years before.[16] According to a member of that firm, "I have never seen such an acceleration of demand for specific board expertise."[17] Faleye, Hoitash, and Hoitash (2013) found that industry expertise at the board level is positively associated with innovation and that it leads to higher firm value among firms where innovation is an important part of the corporate strategy.[18]

In some cases, individuals with specific expertise are not formally elected to the board but instead participate in board meetings as **observer** or **advisory directors**. This practice appears to be common among financial institutions. These directors do not vote on corporate matters, so they are shielded from the potential liability that comes with being an elected director. However, they are available to advise the corporation on important matters. For example, a venture capital firm might invite a partner to sit on the board and an associate to attend board meetings as a nonvoting observer (see the following sidebar). According to survey data, 17 percent of companies have one or more board observers.[19]

Board Observers

In 1997, Excite and Intuit entered into an agreement that, among other things, gave Intuit rights to appoint a boardroom observer:

"For so long as Intuit continues to own at least ten percent (10%) of the outstanding Common Stock of the Company . . . and an Intuit Designee is not a member of the Board of Directors, the Company shall invite a representative of Intuit (the "Representative"), which Representative shall be reasonably acceptable to the Company, to attend all meetings of the Board of Directors and the audit committee thereof in a nonvoting observer capacity and, in this respect, shall give such Representative copies of all notices, minutes, consents, and other Board of Directors' or audit committee members' materials ... provided, however, (i) that the Company reserves the right to withhold any information and to exclude such Representative from any meeting, or any portion thereof, as is reasonably determined by the Chairman of the Board . . . to be necessary for purposes of confidentiality, competitive factors, attorney-client privilege, or other reasonable purposes."[20]

The role of the observer is to monitor various decisions of the board and management. The information the observer obtains then is valuable to outside shareholders in making investment decisions.

Diverse Directors

Companies might seek directors of diverse ethnic origin or female directors when they believe diversity of personal perspective contributes to board deliberation or decision making. According to Spencer Stuart, women and ethnic minorities are the two most sought-after groups of directors. Still, their representation on corporate boards remains low: only 18 percent of directors at large corporations are women, 9 percent African-American, 5 percent Hispanic, and 2 percent Asian.[21] Several cultural and societal factors contribute to this result. For example, individuals from these groups might lack access to the closed networks that lead to board appointment; structural imbalances might exist between supply and demand, given the low representation of these groups among senior management teams; the turnover among existing directors that is required for new board seats to become available is low; and personal biases or prejudices might prevent qualified candidates from receiving an equal opportunity for appointment.

Furthermore, research by Heidrick & Struggles suggests that practitioners don't agree on the value of diversity on the board. Ninety percent of female directors believe that women bring special attributes to the board, whereas only 56 percent of male directors believe this to be true. Similarly, 51 percent of women believe that having three or more female directors on a board makes it more effective, whereas only 12 percent of male directors hold this opinion.[22] These are considerable perception gaps that need to be researched.

Despite the difference of opinions, companies have made significant effort toward recruiting diverse board members. Ninety-three percent of companies have at least one female director on the board, and 87 percent have an ethnic minority director.[23] According to the NACD, more than 75 percent of directors believe that ethnic and gender diversity is a critical factor in board recruitment.[24] (We discuss the impact of diversity on corporate performance in Chapter 5, "Board of Directors: Structure and Consequences.")

Professional Directors

Professional directors are individuals whose full-time careers are serving on boards of directors. They might be retired executives, consultants, lawyers, financiers, or politicians who bring extensive expertise based not only on their professional background but also on the multitude of current and previous board seats. For example, Vernon Jordan (a former legal advisor to Bill Clinton) is considered by some to be a professional director, having served on more than a dozen corporate boards, including American Express, Ashbury Automotive, J.C. Penney, and Xerox.[25] After a successful career in retailing, Allan Leighton of the United Kingdom retired from executive positions at the age of 47 and decided to pursue a career as a professional director (calling the move "going plural"). Subsequently, he served as a board member or an advisor to Royal Mail, Lastminute.com, Scottish Power, and BSkyB.[26] According to a survey by Heidrick & Struggles and the Rock Center for Corporate Governance at Stanford University, 63 percent of companies have one or more professional directors on their board.[27]

Professional directors might be effective as advisors and monitors, given their extensive experience on boards. They have participated in multiple governance systems and have likely witnessed both successes and failures. They might also have more time to dedicate to their board responsibilities because they do not need to balance them with the demands of a "day job." In addition, professional directors bring extensive personal and professional networks.[28]

However, relying on professional directors can be risky. Because they serve on multiple boards simultaneously, professional directors tend to be busy. As we see in the next chapter, "busy" directors are associated with lower governance quality. Professional directors might not have the motivation to be effective monitors if they are attracted to the position for its reputational prestige (such as bragging to their social peers), if they do not attend to all of their directorships with equal effort, or if they view serving on multiple boards as a form of "active retirement." Perhaps validating these concerns, Masulis and Mobbs (2014) found that directors with multiple directorships distribute their efforts unequally, dedicating more time to prestigious corporations than to others.[29] Finally, professional directors might lack independence and may be unwilling to stand up to management or fellow directors if they substantially rely on their director fees for income.[30]

Disclosure Requirements for Director Qualifications

In 2010, the Securities and Exchange Commission (SEC) amended Regulation S–K to require expanded disclosure about the qualifications of directors. Companies must now disclose the specific experience, qualifications, and attributes that make an individual qualified to serve as a director. Companies must also disclose directorships that the individual held during the previous 5 years (instead of only current directorships), legal proceedings involving the director during the previous 10 years, and disciplinary sanctions imposed by regulatory bodies. This information is intended to improve shareholder decisions in a director election.

Regulation S–K was also amended to require disclosure of whether the company has a policy regarding boardroom diversity and, if so, how diversity is considered in identifying director nominees. The SEC did not define *diversity*, but it suggested that the term could be broadly defined to include differences of viewpoint, professional experience, education, and skills, as well as race, gender, and national origin (see the following sidebar).[31]

Director Recruitment and Qualification

Analog Devices

Analog Devices provides a detailed explanation of the criteria that the company uses to identify new directors:

"In considering whether to recommend any candidate for inclusion in the Board of Directors' slate of recommended director nominees . . . the Nominating and

Corporate Governance Committee will apply the criteria set forth in our Corporate Governance Guidelines. These criteria include the candidate's integrity, business acumen, experience, commitment, and diligence, the presence of any conflicts of interest and the ability of the candidate to act in the interests of all shareholders. . . . The Nominating and Corporate Governance Committee seeks nominees with a broad diversity of experience, professions, skills, geographic representation, and backgrounds. The Nominating and Corporate Governance Committee does not assign specific weights to particular criteria and no particular criterion is necessarily applicable to all prospective nominees. Analog Devices believes that the backgrounds and qualifications of the directors, considered as a group, should provide a significant composite mix of experience, knowledge, and abilities that will allow the Board to fulfill its responsibilities." [32]

Covidien

Covidien explains how a director's biography qualifies him to sit on the board of directors and the audit committee:

"Mr. Brust served as the Chief Financial Officer of Sprint Nextel Corporation, a wireless and wireline communications company, from May 2008 until his retirement in April 2011. . . . Mr. Brust is an experienced financial leader. His service as Chief Financial Officer of Sprint Nextel Corporation, the Eastman Kodak Company and Unisys Corporation as well as his 31 years at General Electric Company make him a valuable asset, both on our Board of Directors and on our Audit Committee. Mr. Brust's positions have provided him with a wealth of knowledge in dealing with financial and accounting matters. The depth and breadth of his exposure to complex financial issues at such large corporations makes him a skilled advisor." [33]

Wells Fargo

Wells Fargo explains the role of diversity in board recruitment:

"Although the GNC [governance and nominating committee] does not have a separate policy specifically governing diversity . . . the GNC will consider, in identifying first-time candidates or nominees for director . . . the current composition of the Board in light of the diverse communities and geographies we serve and the interplay of the candidate's or nominee's experience, education, skills, background, gender, race, ethnicity and other qualities and attributes with those of the other Board members. . . . In implementing its practice of considering diversity, the GNC may place more emphasis on attracting or retaining director nominees with certain specific skills or experience, such as industry, regulatory, public policy, or financial expertise, depending on the circumstances and the composition of the Board at the time. Gender, race and ethnic diversity also have been, and will continue to be, a priority for the GNC and the Board in its director nomination process because the GNC and the Board believe that it is essential that the composition of the Board appropriately reflects the diversity of the Company's team members and the customers and communities they serve. The GNC believes that it has been successful in its past efforts to increase gender, race, and ethnic diversity on the Board, and of the 14 director nominees for election at the 2014 annual meeting, nine nominees (64 percent) are women, Asian, African-American and/or Hispanic. . . . The GNC and the Board will continue to monitor the effectiveness of its practice of considering diversity through assessing the results of any new director search efforts and the GNC's and Board's self-evaluation process in which directors discuss and evaluate the composition and functioning of the Board and its committees."[34]

Director Recruitment Process

As we discussed in Chapter 3, "Board of Directors: Duties and Liability," director recruitment is a key responsibility of the nominating and governance committee. The committee is responsible for identifying qualified candidates to serve on the board, interviewing and selecting candidates to be put before shareholders for a vote, hiring a search firm to assist in the recruitment process (if necessary), and managing the board evaluation process.

The process should begin by evaluating the needs of the company and identifying gaps in the board's desired capabilities. A list is then assembled of potential candidates whose qualifications fill the identified gaps. The method for assembling this list varies among companies. Some rely extensively on the personal and professional networks of existing board members and the CEO. Others rely on a third-party consultant or search firm to assemble a list of candidates among a broader pool. According to the NACD, approximately 50 percent of companies use a search firm. However, this varies with firm size. Eighty-two percent of large companies (with market capitalization greater than $10 billion) use a search firm, while smaller firms are considerably less likely to do so.[35]

Although intuition might suggest that board candidates identified by search firms would be more qualified on average than candidates identified through a personal network (because they come from a broader pool and are less likely to be selected because of personal biases of existing board members), this is not necessarily the case. Existing directors often have an extensive network that is equal in breadth and insight to the network a third-party consultant uses. To our knowledge, no rigorous studies have compared the qualification of board candidates deriving from each source, primarily because the role of search firms in selecting directors is not a required disclosure by firms.

The director recruitment process differs from the recruitment process for senior executives in two key manners. First, it is more informal and reliant upon professional networks. Many director candidates are initially referred through the personal and professional connections of current board members (or the CEO) rather than through third-party recruiters. Second, the sequence of steps differs. When recruiting executives, the company assembles a list of top candidates, interviews them, and then makes a selection based on an evaluation of which is best qualified. When recruiting directors, the company assembles a list of top candidates, ranks them in preferential order, and approaches the candidates one at a time. In effect, the board (or the nominating and governance committee) decides who it wants to nominate before meeting face-to-face with the candidates. This requires a more careful evaluation of the skills and experience of the individual, without the benefit of meeting in advance. The meeting is as much an invitation to join the board as it is an interview. This is done because it is considered inappropriate to approach a qualified candidate (one who has been highly successful in a professional career) only to reject him or her in favor of another. It is not clear whether a competitive process would improve board quality or whether the most qualified candidates would choose not to engage in interviews.

The composition of the board should satisfy the diverse strategic, operating, and functional needs of the company. It's also important that the culture of the board reflect that of the organization and that board members have good rapport among themselves and with senior management. Recruiters recommend against companies selecting directors based on regulatory and compliance expertise. (One exception is that a company embroiled in extensive legal troubles might specifically bring on a director to help the company navigate through this period.) Generally, directors can be taught compliance more readily than they can be taught domain expertise. Perhaps for this reason, more than half of all boards are open to recruiting directors with no previous board experience.[36]

According to the NACD, directors are satisfied with the board recruitment process. Eighty-seven percent of directors believe their companies are effective or highly effective in handling director recruitment, and only 13 percent believe they are not effective.[37]

Finally, the director recruitment process is unique in that companies do not tend to engage in succession planning among board members. According to survey data, only half of companies (49 percent) begin the process of identifying potential candidates to serve on the board before an outgoing director announces plans to step down. Fewer than half (40 percent) develop a formal written document to outline the skills, competencies, and experiences required of new director candidates.[38] Although companies might feel that the board can continue to function with the loss of a single member, it seems that director succession planning should be a key responsibility of the nominating and governance committee (see the following sidebar). This is especially true if the company requires directors with a rarified skill set.

Outgoing CEOs on the Board

Should the outgoing CEO remain on the board as a director after stepping down from it as an executive? Proponents of the practice say that it can lend stability to the transition process. The former CEO is available to provide advice and mentor the incoming CEO and can help him or her manage boardroom dynamics. This might be particularly valuable if the incoming CEO has not had previous CEO experience. Critics of the practice say that it undermines the credibility and leadership of the incoming CEO. To the rest of the board, the former CEO might still seem like "the boss" and the incoming CEO a more junior executive.

According to a survey by Korn/Ferry Institute, 72 percent of directors believe that the former CEO should not sit on the board.[39] A separate survey found that only 14 percent of companies have a retired CEO as a board member. This figure has fallen over time as the practice has become less common. Perhaps surprisingly, 20 percent of companies have a policy restricting the former CEO from serving on the board.[40]

Evans, Nagarajan, and Schloetzer (2010) found that companies that retain nonfounder former CEOs on the board exhibit significantly worse operating and stock price performance during the two years following the succession event. By contrast, they see no deterioration in performance when the former CEO was also a founder. They interpret the results "as indicative of a powerful former CEO holding the influential board chairman position but lacking the pecuniary and nonpecuniary attachment to the firm that founder CEOs typically possess."[41] Quigley and Hambrick (2012) found that outgoing CEOs who remain on the board as chair restrict the degree to which their successors make strategic change, measured in terms of business divestiture, investment in advertising or research, and turnover among senior management.[42] Therefore, it might be disadvantageous for some firms to retain an outgoing CEO on the board, although a decision should be based on the company's situation.

Director Compensation

Directors require compensation for the time, responsibility, and expense of serving as directors. Recruiters suggest that most directors would be unwilling to do this work on a *pro bono* basis. (Directors at nonprofits is one exception.) Therefore, the amount of compensation must be sufficient to attract and retain qualified professionals with the knowledge required to advise and monitor the corporation. It should also be structured to motivate directors to act in the interest of shareholders and stakeholders. As a result, understanding the payment structure is important for evaluating the incentives directors have to contribute to a sound governance system.

Director compensation covers not only time directly spent on board matters but also the cost of keeping the director's calendar open in case of unexpected events, such as an unsolicited takeover bid, financial restatement, or emergency CEO succession. In addition, it covers the personal risk that comes with serving on a board. For example, although we have seen that directors are unlikely to be responsible for out-of-pocket payments for legal liability or expenses, lawsuits still demand substantial time and attention. They also bring reputational risk and take an emotional toll on those involved.[43]

Directors of companies in the S&P 1500 Index receive annual compensation of $168,270, on average. Compensation packages comprise approximately 38 percent cash annual retainer and 62 percent equity (stock options and stock awards). Director compensation is $220,000 at large-sized companies, $160,000 at medium-sized companies, and $119,280 at small companies (see Table 4.2).[44]

Compensation mix does not vary significantly by company size. Modest variation exists across industries, with a lower mix of equity awards in stable industries such as consumer goods and utilities and a higher mix of equity in research-intensive industries such as technology and healthcare. This suggests that some relation exists between compensation risk and reward, based on the nature of the industry.

Table 4.2 Director Compensation

	Large Companies (S&P 500)	Medium Companies (S&P 400 Midcap)	Small Companies (S&P 600 Small Cap)	Average (S&P 1500)
Annual retainer	$220,000	$160,000	$119,280	$168,270
Cash (percentage)	38%	38%	39%	38%
Equity (percentage)	62%	63%	63%	63%

Source: Equilar (2013).

Many companies pay directors supplemental fees for serving on committees. These figures are in addition to the compensation figures cited in Table 4.2. Committee fees might be an annual retainer or might be awarded on a per-meeting basis. Committee fees average between $10,000 and $15,000 per year. Fees are higher for directors who serve on the audit committee because committee members are required to have financial expertise. They also bear a higher risk of being named in shareholder litigation, and they might have a bigger workload when assigned to this committee (see Table 4.3).

Table 4.3 Director Committee Fees

	Large Companies (S&P 500)	Medium Companies (S&P 400 Midcap)	Small Companies (S&P 600 Small Cap)	Average (S&P 1500)
Audit Committee				
Retainer	$10,000	$10,000	$9,000	$10,000
Meeting fee	$1,500	$1,500	$1,500	$1,500
Retainer (chair)	$15,000	$15,000	$11,000	$15,000
Compensation Committee				
Retainer	$10,000	$7,500	$6,250	$7,500
Meeting fee	$1,500	$1,500	$1,425	$1,500
Retainer (chair)	$15,000	$10,000	$7,500	$10,000
Governance Committee				
Retainer	$7,500	$6,000	$5,000	$6,000
Meeting fee	$1,500	$1,500	$1,425	$1,500
Retainer (chair)	$10,000	$7,500	$5,000	$10,000

Source: Equilar (2013).

Nonexecutive chairmen and lead independent directors also receive supplemental pay. The average total compensation for nonexecutive chairmen is approximately 60 percent higher than that paid to other directors. Lead independent directors receive total compensation that is approximately 12 percent higher. These pay multiples hold true for small, medium, and large companies and are intended to compensate for the increased responsibilities associated with leadership roles.[45]

One important question is whether the level of director fees is reasonable or appropriate, from the perspective of shareholders. As is the case with most other compensation issues, this is a difficult question to answer. One simple way to think about it is to consider the opportunity cost to these directors. If they were not directors, what might they earn for their services? Directors spend approximately 20 hours per month on board-related duties.[46] At $200,000 per year, this translates into an hourly rate of approximately $800. This is comparable to the hourly rate of individuals with similar professional backgrounds (in fields such as business, finance, consulting, and law).

From the corporation's perspective, the cost of board member compensation can be a significant portion of the total direct cost of maintaining a governance system. (The auditor fee represents another significant direct cost.) According to a study of companies in Silicon Valley, small companies incur total costs for nonexecutive board compensation of around $750,000, and large companies incur $1.8 million. These figures represent 0.5 percent of revenue for the small companies and less than 0.1 percent at the large companies. They also represent 0.16 percent of the market capitalization of the small companies and 0.02 percent of the large companies.[47] Although smaller companies get less leverage out of the direct cost of their board, they are perhaps in a stage of growth in which strong monitoring systems and sound strategic advice are more important. Considering the importance that many experts place on having effective corporate governance, these costs are not very significant.[48]

Another important question is whether the mix of director compensation is appropriate. To answer this, shareholders should consider various factors, including the company's growth prospects, industry, risk profile, and cash position. For example, a small startup might offer a mix that is heavily comprised of stock options if the company is cash starved, in growth phase, and can benefit from the strategic advice of directors. For these companies, cash is critical for survival, and shareholders likely prefer that the cash be invested in the company, not paid out to board members. This type of pay structure also attracts certain types of directors: those who can deal with risk, who have the valuable strategic insights for the company, and who are willing to work hard to make the company a success. Conversely, large, steadily growing companies might choose to offer a high cash component along with some type of equity payment (such as restricted stock units).

Finally, in evaluating compensation, investors should remember that directors are not managers and that their compensation mix should be consistent with their serving an advisory and oversight function (see the following sidebar). We discuss the incentive value of compensation for executives in Chapter 8, "Executive Compensation and Incentives."

Director Compensation

The Coca-Cola Company: All-or-Nothing Plan

In 2006, The Coca-Cola Company adopted a new and unique director compensation plan. Directors did not receive guaranteed cash compensation. Instead, they received equity units with a stated value of $175,000. The equity units came with a three-year performance trigger: They would vest if the company achieved its publicly stated goal of 8 percent per year earnings-per-share growth. If the target was met at the end of three years, the directors would receive $175,000 in cash. If the target was not met, the directors would receive nothing.[49]

Investors evaluating this plan must ask themselves a few questions. First, should director compensation at a large and steadily growing company be entirely performance-based? Step-function payments have the potential to encourage individuals either to bank excess profits when they have overachieved their yearly goals or to get aggressive when they are barely underachieving their yearly goals to meet the cliff payout thresholds. Second, is earnings per share the correct performance measurement for contingent compensation? The risk in using a single performance metric is that it is more easily subject to manipulation. An ethical risk might exist if the performance metric is a GAAP-based metric, which the audit committee of the board is responsible for reviewing. Third, is it in the best interest of the company to compensate a director this way? After all, directors are not in a position to ensure that the company executes its strategic goals (as managers are), so it is hard to see how the directors can directly contribute to achieving the company's performance targets. However, this "all or nothing" plan puts directors in the same financial position as shareholders. In this way, it is a gesture to show that if the shareholders suffer from underperformance, the directors will suffer as well.

Coca-Cola achieved its earnings objective, and directors received the promised equity awards. The company eventually discontinued this program and reverted to a more traditional pay structure.[50]

SPX Corporation

In 2002, SPX Corporation offered cash bonuses to directors and executives in which bonuses were earned based on the company's ability to exceed certain return-on-capital targets. The targets were calculated using the metric **economic value added**. EVA is calculated as after-tax operating profit minus the company's estimated cost of capital. At SPX, if the company was able to generate EVA greater than a certain target, executives and directors earned a cash bonus, some of which was paid out immediately; the rest was deferred for future payout.

For 2003, SPX increased the size of the bonus payments by modifying the calculation used to compute EVA. The company made adjustments to exclude certain pension costs, differences between the cash tax rate and the accrued tax rate assumption, and "the negative impact of industry factors beyond management control." After making these adjustments, the CEO received a total bonus credit of $10.2 million, $6.7 million of which was paid out immediately (his salary was $1.4 million). Independent directors also received a bonus of almost $100,000, five times higher than the annual target, and a $40,000 retainer and 4,000 stock options (estimated fair market value $109,000).[51]

Activist investors targeted the company, alleging that management received unjustified awards, that the bonus plan was unnecessarily complex, and that it provided incentive for value-destroying capital allocation decisions.

Ownership Guidelines

Many companies require that directors maintain personal ownership positions in the company's common stock during their tenure on the board (**ownership guidelines**). Such a requirement is intended to align the interests of directors with those of the common shareholders they represent, thereby giving directors an incentive to monitor management. For somewhat obvious reasons, shareholders (and governance experts) look favorably upon companies whose directors own stock. However, it is an open question what level of ownership is sufficient to mitigate agency problems between the board and shareholders.

According to Equilar, approximately 78 percent of the 100 largest companies in the United States have some form of director ownership guidelines.[52] Companies can structure these guidelines in a few ways. Some companies require that directors accumulate and retain a specified amount of company stock, either through open-market purchases or through the retention of restricted stock grants. The minimum amount of stock that directors are required to hold is defined as a multiple of their annual cash retainer. Other companies require that directors hold restricted stock grants for a minimum number of years. Directors are not required to meet these guidelines immediately upon assuming their board seat but are instead given time to accumulate the minimum ownership amounts. For example, directors at Pitney-Bowes have five years to accumulate their ownership requirement of 7,500 shares (approximately $250,000 in value).[53] Directors at Hewlett-Packard are given five years to accumulate shares valued at five times their annual retainer (approximately $500,000 in share value).[54] On average, companies give directors five years to meet ownership guidelines.[55]

Requiring directors to own company shares might not always be a good idea. First, directors are not managers. They are advisors and monitors. Paying directors similar to management might compromise their ability to provide effective oversight. A director might be unwilling to approve a project or an acquisition that risks depressing the company share price in the near term, even if the project will create long-term value, if the director's personal financial portfolio cannot accommodate stock price volatility. In this way, stock ownership might encourage directors to make decisions through the lens of their personal financial interest instead of the long-term interest of the corporation. Similarly, directors with a large equity position might be less likely to oppose low-level manipulation of accounting results (such as the smoothing of earnings or accelerated booking of revenue) if they believe that stock price will suffer from their detection. Finally, ownership guidelines are not usually calibrated for the wealth of the individual director. A guideline that specifies a $100,000 investment carries a different weight for a director with a net worth of $1 million than it does for a director with a net worth of $100 million.

The evidence on this issue is mixed. Mehran (1995) did not find a relationship between director stock ownership and either increased operating performance or increased firm value.[56] However, Mikkelson and Partch (1989) demonstrated that when a director with a major ownership position sits on the board, the company is more likely to agree to a takeover bid. This suggests that director stock ownership might decrease management entrenchment.[57] Cordeiro, Veliyath, and Neubaum (2005) and Fich and Shivdasani (2005) found that equity ownership among directors is positively associated with future stock price performance and firm value.[58] They saw this as evidence that equity-based compensation gives directors greater incentive to monitor managerial self-interest. However, Brick, Palmon, and Wald (2006) found a positive correlation between director compensation and CEO compensation and that above-average compensation is associated with lower future firm performance. They saw this as evidence of "mutual back scratching or cronyism."[59]

Board Evaluation

A **board evaluation** is the process by which the entire board, its committees, or individual directors are evaluated for their effectiveness in carrying out their stated responsibilities. The concept of a board evaluation was among the key recommendations of the Higgs Report, which stated that "every board should continually examine ways to improve its effectiveness" and remains a recommendation of the U.K. Corporate Governance Code.[60] In the United States, annual board evaluations are a listing standard of the New York Stock Exchange (NYSE), which requires that the nominating and governance committee "oversee the evaluation of the board and management." Furthermore, each committee (audit, compensation, and nominating and governance) is required to perform its own self-evaluation.[61]

That said, companies are not required to perform an evaluation of *individual* directors. Some companies do this, but many do not. According to the NACD, only 38 percent of companies evaluate the performance of individual directors. Large corporations are more likely to do so (47 percent) than small companies (30 percent).[62]

Evaluations—whether at the board, committee, or individual level—are important because they enable the board to understand whether it is meeting its own expectations for performance. For example, a board might discover that it is effective in compliance and regulatory oversight but that it dedicates insufficient time to overseeing the company's operations or strategy. Evaluations also help the board to understand the performance of directors and whether they are exhibiting the skills, knowledge, and expertise that is expected of them. If a director is not adequately engaged, the evaluation process can be an effective tool for initiating a discussion about improvement or replacement.

Furthermore, board evaluations vary significantly in terms of the process and scope. The following is a list of some of the choices companies make in designing evaluations:

- Are the board and committees evaluated only as a whole or at the level of the individual director?

- Is the board evaluated against the company's own policies or against the practices of highly successful peers?
- Are individual directors subjected to peer evaluation, self-evaluation, or a combination?
- Are evaluations conducted by interview or by survey?
- Are evaluations conducted by an internal officer (such as a human resources executive), an outside law firm, or a third-party consultant?

In addition, evaluations can address a variety of topics, including these:

- **Composition**—Does the board have the expertise it needs to fulfill all its responsibilities? Is the process for selecting new directors satisfactory? Are individual board members contributing broadly and in their areas of expertise? Is the board taking full advantage of the skills and experiences of its directors?
- **Accountability**—Is the board effective in fulfilling its responsibilities? Has the board set an appropriate strategy? Has the board ensured the relationship integrity among the company's vision, mission, strategy, business model, and key performance metrics? Has the board set realistic long-term objectives? Does the board successfully monitor performance? Does the board successfully monitor and advise the CEO?
- **Information**—Is the board getting the information it needs? Is information accurate and timely?
- **Meetings**—Are meetings appropriately structured? Is sufficient time dedicated to all necessary topics? Is discussion open and honest? Are directors adequately prepared?
- **Relations**—Are directors honest and open in their discussion with one another? Are directors honest and open in their discussion with management? Do boardroom relations encourage optimum decision making? Does management receive appropriate support from the board? Does management receive sufficient oversight from the board?[63]

Finally, just because an evaluation is comprehensive in scope does not mean that it leads to effective outcomes.[64] Practically speaking, it is difficult for the professionals conducting the evaluation to give constructive feedback, even if they are third-party consultants. The consultants who perform these evaluations indicate that many directors, given the success they have achieved in their professional lives, do not welcome commentary about their shortcomings, and consultants' advice for improvement is often ignored. This is unfortunate, as it can lead to outcomes in which ineffective directors remain on the board when they should either improve or retire. To this end, a survey by *Corporate Board Member* magazine found that almost a quarter of officers have directors on their boards whom they feel should be replaced. Thirty-six percent of those respondents believe the directors lack the necessary skill set, 31 percent believe that the directors are not engaged, and the remainder believe that the directors either are unprepared for meetings or have been on the boards too long.[65] For governance quality to improve, these board members should hear this feedback firsthand.

Removal of Directors

For a variety of reasons, a director might want to leave a corporate board. These reasons can be benign (such as a desire to pursue new opportunities or retire) or more troublesome (such as a fundamental disagreement with fellow board members over the direction of the company—see the following sidebar). Similarly, the company might have either benign or troublesome reasons for wanting to replace a director. The company could decide that, after many years of service, it is time to find a new director who can look at strategy and operations from a different perspective. Or the company might feel that a particular director is negligent in his or her services and is therefore unfit to oversee the organization.

That said, a director leaving unwillingly is extremely rare. (Audit Analytics counts only 106 dismissals out of the entire population of public directors in 2009.)[66] Generally directors leave voluntarily. However, it is usually unclear what has prompted a director to step down when that director leaves for reasons other than reaching a mandatory retirement age.

Director Resignations

Director resignations in protest occur infrequently. However, they send a strong signal to the market that the management or oversight of the company might be deficient.[67]

Fair, Isaac and Company

In 2001, Robert Sanderson resigned from the board of Fair Isaac. As required, the company released a copy of his resignation letter in an 8-K filing with the SEC:

"I hereby resign as a Director of Fair Isaac effective immediately. I am resigning because I disagree with the rest of the Board's willingness to grant 100,000 stock options to [CEO] Tom Grudnowski in fiscal 2001. This was an incorrect decision for two principal reasons. First, the Company's 1992 Long-Term Incentive Plan limits the number of options which may be granted to any one employee to 50,000 a year. While it may be legal to grant Mr. Grudnowski 100,000 options, doing so would violate the spirit of the agreement among the Company, the Board, and the shareholders embodied in the plan. Second, Mr. Grudnowski doesn't deserve the grant. He was hired to get the Company growing again and to develop Internet-based new business. During his tenure as CEO, revenue growth has been below the Company's long-term record, and revenues from new business have been miniscule. He has not earned the reward of an extraordinary option grant. It is my hope that the Board will conclude, as I have, that the Company will not achieve long-term success with Mr. Grudnowski in charge, and that the best way to increase shareholder value is to sell the Company."[68]

Surge Components

In 2001, James Miller sent the following resignation letter to the board of directors:

"Since joining the board of directors of Surge, I have on numerous occasions expressed my belief that I have not been given appropriate and relevant information necessary for me to perform my duties. It has been difficult for me to receive requested information either in a timely manner or at all. Furthermore, it has come to my attention that there were significant events and actions taken which were not properly disclosed to me. Case in point: the company recently filed two Q's without my advice, review, or approval. This is particularly disturbing given the fact that I am chairman of the audit committee. As a result of these and other unacceptable circumstances, I do not believe I can discharge my responsibilities in the manner in which the shareholders deserve."[69]

Agrawal and Chen (2011) found that two-thirds of director resignations are related to governance issues (such as board members being given insufficient information on issues; being asked to vote on a matter that they are unfamiliar with; or having disputes over hiring, compensating, or firing a CEO). The remaining resignations occur because of disagreements over strategy or financing decisions. As we might expect, they found substantial negative abnormal stock price returns surrounding disclosure of a resignation.[70]

Fahlenbrach, Low, and Stulz (2013) found that director resignations are correlated with decreased share price, decreased operating performance, greater likelihood of future financial restatement, and greater likelihood of a securities lawsuit.[71]

The board may not remove a fellow director, even if the director is performing poorly. Shareholders may remove a director at the annual meeting. This is rare, however, outside of a contested election. During 2013, only 44 directors failed to win majority support.[72] Shareholders may also remove a director between annual meetings, if permitted under the company's charter. This, too, is rare. The most common way a director is removed is not to be renominated for election (see the following sidebar).[73]

Director Removal

Dow Chemical

In 2007, J. Pedro Reinhard, director of Dow Chemical and former chief financial officer of the company, negotiated with J.P. Morgan and an Omani sovereign wealth fund to engage in a leveraged buyout of the company. Reinhard did not notify either the CEO of Dow Chemical or his fellow board members of his actions. When the board discovered these actions, Reinhard was fired from his consulting and advisory contract with the company. He remained on the board, however, until the end of his term. At the next annual meeting, the governance committee reduced the number of board seats from 12 to 11, and Reinhard was not renominated.[74]

To our knowledge, a well-developed body of research on the removal of directors does not exist. Most studies focus on the resignation of directors following a significant negative event, such as a lawsuit or financial restatement, and not removal during the due course of business. For example, Srinivasan (2005) found that director turnover is significantly higher for firms that undergo a major financial restatement (48 percent during the subsequent three-year period), compared to firms that undergo a technical restatement (18 percent). Furthermore, he found that these board members tend to lose their other directorships as well. The phenomenon is most pronounced for audit committee members.[75]

Similarly, Arthaud-Day, Certo, Dalton, and Dalton (2006) found that director and audit committee members are 70 percent more likely to turn over if the company experiences a restatement. They explained that forced turnover of senior officers sends a signal that the company is disassociating itself from its past errors and that it is committed to restructuring control and oversight mechanisms to prevent future recurrence. They noted that although these actions do not fully repair reputational damage, they are meant to reassure shareholders that they can rely on the company going forward.[76]

Finally, people debate whether directors and officers of failed companies should be elected to directorships at other firms or whether their failure to properly monitor one firm should disqualify them from other boards. To this end, shareholders raised questions when Xerox named former chairman and CEO of Citigroup Charles Prince to its board and when Alcoa named former chairman and CEO of Merrill Lynch Stanley O'Neil to its board and audit committee. Nonexecutive directors at Lehman Brothers, Wachovia, Washington Mutual, Bear Stearns, and AIG all gained new directorships after their companies failed.[77] On one hand, failure brings meaningful experience that might be valuable in another corporate setting. On the other hand, if the failure was caused by a lapse in judgment or ineffective monitoring, legitimate questions arise over whether a possible recurrence is worth the risk to the corporation. According to one expert, "When selecting individuals to oversee an organization, what criteria should we be using other than their previous performance on a corporate board? [I]f there's no accountability here, then what is the system of accountability?"[78]

Still, survey evidence suggests that business leaders are forgiving of directors of failed companies, certainly more than they are of the senior executives of those same companies. According to one report, only 37 percent of executives and directors believe that the former CEO of a company that experienced significant accounting or ethical problems can be a good board member at another company. By contrast, 67 percent of respondents believe that directors of such a company can be a good board member elsewhere. When asked to elaborate, respondents suggest that the CEO is held to a higher standard of accountability, given his or her position of leadership. By contrast, directors are presumed to have less involvement in potential violations and are also seen as able to learn from mistakes of this nature. However, these opinions are not universal.[79]

Endnotes

1. National Association of Corporate Directors and the Center for Board Leadership, "NACD Public Company Governance Survey" (2008). Accessed October 14, 2010. See www.nacdonline. org.

2. Mark Cheffers and Don Whalen, "Audit Analytics, Director Departures: A Five-Year Overview" (2009). Accessed October 14, 2010. See www.auditanalytics.com/0000/custom-reports.php.

3. Spencer Stuart, "Spencer Stuart U.S. Board Index" (2013). Accessed March 30, 2015. See https://www.spencerstuart.com/research-and-insight/us-financial-services-board-index-2013.

4. Ibid.

5. Ibid.

6. Eliezer M. Fich, "Are Some Outside Directors Better than Others? Evidence from Director Appointments by Fortune 1000 Firms," *Journal of Business* 78 (2005): 1943–1971.

7. Rüdiger Fahlenbrach, Angie Low, and René M. Stulz, "Why Do Firms Appoint CEOs as Outside Directors?" *Journal of Financial Economics* 97 (2010): 12–32.

8. Heidrick & Struggles and the Rock Center for Corporate Governance at Stanford University, "2011 Corporate Board of Directors Survey" (2011). Accessed April 25, 2015. See http://www. gsb.stanford.edu/faculty-research/publications/2011-corporate-board-directors-survey.

9. Charles A. O'Reilly III, Brian G. Main, and Graef S. Crystal, "CEO Compensation as Tournament and Social Comparison: A Tale of Two Theories," *Administrative Science Quarterly* 33 (1988): 257–274.

10. Olubunmi Faleye, "CEO Directors, Executive Incentives, and Corporate Strategic Initiatives," *Journal of Financial Research* 34 (2011): 241–277.

11. Ronald W. Masulis, Cong Wang, and Fei Xie, "Globalizing the Boardroom—The Effects of Foreign Directors on Corporate Governance and Firm Performance," *Journal of Accounting and Economics* 53 (2012) 527–554.

12. Spencer Stuart (2013).

13. Egon Zehnder International, "2012 European Diversity Analysis" (2012). Accessed April 25, 2015. See http://www.egonzehnder.com/files/european_diversity_analysis_2012_1.pdf.

14. Egon Zehnder, "2014 Global Board Index Achieving Global Board Capability: Keeping Pace with Global Opportunity" (2014). Accessed October 1, 2014. See http://www.egonzehnder.com/global-board-index.

15. Lockheed Martin, Form DEF 14A, filed with the Securities and Exchange Commission April 21, 2015.

16. Russell Reynolds, "Digital Economy, Analog Boards: The 2013 Study of Digital Directors" (2013). Accessed December 10, 2014. See http://www.russellreynolds.com/content/digital-economy-analog-boards-2013-study-digital-directors.

17. Joann S. Lublin, "Wanted: More Directors with Digital Savvy," *Wall Street Journal Online* (May 15, 2013, Eastern edition): B.6.

18. Olubunmi Faleye, Rani Hoitash, and Udi Hoitash, "Industry Expertise on Corporate Boards," Northeastern University D'Amore-McKim School of Business Research Paper No. 2013-04 (2013). Accessed April 25, 2015. See http://ssrn.com/abstract=2117104.

19. Heidrick & Struggles and the Rock Center for Corporate Governance at Stanford University (2011).

20. Findlaw, "Nomination and Observer Agreement—Excite Inc. and Intuit Inc" (June 25, 1997). Accessed November 4, 2010. See http://corporate.findlaw.com/contracts/corporate/nomination-and-observer-agreement-excite-inc-and-intuit-inc.html.

21. Spencer Stuart (2013).

22. Boris Groysberg and Deborah Bell, "2010 Board of Directors Survey, Sponsored by Heidrick & Struggles and Women Corporate Directors (WCD)" (2010). Accessed October 7, 2010. See www.heidrick.com/publicationsreports/publicationsreports/hs_bod_survey2010.pdf.

23. Spencer Stuart (2013).

24. National Association of Corporate Directors and The Center for Board Leadership, "NACD Public Company Governance Survey" (2009). Last accessed November 10, 2010. See www.nacdonline.org/.

25. American Express Co., Inc., Form DEF 14A, filed with the Securities and Exchange Commission March 15, 2007.

26. Wikipedia, "Allan Leighton." Accessed November 14, 2010. See http://en.wikipedia.org/wiki/allan_leighton.

27. Heidrick & Struggles and the Rock Center for Corporate Governance at Stanford University (2011).

28. Eugene H. Fram, "Are Professional Board Directors the Answer?" *MIT Sloan Management Review* 46 (2005): 75–77.

29. Ronald W. Masulis and Shawn Mobbs, "Independent Director Incentives: Where Do Talented Directors Spend Their Limited Time and Energy?" *Journal of Financial Economics* 111 (2014): 406–429.

30. However, one could argue that professional directors have greater incentive for this same reason. If they do a poor job at one firm, they might lose multiple directorships.

31. Securities and Exchange Commission, "17 CFR Parts 229, 239, 240, 249, and 274. Proxy Disclosure Enhancements [Release Nos. 33-9089; 34-61175; IC-29092; File No. S7-13-09]." Last accessed November 4, 2010. See www.sec.gov/rules/ final/2009/33-9089.pdf.

32. Analog Devices, Inc., Form DEF 14A, filed with the Securities and Exchange Commission January 30, 2014.

33. Covidien, Form DEF 14A, filed with the Securities and Exchange Commission January 24, 2014.

34. Wells Fargo Inc., Form DEF 14A, filed with the Securities and Exchange Commission March 18, 2014.

35. National Association of Corporate Directors and the Center for Board Leadership (2009).

36. Spencer Stuart (2013).

37. National Association of Corporate Directors and the Center for Board Leadership (2009).

38. Heidrick & Struggles and the Rock Center for Corporate Governance at Stanford University (2011).

39. Korn/Ferry Institute, "34th Annual Board of Directors Study" (2007). Last accessed November 4, 2010. See www.kornferry.com/publication/9955.

40. National Association of Corporate Directors and the Center for Board Leadership (2009).

41. John Harry Evans, Nandu J. Nagarajan, and Jason D. Schloetzer, "CEO Turnover and Retention Light: Retaining Former CEOs on the Board," *Journal of Accounting Research* 48 (2010): 1015–1047.

42. Timothy J. Quigley and Donald C. Hambrick, "When the Former CEO Stays on as Board Chair: Effects on Successor Discretion, Strategic Change, and Performance," *Strategic Management Journal* 33 (2012): 834–859.

43. One example is the board of the Hewlett-Packard Company following the "pretexting" scandal in 2006. See Alan Murray, "Directors Cut: H-P Board Clash over Leaks Triggers Angry Resignation," *Wall Street Journal* (September, 6, 2006, Eastern edition): A.1.

44. Equilar Inc., "2013 S&P 1500 Board Profile Committee Fees (Part 1) Featuring Commentary by Society of Corporate Secretaries & Governance Professionals and Meridian" (2013). Accessed May 5, 2015. See http://info.equilar.com/rs/equilar/images/equilar-2013-board-fees-report.pdf?mkt_tok=3rkmmjwwff9wsrois6xjzkxonjhpfsx57eokx.

45. Equilar Inc., "2013 S&P 1500 Board Profile Committee Fees (Part 2) Featuring Commentary by Semler Brossy" (2013). Accessed December 11, 2014. See http://info.equilar.com/rs/equilar/images/equilar-2013-sp-1500-board-profile-committee-fees-report.pdf?mkt_tok=3rkmmjwwff9wsroisqrmzkxonjhpfsx54ugpx6k3lmi%2f0er3fovrpufgji4fssbli%2bsldweygjlv6sgfs7ffmalt0lgfxby%3d.

46. Spencer Stuart (2013).

47. Compensia, "Silicon Valley 130: Board of Directors Compensation Practices" (October 2007). Accessed April 15, 2015. See www.compensia.com/surveys/sv130-board.pdf.

48. The Sarbanes–Oxley Act of 2002 contributed to a significant rise in director compensation in recent years. Linck, Netter, and Yang (2009) found that director compensation at large companies rose almost 50 percent between 1998 and 2004 (measured as a percentage of sales). They also found a substantial increase in the cost of director and officer (D&O) insurance premiums (which are paid by the firm). See James S. Linck, Jeffry M. Netter, and Tina Yang, "The Effects and Unintended Consequences of the Sarbanes–Oxley Act on the Supply and Demand for Directors," *Review of Financial Studies* 22 (2009): 3287–3328.

49. The Coca-Cola Company, Form DEF 14A, filed with the Securities and Exchange Commission March 13, 2007.

50. Ibid.

51. SPX Corporation, Form DEF 14A, filed with the Securities and Exchange Commission March 17, 2004.

52. Equilar Inc., "2012 Director Stock Ownership Guidelines Report," (2013). Accessed July 28, 2014. See https://insight.equilar.com.

53. Pitney-Bowes Inc., Form DEF 14A, filed with the Securities and Exchange Commission March 27, 2014.

54. Hewlett Packard, Form DEF 14A, filed with the Securities and Exchange Commission February 3, 2014.

55. Equilar Inc., "2012 Director Stock Ownership Guidelines Report," (2013).

56. Hamid Mehran, "Executive Compensation Structure, Ownership, and Firm Performance," *Journal of Financial Economics* 38 (1995): 163–184. As cited in Clifford Holderness, "A Survey of Blockholders and Corporate Control," *Economic Policy Review—Federal Reserve Bank of New York* 9 (2003): 51–63.

57. Wayne H. Mikkelson and Megan Partch, "Managers' Voting Rights and Corporate Control," *Journal of Financial Economics* 25 (1989): 263–290. As cited in Holderness (2003).

58. James J. Cordeiro, Rajaram Veliyath, and Donald O. Neubaum, "Incentives for Monitors: Director Stock-Based Compensation and Firm Performance," *Journal of Applied Business Research* 21 (2005): 81–90. Eliezer M. Fich and Anil Shivdasani, "The Impact of Stock-Option Compensation for Outside Directors on Firm Value," *Journal of Business* 78 (2005): 2229–2254.

59. Ivan E. Brick, Oded Palmon, and John K. Wald, "CEO Compensation, Director Compensation, and Firm Performance: Evidence of Cronyism?" *Journal of Corporate Finance* 12 (2006): 403–423.

60. Financial Reporting Council "The UK-Corporate Governance Code" (2014). Accessed March 31, 2015. See https://www.frc.org.uk/our-work/publications/corporate-governance/uk-corporate-governance-code-2014.pdf.

61. New York Stock Exchange, "Corporate Governance Standards." Accessed March 31, 2015. See http://nysemanual.nyse.com/lcmtools/platformviewer.asp?selectednode=chp_1_4_3_6&manual=%2flcm%2fsections%2flcm-sections%2f.

62. National Association of Corporate Directors, "2013–2014 NACD Public Company Governance Survey" (Washington, D.C.: National Association of Corporate Directors, 2014).

63. Adapted from Richard M. Furr and Lana J. Furr, "Will You Lead, Follow, or Develop Your Board as Your Partner?" (2005). Accessed May 5, 2015. See http://www.leader-values.com/article.php?aid=593.

64. We are not aware of any large-scale research studies on the performance consequences of board member evaluation methods.

65. *Corporate Board Member* and PricewaterhouseCoopers LLC, "Special Supplement: What Directors Think 2009, *Corporate Board Member*/PricewaterhouseCoopers LLC Survey" (2009). Accessed May 5, 2015. See http://rss.boardmember.com/MagazineArticle_Details.aspx?id=4171.

66. Cheffers and Whalen (2009).

67. Anup Agrawal and Mark A. Chen, "Boardroom Brawls: An Empirical Analysis of Disputes Involving Directors," *Social Science Research Network* (2011): 1–60. Accessed May 5, 2015. See http://ssrn.com/abstract=1362143.

68. Fair, Isaac & Co., Form 8-K, filed with the Securities and Exchange Commission June 1, 2001.

69. Surge Components, Inc., Form 8-K, filed with the Securities and Exchange Commission August 1, 2001.

70. Agrawal and Chen (2011).

71. Rüdiger Fahlenbrach, Angie Low, and Rene M. Stulz, "The Dark Side of Outside Directors: Do They Quit When They Are Most Needed?" (July 31, 2013). Charles A. Dice Center Working Paper No. 2010-7; Swiss Finance Institute Research Paper No. 10-17; ECGI - Finance Working Paper No. 281/2010. Accessed April 25, 2015. See http://ssrn.com/abstract=1585192.

72. United States Research Team, "2013 Proxy Season Review United States," ISS (2013). Accessed December 12, 2014. SEE http://www.issgovernance.com/library/united-states-2013-proxy-season-review/.

73. William Meade Fletcher, "§ 351. Common Law Right to Remove for Cause," *Fletcher Cyclopedia of the Law of Corporations* (St. Paul: Homson/West, 1931).

74. Roger Parloff, "Inside Job," *Fortune* (July 7, 2008): 94–108.

75. Suraj Srinivasan, "Consequences of Financial Reporting Failure for Outside Directors: Evidence from Accounting Restatements and Audit Committee Members," *Journal of Accounting Research* 43 (2005): 291–334.

76. Marne L. Arthaud-Day, S. Trevis Certo, Catherine M. Dalton, and Dan R. Dalton, "A Changing of the Guard: Executive and Director Turnover Following Corporate Financial Restatements," *Academy of Management Journal* 49 (2006): 1119–1136.

77. Susanne Craig and Peter Lattman, "Companies May Fail, but Directors Are in Demand," *Dealbook.Nytimes.com* (September 14, 2010).

78. Rakesh Khurana, as cited in Ibid.

79. Heidrick & Struggles and the Rock Center for Corporate Governance at Stanford University (2011).

5

Board of Directors: Structure and Consequences

In this chapter, we examine the structural attributes of the board of directors and provide an assessment of whether these choices contribute to board effectiveness and shareholder value. Despite what you might read in the popular press or professional literature, this is not a simple exercise.

Our objective is to take you through the evidence. We critically examine the importance of several salient features of a board of directors: separation of roles between the chairman and the CEO, the appointment of a lead director, board size, board committee structure, boards with directors that serve on other boards (that is, "busy" directors), female directors and diverse boards, and others. We also examine what impact, if any, these attributes have on the board's ability to perform its advising and monitoring functions. If these attributes are important, we should see that they are associated with improved outcomes (such as superior operating performance or increased stock returns) or other observable metrics (such as higher takeover premiums, fewer accounting restatements, less shareholder litigation, and more rational executive compensation). If no improvements are observed, it is difficult to claim that these attributes are significant.

Two caveats are important. First, we do not provide a complete review of the literature on each topic in this chapter. The relevant body of work is too expansive to be summarized in one place. Still, we aim to provide a fair reflection of the general research results. Second, as mentioned in Chapter 1, "Introduction to Corporate Governance," the results discussed in this chapter are "on average" results across a large sample of companies. They do not tell us what will happen for an individual company. A company might find that a certain board structure is perfectly suitable, given its specific situation, even though the evidence from academic and professional literature suggests that it leads to worse outcomes on average. Where applicable, we cite examples that attempt to draw out these contradictions and, in doing so, enable the reader to draw conclusions about the relative importance of individual attributes.

Finally, it is difficult to infer that any change in the board of directors will "cause" a change in organizational performance. In reading this chapter, keep in mind the famous dictum that "correlation does not imply causation."

Board Structure

The structure of a board of directors is generally described in terms of its prominent structural attributes: its size, professional and demographic information about the directors serving on it, their independence from management, number of committees, and director compensation.

According to Spencer Stuart, the board of an average large U.S. corporation has approximately 11 directors. (Boards usually have an odd number of directors to reduce the likelihood of a tie vote.) The average age of directors is nearly 63 years. More than 85 percent of directors meet the independence standards required by U.S. listing exchanges. Fifty-five percent have a chairman who is also CEO, and only 25 percent have a chairman who is fully independent. Boards meet (in person and by telephone) eight times per year, on average. Audit committee members meet nine times, and compensation committee members six times. The Sarbanes–Oxley Act of 2002 mandates that all members of these committees be independent directors and that at least one member of the audit committee have expertise in finance and accounting. Approximately three-quarters of boards have a mandatory retirement age, which is usually 72 years or older (see Table 5.1).[1] Term limits are relatively rare in the U.S. but are observed outside North America.

Table 5.1 Structure of the Board of Directors of U.S. Corporations

Board Composition	2013	2008	2003	5-year % Change	10-year % Change	Comments
Average board size	10.7	10.8	10.9	–1%	–2%	Slight decrease over 10 years
Boards with 12 or fewer directors	84%	80%	74%	5%	14%	Continued trend toward smaller boards
Independent directors	85%	82%	79%	4%	8%	Boards becoming more independent
Average age of independent directors	62.9	61.2	60.3	3%	4%	Average age continues to increase
New independent directors						
Total number	339	380	393	–11%	–14%	Board turnover has trended down
Women	24%	18%	19%	33%	26%	Female representation has increased
Active CEOs/COOs/presidents/vice chairs	23%	31%	32%	–26%	–28%	Active CEO representation has decreased
Retired CEOs/COOs/presidents/vice chairs	23%	16%	12%	44%	92%	Retired CEO representation has increased
All other corporate executives	21%	19%	12%	11%	75%	Other corporate leaders are being recruited
Women directors						
Women as a percentage of all directors	18%	16%	13%	11%	36%	Female representation increasing but still low
Boards with at least one woman director	93%	89%	85%	4%	9%	Fewer boards have no female directors

continues

Board Composition	2013	2008	2003	5-year % Change	10-year % Change	Comments
CEO profile						
Average number of other corporate directorships	0.6	0.7	1.0	−14%	−40%	CEOs sitting on fewer outside boards
Women CEOs	22	14	9	57%	144%	Number of female CEOs rising but still low
Boards where CEO is the only nonindependent	60%	44%	35%	36%	71%	Increasingly, CEO is sole insider
Average age	56.7	55.4	55.3	2%	3%	Slight decrease over 10 years
Average tenure with company	17.8	14.4	14.7	24%	21%	Average tenure with company has increased
Chairman independence						
CEO is also chairman	55%	61%	77%	−10%	−29%	Fewer companies with dual CEO/chair but still majority
Independent chairman	25%	16%	N/A	56%	N/A	Most companies do not have independent chair
Boards with lead or presiding director	90%	95%	36%	−5%	150%	Nearly all boards have lead or presiding director
Board meetings						
Average number of board meetings	8.0	8.7	7.8	−8%	3%	Fairly stable over 10 years
Median number of board meetings	7	8	7	−13%	0%	Fairly stable over 10 years
Retirement age						
Boards with mandatory retirement age	72%	74%	66%	−3%	9%	Mandatory retirement ages are more common
Boards with mandatory retirement age of 75+	24%	11%	3%	118%	700%	Mandatory retirement ages have increased
Boards with mandatory retirement age of 70	11%	27%	51%	−59%	−78%	Mandatory retirement ages have increased

Board Composition	2013	2008	2003	5-year % Change	10-year % Change	Comments
Committee meetings						
Average number of audit meetings	8.7	9.1	7.3	-4%	19%	Audit committees continue to meet twice per quarter
Average number of compensation meetings	6.3	6.6	N/A	-5%	N/A	Stable over 5 years
Audit committee chairmen						
Active chair/president/CEO/vice chair	10%	15%	28%	-33%	-64%	Fewer active CEOs as audit chair
Retired chair/president/CEO/vice chair	28%	28%	20%	0%	40%	More retired CEOs as audit chair
Financial exec/CFO/treasurer/public accounting	35%	24%	7%	46%	400%	Audit chair more likely to have financial background

Source: Spencer Stuart, "Spencer Stuart U.S. Board Index® 2013" (2013). Copyright © 2013 Spencer Stuart. Reprinted and used by permission. Comments edited by the authors.

Are these the right levels? Would outcomes improve if companies were compelled, through either regulation or shareholder activism, to change the composition of their boards? We consider several attributes:

- Independence of the chairman
- Lead independent director
- Outside (nonexecutive) directors
- Independence standards
- Independent committees of the board
- Representation on the board by selected constituents (bankers, financial experts, politically connected individuals, and employees)
- Companies whose directors sit on multiple boards (**busy boards**)
- Companies whose senior executives sit reciprocally on each other's boards (**interlocked boards**)
- Overlapping committee assignments
- Board size
- Diverse boards
- Boards with female directors

Chairman of the Board

The **chairman** presides over board meetings. He or she is responsible for scheduling meetings, planning agendas, and distributing materials in advance. In this way, the chairman shapes the timing and manner in which the board addresses governance matters and sets the meeting agenda. The chairman also plays a critical role in communicating corporate priorities, both internally and externally, and in managing stakeholder concerns. The chairman is expected to participate in or lead the discussion of several high-level items, including long-term strategic planning, enterprise risk management, management performance evaluation, management and director compensation, succession planning, director recruitment, and merger-related activity.

Professional studies suggest that certain personal characteristics might be correlated with an individual being more effective in this role. These include good communication and listening skills, a clear sense of direction, business acumen, an ability to bring people together, an ability to get to key issues quickly, and an ability to gain shareholder confidence.[2] Although these have not been thoroughly tested, anecdotes of successful public company chairmen tend to support them. For example, John Pepper, former nonexecutive chairman of the Walt Disney Company, was known for being an effective chairman who restored relations with shareholders and stakeholders following the tumultuous ending to Michael Eisner's long run as CEO of that company. As one friend described Pepper, "He is very balanced and mature and can deal with all kinds of people. He can take a position in the middle of a dispute, but people will feel like he's listened and considered a position even if he comes out on the other side."[3]

Many governance experts assert that it is important that the position of chairman be separated from the position of CEO. This approach is widely adopted in the United Kingdom and other countries. It was also required of companies in the United States that received extraordinary assistance under the Troubled Asset Relief Program (TARP) in 2008, and it was proposed as a requirement of all publicly traded companies under Senator Charles Schumer's Shareholder Bill of Rights.[4] Prominent shareholder groups, pension funds, and proxy advisory firms generally support shareholder proposals to create an independent chairman. According to proxy advisory firm Glass, Lewis & Co., "We ultimately believe vesting a single person with both executive and board leadership concentrates too much oversight in a single person and inhibits the independent oversight intended to be provided by the board on behalf of shareholders"[5] According to Spencer Stuart, 25 percent of boards in the United States have an independent chairman.[6]

Having an independent chairman includes several potential benefits:

- It leads to clearer separation of responsibility between the board and management.
- It eliminates conflicts in the areas of CEO performance evaluation, executive compensation, long-term succession planning, and the recruitment of independent directors.
- It gives clear authority to one director to speak to shareholders, management, and the public on behalf of the board.
- It gives the CEO time to focus completely on the strategy, operations, and culture of the company.

Advocates of an independent chairman believe that having one is particularly important in these situations:

- The company has a new CEO, particularly an insider who has been promoted and therefore has no previous experience as CEO.
- Company performance has declined and significant changes to the company's strategy, operations, or culture are needed that require management's complete attention while the board considers whether a change in leadership or sale of the company is necessary (see the accompanying sidebar).

- The company has received an unsolicited takeover bid, which management might not be able to evaluate independently without considerations for their own job status.

However, having an independent chairman can also involve several potential disadvantages:

- It can be an artificial separation, particularly when the company already has an effective chairman/CEO in place.
- It can make recruiting a new CEO difficult when that individual currently holds both titles or expects to be offered both titles.
- It can create duplication of leadership and internal confusion.
- It can lead to inefficient decision making because leadership is shared.
- It can create new costs to decision making because specialized information might not easily transfer from the CEO to the chairman (the **information gap**).
- It can create a second layer of monitoring costs because the new chairman also poses a potential agency problem.
- It can weaken leadership during a crisis.[7]

Separating (Then Combining) the Chairman and CEO

Bank of America

In May 2009, the shareholders of Bank of America voted to strip then-chairman and CEO Ken Lewis of his chairman title following the company's ill-fated acquisition of Merrill Lynch during the financial crisis. By a razor-thin margin (50.3 percent to 49.7 percent), shareholders approved a resolution to amend the company's bylaws and require an independent chairman. "It's an enormous victory for shareholders," said an investor who voted in favor of the move. "Now the CEO will be accountable to a board chaired by an independent director."[8] Later that year, Lewis resigned from the company and was replaced as CEO by Brian Moynihan. The chairmanship passed to Charles Holliday, former chairman and CEO of DuPont.

In October 2014, the company reversed course. The board voted unanimously to remove the bylaw restriction and grant Brian Moynihan the dual chairman/CEO title. According to Holliday, "The board strongly supports the strategy that Brian has set and, after careful deliberation, has decided to take these next steps in our governance responsibilities."[9] Shareholder reaction was mixed. "We think Brian Moynihan has done a great job as CEO and we have no problem with him holding both positions," said one shareholder. Others disagreed: "They have flaunted the will of shareholders. . . . It's like the board poking their finger in the eye of the investors." The California Public Employees' Retirement System (CalPERS) expected that shareholders would sponsor a resolution the following year to undo the board's reversal.[10]

Over the years, several corporations—including Hewlett-Packard, Disney, and Target—have split the roles of chairman and CEO following poor performance or a crisis only to recombine them when stability was restored.

According to Institutional Shareholder Services (ISS), 57 companies held a vote in 2013 on shareholder resolutions to require an independent chairman. Of these, only 4 received majority approval. Average support across all votes was 31.1 percent.[11]

Researchers have studied the impact of separating the chairman and CEO roles. Most studies have found little or no evidence that separation leads to improved corporate outcomes. For example, Baliga, Moyer, and Rao (1996) found that companies that announce a separation (or combination) of the roles do not exhibit abnormal positive (or negative) stock price returns around the announcement date. They also found no evidence that a change in the independence status of the chairman has any impact on the company's future operating performance, and they found only weak evidence that it leads to long-term market value creation. They concluded that although a combined chairman/CEO "may increase potential for managerial abuse, [it] does not appear to lead to tangible manifestations of that abuse."[12] Dey, Engel, and Liu (2011) found that companies that separate the chairman and CEO roles due to investor pressure exhibit negative returns around the announcement date and lower subsequent operating performance.[13] Boyd (1995) provided a meta-analysis of several papers on chairman/CEO duality and found, on average, no statistically significant relationship between the independence status of the chairman and operating performance.[14]

Research also suggests that companies are more likely to separate the chairman and CEO roles for succession purposes and are less likely to do so to improve management oversight. Grinstein and Valles Arellano (2008) examined a sample of companies that created nonexecutive chairs between 2000 and 2004. They found that the majority did so with the outgoing chairman/CEO retaining the title of chairman until his or her successor as CEO gained sufficient experience. In these cases, adopting a nonexecutive chairman was a means of providing stability during a period of transition. Only in a minority (20 percent) of the sample did an independent director assume the chairmanship. In these companies, the appointment of an independent chairman was more likely to follow a period of poor operating performance and, therefore, likely was driven by an attempt to improve corporate oversight.[15]

Brickley, Coles, and Jarrell (1994) reached similar conclusions. They found that firms that separate the chairman and CEO roles almost always appoint a former officer with relatively high stock ownership to the chair. They argued that this structure reduces the cost of sharing information. The authors also found that companies use the chairmanship as a reward to newly appointed CEOs who perform well during a preliminary period. They concluded that a dual chairman/CEO is an important tool in succession planning and that forcing a separation likely creates costs that outweigh the benefits.[16]

The evidence therefore suggests that an independent chairmanship is likely not a governance practice that definitively improves corporate outcomes. However, it is also not a structure that has been shown to destroy shareholder value.[17] The circumstances under which this structure is beneficial will likely vary depending on the specific situation. Research does not support mandating the split for all companies. As a *Wall Street Journal* columnist glibly stated, "It's a good idea for companies for which it is a good idea."[18]

Lead Independent Director

The position of lead independent director has emerged as somewhat of a compromise between allowing companies to maintain dual chairman/CEO positions and forcing companies to separate these roles and appoint an independent chairman. The position evolved from the role served by the director who presides over executive sessions of the board. The New York Stock Exchange (NYSE) requires that nonexecutive directors meet outside the presence of management in regularly scheduled **executive sessions** and that an independent director preside over these meetings. In recent years, this director has assumed a more prominent role with expanded powers and has come to be known as the **lead independent (presiding) director**.

Many corporate governance experts recommend that companies formally appoint a lead independent director, particularly those in which the CEO also serves as chairman of the board. The expectation is that the lead independent director can serve as an important counterbalance to the chairman/CEO. However, beyond presiding over executive sessions, the responsibilities of this role are still being defined and vary widely across companies.

According to Spencer Stuart, the lead director at most companies serves as liaison between the chairman/CEO and independent directors. This person also plays a prominent role in the evaluation of corporate performance, CEO succession planning, director recruitment, and board and director evaluations. Sometimes the lead director serves as the main contact to receive and address shareholder communications.[19] He or she can particularly be important during times of crisis, including periods of increased government or regulatory scrutiny, hostile takeover attempts, and contentious proxy battles. In these situations, the lead director brings clarity of communication and clear leadership to internal and external stakeholders.

To be effective, the lead director needs many of the same attributes required of the chairman, including communication and listening skills, diplomacy, and an ability to gain confidence. The lead director must also be willing to take stands that are counter to those of management and, in doing so, compel change. According to one director, "The person has to care for the spirit of the board. He or she needs to be committed to integrity, loyalty, and equanimity. [Y]ou need someone in this role who calls for candor and makes people feel safe about asking the tough and proverbial 'dumb' questions."[20] However, the lead director should not become too involved in management issues, particularly during a crisis.

Experts believe that lead directors can contribute to improved corporate performance in these ways:

- Taking responsibility for improving board performance
- Building a productive relationship with the CEO
- Supporting effective communications with shareholders
- Providing leadership in crisis situations or in turbulent times
- Ensuring that the board is engaged effectively in developing corporate strategy
- Leading the board in succession planning for the CEO and senior management and for the board and its leaders[21]

Although the board should already be discussing these items, appointing a lead director might accelerate the process. Anecdotal evidence suggests that this can be accomplished by concentrating responsibility for selected matters in the hands of one capable director and granting him or her authority to act. Several examples of successful lead directors can provide a model for other companies to emulate. However, as these examples indicate, the lead director is likely to succeed only if given sufficient autonomy and if the chairman or other board members don't undermine his or her authority (see the following sidebar).

Lead Directors in Action

The Home Depot

Bonnie Hill was head of the compensation committee at Home Depot during the controversy over compensation paid to former CEO Robert Nardelli. In that role, she fielded a large number of complaints from institutional investors who were dissatisfied with the seeming disconnect between pay and performance. Hill decided that it was in the best interest of the company to proactively reach out to investors. She and fellow nonexecutive directors organized a town hall meeting where approximately 40 institutional shareholders were invited to voice their concerns. Management did not participate in the meeting. Following the town hall meeting, the company adjusted its compensation program to better align pay and performance. Because of the positive reception Hill received from shareholders, she was named lead independent director. She used that position to foster closer communication with shareholders on a wide variety of additional governance matters.[22]

Royal Dutch Shell

In 2004, it was revealed that Royal Dutch Shell had overstated its estimate of proved oil and gas reserves by nearly 4 billion barrels, or 20 percent. During the investigation that followed, disturbing details came to light regarding management's complicity in hiding the matter from the board and the public. The board appointed Sir John Kerr, nonexecutive director of Shell Transport and former European diplomat, to lead a steering committee of independent directors in a comprehensive review of the company's organizational structure and governance. In the months that followed, Kerr met with institutional investors who held more than 50 percent of the company's common stock. He met with some investors multiple times. Kerr took detailed notes in these meetings and was able to refer to and follow up on specific suggestions made previously. His approach gained the confidence of investors, who believed that the company was truly listening to them. In October 2004, Kerr's steering committee recommended a complete overhaul of the company's organizational and governance systems, based in part on shortcomings investors had identified.[23]

The research literature on lead independent directors is modest because it is difficult to distinguish between companies that have a truly empowered lead director and those that grant that title to the director who presides over executive sessions. Still, some evidence suggests that lead independent directors improve governance outcomes. Larcker, Richardson, and Tuna (2007) found that appointing a lead independent director, in combination with other factors, is associated with improved future operating performance and stock price returns.[24]

The benefit of a lead director likely will depend on the governance situation of the firm and the personal qualities of the director selected.

Outside Directors

As discussed in Chapter 2, "International Corporate Governance," securities regulations in most developed countries require that companies have a majority of **outside (nonexecutive) directors.** Outside directors are expected to execute their duties without undue influence from management because they have no reporting lines to the CEO and do not rely on the company for their livelihood. They are also expected to draw on their professional backgrounds and lend functional expertise to advise on the company strategy and business model. Therefore, they are expected to be better suited to fulfill the advisory and monitoring functions of the board than inside directors.

However, outside directors are likely to be less informed about the company than inside directors. We referred to this earlier as the "information gap" and noted that such a gap is more likely to occur when specialized knowledge is required to run the company. When an information gap occurs, decision making can suffer. Decision making can also suffer through lack of independence. Although companies are required to meet the independence standards of listing exchanges, outside directors who meet these standards in a technical sense are not guaranteed to be truly independent. Some governance experts point out that insiders can coopt the board by nominating outside directors who appear to be independent but are not.[25] Alternatively, outside directors might be independent but not adequately engaged or qualified. When this occurs, numerical targets for outside representation become ineffective (see the following sidebar).

Independent . . . but Qualified?

Lehman Brothers

In 2008, the board of directors of Lehman Brothers had 11 directors, of which 10 were outsiders and 1 was an insider (chairman and CEO Richard Fuld). Of the 10 outside directors, only 1 had recent experience leading a large U.S. bank (Jerry Grundhofer, former CEO of U.S. Bancorp). The other outside directors were:

- John Macomber, 80, former McKinsey consultant, with experience as a CEO in the chemicals industry
- John Akers, 74, former CEO of IBM
- Thomas Cruikshank, 77, former CEO of Halliburton
- Henry Kaufman, 81, former chief economist of Salomon Brothers
- Sir Christopher Gent, 60, former CEO of Vodafone
- Roger Berlind, 75, theater producer

- Roland Hernandez, 50, former CEO of Telemundo
- Michael Ainslie, 64, former CEO of Sotheby's
- Marsha Johnson Evans, 61, former head of the Red Cross[26]

The composition of this board is notable for the number of retired executives. Although retired executives have more time than current executives to dedicate to board matters, their knowledge of industry dynamics and regulations is potentially outdated. This board is also notable for its average age. Older directors are not necessarily less effective than younger directors, but the ultimate bankruptcy of the company does suggest that this board was not properly equipped to advise on or monitor firm strategy and risk. Indeed, the career profiles of the outside directors indicate that they might have been selected for reasons other than their financial industry expertise.[27]

Research indicates that investors generally look favorably upon companies that add outside directors to the board. Rosenstein and Wyatt (1990) found that adding an outside director to the board leads to a statistically significant increase in stock price around the announcement date.[28] Interestingly, the addition of an insider to the board is greeted with a negative reaction by shareholders if the insider owns only a small amount of company stock but is greeted with a positive reaction if the insider owns a large amount of stock. Apparently, investors understand the potential trade-off between the information advantage of insiders and their potential for self-dealing, and they expect high stock ownership to help mitigate this risk. Nguyen and Nielsen (2010) found that the stock market reacts negatively to the sudden death of an outside board member and that the stock price reaction is more negative when that board member serves a critical role, such as chairman or head of the audit committee or when overall representation on the board by outside directors is low. Conversely, the stock price reaction is less negative when the outside director has been on the board for a long period of time or was appointed during the current CEO's tenure.[29]

The impact of outside directors on the long-term operating performance of the company is less clear. Bhagat and Black (2002) found almost no relationship between the percentage of outsiders on a board and the long-term performance of the company's stock.[30] In contrast, Knyazeva, Knyazeva, and Masulis (2013) found that outside board members have a positive effect on firm value and operating performance.[31] Duchin, Matsusaka, and Ozbas (2010) found that the effectiveness of outside directors depends on the cost of acquiring information about the firm. When it is easy for outsiders to gain expertise on the firm (because the firm is in a straightforward industry), company performance increases following the appointment of outsiders to the board. When it is difficult for outsiders to gain expertise, company performance decreases following their appointment.[32]

Boards with a higher percentage of outside directors might also make better decisions regarding mergers and acquisitions. Cotter, Shivdasani, and Zenner (1997) found that when a company announces an acquisition, the stock price change of the acquiring firm is more negative if its board consists largely of executive directors than if the board consists mostly of nonexecutive directors. The expectation is that an acquisition is more likely to destroy value through empire building if executive directors have negotiated the purchase price. Similarly, companies receive a higher takeover premium if the board of the target company is independent.[33] Byrd and Hickman (1992) found similar results. The results suggest that a board composed of outsiders is more likely to negotiate arm's-length transactions, thereby ensuring that the targets and takeover prices are rational.[34]

Finally, it is not clear whether boards with a higher percentage of outsiders negotiate more rational compensation packages with CEOs. Boyd (1994) found an unexpected positive relationship between the level of CEO compensation and the percentage of outside directors.[35] However, Finkelstein and Hambrick (1989) found no relationship between these variables.[36]

Clearly, outside directorships have both positive and negative aspects. Outsiders have the potential to bring expertise and independence to the board, which can reduce agency costs and improve firm performance. However, outsiders operate at an information disadvantage that can decrease their effectiveness. The research results on this point are mixed, and shareholders should evaluate board members based on their experience and the relevance of that experience in monitoring and advising management.

Board Independence

The NYSE requires that listed companies have a majority of independent directors. **Independence** is defined as having "no material relationship with the listed company (either directly or as a partner, shareholder, or officer of an organization that has a relationship with the company)."[37] A director is not considered independent if the director or a family member:

- Has been employed as an executive officer at the company within the past three years

- Has earned direct compensation in excess of $120,000 from the company in the past three years

- Has been employed as an internal or external auditor of the company in the past three years
- Is an executive officer at another company where the listed company's present executives have served on the compensation committee in the past three years
- Is an executive officer at a company whose business with the listed company has been the greater of 2 percent of gross revenues or $1 million within the past three years

These standards are intended to ensure that directors execute their duties with independent judgment.[38] Independence is important for both the advisory and monitoring functions of the board. It enables a director to objectively evaluate the top executives, strategy, business model, and risk-management policies proposed by senior management. It also enables them to be objective when measuring operating and financial results against predetermined targets. Independence means that compensation arrangements are established through arm's-length negotiation and that acquisitions are determined in the best interest of shareholders. Directors who maintain material relations with the company or otherwise rely on the company for their livelihood are less likely to be independent in these areas. According to MSCI ESG Research, the boards of Cablevision, Kinder Morgan, J.M. Smucker, and Brown-Forman were among the least independent in 2014; MasterCard and Unum Group scored among the most independent.[39]

The risk for investors is that the independence standards of the NYSE (or other listing exchanges) do not reliably produce directors with truly independent judgment. The NYSE acknowledges this risk:

> It is not possible to anticipate, or explicitly to provide for, all circumstances that might signal potential conflicts of interest, or that might bear on the materiality of a director's relationship to a listed company. . . . Accordingly, it is best that boards making "independence" determinations broadly consider all relevant facts and circumstances.[40]

Effectively, NYSE guidelines draw a line in the sand. For investors, this means that some directors will meet independence standards and not be independent in their perspectives, while others will not meet these standards yet be perfectly capable of maintaining independence. Stated differently, there is a risk that the structural characteristics used in the NYSE test for independence are a misleading measure of the independence of an individual director (see the following sidebar).

Business Relations and "Independence"

Three of the NYSE standards for independence are aimed at weeding out individuals who have a personal relationship with C-level executives. These include restrictions on former executives, former auditors, and executives who have a relationship through outside compensation committees. These are reasonable approximations for relationships that might compromise judgment.

However, the other two restrictions are somewhat arbitrary. Why does a $120,000 salary compromise judgment? It is a relatively large figure, but most salaries, regardless of level, are material to the people who earn them. Likewise, why does the fact that a director's firm relies on the company for 2 percent of gross revenue compromise the judgment of that director? Business partners surely want to see their customers or suppliers succeed financially. Although some directors might abuse their position of influence for gain, others will have a vested interest in ensuring that the company on whose board they sit prevents insider abuse and remains viable. (See the sidebar "The Reelection of Warren Buffett" in Chapter 12, "Institutional Shareholders and Activist Investors.")

Most studies fail to find a significant relationship between formal board independence and improved corporate outcomes. We cited some of these studies in the previous section on outside directors. In aggregate, they tend to demonstrate either a modest relationship or no relationship between independence and market returns or long-term performance. Some evidence suggests that independence leads to more rational merger-and-acquisition activity. The relationship between independence and CEO compensation is not clear. We suspect that the structural shortcomings of the NYSE standards of independence confound the data used in most studies and at least partially explain the weak results.

Hwang and Kim (2009) recognized this shortcoming and attempted to correct it by designing a study that takes into account situational or psychological factors beyond NYSE guidelines that risk compromising a director's judgment. The authors made a distinction between directors who are independent according to NYSE standards (**conventionally independent**) and those who are independent in their social relation to the CEO (**socially independent**). They used the board of Cardinal Health to illustrate this distinction:

In the year 2000, this board had 13 directors, 10 of whom were conventionally independent of the CEO. However, one conventionally independent director was not only from the same hometown, but also graduated from the same university as the CEO (incidentally, this director provided a job, at his own firm, for the CEO's son). Another conventionally independent director graduated from the same university and specialized in the same academic discipline as the CEO. Similarly, 3 others shared informal ties with the CEO and, ultimately, only 5 of the 13 directors were conventionally *and* socially independent of the CEO.

The authors identified six areas where the independence standards of the NYSE might fail to take into account social relationships that could compromise independence if the director and the CEO have the following in common:

1. Served in the military
2. Graduated from the same university (and were born no more than three years apart)
3. Were born in the same U.S. region or the same non-U.S. country
4. Have the same academic discipline
5. Have the same industry of primary employment
6. Share a third-party connection through another director to whom each is directly dependent

The authors posit that people who share these social connections feel a psychological affinity that might bias them to overly trust or rely on one another without maintaining sufficient objectivity. Among a sample of directors of Fortune 100 companies between the years 1996 and 2005, the authors found that 87 percent are conventionally independent, but only 62 percent are both conventionally and socially independent. They found that social dependence is correlated with higher executive compensation, lower probability of CEO turnover following poor operating performance, and higher likelihood that the CEO manipulates earnings to increase his or her bonus. They concluded that social dependence compromises the ability of the board to maintain arm's-length negotiations with management.[41]

Other studies that take an unconventional approach to measuring independence reach similar conclusions. Coles, Daniel, and Naveen (2014) hypothesized that directors appointed by the current CEO are more likely to be sympathetic to his or her decisions and therefore less independent ("coopted"). Consistent with this, they found that the greater the percentage of the board appointed during the current CEO's tenure, the worse the board performs its monitoring function—measured in terms of pay level, pay-for-performance sensitivity, the likelihood that an underperforming CEO is terminated, and merger and acquisition activity. They concluded that "not all independent directors are effective monitors" and that "independent directors that are coopted behave as though they are not independent."[42] Similarly, Fogel, Ma, and Morck (2014) found that "powerful" independent directors (directors with a large social network) are associated with more valuable merger-and-acquisition activity, stricter oversight of CEO performance, and less earnings management.[43]

Although this type of analysis is certainly not easy, it demonstrates a level of critical thinking that is sometimes absent in the debate on corporate governance. Their findings suggest that an expanded and more sophisticated assessment of independence is likely to lead to better understanding of governance quality than simply checking for adherence with regulatory guidelines.

Independent Committees

The Sarbanes–Oxley Act of 2002 requires that the audit, compensation, and nomination and governance committees of U.S. publicly traded companies include only independent directors. By contrast, other specialized committees of the board— such as finance and investment committees, credit committees, and science and technology committees—carry no such restrictions and often have a combination of inside and outside directors.

The issues regarding committee independence are similar to those regarding general board independence. Independent committees have the potential to objectively monitor managerial behavior and corporate performance, but committees with inside directors might have firm-specific knowledge that can improve their contribution to long-term operating performance. Independence standards mandated by the Sarbanes–Oxley Act are intended to balance these trade-offs. Committees with a primary charter to monitor the performance of management (audit, compensation, and nomination and governance) carry a legal mandate for independence. All other committees that serve both an advisory and a monitoring function (finance, environmental, science and technology, and others) don't carry these mandates.

The research literature produces some evidence that independent directorships improve the monitoring ability of the audit committee. Klein (2002) found that companies with a majority of independent directors on the audit committee have higher earnings quality than companies with a minority of independent directors on this committee. However, she did not find that a standard of 100 percent independence improves results compared to a simple majority. (The sample period preceded NYSE requirements for 100 percent independence.) She concluded that although independence on the audit committee might be important, "a wholly independent audit committee may not be necessary."[44]

In a separate study, Klein (1998) tested whether having insiders on the investment and finance committees improves firm performance. She reasoned that although the audit committee is intended as an oversight body to mitigate agency costs, investment and finance committees are focused on strategic growth, so they should benefit from an insider's firm-specific knowledge. She found slight evidence in support of this hypothesis: Companies with a higher percentage of executive directors on the investment and finance committees tend to exhibit slightly better operating returns and stock market performance. She did not find this same correlation for audit and compensation committees.[45]

These studies suggest that the independence level of committees bears some influence on corporate outcomes. They also support the thesis that having inside directors on committees is neither uniformly positive nor uniformly negative. As we might expect, it depends on the function of the committee.

Bankers on the Board

Bankers play a prominent role on many corporate boards. They bring expertise regarding a firm's capital structure, financing options, financial risk, and mergers and acquisitions. They also bring industry knowledge gained from serving clients in similar businesses. During times of trouble, they can help facilitate access to capital, particularly when a company is "priced out" of the public markets because of a low credit rating. Bankers also bring monitoring expertise that comes from having a creditor perspective, with an emphasis on compliance with covenants and excess coverage. This enables them to detect and address early signs of trouble.

However, bankers might not be fully independent monitors because they have a divided loyalty between their employers and the company on whose board they sit. Some might use their positions to steer business toward their banks. This violation of fiduciary duty is often hard to detect. Also, when the banker's employer provides financing to the company, the bank's interest as creditor might conflict with the interest of shareholders.

Research on the contribution of bankers to company boards is generally unfavorable. Güner, Malmendier, and Tate (2008) found that companies that add commercial bankers to the board tend to increase their borrowing activity but do not realize a corresponding increase in firm value. The evidence suggests that the increase in borrowing activity is encouraged to generate low-risk profits for the lending institution. Furthermore, the authors found no evidence that companies gain access to funds that they could not otherwise receive on their own. Also, the authors found that companies that add investment bankers to the board tend to make worse acquisitions. Stock price returns for the acquiring firm are about 1 percent less on the announcement date when investment bankers are on the board. This conflicts with the notion that investment bankers can create value by negotiating better deals. The findings suggest that bankers who sit as outside directors put the interest of their employers above their obligation to company shareholders.[46] Studies on the impact of bankers in Germany and Japan arrive at similar conclusions.[47]

Erkens, Subramanyam, and Zhang (2014) also examined the impact of commercial bank representation on governance outcomes. They hypothesized that representation by an affiliated banker on a company's board gives the bank more direct access to information about performance, therefore reducing market pressure to adopt conservative accounting to establish creditworthiness. They found evidence in support of this hypothesis. They also found that banker representation allows lenders to renegotiate debt covenants in a more timely manner, based on private information.[48] This study, too, suggests that bankers use their position to protect the interests of their employers.

At the same time, evidence exists that banking experience on the board can be beneficial to the company when the director is not conflicted by a relationship between his or her employer and the company. Huang, Jiang, Lie, and Yang (2014) found that directors with previous investment banking experience improve the outcome of mergers-and-acquisition activity. Companies with investment banking directors exhibit higher returns when announcing an acquisition, pay lower takeover premiums and advisory fees, and exhibit superior performance post-acquisition. This suggests that directors with investment banking experience might help a firm make better acquisitions by identifying suitable targets and reducing the cost of the deals.[49]

Financial Experts on Board

Section 407(b) of the Sarbanes–Oxley Act requires that companies appoint a **financial expert** to the audit committee. To qualify as a financial expert, the director must have experience as a public accountant, auditor, principal financial officer, comptroller, or principal accounting officer at an issuer. The director also is required to have an understanding of accounting principles, the preparation of financial statements, internal controls, and audit committee functions.[50]

The evidence suggests that adding a financial expert to the audit committee improves governance quality. Defond, Hann, and Hu (2005) found that the market reacts favorably when a financial expert is added to the audit committee. They also divided the sample of financial experts into two groups and found that the market reacts positively to the appointment of experts with accounting backgrounds but not those with nonaccounting financial backgrounds. Their results indicate that shareholders value audit committee members who can directly improve the integrity of financial statements.[51] Similarly, Agrawal and Chadha (2005) found that companies have fewer restatements when an audit committee member has a CPA or similar degree.[52] Krishnan (2005) found that companies that have financial expertise on the audit committee are less likely to have problems with their internal controls.[53]

Politically Connected Boards

Some companies believe that it is beneficial to add a politically connected director to their board. The director can use his or her professional network or knowledge to help secure government contracts or improve relationships with regulators. Other companies establish political connections when a senior officer leaves the company to take a high-level appointment in the administration or a federal agency.

Modest evidence indicates that investors look favorably upon politically connected boards. Faccio (2006) and Hillman, Bierman, and Zardkoohi (1999) found that investors react positively to news that a company CEO or board member has received a political appointment.[54] Similarly, Goldman, Rocholl, and So (2009) found that companies whose board members were affiliated with the Republican party exhibited positive stock price returns following the election of George W. Bush in 2000.[55]

However, these connections might not yield tangible benefits. Fisman, Fisman, Galef, and Khurana (2006) studied the influence of firm connections to former U.S. Vice President Richard Cheney, who previously served as CEO of Halliburton. They found no evidence that companies benefited from these ties.[56] Faccio (2010) found that companies with political connections have lower taxes and greater market power but that they also have lower return on assets and lower market-to-book ratios than peers.[57] Studies of French companies have reached similar conclusions.[58]

Employee Representation

German law requires that the supervisory boards of German corporations have 33 percent employee representation when the company has 500 or more employees and 50 percent employee representation when the company has 2,000 or more employees. This requirement is considered an employee's **right of codetermination** and ensures that employees participate in decisions that impact workplace matters such as work rules and schedules, methods for appraising and hiring personnel, the design of health and safety work standards, wage and benefits agreements, and the process for introducing technology into production. Through board seats, employees also have input into high-level corporate matters such as strategy, operations, capital structure, and management oversight. Codetermination has the potential to give employees a real voice in the governance process.

A prudent level of employee involvement can be desirable for decision making. Employees have valuable information about daily business processes, customers, and suppliers. Board representation can facilitate the flow of this information between employees and management. Employee representation can also improve internal relations and reduce work stoppages. In addition, employee representation can reduce agency costs through better oversight of management compensation and perquisites. However, board representation puts employees in a position to engage in higher levels of rent extraction (such as demanding artificially inflated wages or employment numbers). This can reduce a company's competitive position.

The academic evidence on employee representation is mixed. Gorton and Schmid (2004) found that the stock of German companies with higher levels of employee representation (50 percent of directors) trade at lower prices than the stock of companies with lower levels of employee representation (33 percent of directors).[59] Fauver and Fuerst (2006) found that employee representation is positively related to market valuation in industries that require high levels of coordination (such as manufacturing, transportation, and wholesale or retail trade) and in concentrated industries with less competition. Modest evidence shows that the benefits of employee representation form an "inverse U," meaning that some level of employee representation improves firm valuation, but beyond a certain threshold, it leads to diminishing returns. Companies with employee representation are more likely to pay a dividend, which reduces expropriation of capital by management.[60] Using a sample of publicly traded French corporations, Ginglinger, Megginson, and Waxim (2011) also found modest evidence that employee representation on the board is positively associated with firm value and profitability.[61]

These studies involve European corporations, so it is not clear how they translate to the United States, where employee representation is not required (see the following sidebar). However, studies that have examined firms that are essentially employee owned through employee stock ownership plans (ESOPs) tend to reach negative conclusions. Faleye, Mehrotra, and Morck (2006) examined the performance of companies in which labor owns at least 5 percent of shares and, therefore, has a voice in corporate decision making. They found that such firms have lower valuations, invest less in long-term assets, are more risk averse, exhibit slower growth, have lower employment growth, and have lower labor productivity. They concluded that employee influence conflicts with an objective of maximizing shareholder value.[62]

However, anecdotal evidence suggests that employee participation in corporate decision making, at either the board level or managerial level, can be beneficial in certain circumstances. For example, Southwest Airlines is known for granting significant autonomy to pilots and flight crews to make adjustments that improve efficiency and increase customer satisfaction. Whether board representation is required for operational benefits to be realized is not clear. We suspect that the effectiveness of employee board representation depends on the nature of the existing relations between management and labor, as well as the culture and competitive positioning of the firm.

Union Representatives on the Board

General Motors

In 2014, General Motors nominated Joseph Ashton, vice president of the United Auto Workers (UAW), to the board of directors. At the time, the UAW Retiree Medical Benefits Trust was General Motors' largest shareholder, holding 8.7 percent of the company's stock, valued at roughly $4.9 billion, which the union received as part of the company's emergence from Chapter 11 bankruptcy in 2010. The Trust recommended Ashton as a prospective board member. According to company Chairman Tim Solso, "Joe brings a wealth of knowledge from his work across many industries, especially his deep understanding how labor strategy can contribute to a company's success."[63] The company's proxy statement elaborated that Ashton had "expertise in areas such as manufacturing processes, pension and health care costs, government relations, employee engagement and training, and plant safety."[64]

It is highly unusual for a major U.S. corporation to elect a union representative to the board. Labor representatives hold significantly less than 1 percent of all directorships among publicly traded companies in the U.S.

Experts disagreed on the impact that Ashton's nomination would have on governance quality. According to one, Ashton would be conflicted in situations where the board must decide whether to lay off workers or close plants: "it puts them [labor representatives] in a very different position where they could be forced to choose between loyalties." Others saw it as positive: "having someone in the room who is very informed could be helpful, not just in being forceful about wages, but in what people are thinking about when they're working on the front lines of a company."[65]

Boards with "Busy" Directors

The vast majority (79 percent) of board members in the United States serve on just one corporate board. A fair number sit on two or three boards, but the numbers drop off significantly beyond that. According to *data from Equilar,* fewer than 1 percent of directors sit on five or more boards (see Table 5.2).[66]

Table 5.2 Number of Directorships per Director

Number of Directorships	Directors	%
7 or more	10	0.0%
6	23	0.1%
5	119	0.3%
4	464	1.2%
3	1,794	4.5%
2	6,035	15.3%
1	31,102	78.6%
Total unique directors	39,547	100.0%

Source: Data collected by Equilar and computations by the authors. Data for companies with fiscal year ending between June 2012 and May 2013.

Researchers refer to directors who hold multiple board seats as **busy directors**. The numeric threshold that constitutes a "busy" director is undefined, although researchers generally consider it to be three or more board seats. Similarly, academics refer to a "busy" board as one in which a significant number of directors are busy.

Having a busy director can bring potential benefits. Busy directors are likely to have firsthand access to important information about operations, strategy, and finances at related companies. They are also likely to have broad social and professional networks, which are valuable for recruiting directors, evaluating executive talent, dealing with regulators, and forging partnerships. In addition, busy directors might have high integrity and sound reputations, which are driving factors in the demand for their services. However, busy directors also have the potential to be lax in their oversight or unavailable at critical moments because of outside obligations (see the following sidebar). Recognizing these risks, many companies place restrictions on the number of boards that their directors can sit on simultaneously. According to Spencer Stuart, more than three-quarters (76 percent) of S&P 500 companies had such a restriction in 2013.[67]

Profile of a Busy Director

In 2012, Irvine Hockaday, Jr., was on the board of three publicly traded companies (Crown Media Holdings, Estee Lauder, and Ford Motor). Hockaday is the former president and CEO of Hallmark Cards, a position he held from 1986 to 2001. He is also a lifetime trustee of the Aspen Institute, former chairman of the Federal Reserve Bank of Kansas City, and a prominent citizen in the Kansas City area. Hockaday is described by one colleague as "an independent thinker who doesn't get swept along in the tide. If it doesn't ring right, he's quick to ask for clarification. He sure doesn't sit there like a bump on a log."[68] At one time, Hockaday served on six boards (including Dow Jones, Sprint Nextel, and Aquila).

Hockaday has performed many valuable services as a board member. He was the lead independent director of Ford and instrumental in recruiting Alan Mulally to that company in 2006. He also played an important role in forcing the resignation of Sprint CEO William Esrey and COO Ronald LeMay after it was discovered that the two men used illegal tax shelters designed by the company's tax auditor, Ernst & Young. He was also head of the compensation committee of Dow Jones, where he emphasized pay for performance and reportedly did not miss a board meeting in 12 years. At five of the six public boards he has served on, he took compensation in stock instead of cash, believing that it better aligned his interest with those of shareholders.

However, Hockaday has been involved in controversies. For example, he was the head of the compensation committee of Aquila when it awarded a controversial severance package of $7.6 million to outgoing CEO Robert Green following an ill-timed foray into the energy trading markets and a collapse of the company's stock price.[69]

Recently, Hockaday reduced his directorships. In stepping down from the board of Sprint, he noted that "being a director is more demanding than it once was."[70]

Researchers have studied the relationship between busy boards and governance quality, which is one of the few areas of research on board structure that yields consistent and convincing results: Companies with busy boards tend to have worse long-term performance and worse oversight. Fich and Shivdasani (2006) found that companies with busy boards have lower market-to-book ratios and lower return on assets. They also found that companies with busy boards are less likely to fire an underperforming CEO than companies that do not have busy boards. In addition, they demonstrate that investors react positively to news that a busy director is resigning from the board and negatively to news that an outside director is assuming an additional directorship.

Investor response is most negative if the outside director or the board itself becomes "busy" after assuming the additional directorships.[71]

Many other studies have found similar results. For example, Core, Holthausen, and Larcker (1999) examined a variety of governance variables (busy directors, old directors, directors appointed by the CEO, and so on) to measure their impact on future firm operating performance and other variables, such as CEO compensation. They found that busy boards award larger compensation packages to CEOs than nonbusy boards. Companies with busy boards also exhibit lower one-, three-, and five-year operating performance (measured as return on assets) and stock market returns.[72]

Falato, Kadyrzhanova, and Lel (2013) found that the stock market reacts more negatively to the sudden death of an independent director when the remaining workload has to be redistributed among busy directors than nonbusy directors. Their evidence suggests that the magnitude of the decline depends on the importance of the deceased directors' committee roles in the firm, that the performance deficit among busy boards persists over time, and it is accompanied by reduced board monitoring (that is, higher CEO rent extraction and lower earnings quality). They conclude that "independent director busyness is detrimental to board monitoring quality."[73]

Field, Lowry, and Mkrtchyan (2013) argued that busy directors are ineffective monitors but are important corporate advisors. They cited as evidence the prominence of busy directors among firms undergoing an initial public offering (IPO) and the contribution of those directors to firm value. They note that the benefits of busyness are "lowest among Forbes 500 firms, which likely require more monitoring than advising."[74]

Interlocked (or Connected) Boards

An **interlocked board** is one in which an executive of one firm sits on the board of another and an executive of the second firm sits on the board of the first. According to one estimate, 8 percent of boards are interlocked through reciprocal CEO representation. When the definition is expanded to include retired CEOs and other current senior executives, the percentage of companies with interlocked boards increases to 20 percent.[75]

Interlocking creates a network among directors that can lead to increased information flow, which, in turn, improves decision making. Best practices in corporate strategy and firm oversight can be transferred more efficiently across companies that have shared board representation. Director networks also serve as a source of important business relationships, including new clients, suppliers, sources of capital, political connections, regulators, and director and executive referrals.

However, obvious drawbacks exist in this arrangement. Interlocking can become anticompetitive if proprietary information is shared among competing firms that use this information to collude on market actions.[76] Furthermore, interlocking creates a dynamic of reciprocity. For example, if the CEO of one firm approves a large compensation contract to the CEO of another firm, it is difficult for the second CEO not to reciprocate. As such, interlocks can compromise the objectivity of directors and weaken their monitoring capability.

Research demonstrates the positive effects of network connections among firms. Hochberg, Ljungqvist, and Lu (2007) found that such connections improve performance of companies in the venture capital industry.[77] Fracassi and Tate (2012) found that companies that share network connections at the senior executive and the director level have greater similarity in their investment policies and higher profitability. These effects disappear when the network connections are terminated.[78] Cai and Sevilir (2012) found that board connections between firms lead to higher value creation in mergers and acquisitions.[79] Larcker, So, and Wang (2013) found that companies with a well-connected board have greater future operating performance and higher future stock price returns than companies whose boards are less connected. These effects are most pronounced among companies that are newly formed, have high growth potential, or are in need of a turnaround.[80]

Research also demonstrates the role that network connections play in the dissemination of business practices (good and bad). Bizjak, Lemmon, and Whitby (2009) found that the practice of stock-option backdating, which originated among a localized set of companies, was transferred to many more through boardroom connections.[81] Brown and Drake (2014) found that tax avoidance strategies are shared across board networks.[82] Cai, Dhaliwal, Kim, and Pan (2014) found that corporate disclosure policies—in particular the decision to stop issuing quarterly earnings guidance—are also shared through network connections.[83]

The evidence also indicates that network connections can lead to decreased monitoring. Hallock (1997) found some weak evidence that CEOs of companies with interlocked boards earn higher compensation than the CEOs of companies with noninterlocked boards.[84] Nguyen (2012) found that CEOs whose firms are connected through interlocked boards are less likely to be fired following poor performance.[85] Finally, Santos, Da Silveira, and Barros (2009) found evidence that companies with interlocked boards in Brazil have lower market valuations. The results are especially strong for boards that are both interlocked and busy.[86]

Committee Overlap

A separate body of work examines whether committee overlaps—the degree to which directors serve on multiple committees—improve or impair monitoring functions through better information flow. For example, it might be the case that a director who serves on the audit committee will be a more effective contributor if he or she sits concurrently on the compensation committee. Because compensation contracts are based in part on the achievement of accounting-based performance metrics, a director's understanding of financial accounting might allow for improved compensation contracting. A director with audit committee experience will be in a better position to understand which components of reported earnings are more informative about CEO decisions (and also less susceptible to manipulation), allowing the committee to write bonus contracts with greater weight on these components.

There is some evidence that these benefits do, in fact, manifest themselves. Carter and Lynch (2009) found that concurrent membership on audit and compensation committees is associated with lower weighting placed on discretionary accounting accruals that might be more susceptible to manipulation and greater weight on stock-return metrics in compensation contracts.[87] Similarly, Grathwohl and Feicha (2014) found among a sample of publicly listed firms in Germany that overlap between the audit and compensation committees is associated with higher bonus payments and higher pay-for-performance sensitivity of those bonuses.[88]

Conversely, there are potential benefits to having members of the compensation committee serve on the audit committee. Compensation committee members will have more detailed knowledge about the incentives that executives have to make accounting choices to maximize compensation and to assess the business risk created by the compensation structure. While the research literature in this area is less developed, there is some evidence that this might occur. Chandar, Chang, and Zheng (2012) found that firms with overlapping membership between the two committees are associated, on average, with higher financial reporting quality.[89]

Companies exhibit widely varying practices when it comes to audit and compensation committee overlaps. In 2012, 26 percent of publicly traded companies in the United States had no overlapping members between the compensation and audit committees, 33 percent had one overlap, 25 percent two overlaps, and 16 percent three or more overlaps. In approximately one-third of companies (32 percent), the audit committee chair also served on the compensation committee. In a similar percentage of cases (35 percent), the compensation committee chair served on the audit committee. In 6 percent of companies, the audit committee and compensation committees had exactly the same members.[90]

In the extreme, companies appoint all independent directors to all standing committees so that every committee effectively has 100 percent overlap. This arrangement is known as a "committee of the whole" and is intended to foster knowledge dissemination across the entire board. Because directors participate in all functional discussions, they have greater exposure to the details of the firm's operations and governance. A committee-of-the-whole structure requires significant time commitment.

Only a slim minority of companies (3.4 percent) employ a committee-of-the-whole structure.[91] Goldman Sachs, Coach, Nucor, Moody's, and A.H. Belo are examples of companies that have committees of the whole, although their regulatory filings provide little insight into their decision to adopt this structure.

More research is needed to understand the trade-offs and benefits of committee overlap and the settings in which they are most likely to be beneficial.

Board Size

The size of the board of directors tends to be related to the size of the corporation. Companies with annual revenues of $10 million have 7 directors, on average, and companies with revenues of more than $10 billion have 11 directors, on average.[92]

Large boards have more resources to dedicate to both oversight and advisory functions. They allow for greater specialization to the board through diversity of director experience and through functional committees. However, large boards bring additional costs in terms of compensation and coordination of schedules. In addition, large boards suffer from slow decision making, less candid discussion, diffusion of responsibility, and risk aversion. Given the trade-offs, many experts believe a theoretically optimal board size exists. For example, Lipton and Lorsch (1992) argued that boards of directors should have either 8 or 9 members and should not exceed 10.[93]

Researchers have examined the relationship between board size and corporate performance. Yermack (1996) measured the relationship between board size and firm value (measured as the ratio of market-to-book value). He found that as board size increases, firm value falls (after controlling for factors such as firm size and industry). The largest deterioration in value occurs between boards of 5 and 10 directors, suggesting that inefficiencies grow the most within this range. Yermack (1996) also found that larger boards are less likely to dismiss underperforming CEOs, they are less likely to award compensation contracts that correlate with shareholder value, and shareholders respond negatively to announcements that a company is increasing its board size. The author concluded that "an inverse association between board size and firm value" exists.[94]

However, as with other structural board variables that we have considered, the truth is more complicated. Coles, Daniel, and Naveen (2008) argued that a variety of other factors likely influence the relationship between board size and firm value. They identified "complexity" as one such variable. The authors argued that complex companies (those with many business segments, those that require external contracting relationships, leveraged firms, and those in specialized industries) might benefit from large boards because they bring more information to the decision-making process. As an example, they cited the board of Gulfstream Aerospace, which included at one point Henry Kissinger, Donald Rumsfeld, and Colin Powell. The authors speculated that "most likely these directors were selected not for monitoring, but for their ability to provide advice in obtaining defense contracts." If this is the case, a large board should have positive performance effects at complex companies where incremental expertise is needed. The authors tested this hypothesis by separating complex firms from so-called "simple" firms and repeating Yermack's analysis. They found that complexity brings added explanatory power: Board size is negatively correlated with firm value for simple firms and positively correlated for complex firms (with diminishing benefits beyond a certain point). They concluded, "At the very least, our empirical results call into question the existing empirical foundation for prescriptions for smaller, independent boards. [O]ur evidence casts doubt on the idea that smaller boards with fewer insiders are necessarily value enhancing."[95]

The research conducted by Coles, Daniel, and Naveen (2008) is an excellent example of how multiple factors can influence the relationship between a structural attribute and governance outcomes. At first glance, the data suggest that board size and corporate outcomes are strictly linearly related, but in reality, the relationship is more nuanced. Complexity is one explanatory variable that early research did not properly consider, and other variables also likely bear consideration when exploring composition and structure.

Board Diversity

Many stakeholders advocate that corporate officers should increase the ethnic diversity of their boards so that their composition more closely reflects the diversity of the broader U.S. population. Ethnic diversity might improve decision making by ensuring that the board has the full array of knowledge in terms of market dynamics, customer behavior, and employee concerns to succeed operationally and culturally. According to social psychologists, diversity helps boards overcome tendencies toward **groupthink**, in which directors reach consensus too quickly because of the way social similarities shape their perception and decision making. Diversity can also encourage healthy debate by making directors more likely to challenge one another's viewpoints without excessive concern for maintaining harmony because of social similarity. From the standpoint of public policy, diversity is an important social value and one that is consistent with equality.[96]

However, some evidence suggests that boardroom diversity might detract from the quality of decision making. Social psychologists have shown that heterogeneous groups exhibit lower levels of teamwork. Differences among team members can lead to less information sharing, less accurate communication, increased conflict, lower cohesiveness, and an inability to agree upon common goals.[97] If this dynamic manifests itself in the boardroom, both advice and monitoring might suffer.

Considerable professional and academic research focuses on the relationship between boardroom diversity and corporate outcomes. Not surprisingly, the results are mixed. Erhardt, Werbel, and Shrader (2003) found a significant positive relationship between diverse gender and minority board representation and corporate performance.[98] Similarly, Carter, D'Souza, Simkins, and Simpson (2010) found that board diversity is correlated with higher market-to-book ratios.[99] By contrast, Wang and Clift (2009) found no relationship between boardroom diversity and corporate performance, and Zahra and Stanton (1988) found a negative relationship.[100]

Similarly, the research on diversity and corporate decision making is inconclusive. Westphal and Zajac (1995) found that demographic similarity between the CEO and the board is correlated with higher levels of CEO compensation.[101] This is consistent with the idea that social similarity can lead to reciprocity and implies that diversity in the boardroom might improve independence and oversight. However, Belliveau, O'Reilly, and Wade (1996) found that it is not social similarity but the social status of the CEO relative to other board and compensation committee members that leads to higher compensation.[102] This implies that CEO power is the greater determinant of boardroom dynamics.

Female Directors

Women are significantly underrepresented on boards of directors. According to Catalyst, a nonprofit research organization dedicated to expanding opportunities for women in business, just 17 percent of the directors of Fortune 500 companies are women, compared with 50 percent of the general population and 47 percent of the workforce. Boards might lack female directors because women are underrepresented at the senior executive level. Only 18 percent of corporate officers are women.[103]

In recent years, several countries have made it a priority to increase female representation on corporate boards. Norway was the first country to pass such a law, requiring in 2003 that all listed company boards be composed of at least 40 percent female directors, with full compliance required by 2008. Companies not compliant with the law risk being delisted from exchanges. The law had an immediate impact on female board membership. In 2002, only 7 percent of directors at Norwegian companies were women. By late 2007, the figure had risen to 35 percent.[104] Other European countries followed suit. Spain enacted a 40 percent requirement starting in 2015. France passed similar legislation. Sweden asked companies to voluntarily increase female directorship to 25 percent or risk a legal mandate (see Table 5.3).

Table 5.3   Percentage of Female Directors, by Country

Country	% Female	Country	% Female
Norway	36.1%	Hong Kong	9.5%
Sweden	27.0%	Spain	9.5%
Finland	26.8%	Belgium	9.2%
France	18.3%	China	8.4%
South Africa	17.9%	Italy	8.2%
Denmark	17.2%	Greece	7.0%
Netherlands	17.0%	Singapore	6.9%
Germany	14.1%	Malaysia	6.6%
Australia	14.0%	India	6.5%
United States	14.0%	Indonesia	6.0%
Poland	13.6%	Mexico	5.8%
Canada	13.1%	Brazil	5.1%
Turkey	12.7%	Russia	4.8%
United Kingdom	12.6%	Taiwan	4.4%
Austria	11.3%	Chile	2.8%
Switzerland	10.0%	South Korea	1.9%
Thailand	9.7%	Japan	1.1%

Source: GMI Ratings, 2013 Women on Boards Survey.

Advocates of gender diversity point to the many potential benefits of increasing female representation. Gender balance can enhance board independence by encouraging healthy debate among diverse perspectives and reducing the social similarities among homogeneous groups that can lead to groupthink and premature consensus. Women might have different insights into customer behavior, particularly in industries where women are the primary purchasing agents. Women might also evaluate information and consider risk and reward differently than men, thereby improving decision making. In addition, women may exhibit higher levels of trustworthiness and cooperation, thus improving boardroom dynamics. Finally, social benefits exist for increasing gender equality on the board.

The primary risk to higher female board representation occurs when companies, in an effort to appear more gender-balanced, recruit underqualified directors. This practice, referred to as **tokenism,** is similar to the risk of appointing outside directors with the sole purpose of satisfying perceived external demand for diversity.

Evidence is inconclusive about whether female board representation improves corporate performance. Catalyst (2007) divided Fortune 500 companies into quartiles based on female board representation. It found that the quartile with the highest percentage of females outperformed the lowest quartile in return on equity (13.9 percent versus 9.1 percent), net margin (13.7 percent versus 9.7 percent), and return on invested capital (7.7 percent versus 4.7 percent). It also found that companies with three or more female directors performed well above average along all three financial metrics. Unfortunately, this study did not include control variables, so it likely omits important explanatory factors, such as industry, company size, or capital structure.[105] More rigorous studies find no relationship between female board representation and performance.[106]

However, modest evidence supports the idea that female representation can improve governance quality. Adams and Ferreira (2009) found that female directors have better attendance records than men and that male directors have fewer attendance problems when women also serve on the board. They also found that boards with female representation are more likely to fire an underperforming CEO and award more equity-based compensation. They did not find a positive correlation between female board representation and either operating performance or market valuation.[107]

Finally, evidence suggests that female board representation can be detrimental when encouraged primarily to meet arbitrary quotas. Ahern and Dittmar (2012) examined the impact of the Norwegian law on female board representation. They found that the law led to considerable changes in board composition in terms of not only gender but also age, education, and experience. They found that the somewhat arbitrary governmental constraints of the law led to a significant decrease in firm value. They found that the loss in firm value was not primarily attributable to a greater number of female directors but to the inexperience of new directors.[108]

Summary

Table 5.4 presents a high-level summary of the evidence discussed in this chapter. A casual reading of this information indicates that very modest evidence supports the adoption of many of these attributes. Although this might be surprising to some, it is characteristic of the current debate on governance that is insufficiently grounded in empirical research. (We discuss this in more detail in Chapter 15, "Summary and Conclusions.")

Table 5.4 Summary of Performance Effect for Selected Board Structural Characteristics

Board Attribute	Explanation	Findings from Research
Independent chairman	The chairman of the board meets NYSE standards for independence.	No evidence that this matters.
Lead independent director	The board has designated an independent director as the "lead" person to represent the independent directors in conversation with management, shareholders, and other stakeholders.	Modest evidence that this improves performance.
Number of outside directors	Number of directors who come from outside the company (nonexecutive).	Mixed evidence that this can improve performance and reduce agency costs. Depends primarily on how difficult it is for outsiders to acquire knowledge of the company and its operations.
Number of independent directors	Number of directors who meet NYSE standards for independence.	No evidence that this matters beyond a simple majority.
Independence of committees	Board committees are entirely made up of directors who meet NYSE standards for independence.	Positive impact on earnings quality for audit committee. No evidence for other committees.
Bankers	Directors with experience in commercial or investment banking.	Negative impact on company performance when banker's employer serves as advisor or lender to the company.

continues

Board Attribute	Explanation	Findings from Research
Financial experts	Directors with experience either as public accountant, auditor, principle financial officer, comptroller, or principal accounting officer.	Positive impact for accounting professional only. No impact for other financial experts.
Politically connected directors	Directors with previous experience with the federal government or regulatory agency.	No evidence that this matters.
Busy boards	A "busy" director is one who serves on multiple outside boards (typically three or more). A "busy" board is one that has a majority of busy directors.	Negative impact on performance and monitoring.
Interlocked boards	An executive from Company A sits on the board of Company B, while an executive from Company B sits on the board of Company A.	Positive impact on performance, negative impact on monitoring.
Overlapping board committees	A director sits on more than one committee at the same company.	Positive impact on monitoring.
Board size	The total number of directors on the board.	Positive impact on performance to have small board if company is "simple," larger board if company is "complex."
Diversity	The board has directors that are diverse in background, ethnicity, or gender.	Mixed evidence on performance and monitoring.

Source: Authors.

Endnotes

1. Spencer Stuart, "2013 Spencer Stuart U.S. Board Index" (2013). Accessed January 23, 2015. See www.spencerstuart.com/research/.

2. Directorbank, "What Makes an Outstanding Chairman? The Views of More Than 400 Directors." Accessed May 5, 2015. See http://www.docstoc.com/docs/10282082/What-makes-a-Chairman-Outstanding_Directorbank-Survey_2008.

3. Laura M. Holson, "Former P&G Chief Named Disney Chairman," *New York Times* (June 29, 2006): C13.

4. The final version of the Dodd–Frank Act did not include this provision, although it was included in earlier versions of the legislation.

5. Ross Kerber and Lisa Richwine, "Proxy Advisers Urge Split of Chair, CEO Roles at Disney," *Reuters News* (February 26, 2013).

6. Spencer Stuart (2013).

7. Ira M. Millstein Center for Global Markets and Corporate Ownership, "Chairing the Board: The Case for Independent Leadership in Corporate North America, Policy Briefing No. 4," Columbia Law School (2009). Accessed October 12, 2009. See http://web.law.columbia.edu/sites/default/files/microsites/millstein-center/2009%2003%2030%20Chairing%20The%20Board%20final.pdf.

8. Ieva M. Augstums and Mitch Weiss, "Shareholders Oust BofA Chairman," Associated Press (April 29, 2009).

9. Bank of America, Form 8-K, Exhibit 99.1, filed with the Securities and Exchange Commission October 1, 2014.

10. Christina Rexrode and Dan Fitzpatrick, "Investors Push Back at BofA's Reversal," *Wall Street Journal* (October 31, 2014): C.1.

11. United States Research Team, "2013 Proxy Season Review United States," ISS (2013). Accessed December 12, 2014. See http://www.issgovernance.com/library/united-states-2013-proxy-season-review/.

12. B. Ram Baliga, R. Charles Moyer, and Ramesh S. Rao, "CEO Duality and Firm Performance: What's the Fuss?" *Strategic Management Journal* 17 (1996): 41–53.

13. Aiyesha Dey, Ellen Engel, and Xiaohui Liu, "CEO and Board Chair Roles: To Split or Not to Split?" *Journal of Corporate Finance* 17 (2011): 1595–1618.

14. Brian K. Boyd, "CEO Duality and Firm Performance: A Contingency Model," *Strategic Management Journal* 16 (1995): 301–312.

15. Yaniv Grinstein and Yearim Valles Arellano, "Separating the CEO from the Chairman Position: Determinants and Changes after the New Corporate Governance Regulation," *Social Science Research Network* (2008). Accessed October 10, 2009. See http://ssrn.com/abstract=1108368.

16. James A. Brickley, Jeffrey L. Coles, and Gregg A. Jarrell, "Corporate Leadership Structure: On the Separation of the Positions of CEO and Chairman of the Board," Simon School of Business working paper FR 95-02 (1994). Accessed February 26, 2009. See http://hdl.handle.net/1802/4858.

17. David F. Larcker, Gaizka Ormazabal, and Daniel J. Taylor, "The Market Reaction to Corporate Governance Regulation," *Journal of Financial Economics* 101 (2011): 431–448.

18. Holman W. Jenkins, Jr., "A Non-Revolution at Microsoft," *Wall Street Journal* (February 5, 2014, Eastern edition): A.15.

19. Spencer Stuart, "A Closer Look at Lead and Presiding Directors, Cornerstone of the Board," *New Governance Committee* (2006). Accessed May 5, 2015. See http://content.spencerstuart.com/sswebsite/pdf/lib/Cornerstone_LeadPresiding_Director0306.pdf.

20. Ibid.

21. Jeff Stein and Bill Baxley, "The Role and Value of the Lead Director—A Report from the Lead Director Network," *Harvard Law School Corporate Governance Blog* (August 6, 2008). Accessed May 3, 2015. See http://corpgov.law.harvard.edu/2008/08/06/the-role-and-value-of-the-lead-director-a-report-from-the-lead-director-network/.

22. Joann S. Lublin, "Theory & Practice: New Breed of Directors Reaches Out to Shareholders; Treading a Fine Line between Apologist, Sympathetic Ear," *Wall Street Journal* (July 21, 2008, Eastern edition): B.4.

23. Chris Redman, "Shell Rebuilds Itself," *Corporate Board Member* (March/April 2005). Accessed May 5, 2015. See http://shellnews.net/week12/corporate_board_member_magazine21march05.htm. See also David F. Larcker and Brian Tayan, "Royal Dutch/Shell: A Shell Game with Oil Reserves," Stanford GSB Case No. CG-17 (2009).

24. Those factors include a lead director, greater proportion of blockholders, and a compensation mix that is weighted toward accounting performance, smaller boards, and fewer busy directors. See David F. Larcker, Scott A. Richardson, and İrem Tuna, "Corporate Governance, Accounting Outcomes, and Organizational Performance," *Accounting Review* 82 (2007): 963–1008.

25. Roberta Romano, "The Sarbanes–Oxley Act and the Making of Quack Corporate Governance," *Yale Law Journal* 114 (2005): 1521–1612.

26. Lehman Brothers, Form DEF 14A, filed with the Securities and Exchange Commission March 5, 2008.

27. Dennis K. Berman, "Where Was Lehman Board?" *Wall Street Journal Blog, Deal Journal* (September 18, 2008). Accessed November 9, 2010. See http://blogs.wsj.com/deals/2008/09/15/where-was-lehmans-board/.

28. Stuart Rosenstein and Jeffrey G. Wyatt, "Outside Directors, Board Independence, and Shareholder Wealth," *Journal of Financial Economics* 26 (1990): 175–191.

29. Bang Dang Nguyen and Kasper Meisner Nielsen, "The Value of Independent Directors: Evidence from Sudden Deaths," *Journal of Financial Economics* 98 (2010): 550–567.

30. Sanjai Bhagat and Bernard Black, "The Noncorrelation Between Board Independence and Long-Term Firm Performance," *Journal of Corporation Law* 27 (2002): 231.

31. Anzhela Knyazeva, Diana Knyazeva, and Ronald W. Masulis, "The Supply of Corporate Directors and Board Independence," *Review of Financial Studies* 26 (2013): 1561–1605.

32. Ran Duchin, John G. Matsusaka, and Oguzhan Ozbas, "When Are Outside Directors Effective?" *Journal of Financial Economics* 96 (2010): 195–214.

33. James F. Cotter, Anil Shivdasani, and Marc Zenner, "Do Independent Directors Enhance Target Shareholder Wealth during Tender Offers?" *Journal of Financial Economics* 43 (1997): 195–218.

34. John W. Byrd and Kent A. Hickman, "Do Outside Directors Monitor Managers?" *Journal of Financial Economics* 32 (1992): 195–221.

35. Brian K. Boyd, "Board Control and CEO Compensation," *Strategic Management Journal* 15 (1994): 335–344.

36. Sydney Finkelstein and Donald C. Hambrick, "Chief Executive Compensation: A Study of the Intersection of Markets and Political Processes," *Strategic Management Journal* 10 (1989): 121–134.

37. NYSE, "Corporate Governance Listing Standards, Listed Company Manual Section 303A.02—Corporate Governance Standards (approved January 11, 2013)."Accessed May 3, 2015. See http://nysemanual.nyse.com/LCMTools/PlatformViewer.asp?selectednode=chp_1_4_3_3&manual=%2Flcm%2Fsections%2Flcm-sections%2F.

38. Marty Lipton makes the following historical observation: "It is interesting to note that it is not at all clear that director independence is the fundamental keystone of 'good' corporate governance. The world's most successful economy was built by companies that had few, if any, independent directors. It was not until 1956 that the NYSE recommended that listed companies have two outside directors, and it wasn't until 1977 that they were required to have an audit committee of all independent directors." See Martin Lipton, "Future of the Board of Directors," paper presented at the Chairman & CEO Peer Forum: Board Leadership in a New Regulatory Environment, New York Stock Exchange (June 23, 2010).

39. Note that the companies with low independence levels have considerable inside ownership or are controlled corporations. Tony Chapelle, "Listed: The Least and Most Independent Boards," *Agenda* (January 16, 2015). Accessed January 16, 2015. See http://agendaweek. com/c/1045763/107713/listed_least_most_independent_boards?referrer_module=Twitter&cam pCode=Twitter.

40. NYSE.

41. Byoung-Hyoun Hwang and Seoyoung Kim, "It Pays to Have Friends," *Journal of Financial Economics* 93 (2009): 138–158.

42. Jeffrey L. Coles, Naveen D. Daniel, and Lalitha Naveen, "Co-opted Boards," *Review of Financial Studies* 27 (June 2014): 1751–1796.

43. It might be the case that better companies attract more powerful directors. See Kathy Fogel, Liping Ma, and Randall Morck, "Powerful Independent Directors," European Corporate Governance Institute (ECGI)—Finance 404, *Social Science Research Network* (2014). Accessed January 22, 2015. See http://ssrn.com/abstract=2377106.

44. Earnings quality is measured using the metric abnormal accruals. Generally, abnormal accruals represent the difference between Generally Accepted Accounting Principles (GAAP) earnings, which are measured on an accrual basis, and GAAP cash flow, which represents cash generated by the business. When a large discrepancy exists between these two figures during a sustained period of time, the company's accounting is considered to be lower quality because the company is systematically recording more net income than it is generating on a cash basis. Research has shown that large abnormal accruals are correlated with an increased likelihood of future earnings restatements. This correlation is modest but still significant. Many academic studies that measure accounting quality use abnormal accruals as a measurement. Although not perfect, it is a standard measure that can be applied across firms. See April Klein, "Audit Committee, Board of Director Characteristics, and Earnings Management," *Journal of Accounting and Economics* 33 (2002): 375–400.

45. April Klein, "Firm Performance and Board Committee Structure," *Journal of Law and Economics* 41 (1998): 275–303.

46. A. Burak Güner, Ulrike Malmendier, and Geoffrey Tate, "Financial Expertise of Directors," *Journal of Financial Economics* 88 (2008): 323–354.

47. Ingolf Dittmann, Ernst Maug, and Christoph Schneider, "Bankers on the Boards of German Firms: What They Do, What They Are Worth, and Why They Are (Still) There," *Review of Finance* 14 (2010): 35–71. And Randall Morck and Masao Nakamura, "Banks and Corporate Control in Japan," *Journal of Finance* 54 (1999): 319–339.

48. David H. Erkens, K. R. Subramanyam, and Jieying Zhang, "Affiliated Banker on Board and Conservative Accounting," *Accounting Review* 89 (2014): 1703–1728.

49. Qianqian Huang, Feng Jiang, Erik Lie, and Ke Yang, "The Role of Investment Banker Directors in M&A," *Journal of Financial Economics* 112 (2014): 269–286.

50. Sarbanes–Oxley Act of 2002, Section 407(b).

51. Mark L. Defond, Rebecca N. Hann, and Xuesong Hu, "Does the Market Value Financial Expertise on Audit Committees of Boards of Directors?" *Journal of Accounting Research* 43 (2005): 153–193.

52. Anup Agrawal and Sahiba Chadha, "Corporate Governance and Accounting Scandals," *Journal of Law and Economics* 48 (2005): 371–406.

53. Jayanthi Krishnan, "Audit Committee Quality and Internal Control: An Empirical Analysis," *The Accounting Review* 80 (2005): 649–675.

54. Mara Faccio, "Politically Connected Firms," *American Economic Review* 96 (2006): 369–386. See Amy J. Hillman, Leonard Bierman, and Asghar Zardkoohi, "Corporate Political Strategies and Firm Performance: Indications of Firm-Specific Benefits from Personal Service in the U.S. Government," *Strategic Management Journal* 20 (1999): 67–81.

55. Eitan Goldman, Jörg Rocholl, and Jongil So, "Do Politically Connected Boards Affect Firm Value?" *Review of Financial Studies* 22 (2009): 2331–2360.

56. David Fisman, Ray Fisman, Julia Galef, and Rakesh Khurana, "Estimating the Value of Connections to Vice-President Cheney," Columbia and Yale University, working paper (2006). Accessed August 23, 2008. See http://fairmodel.econ.yale.edu/ec483/ffgk.pdf.

57. Mara Faccio, "Differences between Politically Connected and Nonconnected Firms: A Cross-Country Analysis," *Financial Management* (Blackwell Publishing Limited) 39 (2010): 905–928.

58. Marianne Bertrand, Francis Kramarz, Antoinette Schoar, and David Thesmar, "Politicians, Firms, and the Political Business Cycle: Evidence from France" (2007). Accessed February 23, 2011. See http://www.crest.fr/ckfinder/userfiles/files/Pageperso/kramarz/politics_060207_v4.pdf.

59. Gary Gorton and Frank A. Schmid, "Capital, Labor, and the Firm: A Study of German Codetermination," *Journal of the European Economic Association* 2 (2004): 863–905.

60. Larry Fauver and Michael E. Fuerst, "Does Good Corporate Governance Include Employee Representation? Evidence from German Corporate Boards," *Journal of Financial Economics* 82 (2006): 673–710.

61. Edith Ginglinger, William Megginson, and Timothée Waxin, "Employee Ownership, Board Representation, and Corporate Financial Policies," *Journal of Corporate Finance* 17 (2011): 868–887.

62. Olubunmi Faleye, Vikas Mehrotra, and Randall Morck, "When Labor Has a Voice in Corporate Governance," *Journal of Financial and Quantitative Analysis* 41 (2006): 489–510.

63. General Motors Press Release, "GM Nominates UAW VP Joe Ashton to Board," *Dow Jones Institutional News* (April 25, 2014).

64. General Motors, Form DEF 14A, filed with the Securities and Exchange Commission April 25 2014.

65. Jena McGregor, "Adding a Union Guy to GM's Board," *Washington Post* (April 29, 2014). Accessed January 23, 2015. See http://www.washingtonpost.com/blogs/on-leadership/wp/2014/04/29/adding-a-union-guy-to-gms-board/.

66. Equilar, Inc. Proprietary directorship data for fiscal years from June 2012 to May 2013.

67. Spencer Stuart (2013).

68. Jennifer Mann, "Outgoing Hallmark CEO Reflects on Successes, Setbacks," *Kansas City Star* (October 9, 2001).

69. David F. Larcker and Brian Tayan, "Executive Compensation at Aquila: Moving Utility Services to Power Trading," Stanford GSB Case No. CG-14 (2008).

70. Anonymous, "Hockaday Stepping Down from Sprint's Board," Associated Press (March 27, 2009).

71. They categorize a board as "busy" if 50 percent or more of the outside directors sit on three or more boards. See Eliezer M. Fich and Anil Shivdasani, "Are Busy Boards Effective Monitors?" *Journal of Finance* 61 (2006): 689–724.

72. John E. Core, Robert W. Holthausen, and David F. Larcker, "Corporate Governance, Chief Executive Officer Compensation, and Firm Performance," *Journal of Financial Economics* 51 (1999): 371–406.

73. Antonio Falato, Dalida Kadyrzhanova, and Ugur Lel, "Distracted Directors: Does Board Busyness Hurt Shareholder Value?" *Social Science Research Network* (2013). Accessed January 26, 2015. See http://ssrn.com/abstract=2272478.

74. Laura Field, Michelle Lowry, and Anahit Mkrtchyan, "Are Busy Boards Detrimental?" *Journal of Financial Economics* 109 (2013): 63–82.

75. Kevin F. Hallock, "Reciprocally Interlocking Boards of Directors and Executive Compensation," *Journal of Financial and Quantitative Analysis* 32 (1997): 331–344.

76. For this reason, the Clayton Antitrust Act of 1914 prohibits board locking between directly competing firms (such as railroads, steel producers, or banks). However, the act does not broadly prohibit the practice.

77. Yael Hochberg, Alexander Ljungqvist, and Yang Lu, "Whom You Know Matters: Venture Capital Networks and Investment Performance," *Journal of Finance* 62 (2007): 251–301.

78. Cesare Fracassi and Geoffrey A. Tate, "External Networking and Internal Firm Governance," *Journal of Finance* 67 (2012): 153–194.

79. Ye Cai and Merih Sevilir, "Board Connections and M&A Transactions," *Journal of Financial Economics* 103 (2012): 327–349.

80. David F. Larcker, Eric C. So, and Charles C. Y. Wang, "Boardroom Centrality and Firm Performance," *Journal of Accounting and Economics* 55 (2013): 225–250.

81. John Bizjak, Michael Lemmon, and Ryan Whitby, "Option Backdating and Board Interlocks," *Review of Financial Studies* 22 (2009): 4821–4847.

82. Jennifer L. Brown and Katharine D. Drake, "Network Ties among Low-Tax Firms," *Accounting Review* 89 (2014): 483–510.

83. Ye Cai, Dan Dhaliwal, Yongtae Kim, and Carrie Pan, "Board interlocks and the diffusion of disclosure policy," *Review of Accounting Studies* 19 (2014): 1086–1119.

84. Hallock (1997).

85. Bang Dang Nguyen, "Does the Rolodex Matter? Corporate Elite's Small World and the Effectiveness of Boards of Directors," *Management Science* 58 (2012): 236–252.

86. Rafael Liza Santos, Alexandre Di Miceli Da Silveira, and Lucas Ayres B. de C. Barros, "Board Interlocking in Brazil: Directors' Participation in Multiple Companies and Its Effect on Firm Value," *Social Science Research Network* (2009). Accessed November 9, 2009. See http://ssrn.com/abstract=1018796.

87. Mary Ellen Carter and Luann J. Lynch, "Compensation Committee Attributes and the Treatment of Earnings Management in Bonuses," working paper (October 2011).

88. Julia Grathwohl and Darina Feicha, "Supervisory Board Committee Overlap and Managers' Bonus Payments: Empirical Evidence from Germany," *Schmalenbach Business Review* 66 (2014): 470–501.

89. Nandini Chandar, Hsihui Chang, and Xiaochuan Zheng, "Does Overlapping Membership on Audit and Compensation Committees Improve a Firm's Financial Reporting Quality?" *Review of Accounting and Finance* 11 (2012): 141–165.

90. Note: Data represent 3,011 firms in fiscal year 2012, 4,029 firms in fiscal year 2007, and 3,378 firms in fiscal year 2002. Source: Data from Equilar. Calculations by the authors. See David F. Larcker, Brian Tayan, and Christina Zhu, "A Meeting of the Minds: How Do Companies Distribute Knowledge and Workload Across Board Committees?" Stanford Closer Look Series (December 8, 2014). Accessed May 3, 2015. See http://www.gsb.stanford.edu/faculty-research/centers-initiatives/cgri/research/closer-look.

91. Ibid.

92. *Corporate Board Member* and PricewaterhouseCoopers LLC (2007).

93. Martin Lipton and Jay W. Lorsch, "A Modest Proposal for Improved Corporate Governance," *Business Lawyer* 48 (1992): 59–77.

94. David L. Yermack, "Higher Market Valuation of Companies with a Small Board of Directors," *Journal of Financial Economics* 40 (1996): 185–211.

95. Jeffrey L. Coles, Naveen D. Daniel, and Lalitha Naveen, "Boards: Does One Size Fit All?" *Journal of Financial Economics* 87 (2008): 329–356.

96. Deborah L. Rhode and Amanda K. Packel, "Diversity on Corporate Boards: How Much Difference Does 'Difference' Make?" *Delaware Journal of Corporate Law* 39 (2014): 377–426.

97. Charles A. O'Reilly III, Katherine Y. Williams, and Sigal Barsade, "The Impact of Relational Demography on Teamwork: When Differences Make a Difference," *Academy of Management Proceedings & Membership Directory* (1999): G1–G6.

98. Niclas L. Erhardt, James D. Werbel, and Charles B. Shrader, "Board of Director Diversity and Firm Financial Performance," *Corporate Governance: An International Review* 11 (2003): 102–111.

99. David A. Carter, Frank D'Souza, Betty J. Simkins, and W. Gary Simpson, "The Gender and Ethnic Diversity of U.S. Boards and Board Committees and Firm Financial Performance," *Corporate Governance: An International Review* 18 (2010): 396–414.

100. Yi Wang and Bob Clift, "Is There a 'Business Case' for Board Diversity?" *Pacific Accounting Review* (Emerald Group Publishing Limited) 21 (2009): 88–103. And Shaker A. Zahra and

Wilbur W. Stanton, "The Implications of Board Directors' Composition for Corporate Strategy and Performance," *International Journal of Management* 5 (1988): 229–236.

101. James D. Westphal and Edward J. Zajac, "Who Shall Govern? CEO/Board Power, Demographic Similarity, and New Director Selection," *Administrative Science Quarterly* 40 (1995): 60–83.

102. Maura A. Belliveau, Charles A. O'Reilly III, and James B. Wade, "Social Capital at the Top: Effects of Social Similarity and Status on CEO Compensation," *Academy of Management Journal* 39 (1996): 1568–1593.

103. Catalyst Inc., "Statistical Overview of Women in the Workplace," *Catalyst Quick Takes* (2013). Accessed April 2, 2015. See http://www.catalyst.org/knowledge/statistical-overview-women-workplace.

104. Joann Lublin, "Behind the Rush to Add Women to Norway's Boards," *Wall Street Journal* (December 10, 2007, Eastern edition): B.1.

105. Joy Lois, Nancy M. Carter, Harvey M. Wagner, and Sriram Narayanan, "The Bottom Line: Corporate Performance and Women's Representation on Boards," Catalyst Inc. (2007). Accessed June 10, 2008. See www.catalyst.org/publication/200/the-bottom-line-corporate-performance-and-womensrepresentation-on-boards.

106. Ian Gregory-Smith, Brian G. M. Main, and Charles A. O'Reilly III, "Appointments, Pay and Performance in UK Boardrooms by Gender," *Economic Journal* 124 (2014): F109–F128.

107. Renée Adams and Daniel Ferreira, "Women in the Boardroom and Their Impact on Governance and Performance," *Journal of Financial Economics* 94 (2009): 291–309.

108. Kenneth R. Ahern and Amy K. Dittmar, "The Changing of the Boards: The Impact on Firm Valuation of Mandated Female Board Representation," *Quarterly Journal of Economics* (2012): 137–197.

Interlude

In the preceding chapters, we have taken a critical look at the board of directors. We have examined the operations and legal obligations of the board; the process of recruiting, compensating, and removing directors; and the research evidence on how board structure impacts firm performance. In doing so, we have referenced certain functional responsibilities of the board, such as approving corporate strategy and ensuring the integrity of financial statements. However, we have not yet defined these responsibilities in detail. We focus on these topics next.

In each of the following chapters, we take a specific topic and examine the manner in which the board fulfills its responsibilities:

- Monitor firm strategy and risk (in Chapter 6, "Strategy, Performance Measurement, and Risk Management")
- Plan for and select a new executive (in Chapter 7, "Labor Market for Executives and CEO Succession Planning")
- Structure executive compensation and equity ownership (in Chapters 8, "Executive Compensation and Incentives," and 9, "Executive Equity Ownership")
- Ensure the integrity of published financial statements (in Chapter 10, "Financial Reporting and External Audit")
- Determine whether to restrict acquisition of the company (in Chapter 11, "The Market for Corporate Control")
- Represent the interests of shareholders (in Chapter 12, "Institutional Shareholders and Activist Investors")

Each of these activities has an important bearing on governance quality. When the board performs these functions well, agency costs decrease and firm value is enhanced. When the board performs these functions less well, agency costs increase and firm value is destroyed.

We start with the first major responsibility: the oversight of firm strategy and risk.

6

Strategy, Performance Measurement, and Risk Management

As we mentioned in Chapter 3, "Board of Directors: Duties and Liability," the Organisation for Economic Co-operation and Development (OECD) states that one of the primary responsibilities of the board is to "ensure the strategic guidance of the company." The UK Corporate Governance Code recommends that directors "constructively challenge and help develop proposals on strategy."[1] Furthermore, survey data from the National Association of Corporate Directors (NACD) indicates that directors themselves consider strategic planning and oversight to be their most important responsibility—more than financial oversight, CEO succession planning, compensation, and shareholder relations.[2]

Consensus holds that strategic oversight is crucial, but the manner in which the board is expected to perform this function is less clear. The confusion arises primarily because it is not the board's responsibility to develop the strategy; that is management's job. Instead, the board is expected to scrutinize the strategy to make sure that it is appropriate for the company's shareholders and stakeholders and then to monitor the contribution of corporate activities to the strategic plan.

We break the discussion of strategy development and oversight into four parts:

1. Defining the corporate strategy
2. Developing and testing a business model that verifies how the strategy translates into shareholder or stakeholder value
3. Identifying key indicators to measure corporate performance
4. Identifying and developing processes to mitigate risks to the strategy and business model

Organizational Strategy

Developing the corporate strategy begins with identifying the organization's overarching **mission** and specific objectives. It answers questions such as, "Why are we in business?" and "What do we hope to achieve?" For example, Lockheed Martin publishes on its Web site a mission statement that outlines corporate vision and values:

Lockheed Martin's Vision:

Be the global leader in supporting our customers to strengthen global security, deliver citizen services and advance scientific discovery.

Lockheed Martin's Value Statements:

Do What's Right

We are committed to the highest standards of ethical conduct in all that we do. We believe that honesty and integrity engender trust, which is the cornerstone of our business. We abide by the laws of the United States and other countries in which we do business; we strive to be good citizens and we take responsibility for our actions.

Respect Others

We recognize that our success as an enterprise depends on the talent, skills, and expertise of our people and our ability to function as a tightly integrated team. We appreciate our diversity and believe that respect—for our colleagues, customers, partners, and all those with whom we interact—is an essential element of all positive and productive business relationships.

Perform with Excellence

We understand the importance of our missions and the trust our customers place in us. With this in mind, we strive to excel in every aspect of our business and approach every challenge with a determination to succeed.[3]

The mission statement becomes the basis for developing the corporate strategy. The **corporate strategy** is how a company expects to create long-term value for shareholders and stakeholders, within the confines of the corporate mission. It answers questions such as, "What business are we in?" and "How can we create value by being in this business?" Strategic considerations include new market entry, acquisitions and divestures, branding, reorganizations, and other similar transformational decisions.

An organization considers multiple aspects when developing its corporate strategy:

- **Scope**—What is the scope of activities that the business will participate in over the long term?
- **Markets**—What markets will the business participate in?

- **Advantage**—What advantages does the company have to ensure that it can compete?

- **Resources**—What resources does the company have (in terms of property, plant, and equipment; human and intellectual capital; customer and supplier networks; and finances) that are required to compete?

- **Environment**—What factors in the market environment influence how the company competes?

- **Stakeholders**—Who are the internal and external stakeholders that influence the business, directly or indirectly?[4]

For example, we can imagine that Lockheed Martin's strategy is to provide cutting-edge innovation in defense, equipment, and technology to give its customers (primarily the U.S. government) a competitive advantage in security and combat. The company achieves an advantage by capitalizing on a base of technological sophistication and proprietary knowledge that it has built up during decades of research and development funding and proven success in attracting and retaining highly specialized engineering talent.

As we stated earlier, it is management's responsibility to define the corporate strategy. Various models assist in this task, such as those outlined in *Strategic Management,* by Saloner, Shepard, and Podolny (2005), and *Competitive Strategy,* by Porter (1998).[5] In some cases, a management consulting firm is retained to bring objectivity and third-party expertise to the exercise (see the following sidebar).

Considerations in Developing the Strategy

Many describe the strategy-development process as though it is always produced through a formal, linear, and logical exercise. First agree on corporate objectives, then develop the plan for achieving those objectives, and finally identify and deploy the necessary resources. The reality in most firms is quite different. Many companies develop a strategy through a nonlinear or iterative process. For example, they might develop a pilot program and then improve or refine the strategy based on the results. Other companies stumble upon a strategy, either at inception or over time, and only later articulate it into a clearly defined corporate strategy. In many cases, companies do not have formal strategy (in the sense taught by business school researchers) but instead loose guidelines developed by management and accepted by the board of directors and shareholders.

The strategy-development process can also be biased through cultural and psychological factors. For example, management might anchor on current activities because they are comfortable with them and know how to manage them. Such an approach can lead to modest, incremental strategic change that binds the company's future too closely to its current way of conducting business. Incrementalism can be particularly detrimental when a company is faced with an unanticipated crisis or change in market environment that requires a more radical reassessment of corporate direction. The strategy-development process can also suffer from poor coordination, with the strategy, finance, and operating groups planning in isolation and experiencing serious communication disconnects.[6] Without proper information sharing, corporate planners fail to understand the true dynamics, pressures, and resources required to achieve company objectives. When this occurs, substantial risk exists that corporate strategy will not create shareholder value.[7]

Strategy Implementation Process

The board of directors needs to understand and evaluate the key elements of the strategy identification and implementation process. We illustrate this process using the generic example of a consumer products company. For simplicity, we follow a linear approach:

- Establish the overarching objective of the firm. If the board takes a purely shareholder perspective, the objective might be to produce total shareholder returns (TSR) that are superior to those of its direct competitors. If it takes a stakeholder perspective, it might establish additional objectives that are of concern to nonshareholder constituents (such as maintaining present employment levels, protecting the environment, and so on).

  Example: Target long-term TSR of 10 percent per year.

- Determine the outcomes that are necessary to achieve the TSR target. Management might propose explicit goals for sales growth, return on capital, free cash flow, and other economic metrics that are consistent with the TSR target. The finance group, in consultation with officers in the functional areas of the company, performs the analysis that supports these goals. The group will likely take into account the growth prospects of the industry and the relationship between financial returns and shareholder value. Board members test the assumptions underlying these computations to ensure that these goals are reasonable and that the relationship between the economic results and value creation is correct.

  Example: Sales growth of 6 percent per year, free cash flow growth of 8 percent, and return on equity of 15 percent.

- Assess the viability of specific strategies to achieve the company's economic targets.

  Example: Develop products at three price points: basic, middle-tier, and premium. The company seeks to increase adoption and encourage consumers to migrate up the value chain, thereby delivering increased sales and profitability. Higher margins, productivity increases, and economies of scale will drive growth in free cash flow.

- Assign targets (both financial and nonfinancial) that will enable the company to measure the success of its strategy over time.

  Example: The company might set financial targets for cash flow and revenue growth from new products and nonfinancial targets for market share, pricing, product attributes, advertising support, research and development productivity, customer satisfaction, brand awareness and strength, and so on. If targets are achieved, the company expects to succeed in its revenue and profitability goals and ultimately achieve its TSR target.

To satisfy itself that company goals are achievable, the board needs to review a causal business model of the organization. A **causal business model** links specific financial and nonfinancial measures in a logical chain to delineate how the corporate strategy translates into the accomplishment of stated goals. The board should evaluate the business model for logical consistency, realism of targets, and statistical evidence that the relationships between performance measures and stated goals are valid.

The board might test management assumptions by asking questions such as these: If we launch a product with the desired attributes, backed by a pricing, packaging, and advertising strategy, will we achieve the customer satisfaction levels that we anticipate? Will customers engage in repeat purchases? Will we achieve the desired sales volumes? What evidence (statistical, not anecdotal) do we have that these relationships are valid for our company? What metrics will we put in place to measure our progress, and how will we capture this data?

This task is extremely difficult because it requires input and agreement from all major functional areas of the firm. For example, analysis should be performed by marketing (What does it take to get the right customers?), human resources (What does it take to get the right employees?), manufacturing (What needs to be done so that we can produce the units in a timely manner?), and engineering (How can we increase new product development?).

The business model serves an important purpose: It specifies how management expects to create long-term value. The business model lays out a concrete plan (value propositions) that the board can test and evaluate when approving the corporate strategy. From a governance perspective, the business model is an important tool that the board can rely on to fulfill its oversight function. By examining the logical chain presented by management, the board can challenge assumptions and eventually recognize that the corporate strategy is sound. This model also provides the basis for measuring management performance and awarding compensation. To perform this function adequately, directors must have the requisite industry knowledge and business background to carefully examine the model and use informed judgment (see the following sidebar).

Considerations in Developing the Business Model

Companies that explicitly develop a causal business model will likely encounter substantial challenges. First, instead of dedicating the time necessary to do a thorough job, management might take shortcuts. One example is relying on general "best practice" ideas that are assumed to work without considering whether these ideas actually fit the organization. Sometimes this takes the form of off-the-shelf technology—such as customer resource management (CRM) and enterprise resource programs (ERP)—that alone is not capable of developing business models. Second, relevant data might be difficult to obtain. If the company does not have a system in place for tracking financial and nonfinancial metrics, such a system needs to be established. This might involve breaking down silos within the organization and convincing managers from across the organization to work collaboratively and share data. Third, managers might resist the concept of a formal business model, particularly if it requires that they fundamentally change how they do business. They might also resist implementation if they are underperforming and therefore want to avoid rigorous performance measurement, or if the modeling process leads to a restructuring that dramatically alters or reduces their area of responsibility. It is the board's responsibility to ensure that organizational inertia does not impede the business modeling process.

Business Model Development and Testing

Following are two real-world examples that illustrate how companies have used statistical data analysis to explore the causal relationship between financial and nonfinancial performance drivers and future operating performance.

Example 1: Fast-Food Chain and Employee Turnover

The board of directors and the senior management team at a major fast-food restaurant chain decided that the company was not growing fast enough. At the request of the board, senior-level executives across the various functional areas of the company convened to examine how and why the company was falling short. Executives outlined what they believed to be a simple causal model of how the company made money (see Figure 6.1).[8]

Consensus Business Model

Source: Authors.

Figure 6.1 Consensus business model.

The group built this model based on an assumption that customer satisfaction was a key driver of operating performance. They hypothesized that employee performance played a critical role in influencing customer satisfaction and that hiring and retention practices were the most important determinants of employee performance.

The company acted on this model even though it had not been verified through formal data analysis. Executives launched a series of strategic initiatives to improve employee performance. These initiatives centered on improving employee hiring practices and improving employee satisfaction. They measured the success of these initiatives through a nonfinancial performance indicator: employee turnover. To support a reduction in turnover, the company implemented an expensive human resource program that included retention bonus awards for all restaurant employees.

Only subsequently did the company undertake a detailed statistical analysis at the store level. The results were not what the company had expected. It turned out that groups of stores with the same overall employee turnover rates exhibited very different financial performance. In addition, several high-profit stores had employee turnover that was significantly above average. These findings contradicted the premise of the company's causal model. The expected correlation between employee turnover and store performance did not exist. The true driver of store performance was not general turnover but *turnover among store managers*. A restaurant suffered a drop in performance when the supervisory personnel turned over. This was because a change in manager impacted consistency of training, food preparation, cleanliness, and other operating processes—at least until the new store manager got up to speed with the new responsibilities.

Based on these findings, senior management shifted its priority from reducing the turnover of all store employees to reducing the turnover of store managers. Retention bonuses were put in place at the store manager level. Further analysis provided an estimate for the financial cost of turnover, which was used to create an upper bound for the size of the retention bonus.

This somewhat simple business model provided new insights into the value-creation process at this company. It became a tool for strategic discussions with the board of directors, and the board was provided summary data on the most important performance indicators, including store manager turnover, to measure corporate performance.

Example 2: Financial Services Firm and Investment Advisor Retention

A large financial services organization had a goal of being a "world leader in financial advisory and brokerage services to retail investors." From prior statistical analyses, executives and the board knew that customer retention and assets under management were key success indicators that directly impacted economic results (see Figure 6.2). Furthermore, this analysis revealed that the level of satisfaction with the investment advisor was positively correlated with the level of assets that the customer entrusted to the company.

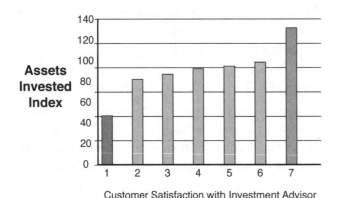

Advisor Rating and Assets Invested

Customer Satisfaction with Investment Advisor

Source: Authors.

Figure 6.2   Relationship between customer satisfaction and asset investment levels.

At the board's request, management undertook further statistical analysis to better understand the factors that contributed to a customer's satisfaction with an investment advisor. They found several, including the advisor's trustworthiness, responsiveness, and knowledge. However, one factor in particular was the most important: advisor turnover. Customers wanted to deal with the same advisor over time, and when they were shuttled around from one advisor to another, they became dissatisfied—even if the new advisor scored high on the personal attributes mentioned earlier (see Figure 6.3).

Management used this knowledge to explore the factors that contributed to advisor turnover. Statistical analysis revealed that they were (in decreasing order) compensation level, work environment, challenging career opportunities, quality of branch management, and work/life balance. The company used these insights to develop a human resources plan to address the compensation issues (changing the level and mix of short- and long-term remuneration). More importantly, senior management and the board now had a rigorous business model to filter strategic planning decisions and key performance metrics to track management performance. Going forward, the board's review of corporate performance included not only the traditional metrics of profitability and assets under management (AUM) but also the newly devised metrics of customer satisfaction, advisor satisfaction, and advisor turnover.

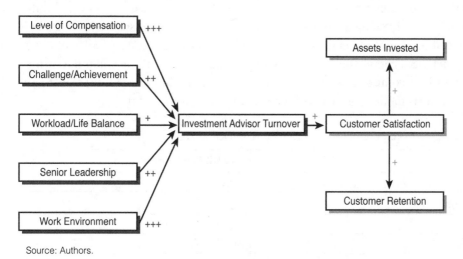

Source: Authors.

Figure 6.3 Statistical analysis of factors contributing to customer satisfaction.

Key Performance Measures

As highlighted in these two examples, an important output from the business model is that it serves as the basis for identifying key performance measures that the board can later use to evaluate management performance and award bonuses. **Key**

performance measures, or **key performance indicators (KPIs)**, include both financial and nonfinancial metrics that validly reflect current and future corporate performance. For example, in the financial services firm example, the business model highlighted the need to use investment advisor turnover and satisfaction, as well as customer satisfaction—in addition to traditional financial measures—as KPIs.

The board also uses key performance measures to evaluate management performance and award compensation. For example, if a company believes that the success of a new product launch should be measured in terms of market share, brand awareness, gross margins, and sale volume, these should be the metrics that the board follows *both* to determine management's success *and* to award compensation.

KPIs are roughly grouped into two categories: financial and nonfinancial. **Financial KPIs** include measures such as total shareholder return; revenue growth; earnings per share; earnings before interest, taxes, depreciation, and amortization (EBITDA); return on capital; economic value added (EVA); and free cash flow. **Nonfinancial KPIs** include measures such as customer satisfaction, employee satisfaction, defects and rework, on-time delivery, worker safety, environmental safety, and research and development (R&D) pipeline productivity. Because of their common usefulness, certain KPIs are broadly used by many companies. Others are used by a more limited set of companies—because of the specificity of their line of business—and include both financial and nonfinancial measures, such as sales per square foot (retailing), R&D productivity (science and technology), and factory downtime (manufacturing). Whatever KPIs a company selects, it is important that they be closely tied to the company business model (see Table 6.1 for commonly used KPIs).

Table 6.1   Measures to Determine Corporate Performance (2012)

	Overall Prevalence
Number of companies	1,128
Accounting metrics	
Earnings	62.1%
Sales	24.1%
Profit margin	6.5%
Return on assets	4.2%
Return on equity	8.0%
Return on investment	17.6%
Cash flow	11.3%
Economic value added (EVA)	1.6%
Other	16.6%

Other metrics	
Business unit related	3.2%
Customer related	4.3%
Individual	12.8%
Operational metrics	8.5%
Same store sales	3.2%
Other	79.8%

Note: Performance measures used to award equity-based performance awards.

Source: J. Carr Bettis, John Bizjak, Jeffrey Coles, and Swaminathan Kalpathy, "Performance-Vesting Provisions in Executive Compensation," Paris December 2014 Finance Meeting EUROFIDAI – AFFI Paper, *Social Science Research Network*, (2013). Accessed May 5, 2015. See http://ssrn.com/abstract=2289566.

Research has shown that companies tend to use multiple performance measures, including a mix of financial and nonfinancial KPIs. de Angelis and Grinstein (2012) found that the KPIs used to award executive bonuses tend to be weighted toward accounting measures, particularly those related to corporate profitability—such as earnings per share, net income growth, and earnings before interest and taxes (EBIT).[9] Ittner, Larcker, and Rajan (1997) and Kim and Yang (2010) found that companies rely on a mix of quantitative and qualitative factors in awarding bonuses. Qualitative factors include those related to strategic development, individual performance, customer satisfaction, employee satisfaction, and workplace safety.[10] Cornelli, Kominek, and Ljungqvist (2013) found that nonquantifiable information (such as leadership style and competence) plays a larger role than so-called hard data in measuring CEO performance.[11]

Although nonfinancial measures are important, boards must be aware of the risks involved in using them. By their nature, nonfinancial measures are more easily subject to measurement error or manipulation. Others are difficult to track with precision. Following are some of the key factors for the board to consider when relying on performance measures:[12]

- **Sensitivity**—How sensitive is the metric to corporate performance? How sensitive is the metric to management action?
- **Precision**—How much measurement error is embedded in the measure? What is the potential for intentional manipulation?
- **Verifiability**—Can the measure be audited or otherwise independently verified?
- **Objectivity**—Is the measure objective (such as number of safety incidents) or subjective (such as level of employee commitment)? Do these different categories of measures have similar sensitivity, precision, and verifiability?

- **Dimension**—Are the results expressed as a percentage, survey scale, number of occurrences, or binary outcome? Would the metric lend itself to different interpretation if expressed in a different manner?
- **Interpretation**—What specific attribute does the data measure? (For example, does product failure rate measure the quality of the manufacturing process or the quality of the product design?)
- **Cost**—What is the cost to develop and track this metric? Does it provide sufficient value to the board, compared to the cost?

Research evidence supports the importance of these efforts. Ittner and Larcker (2003) found that companies that develop a causal business model based on KPIs exhibit significantly higher returns on assets and returns on equity during five-year periods than those that do not.[13] The authors identified three benefits of this process: enhanced internal communication on strategic assumptions, better identification and measurement of strategic value drivers, and improved resource allocation and target setting. Gates (1999) found that companies with a formal set of strategic performance measures tend to exhibit superior stock price returns compared to companies that do not have such measures.[14] Relative performance is even more favorable when such measures are regularly shared with the board of directors, investors, and analysts.

Furthermore, it is important that companies consider using both financial and nonfinancial measures. Researchers have repeatedly shown that nonfinancial KPIs can be a leading indicator of subsequent financial performance. For example, Ittner and Larcker (1998) found that customer satisfaction was a leading indicator of future financial performance in a sample of banking and telecommunications companies.[15] Banker, Potter, and Schroeder (1993) demonstrated a similar relationship between customer satisfaction and future financial results in the hospitality industry.[16] Nagar and Rajan (2001) demonstrated a correlation between manufacturing quality measures and future revenue growth in manufacturing firms.[17] It is therefore critical that boards understand the relationship between nonfinancial measures and subsequent financial performance when deciding on a set of KPIs.

However, the importance of nonfinancial targets depends on the company's strategy and operating environment. For example, Ittner, Larcker, and Rajan (1997) found that nonfinancial measures take on greater importance when a company is pursuing an innovation strategy (such as new ventures that are cash-flow negative) or a quality strategy (such as the implementation of total quality management [TQM] or lean manufacturing).[18] Said, HassabElnaby, and Wier (2003) supported these findings. They found a greater prevalence of nonfinancial measures among companies that are pursuing an "innovation" or "quality" strategy, companies whose products are subject to long development cycles (such as aircraft manufacturers), companies that are in highly regulated industries (such as railroads), and companies in financial distress.[19] These studies suggest that nonfinancial measures are particularly important when a company's current strategy does not lend itself well to short-term financial targets.

How Well Are Boards Doing with Performance Measures and Business Models?

Deloitte undertook one of the most detailed analyses of this subject in a two-part study titled "In the Dark: What Boards and Executives Don't Know about the Health of Their Businesses" (2004 and 2007).[20] Based on a sample of 250 directors and executives at large international corporations, the report found a surprising disconnect between the metrics that board members and executives say are important drivers of firm performance and the KPIs that the companies actually use to track results.

More than 90 percent of respondents claimed that both financial and nonfinancial factors are critical to their company's success. Commonly cited nonfinancial measures included customer satisfaction (97 percent), product or service quality (96 percent), and employee commitment (92 percent). Yet when asked to assess the quality of information they receive regarding each of these measures, respondents claimed to have good visibility into only one: financial results (91 percent). The quality of information regarding nonfinancial measures was rated much lower, including product or service quality (52 percent reporting "excellent" or "good" information), customer satisfaction (46 percent), and employee commitment (41 percent). That is, evidence points to a shockingly large disconnect between the information that is important for understanding value creation and the information that is actually being supplied to the board.

More surprisingly, board members did not appear to have an explanation for why they were not receiving this information. The most frequently cited reason was that the company has "undeveloped tools for analyzing such measures" (59 percent). That is, information on these performance measures was not captured because no one has taken the time to formulate a proper system for tracking them. If true, this is a serious lapse in oversight on the part of directors. The study concluded that a "gap [exists] between awareness and action, rhetoric and reality":

> Until this gap narrows, board directors, managers, and investors remain less well-informed about the true state of their companies' health than they would otherwise. [N]onfinancial measurements of performance . . . can provide the board and management with a vital guide to help steer the company toward long-term success. Yet too many companies focus their attention on financial data and too few rigorously monitor other performance measures.

Ittner, Larcker, and Randall (2003) found similar results. The metrics that are the most important drivers of long-term organizational success suffer from very low measurement quality (see Figure 6.4). According to the study, the only measure that had higher measurement quality than importance is short-term financial accounting results. By contrast, metrics about customer satisfaction, product quality, innovation, and other important drivers were not tracked through reliable metrics. These measures had higher importance than measurement quality.[21]

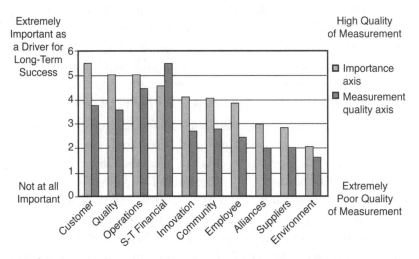

Adapted from Christopher D. Ittner, David F. Larcker, and Taylor Randall (2003).

Figure 6.4   The importance of metrics vs. the quality of their measurement.

All this suggests that many boards might be falling short of their duty to oversee firm strategy and performance. They can redress this deficiency by demanding more detailed information about the full set of KPIs that contribute to future operating success and then tracking those measures to assess the performance of management. With this information, boards can better understand the factors contributing to success or failure, as well as manage organizational risks.

Risk and Risk Management

The notion of risk is largely absent from the preceding discussion. Our focus was on the *desired* outcome instead of the *range* of outcomes that might occur. Although we emphasized the positive outcomes that arise from establishing a sound strategy and valid business model, we did not consider the loss of value that occurs when things do not work out as planned. Nor did we discuss the policies and procedures that a company might put in place to mitigate such losses. Now we take up that discussion.

First, we define the concept of risk in terms of its relationship to the corporate strategy and business model. Then we discuss what is meant by risk management. Finally, we consider the role the board plays in both understanding organizational risk and implementing the policies and procedures necessary to ensure that it is managed properly.

It is important to highlight that when we speak of *risk management* in this chapter, we are not talking about simple compliance with laws and regulations. We are treating it as a minimum standard that organizations attempt to conduct their affairs within the guidelines established by governments and federal agencies. When we speak of risk management, we are addressing the bigger picture involving outcomes or events that can reduce a company's profitability, lead to severe underperformance, or otherwise threaten an organization's success or viability.

The importance of this topic has been underscored by the large number of corporate failures that occurred following the financial crisis of 2008. Many casualties of the crisis—such as American International Group, Bear Stearns, and Lehman Brothers—simply did not understand the risks they were exposed to because of their business models. Had they been aware of these risks in advance, they might have conducted their affairs differently to protect themselves from the collateral damage they ultimately faced. Unfortunately, according to a recent survey, fewer than half of senior executives are confident that their organization understands the range of risks it faces, the severity of those risks, the likelihood of their occurrence, or their potential impact.[22] As might be expected with the financial crisis, Congress has also been actively engaged in the risk-management debate: Risk committee requirements were proposed in—although ultimately omitted from—the Dodd–Frank Act.[23] Risk management is now defined in much broader terms than was formerly the case, and includes CEO succession planning and the structure of executive compensation. (We discuss these issues in Chapters 7, "Labor Market for Executives and CEO Succession Planning," 8, "Executive Compensation and Incentives," and 9, "Executive Equity Ownership.")

Risk and Risk Tolerance

The **risk** facing an organization represents the likelihood and severity of loss from unexpected or uncontrollable outcomes. This includes both the typical losses that occur during the course of business and losses from extremely unlikely and unpredictable events (so-called **black swans**, or **outliers**). Risk arises naturally, both from the nature of the activities that the corporation participates in and from the manner in which it pursues its objectives. Risk cannot be separated from the strategy and operations of the firm but instead is an integral feature of organizational decision making.

Each company must decide how much risk it is willing to assume through its choice of strategy. It is not possible to pursue a risk-free strategy, nor is risk management about removing all risk from the firm. Obviously, if managers were to remove all the risk, they should be able to earn no more than the risk-free interest rate, which is not in the interest of shareholders. Instead, firms succeed when they are better able to manage risk than their competitors.

In making this decision, each company must determine its own tolerance for risk (**risk tolerance—see the following sidebar**). This decision should involve the active participation of the board of directors. If the board (as representatives of shareholders) is willing to accept greater uncertainty and variability in future cash flows in exchange for potentially higher economic returns, then a risky strategy might be appropriate. If not, then either a safer strategy or an entirely new strategy is appropriate. The company must strike its own balance between aggressiveness and conservativeness. This balance can be achieved only when the riskiness of the corporate strategy and business model is properly understood. The risks that the firm is willing to accept should be properly managed in the context of its strategy. The risks that the firm cannot handle on its own or is not good at managing should be hedged or otherwise transferred to a third party. The management of the company and the board of directors need to understand the nature, cost, and repercussions of adverse or unexpected outcomes and manage those accordingly.

Do Risk-Seeking CEOs Create Risky Companies?

Several examples exist of corporate CEOs with a reputation for risk-taking in their personal lives. For example, Richard Branson, the serial entrepreneur and founder of ventures such as Virgin Records and Virgin America airlines, has pursued world records in skydiving, hot air ballooning, and sailing. Larry Ellison, CEO of Oracle Corporation, is an avid sailor and winner of the America's Cup. Steve Appleton, former CEO of Micron, enjoyed flying small aircraft before his untimely death.

Do the personalities of these executives influence the risk tolerance of the organizations they manage? The research into the relation between CEO personality types and corporate governance is in its infancy; still, some evidence suggests that CEO personalities influence the activities of their organizations. For example, Bernile, Bhagwat, and Rau (2014) found that CEOs who in their youth lived through natural disasters without experiencing extremely negative consequences lead organizations that take on more risk (in terms of acquisition activity and capital structure). Conversely, CEOs who witnessed the extreme downside of natural disasters subsequently manage corporations more conservatively.[24] Similarly, Davidson, Dey, and Smith (2013) found that CEOs who spend money lavishly in their personal lives oversee organizations with looser internal controls, as manifested by a higher likelihood of internal employee fraud and unintentional material reporting errors. The authors found other evidence of cultural changes during the tenure of these CEOs, including an increase in equity-based compensation, a decrease in board monitoring, and the appointment of a CFO with similarly lavish personal spending habits. The authors note that "measures of executives' 'off-the-job' behavior capture meaningful differences in managerial style" and that "these measures are [potentially] useful in exploring other aspects of corporate behavior and performance."[25]

Risk to the Business Model

Boards and executives commonly focus on generic risks facing the firm.[26] However, the real risks are extensive and relate to all its activities, including these:

- **Operational risk**—This reflects how exposed the company is to disruptions in its operations. Operational risk is reflected in such factors as concentration of suppliers, concentration of buyers, redundancy in the supply chain, and the extent to which the company monitors its supply chain.

- **Financial risk**—This reflects how much the company relies on external financing (including the capital markets and private lenders) to support its ongoing operations. Financial risk is reflected in such factors as balance sheet leverage, off-balance-sheet vehicles, contractual obligations, maturity schedule of debt obligations, liquidity, and other restrictions that reduce financial flexibility. Companies that rely on external parties for financing are at greater risk than those that finance operations using internally generated funds.

- **Reputational risk**—This reflects how much the company protects the value of its intangible assets, including corporate reputation. Reputational risk is reflected in investing in product brand development, investing in corporate brand development, monitoring the use of brands, monitoring supplier and customer business practices, performing community outreach, and handling stakeholder relations.

- **Compliance risk**—This reflects how much the company complies with laws and regulations that otherwise would damage the firm. Compliance risk is reflected in such factors as labor practices, environmental compliance, and consideration given to the regulatory requirements that govern the company's products, processes, or publicly listed securities.

To understand the risks associated with the organizational strategy, the board must probe deeper than generic risk categories. Survey data suggests that companies are aware of the financial, political, regulatory, and economic risks facing their organizations and the risks associated with loss of human capital. However, they exhibit somewhat lower awareness of—and preparedness for—the risks that are inherent to their business models (see the following sidebar).[27]

A Breakdown in Risk Management

Lululemon

In March 2013, Lululemon Athletica removed from its stores its entire inventory of women's black "luon" yoga pants, which retailed for almost $100 a pair. According to the company, the pants were excessively "sheer" (that is, see-through) and "fall short of our very high standards."[28] In recalling the pants, the company initially blamed its supplier for not meeting technical specifications. Later it alleged that the problem was due to inadequate testing. By June the company returned its pants to shelves, claiming that "our quality testing has never been better than it is now."[29]

The matter, however, did not end there. Complaints about quality continued on blogs and social media Web sites. In one post, a customer demonstrated the sheerness of luon yoga pants by taking a photograph through the fabric. Founder Chip Wilson added fuel to the fire by stating in a television interview that the problem was not the quality of the pants but that certain customers were purchasing pants they should not be wearing: "Quite frankly . . . they don't work for some women's bodies. It's really about the rubbing through the thighs, how much pressure is there over a period of time, how much they use it."[30] Wilson later apologized, but customers were furious. In December, the company lowered profit guidance because of a "meaningful" slowdown in store traffic. CEO Christina Day and CFO John Currie resigned, and Wilson stepped down from the board. By the summer of 2014, the company's stock traded 50 percent below the level at which it had been trading before the initial recall.

The business modeling process discussed earlier provides a rigorous framework for understanding organizational risk. Stress testing the key linkages and assumptions in the business model enable the board and management to better determine what might go wrong with the corporate strategy and the consequences of these problems. A causal business model focuses the risk management discussion by enabling corporate officials to think about how a disruption in one area or function could have cascading effects throughout the organization. The company then can develop policies and procedures to mitigate these risks.

If the company has a well-developed business model, it is possible for the board and management to develop very detailed risk-management analyses of key issues. The company should generally seek to mitigate risk to the extent that it is cost-effective to do so. Risks that the company is not willing to accept should be hedged or otherwise transferred to a third party through insurance or derivative contracts. However, other risks are desirable to retain and might be associated with the firm's competitive advantages, including labor talent, manufacturing processes, brands, patents, and intellectual property. Obviously, good corporate governance requires that risks retained by the company be properly disclosed to shareholders.

Risk Management

Risk management is the process by which a company evaluates and reduces its risk exposure. This includes actions, policies, and procedures that management implements to reduce the likelihood and severity of adverse outcomes and to increase the likelihood and benefits of positive outcomes. To accomplish this, the organization must define and develop a **risk culture**. A **risk culture** sets the tone for risk tolerance in the organization and ensures that risk consideration is a key part of all decisions. Survey data suggests that strong leadership, clear parameters surrounding corporate risk taking, and access to information about potential risks are necessary for this to occur.[31]

Various professional frameworks can guide a company in the risk-management processes. For example, the Committee of Sponsoring Organizations (COSO) framework, originally developed in 1990, has become a respected framework for risk management.[32] COSO recommends that risk management be incorporated into strategy planning, operational review, internal reporting, and compliance. As such, risk should be considered at the enterprise, division, and business unit levels. COSO outlines its recommendations in an eight-step framework:

1. **Internal environment**—Establish the organization's philosophy toward risk management and risk culture.

2. **Objective setting**—Evaluate the company's strategy and set organizational goals based on the risk tolerance of management and the board.

3. **Event identification**—Examine the risks associated with each potential business opportunity.

4. **Risk assessment**—Determine the likelihood and severity of each risk.

5. **Risk response**—Identify the organizational actions taken to prevent or deal with each risk.

6. **Control activities**—Establish policies and procedures to ensure that risk responses are carried out as planned.

7. **Information and communication**—Create an information system to capture and report on the organization's risk-management process.

8. **Monitoring**—Review data from the information system and take actions, as appropriate.

Note that the first steps of this framework are consistent with the argument we have made so far that risk should be discussed in terms of its strategic and operating components. Also note that the information-collection and monitoring steps are consistent with the manner in which we have described performance measurement using KPIs. That is, the risk-management process should be integrated with the processes the company uses for development and oversight of the strategy, business model, and performance measurement (see the following sidebar).

Organizational Risk Management

Heinz Company exemplifies the comprehensive approach to risk management. The company has defined its primary objectives to protect its reputation and shareholder value. To this end, the company's efforts focus on the long-term sustainability of the organization in a manner that enables it to achieve both short-term and long-term financial objectives. *Risk* at Heinz is therefore defined as "anything that can prevent the company from achieving its objectives."

The company groups risk into two categories: operational risk and nonoperational risk. Operational risk areas include product quality, environment and sustainability, employee health and safety, facility and product security, business continuity, and asset conservation. Nonoperational risk areas include strategy and market, corporate governance and ethics, finance, legal, information services, and human resources.

From an organizational perspective, the company maintains an Office of Risk Management, which consists of a chief quality officer, a director of enterprise risk management, and a director of operational risk management and sustainability. The Office of Risk Management has ties to the audit committee of the board, the disclosure committee, and internal audit. In addition, the company maintains a Risk Council, which consists of senior executives in each functional area. As a result, risks are evaluated *both* by compliance officers, whose primary responsibility is risk management, and by functional leaders, whose primary responsibility is managing the company's operations.

The objectives of these two groups (Office of Risk Management and Risk Council) are to identify, prioritize, measure, and manage key risks and to ensure that these processes are owned and understood at the business unit level. Finally, the company emphasizes that its managers be "risk aware but not risk averse, with a primary focus on protecting and thereby maximizing enterprise value and brand equity."[33]

To date, little research rigorously examines the relation between risk management and future firm performance.[34] However, survey data suggests that shareholders place great value on comprehensive risk management. According to a survey by Ernst & Young, more than 80 percent of institutional investors responded that they were willing to pay a premium for companies with good risk-management practices. A majority of respondents claimed that they had passed up the opportunity to invest in a company because they believed risk management was insufficient.[35] Similarly, a survey by PricewaterhouseCoopers found that institutional investors believe that risk management should be the number-one priority of the board of directors, ahead of strategic planning. Investors also believe that risk management expertise is the most important skill that directors should have, ahead of financial, industry, and operational expertise.[36]

Oversight of Risk Management

Although management is ultimately responsible for implementing and enforcing risk management, the board must ensure that these activities are carried out effectively. How is the board expected to satisfy this responsibility? What does it mean to "oversee" risk management?

The risk oversight responsibilities of the board can be roughly divided into four categories. First, the board is responsible for determining the risk profile of the company. As we have discussed, this includes considering macroeconomic, industry-related, and firm-specific risk. The board should determine the risk profile of the company in consultation with management, shareholders, and other key stakeholders. In heavily regulated industries—such as financial services, insurance, and utilities— discussions should include regulators. The board should weigh downside costs against long-term market opportunities and consider the likelihood of both success and failure.

Second, the board is responsible for evaluating the company's strategy and business model to determine whether they are appropriate, given the firm's appetite for risk. The board should be satisfied that the company has identified risks to the strategy and business model and is effectively managing them. The board should confirm that viable contingency plans have been drawn up to deal with potential financial or operational interruptions. In addition, the board should consider whether appropriate hedges and insurance are in place to deal with risks that are not well managed by the firm.

Third, the board is responsible for ensuring that the company is committed to operating at an appropriate risk level on an ongoing basis. Does the company's culture encourage or discourage risky behavior? Are the company's operations assuming more risk than intended by the strategy and business model? Developing internal reporting systems that capture risk data can help answer these questions. Risk metrics should be included among the key performance indicators that the board uses to monitor firm performance. The board should be facile in interpreting this data and attentive to emerging trends (see the following sidebar).

Finally, the board should determine whether management has developed the necessary internal controls to ensure that risk-management procedures remain effective. A lot of this activity is mundane, including ensuring that reporting relationships are well defined, communication channels work, and reporting data is tested for accuracy. Nevertheless, these are important steps for ensuring that risk management practices are effective. Tying executive compensation not only to strategic performance measures but also to the company's risk measures will help ensure that this work is performed appropriately. (This is discussed more fully in Chapters 8 and 9.)

Is Risk the Responsibility of a Committee or the Full Board?

According to a survey by the NACD, 46 percent of companies assign risk management to the audit committee, 11 percent to a special risk committee, and 38 percent to the full board.[37]

A company might assign risk management to the audit committee for several reasons. In recent years, much of the regulatory focus on "risk" has centered on financial statement risk and inaccurate disclosures. In fact, the listing requirements of the New York Stock Exchange (NYSE) require that the audit committee review the firm's risk policies.[38] Companies are also required to disclose "risk factors" that could materially impact financial results; the audit committee oversees this disclosure on the 10-K. The risk-management function within the company typically reports to the chief financial officer and, by extension, the audit committee; the audit committee, therefore, should be well versed in its activities. Finally, the CFO and audit committee are familiar with financial hedges and insurance contracts that the company uses to protect the value of its assets. To reduce redundancies, many companies might choose to consolidate all risk-management activities with the audit committee.

A company might choose to set up a separate risk committee. If risk is operational instead of purely financial, it makes sense that oversight be given to a group of directors who view risk primarily through the lens of operations and firm performance instead of financial results and accounting statements. The audit committee might be burdened with so many regulatory requirements that it cannot possibly dedicate the requisite time to monitor operational risk. Furthermore, much risk is specialized in nature and requires specialized knowledge to evaluate. For this reason, companies such as Aegon (insurance), Duke Energy (utilities), and JPMorgan Chase (banking/finance) all have dedicated risk committees.[39]

However, forming a risk committee does not address a key issue identified earlier in this chapter: Risk management should not be an isolated function within a company. Any consideration of risk—financial or operational—should be made in conjunction with a comprehensive review of the company's strategy, business model, and performance measurement. Therefore, risk management is likely best handled by the entire board, not a subset of directors.

Some research support exists for this position. Ittner and Keusch (2014) conducted a detailed analysis of risk management practices among 676 public, private, and nonprofit organizations in 29 countries. They found that boards of directors have a more consistent understanding of the organization's top risks, a quantified risk appetite, and more extensive and frequent reporting on risk mitigation activities when risk management is assigned to the board as a whole rather than to a committee.[40]

Assessing Board Performance on Risk Management

Little rigorous research assesses the general effectiveness of risk-management programs and the performance consequences of these programs. However, survey data indicates that companies can stand to improve in this area.

A 2014 study by the American Institute of Certified Public Accountants and Chartered Institute of Management Accountants showed that risk-management processes are seriously underdeveloped at many companies. Approximately two-thirds (63 percent) of companies admit that they were caught off guard by a surprise in the previous five years. Almost half have no enterprise risk management processes in place, and only 20 percent describe their organization's level of risk management as "mature" or "robust." Just under half (45 percent) either have no structure in place for identifying and reporting risk to the board, or they track risks by silos, with minimal reporting of aggregate risk exposure to the board. A significant minority (38 percent) do no formal risk assessment when developing strategy, and half fail to consider existing risk exposures.[41]

In particular, the evidence suggests that boards are not effective in understanding or monitoring technological risks to the organization. For example, while 90 percent of companies claim to understand the negative impact that social media can have on their corporate reputation and perceptions of product quality, only 32 percent monitor social media to detect risk.[42] Similarly, CEOs consider the potential loss of customer or proprietary data through a breach of technology systems ("cyber-attacks") to be the largest technological threat facing their organizations, and yet only 20 percent have real-time systems in place to detect threats.[43] These data highlight a very real problem. The board of directors should ensure that its members have adequate risk expertise and that the company has rigorous procedures in place to measure and monitor organizational risks (see the following sidebar).

Risk Management and the Financial Crisis of 2008

The 2008 financial crisis clearly illustrated the failure of risk management at many companies. Major financial institutions—including Lehman Brothers, Bear Stearns, and Citigroup—collapsed in part because their business and trading strategies assumed more risk than either the boards or management realized. Consider a summary report from the OECD:

"When they were put to a test, corporate governance routines did not serve their purpose to safeguard against excessive risk taking in a number of financial services companies. A number of weaknesses have been apparent. The risk management systems have failed in many cases due to corporate governance procedures rather than the inadequacy of computer models alone: Information about exposures in a number of cases did not reach the board and even senior levels of management, while risk management was often activity- rather than enterprise-based. These are board responsibilities. In other cases, boards had approved strategy but then did not establish suitable metrics to monitor its implementation. Company disclosures about foreseeable risk factors and about the systems in place for monitoring and managing risk have also left a lot to be desired, even though this is a key element of the [OECD] Principles. Accounting standards and regulatory requirements have also proved insufficient in some areas, leading the relevant standard setters to undertake a review. Last but not least, remuneration systems have in a number of cases not been closely related to the strategy and risk appetite of the company and its longer-term interests."[44]

As Andrew Ross Sorkin explains in his book *Too Big to Fail* (2009), the management of some of these organizations simply did not understand the risks of their operations. Worse, they took little interest in risk management and even excluded risk officers from important discussions:

"As both Gregory (COO [of Lehman Brothers]) and Fuld (CEO [of Lehman Brothers]) were fixed-income traders at heart, they weren't entirely up to speed on how dramatically that world had changed since the 1980s. Both had started in commercial paper, probably the sleepiest, least risky part of the firm's business. Fixed-income trading was nothing like Fuld and Gregory knew in their day: Banks were creating increasingly complex products many levels removed from the underlying asset. This entailed a much greater degree of risk, a reality that neither totally grasped and showed remarkably little interest in learning more about. While the firm did employ a well-regarded chief risk officer, Madelyn Antoncic, who had a Ph.D. in economics and had worked at Goldman Sachs, her input was virtually nil. She was often asked to leave the room when issues concerning risk came up at executive committee meetings, and in late 2007, she was removed from the committee altogether."[45]

Research suggests that, when properly implemented, risk-management functions can effectively lower the risk levels of the organization. For example, Ellul and Yerramilli (2013) found that bank holding companies with strong risk-management functions had lower enterprise risk.[46] Similarly, Ormazabal (2010) found that firms with observable risk-management activities (such as a risk committee, enterprise risk-management function, chief risk officer, risk-management policies, or other organizational structure related to risk oversight) had less volatility during the financial crisis.[47]

Endnotes

1. Financial Reporting Council, "The UK Corporate Governance Code (2012). Accessed March 16, 2015. See www.frc.org.uk.

2. National Association of Corporate Directors, "2013–2014 NACD Public Company Governance Survey" (Washington, D.C., 2014).

3. Lockheed Martin, "Ethics" (2015). Accessed February 10, 2015. See http://www.lockheedmartin.com/us/who-we-are/ethics.html.

4. Adapted from Gerry Johnson, Kevan Scholes, and Richard Whittington, *Exploring Corporate Strategy: Text & Cases,* 8th ed. (Essex: Pearson Education Limited, 2008).

5. Garth Saloner, Andrea Shepard, and Joel Podolny, *Strategic Management,* rev. ed. (New York: John Wiley & Sons, 2005). And Michael E. Porter, *Competitive Strategy* (New York: Free Press, 1998).

6. Forbes Insights, "The Powerful Convergence of Strategy, Leadership, and Communications: Getting It Right," *FD Corporate Communications* (June 2009). Accessed November 8, 2010. See http://images.forbes.com/forbesinsights/StudyPDFs/PowerfulConvergenceofStrategy.pdf.

7. Eric Olsen, Frank Plaschke, and Daniel Stelter, "The 2008 Value Creators' Report: Missing Link Focusing Corporate Strategy on Value Creation," Boston Consulting Group (2008). Accessed December 8, 2008. See www.bcg.com/documents/file15314.pdf.

8. This is similar to the insightful work done by James L. Heskett, W. Earl Sasser, and Leonard A. Schlesinger, *The Service Profit Chain* (New York: Free Press, 1997).

9. David de Angelis and Yaniv Grinstein "Pay for the Right Performance," Johnson School Research Paper Series No. 03-2011, *Social Science Research Network* (2012). Accessed February 10, 2015. See http://ssrn.com/abstract=1571182.

10. See Christopher D. Ittner, David F. Larcker, and Madhav V. Rajan, "The Choice of Performance Measures in Annual Bonus Contracts," *Accounting Review* 72 (1997): 231–255. Daniel Sungyeon Kim and Jun Yang, "Behind the Scenes: Performance Target Setting of Annual Incentive Plans," *Social Science Research Network* (2012). Accessed June 24, 2014. See http://ssrn.com/abstract=1361814.

11. Francesca Cornelli, Zbigniew Kominek, and Alexander Ljungqvist, "Monitoring Managers: Does It Matter?" *Journal of Finance* 68 (2013): 431–481.

12. Adapted in part from Christopher D. Ittner and David F. Larcker, "Extending the Boundaries: Nonfinancial Performance Measures," in *Handbook of Management Accounting Research,* edited by Christopher S. Chapman, Anthony G. Hopwood, and Michael D. Shields (Oxford: Elsevier, 2009).

13. Christopher D. Ittner and David F. Larcker, "Coming Up Short on Nonfinancial Performance Measurement," *Harvard Business Review* 81 (2003): 88–95. Also see Ittner and Larcker (2005).

14. Stephen Gates, "Aligning Strategic Performance Measures and Results," The Conference Board, research report 1261-99-RR (October 1999). Accessed March 15, 2010. See http://www.conference-board.org/publications/publicationdetail.cfm?publicationid=438.

15. The function linking customer satisfaction to financial performance is "S-shaped" and not a simple linear relation. There are likely to be diminishing returns to increases in customer satisfaction and other similar measures. See Christopher D. Ittner and David F. Larcker, "Are Nonfinancial Measures Leading Indicators of Financial Performance? An Analysis of Customer Satisfaction," *Journal of Accounting Research* 36 (1998): 1–35.

16. Rajiv D. Banker, Gordon Potter, and Roger G. Schroeder, "Reporting Manufacturing Performance Measures to Workers: An Empirical Study," *Journal of Management Accounting Research* 5 (1993): 33–55.

17. Venky Nagar and Madhav V. Rajan, "The Revenue Implications of Financial and Operational Measures of Product Quality," *Accounting Review* 76 (2001): 495–514.

18. Ittner, Larcker, and Rajan (1997).

19. Amal A. Said, Hassan R. HassabElnaby, and Benson Wier, "An Empirical Investigation of the Performance Consequences of Nonfinancial Measures," *Journal of Management Accounting Research* 15 (2003): 193–223.

20. Deloitte Touche Tohmatsu, "In the Dark: What Boards and Executives Don't Know about the Health of Their Businesses. A Survey by Deloitte in Cooperation with the Economist Intelligence Unit" (2004). Last accessed June 24, 2014. See http://www.deloitte.com/assets/Dcom-NewZealand/Local%20Assets/Documents/In%20the%20dark%284%29.pdf. Deloitte Touche Tohmatsu, "In the Dark II: What Many Boards and Executives Still Don't Know About the Health of Their Businesses. Executive Survey Results from Deloitte and the Economist Intelligence Unit" (2007). Accessed September 7, 2010. See http://www2.deloitte.com/content/dam/Deloitte/in/Documents/risk/Board%20of%20Directors/in-gc-in-the-dark-noexp.pdf.

21. Christopher D. Ittner, David F. Larcker, and Taylor Randall, "Performance Implications of Strategic Performance Measurement in Financial Services Firms," *Accounting, Organizations & Society* 28 (2003): 715.

22. Anonymous, "Beyond Box-ticking: A New Era for Risk Governance; A Report from the Economist Intelligence Unit Sponsored by ACE and KPMG," *The Economist* (2009). Accessed November 8, 2010. See https://www.kpmg.com/LU/en/IssuesAndInsights/Articlespublications/Documents/Beyondbox-ticking-final.pdf.

23. Ormazabal (2010) found a positive stock market response to these legislative events for companies that had not disclosed risk-management activities. See Gaizka Ormazabal, "An Examination of Organizational Risk Oversight," Ph.D. dissertation, Stanford University, Graduate School of Business (2010).

24. Gennaro Bernile, Vineet Bhagwat, and P. Raghavendra Rau, "What Doesn't Kill You Will Only Make You More Risk-Loving: Early-Life Disasters and CEO Behavior," *Social Science Research Network* (2014). Accessed March 18, 2015. See http://ssrn.com/abstract=2423044.

25. Robert Davidson, Aiyesha Dey, and Abbie Smith, "Executives' 'Off-the-Job' Behavior, Corporate Culture, and Financial Reporting Risk," *Journal of Financial Economics* (August 1, 2013). Accessed May 5, 2015. See http://dx.doi.org/10.1016/j.jfineco.2013.07.004.

26. Public companies give a laundry list of "risk factors" in the annual 10-K. It is unclear whether these are the real risks the company faces or disclosures that provide the basis of a legal defense in case something bad happens to the firm. The challenge for the board is to push management to precisely articulate the fundamental risks that can have a devastating impact on shareholders and stakeholders.

27. *The Economist* (2009).

28. Lululemon Athletica, "Black Luon Pants Shortage Expected," press release (March 18, 2013). Accessed June 3, 2013. See http://investor.lululemon.com/releasedetail.cfm?ReleaseID=749315. For more on this topic, see David F. Larcker, Sarah M. Larcker, and Brian Tayan, "Lululemon: A Sheer Debacle in Risk Management," Stanford Closer Look Series (June 17, 2014). Accessed May 3, 2015. See http://www.gsb.stanford.edu/faculty-research/centers-initiatives/cgri/research/closer-look.

29. Lululemon Athletica, "Black Luon Pants—FAQ," (March 2013; updated, November 5, 2013). Accessed November 5, 2013. See http://files.shareholder.com/downloads/LULU/0x0x646646/544213e5-7e6d-4f87-8707-cf05d665c8eb/Black_luon_Pant_Shortage_UPDATED_Nov5_FAQ_only.pdf.

30. Bloomberg Television, "Lululemon Pants Don't Work for Some Women: Founder" (November 5, 2013). Accessed November 5, 2013. See http://www.bloomberg.com/news/videos/b/0132a382-cee3-41db-88af-fa2ed73f1762.

31. *The Economist* (2009).

32. Committee of Sponsoring Organizations of the Treadway Commission, "About Us." Accessed May 3, 2015. See www.coso.org/aboutus.htm.

33. Jim Traut, "Enterprise Reputation and Risk Management at H. J. Heinz," *Enterprise Risk Management Initiative* (October 3, 2008). Accessed June 24, 2014. See http://erm.ncsu.edu/library/article/jim-traut-roundtable#.U6nuufk7tcY.

34. Ormazabal (2010) found some evidence that volatility decreases when firms include risk management. His risk-management index is computed using publicly available data on the existence of a risk-management board committee, whether this committee has any members that have risk-management expertise, and other similar variables. See Ormazabal (2010).

35. Ernst & Young, "Investors on Risk: The Need for Transparency," *Ernst & Young Risk Survey Series* (2006). Accessed April 3, 2015. See https://www2.eycom.ch/publications/items/brs/investors_on_risk/en.pdf.

36. PricewaterhouseCoopers LLP, "Through the Investor Lens: Perspectives on Risk & Governance," *PwC's Investor Survey* (2013). Accessed March 29, 2014. See http://www.pwc.com/en_US/us/pwc-investor-resource-institute/publications/assets/pwc-investor-survey.pdf.

37. National Association of Corporate Directors (2014).

38. New York Stock Exchange (NYSE) regulations require that the audit committee discuss risk-management policies and practices. However, the NYSE allows companies to assign primary responsibility for risk management to another committee, as long as the audit committee plays a continuing role in the process.

39. Financial companies, in particular, are likely to have a risk committee because financial risk is almost the same as operational risk for these companies. Even energy companies such as Duke Energy are exposed to commodity price risk, which is both financial and operational.

40. Christopher D. Ittner and Thomas Keusch, "The Determinants and Implications of Board of Directors' Risk Oversight Practices," *Social Science Research Network* (2014). Accessed April 3, 2014. See http://ssrn.com/abstract=2482791.

41. American Institute of Certified Public Accountants (AICPA), "Report on the Current State of Enterprise Risk Oversight: Opportunities to Strengthen Integration with Strategy," 5th edition (2014). Research conducted by the ERM Initiative at North Carolina State University on behalf of the American Institute of CPAs Business, Industry & Government Team. Accessed March 18, 2015. See http://www.aicpa.org/interestareas/businessindustryandgovernment/resources/erm/downloadabledocuments/aicpa-erm-research-study-2014.pdf.

42. David F. Larcker, Sarah M. Larcker, and Brian Tayan, "What Do Corporate Directors and Senior Managers Know about Social Media?" The Conference Board, research report No. DN-V4N20 (October 2012). Accessed May 3, 2015. See http://www.gsb.stanford.edu/sites/gsb/files/publication-pdf/cgri-survey-2012-senior-management-social-media_0.pdf.

43. PricewaterhouseCoopers LLP, "A Marketplace without Boundaries? Responding to Disruption: PWC 18th Annual Global CEO Survey (2015)." Accessed March 17, 2015. See https://www.pwc.com/gx/en/ceo-survey/2015/assets/pwc-18th-annual-global-ceo-survey-jan-2015.pdf; Ernst & Young, "Get Ahead of Cybercrime: EY's Global Information Security Survey (2014)." Accessed March 18, 2015. See http://www.ey.com/Publication/vwLUAssets/EY-global-information-security-survey-2014/$FILE/EY-global-information-security-survey-2014.pdf.

44. Grant Kirkpatrick, "The Corporate Governance Lessons from the Financial Crisis," *OECD Journal: Financial Market Trends* (2009): 1–30. Accessed May 3, 2015. See http://dx.doi.org/10.1787/fmt-v2009-art3-en.

45. Andrew Ross Sorkin, *Too Big to Fail: The Inside Story of How Wall Street and Washington Fought to Save the Financial System—and Themselves* (New York: Penguin, 2009).

46. Andrew Ellul and Vijay Yerramilli, "Stronger Risk Controls, Lower Risk: Evidence from U.S. Bank Holding Companies," *Journal of Finance* 68, no. 5 (October 2013): 1757–1803.

47. Ormazabal (2010).

7

Labor Market for Executives and CEO Succession Planning

In this chapter, we examine the labor market for executives and the CEO succession process. Corporations have a demand for qualified executives who can manage an organization at the highest level. A supply of individuals exists who have the skills needed to handle these responsibilities. The **labor market for chief executives** refers to the process by which the available supply is matched with demand. For the labor market to function properly, information must be available on the needs of the corporation and the skills of the individuals applying to serve in executive roles.

The efficiency of this market has important implications on governance quality.[1] When it is efficient, the board of directors will have the information it needs to evaluate and price CEO talent. This leads to improved hiring decisions and reasonable compensation packages. It also tends to increase discipline on managerial behavior; that is, when managers know they can lose their jobs for poor performance, they have greater incentive to perform. When this market functions inefficiently, management faces less pressure to perform, and distortions can arise in the balance of power between the CEO and the board or in excessive compensation. Executives can also be matched to the wrong job, causing inefficiencies and loss of shareholder value.[2]

In this chapter, we start by considering the factors that contribute to CEO turnover and evidence on how likely boards are to terminate underperforming CEOs. Next, we examine the CEO selection process. We then evaluate the manner in which companies plan for and implement succession at the CEO level, including both internal and external candidates.

Labor Market for Chief Executive Officers

A discussion of the labor market for CEOs is relevant in a book about governance for several reasons. First, the chief executive officer is the primary agent responsible for managing the corporation and ensuring that long-term value is preserved and enhanced. The board of directors has a "duty" to make sure that the right person is selected for the job.

Second, if a manager knows that he or she can be replaced for poor performance, self-interested behavior is limited. In this way, the concept of a "market for labor" is similar to the concept of a "market for corporate control" (which we discuss in Chapter 11, "The Market for Corporate Control"). In the market for corporate control, the board must decide whether the company is better off under current ownership or whether it should be sold to a third party that can better manage the assets. In the labor market for chief executives, the board is asked to determine whether it is economically better to retain the current CEO, given his or her performance, or try to replace that individual with someone who may be better suited to the company's needs. In both cases, the CEO is aware that a failure to perform can lead to loss of employment, through either termination or the sale of the company.

Third, the efficiency of the labor market sets the stage for how much compensation is required to attract and retain a suitable CEO. Ultimately, a matching process takes place between the attributes that the company desires (in terms of skill set, previous experience, risk aversion, and cultural fit), the price the company is willing to pay for these attributes, and the compensation package executives are willing to accept. If these issues are clear and the relevant information is available to all parties, the market has the potential to be efficient. In principle, executives and the board will engage in an arm's-length negotiation, and the resulting pay levels will be neither too high nor too low.[3]

However, it is not at all clear that the labor market for CEOs is especially efficient. For starters, executive skill sets can be difficult to evaluate. An executive who performs effectively at one company is not necessarily guaranteed to repeat this performance at another company. Even if the executive has the requisite qualifications, the board needs to control for differences in industry, the operating and financial condition of the previous employer, cultural fit, work style, predilection for risk taking, and competitive drive before it can make a selection. For these reasons, it is difficult to predict in advance whether a candidate will succeed. This contrasts with many other labor markets, such as those for accountants or factory workers, in which the skills of an employee are more readily identifiable and easier to transfer across companies.

In addition, the efficiency of the CEO labor market is limited by its size and by the ability of executives to move among companies. A job opening for a sales manager might attract hundreds of applicants, dozens of whom have the requisite skills and are willing to consider an offer. If the company's preferred candidate turns down an offer for salary reasons, the company can either increase its offer or make an offer to a second- or third-choice candidate. Contrast this with the search for the head of a publicly traded multinational corporation, such as IBM. How many executives were capable of managing IBM when Lou Gerstner was brought in to turn the company around in 1993? Some executive recruiters have speculated that the number might have been no more than 10.[4] Regardless of whether this estimate is accurate, the limited size and liquidity of the labor market clearly influences the CEO recruitment process (see the following sidebar).

"Brain Drain" to Private Equity

The balance between supply and demand for executive talent appears to have been altered in recent years through the trend of successful CEOs moving from publicly traded companies to private equity–owned firms. Although this can potentially further distort labor market efficiency, the actual impact has not been clearly measured.

Still, some prominent examples signal just how significant the trend has been. James Kilts, former executive at both Kraft Foods and Nabisco Holding Company, later led a successful turnaround at Gillette. After the sale of Gillette to Procter & Gamble in 2005, Kilts' name surfaced as a leading CEO candidate for several consumer product companies. Instead, he left the sector of public companies and joined the advisory board of private equity firm Centerview Partners. David Calhoun, former vice chairman of General Electric, was in similar demand as a CEO candidate. Having turned down several offers, he ultimately accepted a position at market research firm VNU (owners of A.C. Nielsen and Nielsen Media Research), which was private equity owned. He reportedly received a compensation package worth $100 million, significantly above what most public corporations can afford.[5] In 2014, Michael Cavanaugh, rumored to be the leading candidate to one day succeed Jamie Dimon as CEO of JPMorgan Chase, resigned to become co-chief operating officer of private equity firm Carlyle Group. Examples such as these reinforce the notion that boards of directors compete with private as well as publicly held corporations to recruit qualified senior executives.

The efficiency of the labor market is also limited by a lack of uniformity among corporate circumstances and practices. Some companies are looking to develop and promote talent from within; others are looking to bring in an outsider as a catalyst for needed change. If the company is in crisis, an emergency CEO might be required to serve on an interim basis while a long-term successor is groomed. The CEO being replaced may be one who has suddenly died, been forced out for underperformance, or been long scheduled to step down on a specific retirement date. In all these situations, the board is charged with finding a successor; however, the number and quality of candidates available may vary, thereby limiting the company's options. Nickerson (2013) estimated that labor market inefficiencies cost the average company 4.8 percent of its market cap when hiring a new CEO.[6]

Labor Pool of CEO Talent

The United States has approximately 5,000 CEOs of publicly traded companies.[7] According to data from The Conference Board, the average CEO serves in that role between 7 and 10 years (see Figure 7.1).[8]

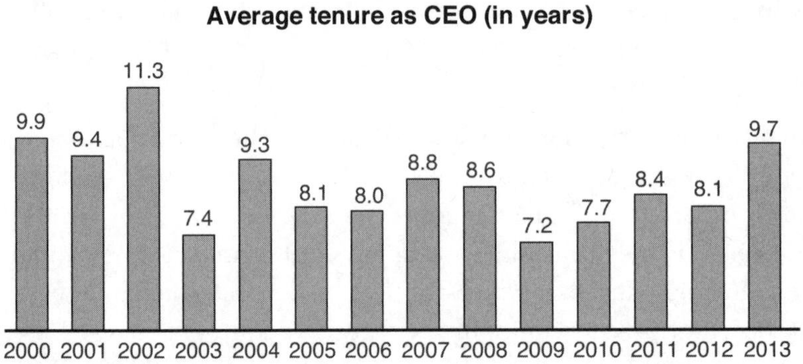

Average tenure as CEO (in years)

Source: The Conference Board, CEO Succession Practices (2014).

Figure 7.1   Departing CEO Tenure (2000–2013).

In terms of experiential background, no standard career path to becoming a CEO exists. According to one study, 22 percent of the CEOs of large U.S. corporations had a background in finance, 20 percent in operations, 20 percent in marketing, 5 percent in engineering, 5 percent in law, 4 percent in consulting, and 6 percent in "other."[9] Only a third of U.S. CEOs have international experience.[10]

In terms of educational background, 21 percent of CEOs earned an undergraduate degree in engineering, 15 percent in economics, 13 percent in business administration, 8 percent in accounting, and 8 percent in liberal arts. The most commonly attended undergraduate institutions are Harvard, Princeton, Stanford, University of Texas, and University of Wisconsin. Just less than half have a master's degree in business administration. Only a small fraction of CEOs have military experience.[11] Based on interview data, executive recruiters believe that educational background is an important indicator of an individual's ability to deal with the higher levels of complexity and decision making that are required as the head of a corporation. They also believe that personal attributes, such as whether a candidate played team sports in college or whether he or she was the oldest child—are indicative of an individual's leadership ability. (Of course, it is not clear whether these attributes translate into better performance.) Still, primary emphasis is placed on the executive's professional track record and management style.

Some evidence exists that personal and professional experience are related to the future performance of a CEO. Cai, Sevilir, and Yang (2014) examined the employment history of CEOs at large U.S. corporations between 1992 and 2010 and found that a disproportionate number (20.5 percent) had previous work experience at a small number of high-profile companies, which the authors describe as "CEO factory firms" (see Table 7.1). They found that the market reacts favorably to the recruitment of CEOs from these firms. They also found that companies that recruit a CEO from these firms exhibit better long-term operating performance and award these executives higher compensation.[12]

Similarly, Falato, Li, and Milbourn (2012) found that the compensation of newly appointed CEOs is correlated with the executive's credentials (reputation with the media, age, and education) and that these credentials are positively associated with long-term firm performance.[13]

Finally, Kaplan, Klebanov, and Sorensen (2012) examined a set of 30 attributes relating to CEO interpersonal, leadership, and work-related skills. They found some evidence that attributes having to do with work style (such as speed, aggressiveness, persistence, work ethic, and high standards) are more predictive of subsequent performance as CEO than interpersonal skills (such as listening skills, teamwork, integrity, and openness to criticism). Still, they caution that research related to CEO characteristics has limitations and that "the generality of our results remains an open empirical question."[14]

Table 7.1   CEO Factory Firms (1992–2010)

Company Name	Number of CEOs	CEO Factory Rank
General Electric	49	1
International Business Machines (IBM)	47	2
Procter & Gamble	28	3
AT&T	21	4
Hewlett-Packard (HP)	21	4
PepsiCo	21	4
Ford Motor	19	7
Honeywell International	19	7
Motorola	18	9
Lucent Technologies	14	10
General Motors (GM)	13	11

Company Name	Number of CEOs	CEO Factory Rank
Johnson & Johnson	13	11
Xerox	13	11
Exxon	13	11
Macy's	12	15
American Express	11	16
Intel	11	16
Kraft Foods	11	16
Rockwell Automation	11	16
United Technologies (UTC)	11	16
Bristol-Myers Squibb	10	21
Sears Roebuck	10	21
Baxter International	9	23
Dow Chemical	9	23
DuPont (E.I.) de Nemours	9	23
International Paper	9	23
Sprint	9	23
Texas Instruments	9	23
Albertsons	8	29
Corning	8	29
Eastman Kodak	8	29
Emerson Electric	8	29
Kroger	8	29
Eli Lilly	8	29
Merrill Lynch	8	29
Sara Lee Corp.	8	29

Source: Cai, Sevilir, and Yang (2014).

CEO Turnover

A CEO may leave the position for a variety of reasons, including retirement, recruitment to another firm, dismissal for poor performance, or departure following a corporate takeover. In 2013, CEO turnover was 14.4 percent on a worldwide basis. Over the last decade, this figure has fluctuated between 9 percent and 15 percent (see Figure 7.2).[15]

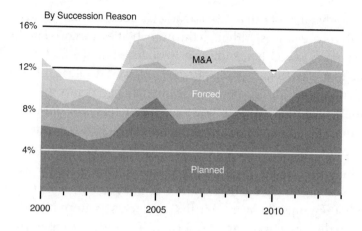

Source: Favaro, Karlsson, and Neilson (2014). Reprinted with permission from PwC Strategy & LLC. © 2014 PwC. All rights reserved.

Figure 7.2   CEO turnover rate, 2000–2013.

Extensive research has examined the relationship between CEO turnover and performance.[16] Studies show that CEO turnover is inversely proportional to corporate operating and stock price performance.[17] That is, CEOs of companies that are not performing well are more likely to step down than CEOs of companies that are performing well. We would expect this from a labor market that rewards success and punishes failure. However, the literature also finds that CEO termination is not especially sensitive to performance. Some CEOs are unlikely to be terminated no matter how poorly they perform.[18]

This point is clearly illustrated in a study by Huson, Parrino, and Starks (2001). The authors grouped companies into quartiles based on their operating performance during rolling five-year periods. They then compared the frequency of forced CEO turnover (terminations) across quartiles. They found that, although considerable disparity in operating performance exists between the top and bottom quartiles, termination rates are not materially different. For example, during the measurement period 1983–1988, companies in the bottom quartile realized an average annual return on assets (ROA) of –3.7 percent, while companies in the highest quartile realized an average ROA of 12.0 percent, a difference of almost 16 percentage points. Still, the termination rate in the lowest quartile was a meager 2.7 percent per year, versus 0.8 percent in the highest quartile. That is, the probability of the CEO being terminated increased by only 2 *percentage points,* even though the lowest quartile delivered significantly worse profitability. Results were similar in different measurement periods and when companies were grouped by stock market returns.[19]

For our purposes, this study suggests that labor market forces are not always effective in removing senior-level executives. Although the probabilities are correlated with performance, they remain very low. Other studies have produced similar findings. A study by Booz & Co. found that even though companies in the lowest decile in terms of stock returns underperform their industry peers by 45 percentage points over a two-year period, the probability that the CEO is forced to resign increases by only 5.7 percent. Booz & Co. concluded that despite corporate governance getting "better" over time, little change has occurred in the sensitivity of termination to performance.[20]

More recent research by Jenter and Lewellen (2014) found greater sensitivity between performance and forced termination. The authors found that 59 percent of CEOs who perform in the bottom quintile over their first five years are terminated, whereas 17 percent of those in the top quintile are terminated. The difference is even greater for "higher-quality" boards (defined as smaller boards with fewer insiders and higher stock ownership among directors). These findings differ from those of previous studies because Jenter and Lewellen measured CEO-specific relative performance over a longer time period and had a more refined measure of involuntary turnovers.[21]

Similarly, a proprietary survey by one of the authors found that 50 percent of professional executives and board members say they would terminate a CEO after four quarters of poor earnings performance. "Poor earnings performance" is defined as failure to meet internal and analyst forecasts for quarterly earnings. More than 90 percent say they would terminate a CEO after eight quarters of poor results. This data also suggests that termination is perhaps more closely related to performance than in some of the studies cited earlier.[22]

Furthermore, evidence suggests that companies with strong governance systems are more likely to terminate an underperforming CEO. Mobbs (2013) found that companies with a credible CEO replacement on the board are more likely to force turnover following poor performance.[23] Fich and Shivdasani (2006) found that busy boards (boards on which a majority of outside directors serve on three or more boards and presumably do not have the time to be an effective monitor for shareholders) are significantly less likely to force CEO turnover following a period of underperformance than are boards that are not busy.[24] This is consistent with evidence that we saw in Chapter 5, "Board of Directors: Structure and Consequences," that busy boards are less attentive to corporate performance than are boards whose directors have fewer outside responsibilities.

Studies have also found that companies with a high percentage of outside directors, companies whose directors own a large percentage of shares, and companies whose shareholder base is concentrated among a handful of institutional investors are all more likely to terminate an underperforming CEO. This is consistent with a theory that independent oversight reduces agency costs and management entrenchment.

Companies with lower-quality governance tend to "hold on" to underperforming CEOs too long. Strong oversight (by either the board or shareholders) is critical to holding CEOs accountable for company performance. Conversely, companies whose managers own a significant percentage of equity and companies whose CEO is a founding family member are less likely to see their chief executive terminated.[25]

As we would expect from even modestly efficient capital and labor markets, shareholders react positively to news that an underperforming CEO has been terminated and replaced by an outside successor. Huson, Parrino, and Starks (2001) found excess stock returns of 2 to 7 percent following such announcements.[26]

Newly Appointed CEOs

Most newly appointed CEOs are internal executives. According to The Conference Board, between 70 and 80 percent of successions involve an internal replacement.[27] A variety of reasons explain why shareholders and stakeholders might prefer an insider. Internal executives are familiar with the company, and the board has the opportunity to evaluate their performance, leadership style, and cultural fit on a firsthand basis, giving them greater confidence that the executives will perform to expectations. Insiders bring continuity, which, if the company has been successful, can lead to a smooth transition and less disruption to operations and staffing. For this reason, well-managed companies invest in developing internal talent so that key positions can be filled following unexpected departures.

An external successor might be preferable under other circumstances. The board might be dissatisfied with recent performance or decide that the company needs to change direction. The company might lack insiders with sufficient talent or might prefer an outsider with unique experience (such as one who has successfully navigated an operational turnaround, financial restructuring, regulatory investigation, or international expansion), given the current state of the company. Because an outsider is not wedded to the company's current mode of operations or to its existing management team, an executive from outside the company might be more effective in bringing change.

The decision to recruit an external candidate, however, generally comes at a cost. According to Equilar, external CEOs receive first-year total compensation that is approximately 35 percent higher (median average) than that given to internal candidates.[28] This differential is fairly consistent across companies by market capitalization sizes (see Figure 7.3). Part of the premium comes from the fact that external candidates tend to have proven experience as CEO, whereas internal candidates are promoted to the position for the first time. Furthermore, companies that recruit a candidate from the outside tend to be in financial trouble. Therefore, these executives require some sort of "risk premium" to take on a job that involves a higher chance of failure. Finally, external candidates must be bought out of existing employment agreements. This involves making them whole for unvested, in-the-money options, the value of which can be quite substantial. For example, when Target recruited Brian Cornell to be CEO in 2014, it offered equity incentives worth almost $20 million, partly to compensate him for options forfeited at his former employer, PepsiCo.[29]

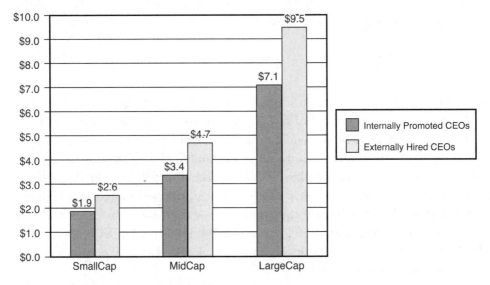

Source: Equilar Inc., "Paying the New Boss: Compensation Analysis for Newly Hired CEOs" (June 2013). Equilar is an executive compensation and corporate governance data firm.

Figure 7.3 CEO median total compensation ($MM).

The trend of looking outside the company for a CEO has increased in recent years. Murphy (1999) found that only 8.3 percent of new CEOs at S&P 500 companies were outsiders during the 1970s. By the 1990s, that figure had risen to 18.9 percent.[30] Studies have also shown that the likelihood of appointing an external successor is inversely related to firm performance. Parrino (1997) found that approximately half of all CEOs who were forced to resign for performance reasons were replaced by an outsider, compared with only 10 percent of CEOs who voluntarily resigned or retired.[31]

Despite the promise that an outside CEO brings to many companies, considerable evidence indicates that external CEOs perform worse than internal CEOs. For example, a 2010 study by Booz & Co. found that internal CEOs delivered superior market-adjusted returns in 7 out of the previous 10 years.[32] Huson, Malatesta, and Parrino (2004) found improvements in operating performance (measured as ROA) following forced termination but only mixed evidence that stock price improved.[33] However, results from these studies could be confounded by the fact that companies that require external CEOs tend to be in worse financial condition. Nevertheless, it is possible that either the practice of recruiting external candidates or the process itself is at least partly responsible for poor subsequent performance.

Models of CEO Succession

Broadly speaking, four general models of CEO succession exist:[34]

- External candidate
- President and/or COO
- Horse race
- Inside–outside model

External Candidate

The first model involves recruiting an external candidate. As discussed earlier, an external candidate is preferable when a company lacks sufficient internal candidates. Unlike internal executives, candidates recruited from the outside tend to have proven experience in the CEO role, thereby reducing the risk that they are unprepared for the responsibility. Also, because external executives are not involved in the decisions of their predecessors, they may have more freedom in making strategic, operational, or cultural changes to the firm. However, external candidates carry significant risk. Even though they are proven in terms of their ability to handle CEO-level responsibilities, they are not proven in terms of organizational fit. The work style that was successful in their previous environment might not necessarily translate well to another (see the following sidebar). External candidates are also more expensive because they need to be bought out of an existing employment contract. External candidates have greater bargaining power to negotiate compensation when they have no viable internal candidates to compete against.

CEO Selection and "Cultural Fit"

Nike

In November 2004, Nike announced the appointment of William Perez as president and CEO. Perez would succeed company founder Phil Knight, who retained the position of chairman.

It was not the first time Knight had tried to step away from the company he had closely managed for more than 30 years. In 1994, he had promoted insider Thomas Clarke to the position of president so he could assume a long-term strategic role as chairman and CEO. By 2000, it was clear that corporate performance was suffering, and Knight resumed control of day-to-day operations.

However, many were optimistic that the appointment of Perez would be different. First, Perez had enjoyed great success at family-controlled SC Johnson & Son, a company he had joined in 1970 and headed since 1996. His extensive experience in consumer marketing was seen as positive for a company that relied heavily on brand perception. He also had international experience, which was important as Nike expanded into new markets.

Some analysts, however, cautioned that Perez might have trouble fitting into the intensely sports-loving culture at Nike. Of particular concern was whether Perez would work well with Knight. Gerry Roche, the executive recruiter who conducted the search, was optimistic: "He gets along well with Phil. They click."[35]

Despite the optimism, Perez announced that he was stepping down just one year later. In his official statement, Perez said, "Phil and I weren't entirely aligned on some aspects of how to best lead the company's long-term growth. It became obvious to me that the long-term interests of the company would be best served by my resignation." For his part, Knight stated, "Succession at any company is challenging, and unfortunately the expectations that Bill and I and others had when he joined the company a year ago didn't play out as we had hoped."[36] It was an unusually candid assessment by both individuals.

The situation at Nike is one that recurs at many corporations when a founder or long-time CEO steps down but does not cede full control to the successor. Conflicts can result that disrupt the ability of the successor to implement new strategies or objectives. Perez touched upon this point in a subsequent interview:

"The fundamental issue was very basic. Phil didn't retire. When I joined Nike it was with the understanding that Phil was going to retire. I honestly believed he was going to step aside and let me move the ship in the right direction. . . . You don't need two CEOs. One is redundant, and I happened to be the redundant one."[37]

Perez was replaced by long-time insider Mark Parker, who had a more constructive relationship with Knight. Perez went on to become CEO of family-controlled Wrigley, where he successfully led the company until its sale to privately held Mars in 2008. Parker, meanwhile, had a successful career as the CEO of Nike. Under his leadership through 2014, Nike stock outperformed the S&P 500 Index by almost 200 percentage points.[38]

President and/or Chief Operating Officer

The second model of CEO succession is promoting a leading candidate to the position of president and/or chief operating officer (COO), where the executive can be groomed for eventual succession (see the following sidebar). This approach allows a company to observe how an executive performs when given CEO-level responsibility without having to first promote that individual. In addition, it gives the executive experience interacting with the board, analysts, the press, and shareholders— constituents to whom he or she may not previously have had exposure. Because no standard set of responsibilities is associated with the COO role, the scope of the position can be customized to meet the needs of the company. In this way, the executive can be specifically tasked with overseeing a firmwide initiative—such as product launch, international expansion, or restructuring—or trained to overcome a weakness or shortcoming. If he or she is successful, the executive can then be promoted.

At the same time, using a COO appointment in the succession process involves risks. Because it is not a standard role, the responsibilities of the position need to be well defined up front and clearly differentiated from those of the CEO. If not, decision making can suffer. Furthermore, the COO role adds structural and cultural complexity to the organization. If the direct reports of both the CEO and the COO do not clearly understand and support the leadership model of the company, internal divisions can form that undermine the success of the COO. Finally, a clear timeline for succession needs to be established. If the COO remains in the position too long, he or she may become perceived as a "lifetime COO" and lose the internal and external support needed to win promotion.

President and COO as Chosen Successor

Kroger

In 2009, Kroger announced the appointment of Rodney McMullen as president and COO. McMullen had previously served as executive vice president in charge of strategy, planning, and finance. He was also executive vice chairman of the board. In his new role, McMullen would oversee all aspects of the grocery store company's operations and more than two dozen local chains, reporting to company chairman and CEO David Dillon. Four years later, McMullen replaced Dillon as CEO. According to Dillon, "He gives us new energy. It's a good time for the organization to re-energize itself. Rodney is ready and change is often good."[39]

The Walt Disney Company

In 2010, The Walt Disney company reshuffled its executive ranks, announcing that Tom Staggs, chief financial officer, and Jay Rasulo, head of parks and resorts, would switch roles, setting up a succession race to succeed CEO Robert Iger. The move gave both executives a chance to learn new skills, with Staggs placed in a high-profile operating role and Rasulo in a strategic and financial role.

In 2015, Staggs was named chief operating officer, responsible for all of the company's operating divisions, including movies, television, consumer products, and parks and resorts. While the move did not guarantee Staggs the CEO role, his appointment was widely viewed by analysts as an indication that he was the chosen frontrunner to succeed Iger upon his planned retirement in 2018.[40]

Horse Race

The third model of CEO succession is the **horse race**. This model was famously used at General Electric to determine the successor to CEO Jack Welch in 2001, and it has subsequently been used at companies including GlaxoSmithKline, Johnson & Johnson, Microsoft, and Procter & Gamble. In a horse race, two or more internal candidates are promoted to high-level operating positions, where they formally compete to become the next CEO. Each is given a development plan to improve specific skills. Progress is measured over a specified period, with evaluations and feedback provided at predetermined milestones. At the end of the evaluation period, a winner is selected.

As with a COO appointment, a horse race allows the board to test primary candidates before granting a promotion. With this model, however, the board is not committing to a preferred successor in advance. Instead, the board has time to build consensus around a favorite.

The horse-race model also has drawbacks. Horse races tend to be highly public and bring unwanted media attention. They create a politicized atmosphere, in which board members, senior executives, and the CEO jockey to position their favored candidate to win. As such, they can be distracting to management and the organization. In addition, a horse race risks the precipitation of a talent drain. Losers of the race often leave because they do not want to report to the person they lost to and because they feel their only legitimate chance of becoming a CEO is with another company.[41]

Inside–Outside Model

In an **inside–outside model**, the company develops a forward-looking profile that lays out the skills and experiences required of the next CEO, based on the future needs of the company. Internal candidates are selected based on their potential fit with this profile. Each is given a preliminary assessment, and areas for development are identified. The candidates are then rotated into new positions where they can develop the skills and experiences needed to fill any gaps in their background. The inside–outside model is different from a horse race: While the internal evaluation is under way, the company identifies promising external candidates, who are also compared against their fit with the CEO profile. If an external candidate is demonstrably better, he or she is recruited to be CEO. If no external candidate is deemed demonstrably better, the leading internal candidate is selected. An external validation is useful in assuring the board that it is selecting the best CEO out of the entire labor market.

The inside–outside model neutralizes certain inefficiencies in the succession process. It levels the playing field between internal and external candidates. Interview data suggests that in many companies, board members are biased against internal executives because they first became acquainted with them in more junior roles and still think of them in a junior capacity. Board members do not have this bias against external candidates, even though external candidates have developed along similar career paths. The inside–outside model reduces this risk by giving the board significant exposure to internal candidates, where their leadership skills can be fully appreciated before they are compared to the external market. Experts recommend that an external candidate be selected only if he or she is 1.5 to 2 times better than the leading internal candidate.[42]

The risk of using the inside–outside model is that it requires significant planning and oversight. A common mistake occurs when the board lets the external process go on too long. When this occurs, internal candidates may feel that they are not the top choice, even if ultimately selected. This leads to an erosion of trust that affects the working relationship between the board and the new CEO well beyond the transition date.

The Succession Process

The succession-planning process relies on the full engagement of both the board of directors and senior management of the company. As a best practice, succession planning is an ongoing activity and includes preparation for both scheduled and unscheduled transitions. The most critical element of this is the continued development of internal talent. At any time, the company maintains a list of candidates that it can turn to in an emergency. It also maintains a list of primary candidates in line to replace the CEO in a planned succession.

At 37 percent of companies, the full board of directors has primary responsibility for succession; at 31 percent of companies, succession is the responsibility of the nominating and governance committee. Twenty percent of companies assign this duty to the chairman or lead director, and 11 percent of companies look to the CEO for this responsibility.[43]

When a succession event is scheduled, the board might choose to convene an ad hoc committee specifically tasked with handling the process. This committee is generally chaired by the most senior independent director. Experts recommend that directors be selected based on their qualifications and engagement rather than their availability. Qualified directors have overseen a succession or have participated in one as a CEO.[44] Because the new CEO will ultimately be selected by a vote of the full board, however, committee meetings should be open to all interested directors (see the following sidebar).

The Board-Led Search

Ford Motor

In 2006, William Ford, Jr., chairman and CEO of the company his great-grandfather Henry Ford had founded more than 100 years before, hired a former Goldman Sachs executive to conduct a review of the company's operations. The review concluded that Ford's current strategy was insufficient to stem losses and that the senior executive team likely did not have the experience to bring needed change. As a result, William Ford decided to voluntarily step down as CEO and bring in an outsider to accelerate a turnaround.

Ford's actions were noteworthy in that it is rare for a founding-family CEO to voluntarily seek his or her own replacement. As Ford himself stated, "I have a lot of myself invested in this company, but not my ego."[45] The search process was also noteworthy in that it was entirely led by the board, without the help of an executive recruiter to source and screen candidates. Instead, the board identified one man—Alan Mulally of Boeing—to be Ford's chosen successor. Many boards would consider such an approach risky because it did not include a third-party expert to validate its decision.

At the time, Mulally was the head of the commercial airline division of Boeing. Although Mulally did not have experience in the automotive industry, he had significant experience at Boeing, where he had led product development for the company's 777 airline model. The board believed the two companies had many similarities: Both had long product cycles; capital-intensive operations; complex manufacturing; and similar management relations with customers, suppliers, and union employees.

As a first step, John Thornton, Ford Motor director and former president of Goldman Sachs, suggested that the company rely on an intermediary to gauge Mulally's interest. Richard Gephardt, former congressional leader, made the initial approach because the two men had worked together on labor issues. After those conversations, Thornton spoke directly with Mulally. Mulally expressed interest but noted that he had been at Boeing for almost 37 years and that he was excited to work on the company's fuel-efficient model, the 787 "Dreamliner." He agreed to discuss the opportunity further with William Ford.

Ultimately, Mulally accepted Ford's offer, and the company's head of human resources finalized the details. It was important to Mulally that he be made whole for the compensation he was forgoing by leaving Boeing. He also requested a significant incentive component that would reward him if his efforts were successful. His first-year compensation was $28 million: $2 million annual salary (prorated to $0.7 million), $18.5 million signing bonus, $1.0 million in stock awards, $7.8 million in options, and $0.3 million in other benefits.[46]

The selection of Mulally was ultimately deemed a success, as Ford was the only one of the Big Three Detroit automakers to avoid bankruptcy in 2009. In 2014, Mulally retired as CEO and was replaced by former chief operating officer Mark Fields in a planned transition.

The outgoing CEO also plays an important role in the succession process. The CEO is responsible for developing talent, in the form of coaching and mentoring, and for assigning executives to areas of the organization where they can be challenged to learn new skills. This includes both job rotations and project-based work. Despite the important role the CEO plays, it is important that the board maintain primary control over the process because the board is responsible for its eventual success. This includes making sure that the CEO does not disrupt or influence the objectivity of the evaluation by advocating on behalf of a favored candidate or undermining a disfavored candidate (see the following sidebar).

Outgoing CEO Behaviors

According to research by Larcker, Miles, and Tayan (2014), the personality of the outgoing CEO can have an important impact on the success of a transition. To this end, they categorize CEOs into six groups, based on the behaviors they exhibit during the succession process:

- **Active advisor**—The sitting CEO accepts that it is time to step down and is ready to do so. The CEO provides thoughtful insight into the selection process but does not overstep his or her role. The CEO limits opinions to when they are solicited and does not impose his or her "will" on the board. Disciplined, self-aware, and satisfied with the role as advisor, the CEO has full acceptance that the board will make the final decision.

- **Aggressor**—The sitting CEO is relatively overt in his or her attempt to influence the selection decision. This type of CEO will "play nice" for most of the process, only to attempt to steer the selection toward a handpicked candidate at a key decision point, undermining other candidates in the process. The CEO will take a strong position with the board and try to force the outcome he or she favors.

- **Passive aggressor**—The sitting CEO tries to influence the selection process in a covert manner. The CEO subtly undermines certain candidates with the way he or she positions them to the board. He or she will come across not as manipulative but instead as an advisor. If this behavior is undetected until late in the process, the board might have to start from the beginning and exclude the CEO.

- **Capitulator**—When the board is close to making the final decision on a successor, the CEO changes his or her mind about retirement and requests to stay longer. This behavior essentially forces the board to choose between the present and future leadership of the company. A nonexecutive director will need to meet with the CEO and firmly inform him or her that the board is moving forward with a successor.

- **Hopeful savior**—The sitting CEO largely identifies with the role of CEO and does not really want to retire. The CEO might actively promote successors in his or her own likeness. Alternatively, he or she might promote someone less capable in the hope that the successor will fail so that he or she can be swept back in to "save" the company.

- **Power blocker**—The sitting CEO also does not want to leave. He or she will throw up obstacles to slow or derail the process. The power blocker is different from the hopeful savior in the aggressiveness of approach. Whereas the hopeful savior is subtle, the power blocker is overt. He or she calls in favors with the board, makes direct personal appeals, or demands to stay.

Larcker, Miles, and Tayan recommend that rather than overlook the personality of the outgoing CEO, companies should tailor their succession plan in part based on an assessment of how the outgoing executive might or might not attempt to influence the selection process.[47]

The next step in the succession process is to create a skills-and-experience profile. This profile is based on a forward-looking view of the company. If the future needs of the company are different from its present ones, the profile of the next CEO will be quite different from that of the outgoing CEO. The skills-and-experience profile is rooted in the company's strategy. The board identifies the attributes in terms of professional background and personal qualities required to successfully execute the strategy and achieve organizational objectives. The profile is used as a yardstick against which both internal and external candidates are benchmarked. In the case of long-term succession planning, the progress of internal candidates is measured over time. When it comes time for a succession event, either scheduled or unscheduled, the board will have a list of viable candidates, ranked in order of preference.[48]

After a new CEO has been selected and approved by a vote of the full board, the transition begins. Interviews with boards and search consultants indicate that transitions can be improved through open and honest dialogue between the CEO-elect and the board. Topics of discussion include how management and the board should interact on an ongoing basis, what each party expects from the other, the requirements for communication, what each party liked and did not like about the previous management, and how the board can support the CEO during both the transition and the tenure. This type of on-boarding activity builds trust and transparency and lays the groundwork for a constructive relationship. The CEO-elect may also choose to improve his or her skills by engaging in coaching by a third-party professional. This allows him or her to collect additional feedback on leadership style and learn to correct behaviors that are not working. Finally, the outgoing CEO can facilitate the transition by remaining behind the scenes but accessible to the new CEO to answer questions that arise.

Interviews suggest that retaining ties to the former CEO is beneficial to the firm. This can be achieved either by inviting the departing CEO to serve (or remain) on the board or by establishing a consulting relationship. Such connections can be beneficial for two reasons. First, the outgoing CEO has unique insight into the firm that can improve the monitoring and advising functions of the boards. Second, extending ties to the outgoing CEO gives that person less incentive to take actions that boost short-term results at the expense of long-term performance in the months prior to departure. At the same time, companies face a risk that the outgoing CEO will exploit a position with the firm to extract agency costs (such as excessive perquisites) without providing substantive value to the firm.

Evans, Nagarajan, and Schloetzer (2010) found that 36 percent of companies invite the outgoing CEO to remain as director.[49] The study found that companies are more likely to retain the outgoing CEO as director when he or she retires voluntarily, is a founder or founding family member, or is succeeded by an insider without CEO experience. The company is also more likely to retain the outgoing CEO if the company has had strong stock price performance in the periods preceding the CEO transition.[50] (The performance implications of retaining a nonfounder CEO on the board are discussed more fully in Chapter 4, "Board of Directors: Selection, Compensation, and Removal.")

How Well Are Boards Doing with Succession Planning?

A survey by Heidrick & Struggles and the Rock Center for Corporate Governance at Stanford University took an inside look at CEO succession planning. Based on a sample of directors and CEOs at 140 public and private companies, the survey found a surprising lack of preparedness when it comes to succession. Only 51 percent of respondents reported that their company could name a permanent successor if called upon to do so immediately. A full 39 percent of respondents claimed to have zero viable internal candidates. Instead, respondents expected that it would take 90 days, on average, to find a permanent CEO. This raises serious questions about the attention boards are paying to this critical oversight responsibility.[51]

The shortcomings appear to stem from a lack of focus. On average, boards spend only two hours per year on succession planning. At most companies, the emphasis appears to be on planning for an emergency but not a permanent successor. A full 70 percent of companies have identified an emergency candidate to serve as CEO on an interim basis if the current CEO needed to be replaced immediately; however, the majority (68 percent) reported that the emergency candidate is not a candidate for the permanent position (see the following sidebar).

Ballinger and Marcel (2010) studied the practice of appointing an emergency—or interim—CEO. They found that it is negatively associated with firm performance and increases a company's long-term risk of failure, particularly when someone other than the chairman is appointed to the interim position. They conclude that "the use of an interim CEO during successions is an inferior *post hoc* fix to succession planning processes that boards of directors should avoid."[52]

When a Current Director Becomes CEO

An interesting situation arises when the CEO resigns from the company and is replaced by a current director. Such a situation occurred at Hewlett-Packard in 2011, when board member Meg Whitman succeeded Léo Apotheker as CEO. The benefit of appointing a current director to the CEO position is that the director can act as a hybrid inside–outside CEO. He or she is likely well versed in all aspects of the company, including its strategy, business model, and risk-management practices. A current director likely also has personal relationships with both the executive team and fellow board members. At the same time, this individual has not participated in the senior management team and thus does not have the legacy ties to the company that an insider would bring. On the other hand, appointing a current director to the CEO position has potential drawbacks. The most obvious of these is that it signals a lack of preparedness on the company's part to properly groom internal talent. It may also signal a lack of preparedness among the board to carry out a rigorous review process. Therefore, appointing a director to the CEO role could actually be an "emergency" succession in disguise.

Citrin and Ogden (2010) found that board members who become the CEO outperform all other types of candidates (including insiders, outsiders, former executives, and COO appointments). They measured performance using a combination of relative stock price returns, revenue growth, and profit growth. They concluded that "directors-turned-CEOs represent a strong blend of insider and outsider [attributes]."[53]

Survey data also suggests that companies fall short on internal talent development. According to the survey cited above, only 58 percent of companies rotate internal candidates into new positions to test their skills and further their growth as part of the grooming process, and only half provide the new CEO with support during the on-boarding and transition process.[54] A separate study found that deficiencies in internal talent development extend to the board level. According to The Conference Board, the Institute for Executive Development, and the Rock Center for Corporate

Governance at Stanford University (2014), only 55 percent of directors understand the strengths and weaknesses of the senior executive team "extremely well" or "very well." Fewer than a quarter of directors (23 percent) formally participate in senior executive performance reviews, and only 7 percent act as a professional mentors to these individuals. Without more regular exposure, it is difficult for the board to fully appreciate the leadership potential of internal candidates.[55]

As these data indicate, many boards do not engage in rigorous succession planning. Instead, succession planning appears often to consist merely of "names in a box," aimed to satisfy compliance requirements but insufficient to handle an inevitable change in senior management. This may explain why so many companies seem ill-prepared when a CEO suddenly steps down. Succession planning would be improved if it were treated instead as an important element of risk management, with potential disruptions to the organization minimized by ensuring that internal talent is always being developed and external talent identified to manage the company in case of a sudden transition (see the following sidebar).

Succession as a Risk-Management Issue

In recent years, more attention has been paid to succession planning as a risk-management issue. In 2009, the Securities and Exchange Commission (SEC) began allowing shareholders to sponsor proposals on the annual proxy requiring companies to develop succession plans and disclose these plans to investors. Previously, such proposals could be excluded from the proxy under Rule 14a-8(i)(7), which allowed omission for matters "relating to the company's ordinary business operations."[56] In explaining its change of position, the SEC wrote that "we now recognize that CEO succession planning raises a significant policy issue regarding the governance of the corporation that transcends the day-to-day business matter of managing the workforce."[57] A handful of such proposals have been put before shareholders, but the majority do not receive approval.[58]

Similarly, Moody's Investors Services includes CEO succession planning as one factor contributing to a company's overall credit rating: "effective succession planning—especially CEO succession planning—[is] critical to the sound management and oversight of an organization." Moody's lists the practices it sees as important for reducing transition risk:

- A track record of smooth transitions
- Active leadership-development programs
- Board involvement in succession, including frequent discussion and interaction with key executives

- An independent board
- Active CEO involvement
- Emergency plan in place[59]

The External Search Process

Approximately 10 to 20 successful external searches for a new CEO take place among Fortune 500 companies each year. In most of these searches, the board of directors hires a third-party recruiter. The need for an external search indicates that either these companies did not have sufficient internal talent development programs in place to groom a successor, the boards felt their companies required an external candidate to bring about change, or simply the use of an external expert was a necessary part of the due diligence process for selecting a CEO.

The external search market in the United States is characterized by significant concentration. Two firms handle the vast majority of external searches: Heidrick & Struggles and Spencer Stuart. Furthermore, searches are concentrated among just a few influential consultants within these firms.

Potential benefits come from a system dominated by a few well-connected search firms and consultants. Well-connected individuals can efficiently assemble information about the needs and capabilities of a vast number of companies and executives. Through their social and professional networks, they gain access to qualitative information about an executive's reputation and potential cultural fit with various firms. This information can be critical to understanding how an executive's proven track record and operation skills will translate into a different environment.

At the same time, market concentration has potential shortcomings. By relying on a select group of recruiters, companies could be limiting the size of the candidate pool. Despite the extensive networks of certain recruiters, experienced talent could be excluded while an established set of executives is recycled among firms. Stated another way, lack of competition among search firms may limit the competition among executives for CEO positions. Other potential shortcomings of the external search market include the following:

- The search consultant may have excessive influence over the selection of candidates. Although directors and other senior executives are invited to nominate qualified external candidates, the search consultant tends to determine who is identified and contacted.

- The search consultant is given considerable responsibility for assessing the pool of candidates and reducing it to a group of finalists. Board members generally do not participate in preliminary interviews, which are handled by the consultant.

- The board might not see enough finalists to make an informed decision. Typically, only three or four finalists are brought before the board committee for in-person interviews (and sometimes only one candidate is). The board tends to make a decision after a handful of interviews, each lasting a few hours. Members of the senior management team are generally not invited to interview the finalists, and interaction with the broader team is not assessed to determine fit.

- The process for determining fair compensation might not be efficient. The search consultant (sometimes in conjunction with the candidate's personal compensation consultant or lawyer) provides input to the company regarding the necessary compensation for the deal to be consummated. Third parties might have a conflict of interest in negotiating compensation if their own compensation is expressed as a percentage of the CEO-elect's first-year compensation. Furthermore, both sides know that once a preferred candidate is identified, the board is unlikely to let the deal fall apart for salary reasons, given how time-intensive the search process is.

Despite these concerns, some research evidence suggests that third-party consultants contribute positively to the recruitment process. Rajgopal, Taylor, and Venkatachalam (2012) found a positive association between the use of third-party consultants and the future operating and stock price performance of the hiring firm. The authors found that third-party intermediaries negotiate significantly higher compensation on behalf of clients but that these pay packages have higher equity-based components and are justified based on subsequent performance. They conclude that "skilled CEOs retain talent agents to signal their skill and [their higher pay] is not consistent with rent extraction."[60]

Severance Agreements

Under a **severance agreement** (or **golden parachute**), a CEO is entitled to additional compensation upon resignation or dismissal. The terms of the agreement are typically included in the broader employment agreement and must be disclosed to shareholders through SEC filings. The following are examples:

- **American Electric Power**—"In the event the Company terminates the Agreement for reasons other than cause, [CEO Michael] Morris will receive a severance payment equal to two times his annual base salary. . . . In January

2005, the Board adopted a policy to seek shareholder approval for any future severance agreement with any senior executive officer of the Company when any such agreement would result in specified benefits provided to the officer in excess of 2.99 times his or her salary and bonus."[61]

- **Home Depot**—"Mr. Nardelli and the Company have agreed in principle to the terms of a separation agreement which would provide for payment of the amounts he is entitled to receive under his pre-existing employment contract entered into in 2000. Under this agreement, Mr. Nardelli will receive consideration currently valued at approximately $210 million (including amounts which have previously been earned or vested). This consideration will include a cash severance payment of $20 million, the acceleration of unvested deferred stock awards currently valued at approximately $77 million and unvested options with an intrinsic value of approximately $7 million, the payment of earned bonuses and long-term incentive awards of approximately $9 million, the payment of account balances under the Company's 401(k) plan and other benefit programs currently valued at approximately $2 million, the payment of previously earned and vested deferred shares with an approximate value of $44 million, the payment of the present value of retirement benefits currently valued at approximately $32 million, and the payment of $18 million for other entitlements under his contract which will be paid over a four-year period and will be forfeited if he does not honor his contractual obligations."[62] The board agreed to these terms in part to compensate Nardelli for compensation that he had accrued at his former employer (General Electric) and forfeited upon his recruitment to Home Depot.

Considerable controversy exists over the use of severance agreements. Critics assert that severance payments have little incentive value because they are not associated with job performance (sometimes labeled as **pay for failure**). Severance agreements might also discourage or retard the process of dismissing an underperforming CEO.

On the other hand, severance agreements may provide benefits to the firm. By promising compensation upon leaving the firm, severance agreements discourage management entrenchment (that is, there are financial incentives for the executive to leave the firm voluntarily). They also allow CEOs to take calculated risks to build shareholder value by promising compensation even if the efforts fail and result in termination. These incentives may be particularly valuable for younger CEOs who have not yet accumulated substantial wealth or reputation and would otherwise be more risk averse. Severance agreements also provide the board with a hard number for what it is going to cost to remove an unacceptable CEO. Without such a contract, the termination would almost certainly go into litigation with an uncertain financial outcome.

Yermack (2006) studied the use of severance agreements among Fortune 500 companies. He found that severance agreements are in place among 80 percent of executives, with a mean present value of $5.4 million. Payments made under these agreements take various forms: ongoing consulting or noncompete agreements (30 percent), lump-sum payments (21 percent), increases in the defined benefit pension plan (18 percent), equity award adjustments (16 percent), and other contracted severance payments (13 percent). Yermack found that shareholders tend to react negatively to the announcement of a severance agreement, suggesting that they are seen as destroying value or a form of rent extraction.[63]

One potential remedy for balancing the conflicting incentives of severance agreements is to assign them a limited term (say, the first three years of a new CEO's tenure). Such a sunset provision would protect the CEO from legitimate risks such as early sale of the company or irrational termination but would be phased out after the period of heightened risk has passed.

Endnotes

1. We loosely define an efficient labor market as one in which the right candidates are recruited into the right positions at the right compensation levels.

2. One method for estimating the efficiency of labor markets is to look at stock price performance following the unexpected death of a CEO. If the "right" executive is in the CEO position, the stock price should go down following an unexpected death. If the "wrong" executive is in the CEO position, the stock price should go up. Johnson, Magee, Nagarajan, and Newman (1985) found no uniform pattern across a sample of sudden deaths but did find evidence that inappropriate appointments might take place at the company-specific level. Salas (2010) found similar results. See W. Bruce Johnson, Robert P. Magee, Nandu J. Nagarajan, and Harry A. Newman, "An Analysis of the Stock-Price Reaction to Sudden Executive Deaths—Implications for the Managerial Labor Market," *Journal of Accounting and Economics* 7 (1985): 151–174. And Jesus M. Salas, "Entrenchment, Governance, and the Stock Price Reaction to Sudden Executive Deaths," *Journal of Banking and Finance* 34 (2010): 656–666.

3. Third-party agents are often involved in contract negotiations, which can distort the size and structure of compensation packages. Rajgopal, Taylor, and Venkatachalam (2012) found that CEOs who use a third-party agent receive first-year compensation that is significantly higher ($10 million) than those who do not. The study found that CEOs who use such agents tend to deliver superior operating and stock price performance, suggesting that premium compensation could be merited. See Shivaram Rajgopal, Daniel Taylor, and Mohan Venkatachalam, "Frictions in the CEO Labor Market: The Role of Talent Agents in CEO Compensation?" *Contemporary Accounting Research* 29 (2012): 119–151.

4. Interviews by the authors with executive recruiters, September 2008; proprietary data.

5. Rik Kirkland, Doris Burke, and Telis Demos, "Private Money," *Fortune* 155 (2007): 50–60.

6. Jordan Nickerson, "A Structural Estimation of the Cost of Suboptimal Matching in the CEO Labor Market," *Social Science Research Network* (November 18, 2013). Accessed February 10, 2015. See http://ssrn.com//abstract=2356680.

7. Based on listings of companies trading on the NYSE (1,800) and NASDAQ (3,100). See NYSE, "NYSE Composite Index." Accessed May 5, 2015. See http://www1.nyse.com/about/listed/nya_characteristics.shtml. And NASDAQ, "Get the Facts." Accessed May 5, 2015. See http://www.nasdaq.com/reference/market_facts.stm.

8. Jason D. Schloetzer, Matteo Tonello, and Melissa Aguilar, "CEO Succession Practices 2014 Edition," The Conference Board (2014). Accessed June 3, 2014. See https://www.conference-board.org/publications/publicationdetail.cfm?publicationid=2731.

9. Burak Koyuncu, Shainaz Firfiray, Björn Claes, and Monika Hamori, "CEOs with a Functional Background in Operations: Reviewing Their Performance and Prevalence in the Top Post," *Human Resource Management* 49 (2010): 869–882.

10. Meghan Felicelli, "Route to the Top," Spencer Stuart (November 1, 2007). Accessed April 6, 2015. See http://content.spencerstuart.com/sswebsite/pdf/lib/Final_Summary_for_2008_publication.pdf.

11. Ibid. See also Efraim Benmelech and Carola Frydman, "Military CEOs," *Journal of Financial Economics*, available online 10 May 2014. See http://www.sciencedirect.com/science/article/pii/S0304405X14000932.

12. Ye Cai, Merih Sevilir, and Jun Yang, "Are They Different? CEOs Made in CEO Factories," Kelley School of Business Research Paper No. 15-13, *Social Science Research Network* (2014). Accessed February 10, 2015. See http://ssrn.com/abstract_id=2549305.

13. Antonio Falato, Dan Li, and Todd T. Milbourn, "CEO Pay and the Market for CEOs," Feds Working Paper No. 2012-39, *Social Science Research Network* (2012). Accessed February 16, 2015. See http://ssrn.com/abstract=2191192.

14. Steven N. Kaplan, Mark M. Klebanov, and Morten Sorensen, "Which CEO Characteristics and Abilities Matter?" *Journal of Finance* 67 (2012): 973–1007.

15. The sample included CEOs of the 2,500 largest publicly traded companies globally. See Ken Favaro, Per-Ola Karlsson, and Gary L. Neilson, "The Lives and Times of the CEO," *strategy+business* 75 (2014). Accessed January 28, 2015. See http://www.strategy-business.com/article/00254?pg=all.

16. James A. Brickley, "Empirical Research on CEO Turnover and Firm Performance: A Discussion," *Journal of Accounting and Economics* 36 (2003): 227–233.

17. Srinivasan (2005) found that more than half of CEOs step down following a restatement that requires the company to reduce net income. Similarly, Arthaud-Day, Certo, Dalton, and Dalton (2006) found that CEOs are almost twice as likely to be terminated in the two years following a major financial restatement; CFOs are almost 80 percent more likely to be terminated. See Suraj Srinivasan, "Consequences of Financial Reporting Failure for Outside Directors: Evidence from Accounting Restatements and Audit Committee Members," *Journal of Accounting Research* 43 (2005): 291–334. And Marne L. Arthaud-Day, S. Trevis Certo, Catherine M. Dalton, and Dan R. Dalton, "A Changing of the Guard: Executive and Director Turnover Following Corporate Financial Restatements," *Academy of Management Journal* 49 (2006): 1119–1136.

18. It is difficult to determine from public sources whether a CEO has been terminated or has voluntarily resigned. Most public announcements refer to CEO departures as retirements, and some "educated guesses" are needed to determine whether a departure was involuntary.

19. Mark R. Huson, Robert Parrino, and Laura T. Starks, "Internal Monitoring Mechanisms and CEO Turnover: A Long-Term Perspective," *Journal of Finance* 56 (2001): 2265–2297.

20. Per-Ola Karlsson, Gary L. Neilson, and Juan Carlos Webster, "CEO Succession 2007: The Performance Paradox," *strategy+business* (2008). Accessed April 6, 2015. See http://www.strategyand.pwc.com/media/file/CEOSuccession2007.pdf.

21. Dirk Jenter and Katharina Lewellen, "Performance-Induced CEO Turnover," Stanford University, Tuck School at Dartmouth working paper (2014). Accessed February 4, 2015. See http://www.gsb.stanford.edu/faculty-research/working-papers/performance-induced-ceo-turn-over.

22. David F. Larcker and Burson-Marsteller, proprietary study (2001).

23. Shawn Mobbs, "CEOs under Fire: The Effects of Competition from Inside Directors on Forced CEO Turnover and CEO Compensation," *Journal of Financial and Quantitative Analysis* 48 (2013): 669–698.

24. Eliezer M. Fich and Anil Shivdasani, "Are Busy Boards Effective Monitors?" *Journal of Finance* 61 (2006): 689–724.

25. Brickley (2003).

26. Huson, Parrino, and Starks (2001).

27. Jason D. Schloetzer, Matteo Tonello, and Melissa Aguilar (2014).

28. Equilar Inc., "Paying the New Boss: Compensation Analysis for Newly Hired CEOs" (June 2013). Accessed May 5, 2015. See http://www.equilar.com.

29. Patrick Kennedy, "New Target CEO Signs for up to $36.6M," *Star Tribune* (August 1, 2014): 1.D.

30. Kevin J. Murphy, "Executive Compensation," *Social Science Research Network* (1999). Accessed July 27, 2010. See http://ssrn.com/abstract=163914.

31. Robert Parrino, "CEO Turnover and Outside Succession: A Cross-Sectional Analysis," *Journal of Financial Economics* 46 (1997): 165–197.

32. Ken Favaro, Per-Ola Karlsson, and Gary L. Neilson, "CEO Succession 2000-2009: A Decade of Convergence and Compression," *strategy+business* 59 (Summer 2010). Accessed May 5, 2015. See http://www.strategy-business.com/article/10208.

33. Comparisons were made to industry benchmarks. See Mark R. Huson, Paul H. Malatesta, and Robert Parrino, "Managerial Succession and Firm Performance," *Journal of Financial Economics* 74 (2004): 237–275.

34. Content in the following two sections is adapted with permission from David F. Larcker and Brian Tayan, "Multimillionaire Matchmaker: An Inside Look at CEO Succession Planning," Stanford GSB Case No. CG-21 (April 15, 2010).

35. Stephanie Kang and Joann S. Lublin, "Nike Taps Perez of S.C. Johnson to Follow Knight," *Wall Street Journal* (November 19, 2004, Eastern edition): A.3.

36. Joann S. Lublin and Stephanie Kang, "Nike's Chief to Exit After 13 Months: Shakeup Follows Clashes with Co-Founder Knight; Veteran Parker to Take Over," *Wall Street Journal* (January 23, 2006, Eastern edition): A.3.

37. Stephanie Kang, "He Said/He Said: Knight, Perez Tell Different Nike Tales," *Wall Street Journal* (January 24, 2006, Eastern edition): B.1.

38. Data from Yahoo Finance! Calculations by the authors. Stock price performance only. Calculations do not include dividends.

39. Edited for clarity. Quote from Steve Watkins, "Kroger's Dillon on Succession: 'You Ain't Seen Nothin' Yet,'" *Business Courier of Cincinnati Online* (November 7, 2013).

40. Ben Fritz, "Disney Picks Staggs as No. 2 Executive," *Wall Street Journal* (February 6, 2015, Eastern edition): B.1.

41. See also James M. Citrin, "Is a 'Horse Race' the Best Way to Pick CEOs?" *Wall Street Journal Online* (August 3, 2009). Accessed November 10, 2010. See http://online.wsj.com/article/SB124898329172394739.html.

42. Stephen A. Miles and Jeffery S. Sanders, "Creating CEO Succession Processes," *Directorship.com* (posted January 27, 2010). Last accessed November 10, 2010. See www.directorship.com/creating-ceo-succession/.

43. Heidrick & Struggles and the Rock Center for Corporate Governance at Stanford University, "2010 CEO Succession Planning survey," (2010). Accessed May 3, 2015. See http://www.gsb.stanford.edu/faculty-research/publications/2010-ceo-succession-planning-survey.

44. Author interview with Stephen A. Miles, vice chairman of Heidrick & Struggles, September 30, 2009.

45. Monica Langley and Jeffrey McCracken, "Designated Driver Ford Taps Boeing Executive as CEO; Alan Mulally Succeeds Bill Ford, Who Keeps Post of Chairman; A Board Swings into Action," *Wall Street Journal* (September 6, 2006, Eastern edition): A.1.

46. Ford Motor Company, Form DEF 14A, filed with the Securities and Exchange Commission April 4, 2008.

47. David F. Larcker, Stephen A. Miles, and Brian Tayan, "Seven Myths of CEO Succession," Stanford Closer Look Series (March 19, 2014). Accessed May 3, 2015. See http://www.gsb.stanford.edu/faculty-research/centers-initiatives/cgri/research/closer-look.

48. The board should not presume that its favored candidate, internal or external, will accept the job. For this reason, multiple candidates should always be considered, and contingency plans should be in place in case events do not unfold as anticipated. Recruiters recommend that companies engage in regular communication with internal candidates, but survey results suggest that only half of companies do so. A majority (65 percent) have not asked internal candidates whether they want the CEO job or, if offered, whether they would accept. See Heidrick & Struggles and the Rock Center for Corporate Governance at Stanford University (2010).

49. This study is based on John Harry Evans, Nandu J. Nagarajan, and Jason D. Schloetzer, "CEO Turnover and Retention Light: Retaining Former CEOs on the Board," *Journal of Accounting Research* 48 (2010): 1015–1047.

50. Jason D. Schloetzer, "Retaining Former CEOs on the Board," The Conference Board, Director Notes, no. DN-015 (September 2010). Last accessed October 1, 2010. See www.conference-board.org/publications/publicationdetail.cfm? publicationid=1854.

51. Heidrick & Struggles and the Rock Center for Corporate Governance at Stanford University (2010).

52. Gary A. Ballinger and Jeremy J. Marcel, "The Use of an Interim CEO during Succession Episodes and Firm Performance," *Strategic Management Journal* 31 (2010): 262–283.

53. James M. Citrin and Dayton Ogden, "Succeeding at Succession," *Harvard Business Review* 88 (November 2010): 29–31. Accessed November 17, 2010. See http://hbr.org/2010/11/succeeding-at-succession/ar/1.

54. Heidrick & Struggles and the Rock Center for Corporate Governance at Stanford University (2010).

55. The Conference Board, the Institute of Executive Development, and the Rock Center for Corporate Governance at Stanford University, "How Well Do Corporate Directors Know Senior Management?" (2014). Accessed May 3, 2015. See http://www.gsb.stanford.edu/faculty-research/publications/2014-how-well-do-corporate-directors-know-senior-management.

56. Securities Lawyer's Deskbook, "Rule 14-8: Proposals of Security Holders." Accessed May 3, 2015. See https://www.law.cornell.edu/cfr/text/17/240.14a-8.

57. SEC Staff Legal Bulletin 14E (CF), "Shareholder Proposals" (October 27, 2009). Accessed May 3, 2015. See www.sec.gov/interps/legal/cfslb14e.htm.

58. See David F. Larcker and Brian Tayan, "CEO Succession Planning: Who's Behind Door Number One?" Stanford Closer Look Series (June 24, 2010). Accessed May 3, 2015. See http://www.gsb.stanford.edu/faculty-research/centers-initiatives/cgri/research/closer-look.

59. Christian Plath, "Moody's Corporate Governance: Analyzing Credit and Governance Implications of Management Succession Planning," Moody's Investor Service (May 15, 2008). Accessed November 6, 2010. See http://ssrn.com/ abstract=1285082.

60. Shivaram Rajgopal, Daniel Taylor, and Mohan Venkatachalam, "Frictions in the CEO Labor Market: The Role of Talent Agents in CEO Compensation?" *Contemporary Accounting Research* 29 (2012): 119–151.

61. American Electric Power, Form DEF 14A, filed with the Securities and Exchange Commission March 14, 2005. The IRS prohibits the tax deductibility of severance agreements that exceed 2.99 times the executive's base salary and bonus. See Internal Revenue Code Section 280G, "Golden Parachute Payments."

62. The Home Depot, Form 8-K, filed with the Securities and Exchange Commission January 4, 2007.

63. David Yermack, "Golden Handshakes: Separation Pay for Retired and Dismissed CEOs," *Journal of Accounting and Economics* 41 (2006): 237–256.

8

Executive Compensation and Incentives

In this chapter, we examine executive compensation and incentives. Executive officers develop the corporate strategy and business model, and they oversee daily management of the firm. Like other employees, executives require monetary compensation for their work.[1] Compensation packages must be sufficient in terms of their level and structure to attract, retain, and motivate qualified executives to create shareholder or stakeholder value.

The compensation committee and the independent directors on the board approve the compensation program. In theory, this should be a simple exercise. The "right" amount of compensation to be paid is the minimum amount it takes to attract and retain a qualified individual. After all, this is the same calculus that goes into setting compensation for all other job functions. However, several factors complicate how this works in practice. As we discussed in the previous chapter, the labor market for chief executive officers does not appear to be highly efficient. Because of potential imbalances between supply and demand and the difficulty in evaluating the quality of candidates, it is not always easy for boards to identify the appropriate executive or the market wage necessary to attract this individual. Moreover, some board members might provide insufficient oversight (because of a lack of independence, insufficient engagement, or a lack of power relative to the CEO) during the compensation-setting process. These factors have the potential to distort executive compensation packages in terms of both size and structure.

Further complicating the process is the large amount of scrutiny this issue receives from the media and Congress.[2] Although some of this attention is merited, the intensity with which many observers have established their position has influenced the tone of the debate, making it difficult to arrive at a reasoned decision about how much compensation is appropriate.

The Controversy over Executive Compensation

Executive compensation has long been a controversial topic in corporate America. In the 1930s, economic depression coupled with enhanced disclosure laws mandated by the Securities and Exchange Commission (SEC) stoked popular outrage over some executive compensation packages. Particular ire was reserved for the compensation paid to executives of the industrial and financial powerhouses of the time, including Bethlehem Steel, General Motors, American Tobacco, and National City Bank, who each received compensation in excess of $1 million. The sentiment of the era is perhaps best encapsulated by Justice Thomas Swan of the Circuit Court of Appeals, who wrote that "no man can be worth $1,000,000 a year."[3]

However, the debate was more muted in the decades following World War II. This is primarily because executive compensation grew at more modest rates between the 1950s and 1970s, well below those of inflation and general wages.[4] High marginal income tax rates (more than 70 percent for top earners) helped to lower the overall size of executive salaries. Few executives received compensation more than the psychologically important $1 million mark.

However, the trend reversed in the 1980s. During a period characterized first by high inflation and then by rapid economic growth, executive compensation ballooned. The trend coincided with a compensation shift away from fixed salaries and annual bonuses toward variable pay tied to long-term performance targets and stock options.[5] Several executives received generous payouts. For example, in 1987, Charles Lazarus of Toys R Us, Michael Blumenthal of Unisys, and Lee Iacocca of Chrysler all received bonuses in excess of $10 million.[6] Investment bankers, Wall Street traders, and private equity partners saw similar increases in pay.

In the 1990s and 2000s, the widespread adoption of stock options accelerated the trend. Exploding corporate profits and a strong bull market enabled several executives to profit handsomely. According to the *Wall Street Journal*, 16 executives of major corporations received total stock option compensation in excess of $500 million between 1992 and 2005, including William McGuire of HealthSouth ($2.1 billion), Larry Ellison of Oracle ($1.5 billion), Sandy Weill of Citigroup ($980 million), and Michael Eisner of Disney ($920 million).[7] Furthermore, total compensation figures were increased by supplemental payments (those made beyond salary and bonuses) that were not always transparently disclosed to investors. Examples included deferred compensation, golden parachutes, and supplemental executive retirement plans (SERPs). The most famous payouts were made to Robert Nardelli of Home Depot ($210 million), Hank McKinnell of Pfizer ($83 million), Lee Raymond of ExxonMobil ($405 million), and Dick Grasso of the New York Stock Exchange ($187.5 million), all in conjunction with their retirements.[8]

Executive compensation levels tapered off during the financial crisis of 2008 and the subsequent recession. The change was most notable among bank executives, such as Jamie Dimon of JPMorgan Chase, whose total compensation decreased from $28 million in 2007 to $21 million in 2010, and Kenneth Chenault of American Express, whose total compensation decreased from $34 million to $17 million over the same time period.[9] New rules, including a requirement under the Dodd–Frank Act that companies grant shareholders an advisory "say on pay" vote, were intended to stem the tide of rising compensation. However, when the recession ended, downward pressure on executive compensation waned, and pay levels reached new heights.

Critics believe that current CEO compensation levels are not justified based on performance and value creation but are instead indicative of a market failure. Bebchuk and Fried (2006) succinctly expressed this view:

> Flawed compensation arrangements have not been limited to a small number of "bad apples"; they have been widespread, persistent, and systemic. Furthermore, the problems have not resulted from temporary mistakes or lapses of judgment that boards can be expected to correct on their own; rather, they have stemmed from structural defects in the underlying governance structures that enable executives to exert considerable influence over their boards.[10]

Is this true? To find out, we review the size and structure of compensation packages. We consider the incentive value of certain compensation elements, including annual bonuses and equity-based pay. We also evaluate the relations between compensation, performance, and risk. We end with a discussion of shareholder perspective on executive compensation and disclosure.

Components of Compensation

The compensation committee of the board of directors recommends the compensation of the chief executive officer and other senior executives. This work is typically performed in consultation with the human resources and finance departments and third-party compensation consultants. Compensation packages are approved by a vote of the independent directors of the full board of directors. A vote of shareholders must generally approve equity-based compensation plans (such as stock option plans and restricted stock awards).

The details of the compensation plan—including those that require shareholder approval and those that do not—are described in the annual proxy. This includes the "fair value" of the total compensation awarded to the chief executive officer and other named officers in each of the previous three years, and values realized by these individuals through the exercise or vesting of equity-based grants. The SEC requires that corporations also include a Compensation Discussion & Analysis (CD&A) section in the proxy. The CD&A includes information that might be useful to shareholders in evaluating the compensation program, including the company's compensation philosophy, elements of the pay package, total compensation awarded, the peer groups used for comparative purposes in designing compensation and measuring performance, performance metrics used to award variable pay, pay equity between the CEO and other senior executives, stock ownership guidelines, pledging activity by officers and directors, clawback policies, severance agreements, golden parachutes, and post-retirement compensation.[11]

A compensation plan serves three primary purposes.[12] First, it must *attract* the right people—those with the skill set, experience, and behavioral profile necessary to succeed in the position. Second, it must be sufficient to *retain* those individuals; otherwise, they will leave to work at another organization that offers more appropriate compensation for their talents. Third, it must provide the right incentives to *motivate* them to perform appropriately. This includes encouraging behaviors that are consistent with the corporate strategy and risk profile of the organization and discouraging self-interested behavior.

The executive compensation package generally includes some or all of the following elements:

- **Annual salary**—Fixed cash payment made evenly during the course of the year. Section 162(m) of the Internal Revenue Code limits the tax deductibility of executive compensation greater than $1 million unless such compensation is performance driven. The fixed salary is typically set at the beginning of the year.

- **Annual bonus**—Additional payment, usually in the form of cash awarded if the yearly performance of the company exceeds specified financial and nonfinancial targets. The size of the bonus is commonly expressed as a percentage of base salary and might include a guaranteed minimum and specified maximum.

  The bonus computation might also include a discretionary element. This can be desirable because all aspects of performance cannot be forecast perfectly (for example, reasonable targets might be impossible to achieve when macroeconomic or industry factors change in a negative way). The board might want to reward executives for their efforts if they do well in a year when economic conditions impact their performance relative to what was expected when the goals were first established.[13] However, discretionary elements can have negative consequences if they reward executives without regard to performance. In this case, discretionary bonuses might indicate that the board has been coopted by management. The compensation committee must make the important choice of a formulaic versus subjective bonus plan, which is a necessary disclosure in the CD&A. Furthermore, a discretionary cash bonus requires disclosure through Form 8-K upon adoption.[14]

- **Stock options**—The right to buy shares in the future at a fixed exercise price, generally equal to the stock price on the grant date. Stock options typically have vesting requirements (that is, they are "earned" in even batches over time or in blocks, such as 25 percent at the end of each of the next 4 years) and expire after 10 years (with 7 years being the next-most-popular term). Some companies adopt "hold to retirement" or "hold past retirement" requirements for equity awards. These features encourage long-term equity ownership and are intended to align the interests of executives with those of shareholders.

- **Restricted stock**—An outright grant of shares that are restricted in terms of transferability and are subject to a time-based vesting schedule. When vested, they are economically equivalent to a direct investment in company stock.

- **Performance shares (units)**—Equity (or cash) awards granted only after specified financial and nonfinancial targets are met during a three- to five-year time period. Performance shares and performance units work the same way except for how the final award is paid—in stock or in cash. The size of the award is generally based on a percentage of base salary, similar to the method used to calculate the annual cash bonus. The maximum award is usually 200 percent of the target. In many ways, performance plans are simply a longer-term version of the annual bonus plan. The performance criteria generally include some type of profit measure (such as earnings-per-share growth or return on assets) or total shareholder return. According to Equilar (2014), 64 percent of companies in the S&P 1500 include long-term performance awards in their CEO compensation package, compared with 57 percent restricted stock, and 50 percent stock options.[15]

- **Perquisites**—Other amenities purchased or provided by the company, such as personal use of a company car or airplane, club memberships, or a home or an apartment.

- **Contractual agreements**—Other cash or stock payments stipulated in the employment agreement, such as severance agreements, post-retirement consulting agreements, and golden parachutes (payments made upon a change in control).

- **Benefits**—Other benefits provided with employment, such as health insurance, post-retirement health insurance, defined contribution retirement accounts (401[k]), supplemental executive retirement plans (SERPs), life insurance, payment for the use of a personal financial planner, and reimbursement of taxes owed on taxable benefits.

The compensation package might also be subject to certain contractual restrictions:

- **Stock ownership guidelines**—The minimum amount of stock that an executive is required to hold during employment, generally expressed as a multiple of base salary. Among the Fortune 100 companies, 84 percent have stock ownership guidelines, typically of an amount equal to five or six times base salary.[16] (Executive stock ownership guidelines are discussed more fully in

Chapter 9, "Executive Equity Ownership." Director stock ownership guidelines are discussed in Chapter 4, "Board of Directors: Selection, Compensation, and Removal.")

- **Pledging restrictions**—The use of shares as collateral for a personal loan, margin loan through a brokerage account, or other type of financial transaction. The Dodd–Frank Act requires companies to disclose pledging activity by officers and directors. (We discuss pledging in Chapter 9.)

- **Clawbacks and deferred payouts**—A contractual provision that enables the company to reclaim compensation in future years if it becomes clear that bonus compensation should not have been awarded previously (see the following sidebar). Section 304 of the Sarbanes–Oxley Act enables companies to reclaim bonuses from the CEO and CFO if it is later determined that the bonuses were awarded on the basis of manipulated earnings.[17] The Dodd–Frank Act broadened the use of clawbacks by requiring companies to develop, implement, and disclose a clawback policy. According to Equilar, the most common triggers of a clawback are a financial restatement, ethical misconduct, and violation of a noncompete clause.[18] Some companies defer the payout of bonuses until sufficient time has elapsed to determine whether the payment is economically justified.

Clawback and Deferred Payout Provisions

ExxonMobil

"[Annual cash bonus payments] are subject to recoupment in the event of material negative restatement of the Corporation's reported financial or operating results. Even though a restatement is unlikely given ExxonMobil's high ethical standards and strict compliance with accounting and other regulations applicable to public companies, a recoupment policy was approved by the Board of Directors to reinforce the well-understood philosophy that incentive awards are at risk of forfeiture and that how we achieve results is as important as the actual results."[19]

Citigroup

"All deferred incentive compensation awarded to any Citi employee, including the named executive officers, is subject to the Citi Clawbacks. The Citi Clawbacks require the forfeiture or cancellation of nonvested incentive compensation when the [Compensation] Committee determines that an employee (a) received an award based on materially inaccurate publicly reported financial statements, (b) knowingly engaged in providing materially inaccurate information relating to publicly reported financial statements, (c) materially violated any risk limits established or revised by senior management and/or risk management, or (d) engaged in gross misconduct. Citi may also seek to recover previously delivered compensation, where permitted by law."[20]

McKesson

"Our executive incentive plans provide that the Compensation Committee may also seek to recoup economic gain from any employee who engages in conduct that is not in good faith and which disrupts, damages, impairs or interferes with the business, reputation or employees of the Company."[21]

Apple

"The named executive officers' [restricted stock unit] RSU awards are granted under the Company's standard RSU agreements. These agreements require an employee to deliver or otherwise repay to the Company any shares or other amount that may be paid in respect of an RSU award in the event the employee commits a felony, engages in a breach of confidentiality, commits an act of theft, embezzlement or fraud, or materially breaches any agreement with the Company."[22]

Research suggests that clawbacks can be an effective tool to reduce agency costs. Iskandar-Datta and Jia (2013) found that companies that adopt clawback provisions in executive compensation contracts experience statistically significant positive excess returns on the announcement. They attribute their results to shareholder perception that clawbacks reduce financial reporting risk.[23]

Chan, Chen, Chen, and Yu (2012) found that the adoption of clawback provisions is associated with a subsequent reduction in accounting restatements. They also found that the auditors of firms that have clawback provisions are less likely to report material internal control weaknesses, charge lower audit fees, and issue audit reports more quickly. The authors concluded that "managers have lower incentives to engage in earnings manipulation when they are subject to clawbacks . . . [and that] clawbacks are consistent with real improvements in reporting integrity."[24]

Determining Compensation

The compensation committee and the board of directors are responsible for determining the level of compensation paid to the CEO and other officers. They must also select the mix of short-term and long-term elements to achieve a payout structure that is consistent with the firm's strategy. In theory, this should be a straightforward exercise, with the level of total compensation set to be commensurate with the value of services received. The process might work as follows: First, determine how much value the company expects to create during a reasonable time horizon (for example, five years). Then determine how much of this value should be attributable to the efforts of the CEO. Finally, determine what percentage of that value should be fairly offered to the CEO as compensation. Although many boards may implicitly follow this type of approach, it is exceedingly difficult to measure the value creation attributable to the efforts of a specific executive.

Instead, most boards determine compensation levels by benchmarking their CEO's pay against that of a set of companies that are comparable in size, industry, and geography (**peer group**). Interviews with compensation consultants reveal that companies commonly aim to provide cash compensation (base salary and annual bonus) at the 50th or lower percentile of the peer group and long-term incentives (primarily equity-based compensation) at the 75th percentile. These figures represent the board's assessment of the market wage opportunity of the CEO and other executive officers. The compensation committee also needs to make sure that the level of pay suggested by the benchmark has a similar level of risk as the compensation package being considered for the executive.

Although benchmarking presumably enables a company to remain competitive regarding the level of compensation, it has some obvious drawbacks. First, compensation levels might become inflated over time as companies increase pay to match amounts paid by peers. When multiple companies within a group try to meet or exceed the median, the median itself tends to increase, creating the well-known **ratcheting effect**. Second, benchmarking determines pay without explicit regard to value creation. This might encourage executives to engage in uneconomic behavior, such as acquiring a competitor purely to increase the size of the overall organization, resulting in a shift in the perceived peer group and, therefore, the CEO's own pay. Third, benchmarking can lead to very different pay packages, depending on the specific companies included in the peer group.

According to Equilar, the median peer group includes 16 companies. Companies tend to select peers with revenues larger than their own. Nearly two-thirds (64 percent) of companies had revenue at or below the median of their group.[25] Because compensation levels are correlated with size of the organization, selecting peers with larger revenues tends to increase the pay packages of senior executives.

Researchers have studied whether peer groups are selectively designed to extract excess pay. The results of these studies are mixed. Bizjak, Lemmon, and Naveen (2008) concluded that peer-group selection is a "practical and efficient mechanism" to determine the market wage for executives and that it is not indicative of manipulation for personal gain.[26] However, Faulkender and Yang (2010) found that companies include unrelated firms in the peer group and that the inclusion of these firms increases pay.[27] Therefore, the process of peer group selection is under considerable scrutiny by securities regulators and shareholder activists (see the following sidebar).

Benchmarking Compensation at Kroger and Safeway

Kroger and Safeway are two grocery store chains that are direct competitors and fairly similar in terms of corporate strategy. However, they use very different peer groups for compensation benchmarking. Kroger has a much smaller peer group, composed of mostly retail and grocery companies, but Safeway has a broader peer group consisting of department stores, food and consumer product manufacturers, and clothing retailers (see Table 8.1).[28]

Table 8.1 Kroger and Safeway, Comparative Statistics

	Kroger	Safeway
CEO total compensation	$11.1 million	$11.3 million
Revenues	$96.7 billion	$44.2 billion
Net income	$1.5 billion	$0.6 billion
Five-year stock return (company)	17 percent	–41 percent
Five-year stock return (peer group)	39 percent	10 percent
Peer group	Costco	Best Buy
	CVS Caremark	Colgate Palmolive
	Rite Aid	Costco
	Safeway	CVS Caremark
	SuperValu	General Mills
	Target	Gap
	Wal-Mart	Home Depot
	Walgreens	Kohl's
		Kroger
		Limited Brands
		Lowe's
		Macy's
		McDonald's
		JC Penney
		Staples
		SuperValu
		Target
		Walgreens

Source: The Kroger Company, Form DEF 14A, filed with the Securities and Exchange Commission May 14, 2013; Safeway, Inc., Form DEF 14A, filed with the Securities and Exchange Commission April 1, 2013.

It is interesting to speculate which company has the more appropriate peer group and why, given that they are in the same industry.

Compensation Consultants

Another area of popular concern is the use of third-party consultants to assist in the process of setting compensation. In 2014, the most frequently used consulting firms were Frederic W. Cook (16 percent), Pearl Meyer (11 percent), Towers Watson (9 percent), Meridian (8 percent), and Compensia (7 percent).[29] At 74 percent of companies, the board of directors selects which firm to use, and at 7 percent of companies, management makes this selection; 20 percent of firms do not disclose this information in the annual proxy.[30]

Critics claim that a conflict of interest arises when the consulting firm used to structure the CEO compensation package is also used for other corporate services, such as designing benefits plans or managing pension assets. They allege that such consultants are less likely to recommend lower pay, for fear of losing contracts for the other services they provide to the company.[31] Although conflicts of interest should be a source of concern, most academic evidence suggests that compensation consultants who provide other services do not allow conflicts of interest to influence their determination of executive pay levels (see the following sidebar).

Conyon, Peck, and Sadler (2009) and Cadman, Carter, and Hillegeist (2010) found that total CEO pay is higher than predicted by economic determinants among companies that use compensation consultants, but they found no evidence that the higher pay is associated with governance quality. Murphy and Sandino (2010) examined CEO pay levels in a sample of companies that have all used compensation consultants. They found that CEO pay increases with the level of "influence" that the CEO has over the board, with influence measured by whether the CEO is also chairman and whether the CEO has appointed a high percentage of directors to the board. Similarly, Chu, Faasse, and Rau (2014) found that compensation consultants retained solely by the board of directors are associated with lower pay than compensation consultants hired by management.[32]

A study by Armstrong, Ittner, and Larcker (2012) found that CEO pay is determined by the quality of governance at the firm and not by the use of a compensation consultant. Companies with weaker governance are more likely to both use compensation consultants and grant higher pay levels. Armstrong et al. concluded that the difference in pay levels is driven by governance differences of the firms, not by the use of a consultant. Moreover, the authors found that pay levels do not vary between companies that retain specialized compensation consultants (who provide only compensation services) and those that use general human resources consultants (who offer a broad array of services). This finding raises some doubt about the belief that conflicts of interest facilitate excess pay levels.[33]

Disclosure on Compensation Consultants

Symantec

Companies are required to disclose whether they use a compensation consultant, the full set of services that the consultant provides, and the total payments made. For example, Symantec notes:

"Since fiscal 2004, the Compensation Committee has engaged Mercer, an outside consulting firm, to provide advice and ongoing recommendations on executive compensation matters. The Compensation Committee oversees Mercer's engagement. Mercer representatives meet informally with the Compensation Committee Chair and the Chief Human Resources Officer and also with the Compensation Committee during its regular meetings, including in executive sessions from time to time without any members of management present. . . .

"We paid Mercer approximately $203,500 for executive compensation services in fiscal 2014. In addition, with the Compensation Committee's approval, management engaged and Symantec paid Mercer and its affiliates for other services, including approximately $2.057 million for other unrelated consulting and business services. . . .

"Based in part on policies and procedures implemented by Mercer to ensure the objectivity of its executive compensation consultants and the Compensation Committee's assessment of Mercer's independence pursuant to the SEC rules, the Compensation Committee concluded that the consulting advice it receives from Mercer is objective and not influenced by Mercer and its affiliates' other relationships with Symantec and that no conflict of interest exists that will prevent Mercer from being independent consultants to the Compensation Committee."[34]

Compensation Levels

Based on a sample of 4,000 publicly traded U.S. companies, the median CEO receives expected total annual compensation of about $2.9 million. Among the largest companies, total compensation is $13.7 million.[35] Total compensation includes salary, cash bonuses, the fair value of equity-based incentives, pensions, benefits, and perquisites (see Table 8.2). Note that the table includes median rather than mean average figures. Mean averages are influenced by a relatively small number of "outliers," and for this reason, median average is a better descriptor of general compensation levels. It represents the amount awarded at a typical company.

Table 8.2   Compensation Paid to CEOs in the United States

Firms (Grouped by Size)	Median Total Expected CEO Compensation ($ thousands)	Median Market Value ($ millions)
Top 100	$13,713	$104,413
101 to 500	$10,656	$21,710
501 to 1,000	$6,458	$6,086
1,001 to 2,000	$3,981	$2,106
2,001 to 3,000	$2,092	$624
3,001 to 4,000	$900	$144
1 to 4,000	$2,869	$1,143

Total compensation includes salary, annual bonus, other bonus, expected value of stock options, performance plans, restricted stock grants, pensions, benefits, and perquisites. In calculating stock option fair value, remaining terms are reduced by 30 percent to adjust for potential early exercise or termination. Market value is the value of common shares outstanding at fiscal year end.

Source: Equilar, proprietary compensation and equity ownership data for fiscal years from June 2013 to May 2014.

Note also that the calculation for compensation reflects the expected fair value of compensation *awarded* during the year. It does not reflect the value executives *realized* during that year. This is an important distinction. The fair value awarded is the value of compensation that the committee intends to pay to the executive in a given year. It measures equity-based incentives according to their expected value, with restricted stock valued at current market prices and stock options valued using an approved valuation method (either Black–Scholes or the binomial pricing model). The actual compensation that the executive receives when he or she ultimately sells the stock or exercises the options will likely be very different from the expected value. Realized compensation is a potentially problematic measure because it often reflects the combined value of stock and options granted during multiple years but exercised in a single year (see the following sidebar).

What Is the "Right" Measure of Pay?

There are three basic ways to measure executive compensation:

- **Expected compensation** represents the expected value of compensation promised to an executive in a given year. This includes the sum value of the salary, annual bonus, long-term cash plan, stock option awards, and restricted stock awards in the year they are granted. Because some of these elements are contingent on future outcomes (such as operating performance or stock price), their expected value must be estimated. The accuracy of these estimates will vary depending on the type of compensation award that is offered.

- **Earned (realizable) compensation** represents the total value of compensation that an executive "earns the right to keep" as cash is delivered and vesting restrictions are removed. In most cases, the total compensation earned in a year includes compensation elements that were awarded in the current year and other elements that were awarded in previous years—such as long-term equity awards and performance units. That is, some of the money that an executive "earns" today is money that was promised long ago.

- **Realized compensation** represents the total value of compensation that an executive takes home as cash in a given year. For equity awards, the realized value is the amount of cash received when the executive ultimately sells shares or exercises and sells stock options. Like earned compensation, realized compensation often comprises pay elements awarded over multiple years, and the realized amount is a function of firm performance over this period.

Total compensation figures disclosed in the company proxy rely on a combination of these measures. Table 8.3 illustrates the differences.

Table 8.3 Compensation of Harley-Davidson CEO Keith Wandell, 2010

	Expected	Earned	Realized	Proxy
Salary	$975,000	$975,037	$975,037	$975,037
Bonus	0	0	0	0
Stock awards	1,381,199	0	0	1,381,199
Option awards	1,636,681	698,906	0	1,636,681
Performance plans	2,600,357	2,340,090	2,340,090	2,340,090
Pension	0	0	0	0
Other benefits	83,490	83,490	67,289	83,490
Total	$6,676,727	$4,097,523	$3,382,416	$6,416,498

Source: Larcker, McCall, and Tayan (2011).

So which of these is the "right" number? Expected compensation is a forward-looking view of the rewards available to an executive and can be used to assess the incentive value of compensation. Earned and realized compensation are backward-looking views of the rewards that an executive actually received and can be used to assess pay for performance.[36]

In recent years, some companies have taken steps to disclose additional information about executive pay. A study of the disclosure practices of S&P 100 companies found that 34 percent provided calculations for "realized pay" in 2014, up from only 9 in 2009; 19 percent provided "realizable pay" in 2014, up from zero in 2009.[37]

Company size (along with industrial sector) is a major determinant of executive compensation levels. Gabaix and Landier (2008) found that an increase in company size can almost entirely explain the increase in executive compensation in recent years. For example, they found that although CEO pay increased sixfold between 1980 and 2003, the market value of the companies they managed also increased sixfold during this period. They concluded that "the rise in CEO compensation is a simple mirror of the rise in the value of large U.S. companies since the 1980s."[38] Of course, demonstrating the correlation between compensation growth and company growth does not indicate that the compensation levels themselves are appropriate.

In a related study, Kaplan and Rauh (2010) found that the growth in executive compensation is largely consistent with the growth in compensation for other highly paid professionals, such as hedge fund managers, private equity managers, venture capitalists, lawyers, and professional athletes. The authors calculated that pay among these groups all grew by roughly the same order of magnitude during 1994–2005. They concluded that CEO compensation has increased because of market forces that contribute to general wage inflation among highly paid professionals and that extreme compensation growth is not limited to the business world.[39]

However, examples exist of individual companies that pay their CEOs more than the normalized level that might be expected, given their size and performance. Research suggests that weak governance systems are correlated with excessive compensation. Core, Holthausen, and Larcker (1999) found an inverse relationship between the quality of oversight that a board provides and the level of compensation within the firm.[40] They also found that companies that award inflated compensation tend to underperform their peers in terms of subsequent operating performance and stock price returns. They concluded that "firms with weaker governance structures have greater compensation and that firms with greater agency problems perform worse." That is, governance quality clearly has an impact on executive compensation levels.

Ratio of CEO Pay to Other Top Executive Pay

Critics of executive compensation levels point to two statistics to support their position. One is the large differential between the pay granted to the CEO and the pay granted to other senior executives (see the following sidebar). The other is the large differential between CEO pay and average employee pay.

C-Suite Pay Differential

Abercrombie & Fitch

In 2008, the Connecticut Retirement Plans and Trust Funds, which manages pension assets on behalf of state and municipal workers in Connecticut, filed a shareholder resolution at Abercrombie & Fitch that would require the company to adopt a policy to encourage greater pay equity between the CEO and other named executive officers (NEOs).[41] According to State Treasurer Denise Nappier:

"Large gaps in pay between the chief executive officer and other NEOs may signal that the CEO is earning an excessively large share of the compensation paid to top executives or that the pay is not tied to performance, and this is rightly of concern to shareholders. It may also be a red flag for inadequate succession planning, as wide pay differentials sometimes reveal significant differences in contribution and ability, and this, too, is troubling."[42]

During fiscal year 2006, Abercrombie & Fitch Chairman and CEO Michael Jeffries earned total compensation of $26.2 million, compared with total compensation of between $2.4 million and $4.3 million for the other NEOs of the company.[43] After negotiation with Nappier, the company agreed to enhance disclosure on the compensation paid to their CEOs relative to other NEOs, and the Connecticut Retirement Plans and Trust Funds dropped its shareholder resolution.

Table 8.4 shows that the typical CEO of a publicly traded U.S. corporation earns roughly 1.8 times the total compensation of the second-highest-paid NEO.[44] The second- highest-paid NEO earns roughly 1.2 times as much as the third-highest-paid NEO. These figures do not vary considerably by company size.

Table 8.4 The Ratio of Pay among Senior Executives

Firms (Grouped by Size)	Ratio of Pay: CEO to Second-Highest-Paid Executive	Ratio of Pay: Second- to Third-Highest-Paid Executive
Top 100	1.75	1.16
101 to 500	2.11	1.22
501 to 1,000	2.07	1.23
1,001 to 2,000	1.96	1.21
2,001 to 3,000	1.80	1.20
3,001 to 4,000	1.58	1.19
1 to 4,000	1.83	1.20

Based on median total compensation.

Source: Equilar, proprietary compensation and equity ownership data for fiscal years from June 2013 to May 2014.

Several factors might contribute to pay inequity within the executive suite. From a purely economic standpoint, the relative pay packages might simply reflect the different levels of value creation within the organization. The success of a very complex company might more heavily rely on the efforts of the CEO, so it might be appropriate to have a greater pay differential to attract a qualified leader.

Furthermore, large pay differentials might also reflect competitive dynamics within the organization. This explanation, known as **tournament theory**, was proposed by Lazear and Rosen (1981), who pointed out that senior executives not only serve a current operating function but also compete in a tournament for promotion.[45] According to the authors, pay inequity serves as an incentive for executives to compete more aggressively for promotion. If they are successful, they receive a large payoff in terms of compensation. As a result, the executive's current salary is not his or her only incentive to perform. The potential for promotion is itself an incentive, and the value of this incentive is reinforced by a large pay differential between the current and potential positions.

However, pay inequity might indeed signal real problems within the company. Large pay differentials might indicate **management entrenchment** (the ability of management to shield itself from market forces and pressures to perform from the board, shareholders, and stakeholders).[46] In this way, large differentials might indicate that the CEO is able to engage in rent extraction, which the corporate governance system has not adequately controlled against. Pay inequity might also be a source of discouragement for executives who believe they are not fairly compensated. If this is the case, talented senior executives might become unmotivated, which leads to higher turnover, reduced productivity, and a decrease in shareholder value. Finally, pay inequity might reflect a lack of talent development within the organization. That is, the NEOs of the company might simply receive low compensation because they have lower talent levels. If this is the case, the company might be at greater risk of a failed transition because it lacks a viable successor when the current CEO eventually steps down.

Research evidence on pay inequity is mixed. Kale, Reis, and Venkateswaran (2009) found that tournament incentives are positively correlated with firm performance, measured in terms of operating returns and market-to-book values.[47] Bebchuk, Cremers, and Peyer (2011), however, found that pay inequity at the senior level is associated with lower firm value and greater risk of agency problems.[48] Kini and Williams (2012) found that tournament incentives are positively associated with firm risk, measured in terms of leverage, operating focus, and reliance on research and development expenditures. They concluded that "while the design of a promotion-based incentive system can be employed to induce senior executives to expend greater effort, it can also be used to shape the amount of risk taken by them."[49]

To reduce the potential for negative effects due to internal pay inequity, some companies place limits on the ratio of CEO compensation to compensation of named executive officers. For example, healthcare information technology company Cerner Corporation limits the cash compensation of the CEO to no more than three times that of the second-highest-paid NEO. The board must approve exceptions to this policy in advance.[50] DuPont has also instituted "pay equity multiples" that limit total annual compensation of the CEO relative to that of the other NEOs. CEO cash compensation is limited to between two and three times the cash compensation paid to the other NEOs, and total compensation (which includes long-term incentives) is limited to between three and four times.[51]

Ratio of CEO Pay to Average Employee Pay

Critics of executive compensation also point to the large differential between the compensation paid to the CEO and the average employee. According to one critic: "If the CEO is going to be paid more than 100 times the average worker, we want to know why. . . . We are trying to get at the notion of economic injustice in what the CEO is making compared to the average worker. It's bad for the long-term performance of a company because it breaches the trust between top management and people who work for them."[52] The Dodd–Frank Act requires companies to disclose the ratio of CEO pay to average employee pay in the annual proxy.

Because of delays implementing the rule, broad descriptive statistics are not available. However, recent estimates have pegged this ratio between 200 times to 500 times.[53] Differences in methodology and sample selection contribute to the disparity. Results vary depending on whether the researcher uses mean or median compensation figures; mean averages can skew results by overweighting outliers. Results also vary depending on whether the researcher uses expected or realized pay; realized compensation can overstate CEO pay in a given year if it includes grants awarded in multiple years but exercised in a single year. The ratio is also influenced by a company's industry, size, location, workforce composition, and measurement period.

For example, Crawford, Nelson, and Rountree (2014) calculated the CEO-to-employee pay ratio among commercial banks using a sample of 10,581 firm-year observations between 1995 and 2012. They found the mean (median) ratio to be 16.6 (8.4) times. At the 90th percentile, the pay ratio was still only 32.8 times. Only at the largest observation did the ratio rise to 821 times.[54]

Still, some companies worry that internal pay inequities can be harmful to the corporation and therefore seek to limit CEO pay. For example, Whole Foods limits the cash compensation of any employee (including the CEO) to no more than 19 times the average annual wage of all full-time employees. The company explains that its compensation programs "reflect our philosophy of egalitarianism."[55]

Compensation Mix

In addition to determining the level of compensation, the compensation committee must decide how to *structure* the compensation package to ensure that it provides incentives that are in line with the company's objectives. Ultimately, this is done by arriving at a mix of cash, equity, and other benefits with appropriate performance targets to attract, retain, and motivate qualified executive officers, across both short-term and long-term horizons.

Table 8.5 shows that the average company pays roughly 29 percent of the CEO's compensation in the form of salary, 20 percent in bonus, 14 percent in stock options, 32 percent in restricted stock and long-term performance plans, and 6 percent in pension and benefits. One interesting statistic is that smaller companies appear to reduce bonuses and performance-based compensation in their compensation and increase the proportion from salary. This might be driven by personal consumption (that is, because the compensation packages are smaller, the executives need a higher mix of cash to support their living expenses).

How appropriate are these compensation mixes? Do they encourage behaviors that appropriately balance risk and reward in pursuit of the corporate strategy? When should the board think about using a different mix of compensation?

Table 8.5 Mix of Compensation Paid to CEOs in the United States

Firms (Grouped by Size)	Salary	Bonus	Stock Options	Restricted Stock and Long-Term Awards	Change in Pension and Other
Top 100	18.9%	23.4%	8.6%	38.8%	10.3%
101 to 500	14.3%	20.5%	14.8%	43.3%	7.2%
501 to 1,000	16.1%	21.1%	14.1%	42.1%	6.6%
1,001 to 2,000	21.1%	22.0%	13.2%	38.4%	5.3%
2,001 to 3,000	30.4%	19.7%	15.6%	29.5%	4.8%
3,001 to 4,000	46.9%	15.9%	14.5%	16.0%	6.8%
1 to 4,000	28.5%	19.6%	14.3%	31.5%	6.0%

Source: Equilar, proprietary compensation and equity ownership data information for fiscal years from June 2013 to May 2014.

Short-Term Incentives

Short-term incentives offer an annual payment (usually cash) for achieving predetermined performance objectives. The size of the bonus is expressed in terms of a **target award**. Most companies define the size of the target award as a percentage of the base salary (for example, the target award might be equal to 200 percent of the base salary). The actual payment that the executive receives might be limited by upper and lower bounds, in which case a minimum award and a maximum award are established. (The minimum award might be equal to 50 percent of the target and the maximum award equal to 200 percent of the target.) As a result, the executive stands to receive a cash payment with a payoff that increases in a stepwise function, with bounded upper and lower limits (see Figure 8.1.)

The bonus payment is awarded if certain performance criteria are achieved during the year. The compensation committee determines the performance criteria. As discussed in Chapter 6, "Strategy, Performance Measurement, and Risk Management," one way to select the measures used to award compensation is to use those that were identified during the business modeling process as being correlated with success in the corporate strategy. In general, these include a mix of accounting measures (such as economic value added, earnings-per-share growth, and return on assets), stock market measures (such as total shareholder return), and nonfinancial measures (such as customer satisfaction, product defect rates, and market share). As such, bonus plans provide executives with an explicit monetary incentive to improve the short-term performance of the firm by achieving operating targets that are known to be correlated with increased shareholder value (see the next sidebar).

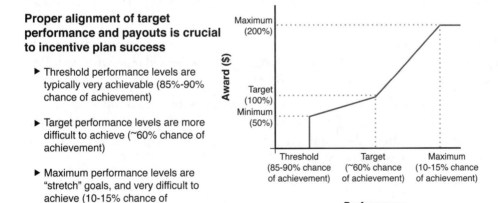

Proper alignment of target performance and payouts is crucial to incentive plan success

▶ Threshold performance levels are typically very achievable (85%-90% chance of achievement)

▶ Target performance levels are more difficult to achieve (~60% chance of achievement)

▶ Maximum performance levels are "stretch" goals, and very difficult to achieve (10-15% chance of achievement)

Source: Michael Benkowitz, Mark A. Borges, and Thomas G. Brown, "Mastering Performance-Based Equity: New Frontiers in Executive Pay," Compensia, Inc. (2008). Accessed May 5, 2015. Available at: http://www.compensia.com/events/breakfastbriefingpres_111208.pdf.

Figure 8.1   Minimum, target, and maximum awards for typical short-term bonus plans.

One potential concern with bonus plans is that annual performance targets might not be very difficult to achieve. According to a 2005 proprietary survey by a major compensation consulting firm, on average, companies pay bonuses equal to 103 percent of the target level. Only 20 percent of executives receive a bonus less than 75 percent of target levels. That is, bonus plans do not appear to be based on "stretch" goals. Research studies arrive at similar conclusions. Merchant and Manzoni (1989) found that internal budget targets used to award performance bonuses are met 80 percent to 90 percent of the time.[56] Indjejikian, Lenk, and Nanda (2000) found that performance targets are achieved 60 percent of the time.[57] As such, it is not clear that average performance hurdles are difficult to achieve or encourage above-average performance. It is important for the board to assess whether the performance targets are sufficiently difficult to attain so that what is termed a "performance-based" bonus is not actually some type of "disguised fixed salary."

In addition, bonus plans have the potential to produce a variety of undesirable executive behaviors. For example, the annual nature of bonus plans can give rise to excessive focus on short-term accounting results at the expense of long-term value creation. One example is delaying the investment in important projects with positive net present value to improve current-period net income. This is of special concern when an executive is in the final few years with the company and is therefore unlikely to see the economic benefit of a long-term investment in his or her annual bonus.[58]

Similarly, the practice of bounding annual bonus plans with a stated maximum can also encourage inappropriate behavior. Healy (1985) and Holthausen, Larcker, and Sloan (1995) found that executives are more likely to manipulate earnings downward after they have achieved their maximum bonus payment.[59] They do so to defer corporate earnings to a later period because they no longer contribute toward their current bonus.

Finally, it is plausible that bonus plans can provide incentives for managers to manipulate accounting results to achieve targets that they would otherwise miss. (We discuss this topic in greater detail in Chapter 9.)

These are all real concerns for the board of directors to consider, given the important role that the bonus plays in the overall compensation package. Fortunately, compensation committees also grant a variety of long-term compensation awards that can mitigate these potential problems.

Annual Incentives

Northrop Grumman

In 2013, Northrop Grumman used the following financial performance metrics in calculating the annual performance bonus for the CEO and other named executive officers of the company:[60]

- *Pension-adjusted operating margin* is calculated as operating margin rate (operating margin divided by sales) adjusted for net FAS/CAS pension income or expense. The net FAS/CAS pension adjustment is the difference between pension expense determined in accordance with GAAP under Financial Accounting Standards (FAS) and pension expense allocated to the business segments under U.S. Government Cost Accounting Standards (CAS).

- Free cash flow conversion is calculated as free cash flow provided by operating activities before the after-tax impact of discretionary pension contributions divided by net income from continuing operations.

- Awards (book-to-bill) represents the total new contracts awarded to the company during the year, net of backlog adjustments, divided by sales during the year.

- Pension-adjusted net income is calculated as net income adjusted for net FAS/CAS pension income or expense after tax.

The company also used the following nonfinancial performance metrics, noting that nonfinancial metrics can only reduce and not raise the bonus:

- Customer satisfaction, measured in terms of customer feedback

- Quality, measured using program-specific objectives within each of our sectors

- Engagement, as reported by employees in a company-wide engagement survey

- Diversity, measured in terms of improving representation of females and people of color in mid-level and senior-level management positions

- Safety, measured by recordable injuries and lost work day rate associated with those injuries

- Environmental sustainability, measured in terms of reduction of greenhouse gas emissions, solid waste, and water utilization

This is a complex annual bonus plan. Are the large number of financial and nonfinancial measures in this annual bonus plan really necessary? When does a plan become too complicated?

Long-Term Incentives

Long-term incentives are added to the compensation mix to encourage executives to select long-term investments that increase shareholder value. Long-term incentives extend the time horizon of the executive and mitigate the natural tendency of a risk-averse executive to reject risky investments. In Table 8.5, we saw that the value of long-term awards (in the form of stock options, equity, and performance plans) is equal in size to the value of short-term awards—46 percent versus 48 percent at the average company. As such, long-term incentives can help mitigate short-term gamesmanship by refocusing the emphasis on long-term performance.[61]

For example, as executives approach retirement, they might be expected to reduce a company's investment in research and development to hit earnings targets that increase their own annual bonus. Because the annual bonus (along with salary) is a key input in calculating their pension benefits, the CEO will benefit by receiving larger annual payments throughout retirement. This is part of the reason firms put "hold until or past retirement" features in stock option and restricted stock programs. That way, if the CEO rejects valuable research and development to boost the value of his or her pension, the executive will, in theory, be punished through a corresponding loss in the eventual value of options and shares owned.

Stock options are an important compensation element that many companies use to create this longer-term horizon for value creation. Options have several desirable features that can help align the interests of executives with those of shareholders. First, options increase in value as the stock price increases. This motivates executives to add corporate value by identifying and implementing investments with positive net present value (NPV). Second, options increase in value with stock-price volatility. This motivates executives to accept risky, positive NPV investments that might otherwise be rejected if the compensation program were instead mostly fixed salary or short-term incentives. Third, because of vesting requirements, options have deferred payoffs that encourage a focus on long-term results. As such, stock options tend to be used in companies where there are substantial investment opportunities that are associated with considerable risk. Stock options will attract highly skilled executives with moderate risk tolerance who want to share in the value created by their work. Whether the company wants this type of employee depends on the firm's strategy. A firm operating in a stable and predictable environment might use more fixed salary and annual bonus compensation, but a company in a highly dynamic and risky industry might place greater emphasis on long-term equity-based compensation.

On the other hand, stock options can offer capricious financial rewards to executives when broad market factors cause changes in stock price that are not the result of the executive's individual effort. During much of the 1990s, a rising market tended to reward most executives who received options, regardless of the firm's operating performance. Conversely, most stock options granted in the late 1990s expired with zero value because of significant market declines, even in cases when some sort of payout was merited based on relative performance. This concern has motivated some companies to replace stock options with restricted stock grants and long-term performance awards.

Some evidence suggests that stock options encourage the investment in new, risky projects. (Risky projects are desirable to shareholders when they are consistent with the strategy and business model of the organization and when such investments have expected positive net present value. They are negative when they are inconsistent with the company's business model or are unlikely to bring rewards that compensate for the associated risk.) Rajgopal and Shevlin (2002) found that stock options are an effective tool to encourage risk-averse managers to invest in higher-risk, higher-return investments. Executives understand that the expected value of a stock option increases with the volatility of the stock price, and they tend to respond to stock option awards by investing in riskier projects to create this volatility.[62] Sanders and Hambrick (2007) found that executives who receive stock options are more likely to increase investment in risky research and development, capital expenditures, and acquisitions. In addition, total shareholder returns at these companies are more likely to be extreme in their outcomes (extremely positive or extremely negative). Unfortunately, the authors found that results are more likely to be extremely negative than extremely positive. They concluded that "high levels of stock options appear to motivate CEOs to take big risks . . . to 'swing for the fences.'"[63] The issue of whether stock options might be related to excessive risk taking is an important consideration that we will consider in greater detail in Chapter 9.

Another tool that companies use is performance awards. Performance awards tie the value of long-term compensation to the achievement of predetermined goals or performance metrics. In recent years, performance awards have come to be a significant portion of the compensation mix. Along with restricted stock, performance awards represent 32 percent of a typical company's CEO compensation program.

de Angelis and Grinstein (2014) examined the use of performance awards among S&P 500 companies. They found that all companies that grant performance awards use at least one accounting-based metric; market-based measures are used less frequently—30 percent of the time; 40 percent of firms use nonfinancial performance measures. Among accounting measures, 87 percent are income based (for example, earnings per share or net income growth), 39 percent are based on revenue, 37 percent on return metrics (for example, return on equity or assets), 23 percent on cash flow, 9 percent on margin, 6 percent on cost reduction targets, and 5 percent on economic value added (EVA). More than half of the sample used between two and four different measures. The weighted-average performance horizon taking into account both short-term and long-term performance awards was slightly less than two years. In addition, the authors found that the size of discretionary bonuses (not tied to predetermined targets) was not correlated with performance awards and concluded that these bonuses were granted for reasons other than performance (such as retention purposes).[64]

Benefits and Perquisites

The CEO compensation package generally includes a mix of benefits, perquisites, and other contingent payments. The value of these awards is not negligible. On average, they constitute 6 percent of the total compensation (see Table 8.5). In some of the more extreme cases cited at the beginning of this chapter, they can ultimately prove to be quite valuable.

The research evidence on the incentive value of these payments is quite mixed. Rajan and Wulf (2006) found that companies consistently use perks as a means to improve executive productivity. They found that perks such as use of aircraft and chauffeur drivers are predominantly awarded to executives who stand to benefit the most from free time.[65] Sundaram and Yermack (2007) argued that defined benefit pension plans (which are a fixed claim on the firm similar to salary) can be seen as a risk-reducing form of compensation that offsets the risk-seeking incentives of equity compensation.[66]

However, other researchers argue that these perquisites and benefits are a form of "stealth compensation" that enriches executives at the cost of shareholders. As such, they can be seen as the very agency costs that corporate governance systems are meant to preclude. To this end, Yermack (2006) found that shareholders react negatively to disclosure that an executive is allowed personal use of company aircraft.[67] Grinstein, Weinbaum, and Yehuda (2010) found that the reported value of perquisites increased by 190 percent following enhanced SEC disclosure rules in 2006. They also found that the reduction in shareholder value following the disclosure significantly exceeded the actual value of the perquisites, indicating that shareholders saw them as value destroying. They concluded that perquisite disclosure "conveys a more fundamental negative signal about the agency conflicts in these firms."[68] Perquisites might not be an especially large dollar amount relative to the market capitalization of the firm, but they might provide a window into the workings of the board and governance quality of the firm.

Compensation Disclosure

As the preceding discussion suggests, the typical executive compensation program is quite complicated. In recent years, the SEC has taken steps to improve the quality of information disclosed to investors in the annual proxy. The most significant of these is the inclusion of a Compensation Discussion & Analysis (CD&A) section that explains in detail the company's compensation philosophy, the elements of the compensation program, the total compensation offered, performance metrics used to award variable pay, and other details of the company's compensation program. The SEC intended the CD&A to provide a "plain English" discussion of these items.

Subsequent research, however, suggests that companies have considerable room to improve the clarity of disclosure about executive pay. Beucler and Dolmat-Connell (2007) found that the median disclosure length is nearly five times longer than the SEC envisioned (4,726 words versus an expectation of 1,000). They concluded that current disclosure is not very accessible to the average investor.[69]

Survey data also finds that institutional investors are dissatisfied with the quality of information they receive about executive compensation in the annual proxy. According to a study by RR Donnelley, Equilar, and the Rock Center for Corporate Governance at Stanford University (2015) fewer than half (38 percent) of institutional investors believe that executive compensation is clearly and effectively disclosed in the proxy. Responses are consistently negative across all elements of compensation disclosure. Sixty-five percent say that the relation between compensation and risk is "not at all" clear. Forty-eight percent say that it is "not at all" clear that the size of compensation is appropriate. Forty-three percent believe that it is "not at all" clear whether performance-based compensation plans are based on rigorous goals. Significant minorities cannot determine whether the structure of executive compensation is appropriate (39 percent), cannot understand the relation between compensation and performance (25 percent), and cannot determine whether compensation is well aligned with shareholder interests (22 percent). Investors also express considerable dissatisfaction with the disclosure of potential payouts to executives under long-term performance plans.[70]

The fundamental complaint about proxies is rooted in a perception that companies are not communicating candidly with owners. Shareholders want corporations to explain information rather than disclose it (see the following sidebar). Investors view corporations as using the proxy as a vehicle to meet disclosure obligations without a willingness to provide information in a format that is clear and understandable to a typical—or even sophisticated—owner.

Shareholder Engagement on Pay

Amgen

Amgen has implemented a unique method for soliciting shareholder feedback on executive compensation. The company's proxy invites shareholders to fill out a survey to provide input and feedback to the compensation committee regarding executive compensation.[71]

The survey asks questions such as:

- Is the compensation plan performance based?
- Is the plan clearly linked to the company's business strategy?
- Are the plan's metrics, goals, and hurdles clearly and specifically disclosed?
- Are the incentives clearly designed to meet the company's specific business challenges, in both the short term and long term?
- Does the compensation of senior executives complement the company's overall compensation program, reinforce internal equity, and promote the success of the entire business enterprise?
- Does the plan promote long-term value creation, which is the primary objective of shareholders?
- Does the plan articulate a coherent compensation philosophy appropriate to the company and clearly understood by directors?[72]

Each question allows for an open-text-field response and links to a pop-up box where shareholders are given expanded information.

This type of survey raises a variety of important questions. Do shareholders have the necessary information to make a correct judgment about these issues? What happens if shareholders indicate that they do not like some part of the compensation program? When does the board have a "duty" to make changes? What type of investor relations activity is needed to support this survey?

Say-on-Pay

Say-on-pay is the practice of granting shareholders the right to vote on a company's executive or director compensation program at the annual shareholder meeting. Say-on-pay is a relatively recent phenomenon, having first been required by the United Kingdom in 2003 and subsequently adopted in countries including the

Netherlands, Australia, Sweden, and Norway. The use and terms of say-on-pay vary across nations (see Table 8.6)

Table 8.6 Say-on-Pay around the World

Country	Year Adopted	Directors or Executives	Binding or Advisory	Frequency	Required or Voluntary
United Kingdom	2003	Directors	Advisory	Annually	Required
The Netherlands	2004	Executives	Binding	Upon changes	Required
Australia	2005	Directors	Advisory	Annually	Required
Sweden	2006	Executives	Binding	Annually	Required
Norway	2007	Executives	Binding	Annually	Required
Denmark	2007	Executives	Binding	Upon changes	Required
United States	2011	Executives	Advisory	Annually/ biennially/ triennially	Required
Switzerland	2014	Directors	Binding	Annually	Required
Germany	None	Executives	Advisory	Annually	Voluntary
Canada	None	Executives	Advisory	Annually	Voluntary

Note: Because the CEO usually serves on the board of directors, a "say-on-pay" vote on director compensation implicitly expresses shareholder opinion on CEO pay as well as director pay.

Source: Authors.

The U.S. adopted say-on-pay in 2011, pursuant to the Dodd–Frank Act. Under Dodd–Frank, companies are required to hold an advisory (nonbinding) vote on compensation at least once every three years. At least once every six years, companies are required to ask shareholders to determine the frequency of future say-on-pay votes (with the options being every one, two, or three years but no less frequently). Advocates of say-on-pay contend that the practice of submitting executive compensation for shareholder approval increases the accountability of corporate directors to shareholders and leads to more efficient contracting, with rewards more closely aligned with corporate objectives and performance.

Despite anticipation that shareholders would take advantage of their right to vote on executive compensation to register dissatisfaction with pay levels, voting results have not conformed to this expectation. Among approximately 2,700 public companies that put their executive compensation plans before shareholders for a vote in 2011, only 37 (1.4 percent) failed to receive majority approval. Support levels across all companies averaged 90 percent. Results in 2014 were little changed: Only 60 out of approximately 2,600 companies (2.4 percent) did not receive majority approval, and the average support level across all companies was 91 percent (see Figure 8.2).[73] Say-on-pay voting results have held steady despite the fact that average compensation levels continue to rise. According to Equilar, median CEO compensation rose by 25 percent between 2010 and 2013.[74]

Research provides mixed evidence on whether say-on-pay leads to improved compensation practices. Ertimur, Ferri, and Muslu (2011) examined the impact of "vote no" campaigns and compensation-related shareholder proposals in the United States. They found that support for shareholder initiatives restricting compensation is higher among companies with above-average CEO pay. Furthermore, they found that vote-no campaigns are associated with a subsequent reduction of $2.3 million in CEO pay—but only when institutional investors initiated the proxy proposal.[75] Cai and Walkling (2011) examined shareholder returns following the passage of say-on-pay legislation by the U.S. House of Representatives. They found some evidence that share prices for firms with high excess compensation reacted in a positive manner to the regulatory announcement.[76] Ferri and Maber (2013) found that say-on-pay regulation in the United Kingdom had some impact on the level of severance pay awarded to CEOs. It also reduced stock option "retesting," in which a company extends the time period of a performance-based grant to give the executive more time to meet the performance threshold. These effects began to show up when at least 20 percent of shareholders voted against the plan. However, the authors did not find evidence that say-on-pay reduced overall pay levels in the United Kingdom.[77] Larcker, Ormazabal, and Taylor (2011) found evidence that capping or regulating executive pay results in less efficient contracts and negatively affects shareholder wealth in firms that are likely to be affected.[78]

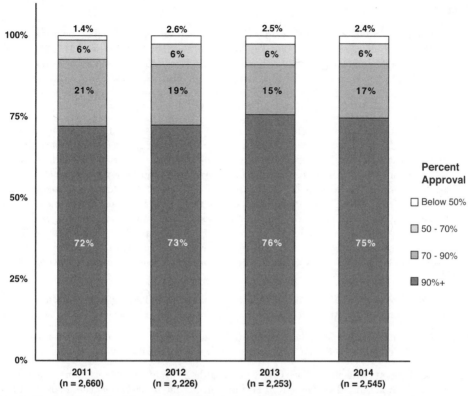

Figure 8.2   Say-on-Pay Vote Results (2011–2014)

Notes: As of December 31, 2014. The 2014 sample includes companies that had an Annual Meeting and Say on Pay vote in calendar year 2014. Year over year data presented in this document does not reflect a constant sample given turnover in the Russell 3000 used for each year as well as differences in how frequently companies hold votes.

For FY 2014, Russell 3000 sample effective as of June 28, 2013.

Source: Semler Brossy Consulting Group, LLC. (2015).

Shareholders, too, express skepticism that say-on-pay leads to improved compensation. According to the survey cited in the previous section, only 58 percent of institutional investors believe that say-on-pay is effective in influencing or modifying pay.[79]

Finally, proxy advisory firms, including ISS and Glass Lewis, have considerable influence over say-on-pay voting. Their ability to sway voting outcomes influences corporate decisions on CEO pay levels and design. We discuss this in greater detail in Chapter 12, "Institutional Shareholders and Activist Investors."

Endnotes

1. Exceptions do exist in which CEOs work for no pay, as a result of either public pressure or moral duty, but they are obviously rare. See Moira Herbst, "The Elite Circle of $1 CEOs: Apple's Steve Jobs and Google's Eric Schmidt Are Just Two of the CEOs Who Work for a Buck. Why Do Top Executives Give Up Their Salaries?" *Business Week Online* (May 10, 2007). Accessed June 27, 2014. See http://www.businessweek.com/stories/2007-05-10/the-elite-circle-of-1-ceosbusinessweek-business-news-stock-market-and-financial-advice.

2. A 2007 report prepared by Congressman Waxman (California) asserted that compensation consultants were a cause of excessive CEO compensation. However, the analysis did not control for other explanatory factors (such as size of the company). When properly controlled, these associations disappear. As a result, the causality attributed in this report was misleading, at the very least. See Henry A Waxman, et al., "Executive Pay: Conflicts of Interest among Compensation Consultants," U.S. House of Representatives Committee on Oversight and Government Reform (December 2007). Separately, Core, Guay, and Larcker (2008) found that while the media places a lot of attention on executive compensation, it actually has relatively little influence in affecting compensation levels. See John E. Core, Wayne Guay, and David F. Larcker, "The Power of the Pen and Executive Compensation," *Journal of Financial Economics* 88 (2008): 1–25.

3. See Harwell Wells, "No Man Can Be Worth $1,000,000 a Year: The Fight over Executive Compensation in 1930s America," *University of Richmond Law Review* 44 (January 2010): 689.

4. Carola Frydman and Raven E. Saks, "Executive Compensation: A New View from a Long-Term Perspective, 1936–2005," *Review of Financial Studies* 23 (2010): 2099–2138.

5. Amanda Bennett, "Executives Face Change in Awarding Pay, Stock Options: More Managers Find Salary, Bonus Are Tied Directly to Performance," *Wall Street Journal* (February 28, 1986, Eastern edition): 1.

6. Anonymous, "Highest Paid CEOs," *USA Today* (May 17, 1988). Last accessed November 10, 2010. See http://infoweb.newsbank.com/iw-search/we/InfoWeb.

7. Measured in terms of the amount realized through stock option exercises and the value of unexercised in-the-money options. See Standard & Poor's ExecuComp data, cited in Mark Maremont and Charles Forelle, "Open Spigot: Bosses' Pay: How Stock Options Became Part of the Problem; Once Seen as a Reform, They Grew into Font of Riches and System to Be Gamed; Reload, Reprice, Backdate," *Wall Street Journal* (December 27, 2006, Eastern edition): A.1.

8. David F. Larcker and Brian Tayan, "Executive Compensation at Nabors Industries: Too Much, Too Little, or Just Right?" Stanford GSB Case No. CG-5 (February 2, 2007).

9. JPMorgan Chase and American Express, Form DEF 14A, filed with the Securities and Exchange Commission during 2008 and 2011.

10. Lucian A. Bebchuk and Jesse M. Fried, "Pay without Performance: Overview of the Issues," *Academy of Management Perspectives* 20 (2006): 5–24. Lucian A. Bebchuk and Jesse M. Fried, *Pay without Performance: The Unfulfilled Promise of Executive Compensation* (Cambridge, Mass.: Harvard University Press, 2006).

11. For examples of each of these, see Equilar, Inc., "CD&A Overview: An Examples-Based Review of Key CD&A Elements" (2009). Accessed June 23, 2009. See www.equilar.com.

12. When reading this section, it is useful to consider whether all the different components of compensation are really necessary. For a comparison of compensation packages paid today against those of 50 years ago, see David F. Larcker and Brian Tayan, "A Historical Look at Compensation and Disclosure," Stanford Closer Look Series (June 15, 2010). Accessed May 5, 2015. See http://www.gsb.stanford.edu/faculty-research/centers-initiatives/cgri/research/closer-look.

13. For an excellent analysis regarding the role of discretion, see Madhav V. Rajan and Stefan Reichelstein, "Subjective Performance Indicators and Discretionary Bonus Pools," *Journal of Accounting Research* 44 (2006): 585–618. See also Christopher D. Ittner, David F. Larcker, and Marshall W. Meyer, "Subjectivity and the Weighting of Performance Measures: Evidence from a Balanced Scorecard," *Accounting Review* 78 (2003): 725–758.

14. U.S. Securities and Exchange Commission (SEC), Division of Corporate Finance, "Current Report on Form 8-K: Frequently Asked Questions" (November 23, 2004): Question 12. Accessed May 5, 2015. See https://www.sec.gov/divisions/corpfin/form8kfaq.htm.

15. Equilar Inc., "CEO Pay Strategies Report" (2014). Accessed February 18, 2015. See www.equilar.com.

16. Equilar Inc., "Executive Stock Ownership Guidelines Report," Equilar (2013). Accessed February 18, 2015. See www.equilar.com.

17. Sarbanes–Oxley Act of 2002 §304, 15 U.S.C. § 7243 (2006).

18. Equilar Inc., "Clawback Policy Report" (2013). Accessed February 18, 2015. See www.equilar.com.

19. Exxon Mobil Corp., form DEF 14A, filed with the Securities and Exchange Commission April 11, 2014.

20. Citigroup, Inc., Form DEF 14A, filed with the Securities and Exchange Commission March 18, 2014.

21. McKesson, Inc., Form DEF 14A, filed with the Securities and Exchange Commission June 19, 2014.

22. Apple Inc., Form DEF 14A, filed with the Securities and Exchange Commission January 22, 2015.

23. Mai Iskandar-Datta and Yonghong Jia, "Valuation Consequences of Clawback Provisions," *Accounting Review* 88 (2013): 171–198.

24. Lilian H. Chan, Kevin C.W. Chen, Tai-Yuan Chen, and Yangxin Yu, "The Effects of Firm-Initiated Clawback Provisions on Earnings Quality and Auditor Behavior," *Journal of Accounting and Economics* 54 (2012): 180–196.

25. Equilar, Inc., "S&P 1500 Peer Group Report: An Analysis of Peer Groups at S&P 1500 Companies" (2014). Accessed February 18, 2015. See www.equilar.com.

26. John M. Bizjak, Michael L. Lemmon, and Lalitha Naveen, "Does the Use of Peer Groups Contribute to Higher Pay and Less Efficient Compensation?" *Journal of Financial Economics* 90 (2008): 152–168.

27. Michael Faulkender and Jun Yang, "Inside the Black Box: The Role and Composition of Compensation Peer Groups," *Journal of Financial Economics* 96 (2010): 257–270.

28. The Kroger Company, Form DEF 14A, filed with the Securities and Exchange Commission May 14, 2013; Safeway, Inc., Form DEF 14A, filed with the Securities and Exchange Commission April 1, 2013.

29. Equilar, Inc., "Compensation Consultant League Table" (2014). Accessed February 19, 2015. See www.equilar.com.

30. Chris S. Armstrong, Christopher D. Ittner, and David F. Larcker, "Corporate Governance, Compensation Consultants, and CEO Pay Levels," *Review of Accounting Studies* 17 (June 2012): 322–351.

31. A similar argument has been made about the same firm providing both audit- and nonaudit-related services to a client. We discuss this in greater detail in Chapter 10, "Financial Reporting and External Audit."

32. See Martin J. Conyon, Simon I. Peck, and Graham V. Sadler, "Compensation Consultants and Executive Pay: Evidence from the United States and the United Kingdom," *Academy of Management Perspectives* (2009): 2343–2355; Brian Cadman, Mary Ellen Carter, and Stephen Hillegeist, "The Incentives of Compensation Consultants and CEO Pay," *Journal of Accounting and Economics* 49 (2010): 263–280; Kevin J. Murphy and Tatiana Sandino, "Executive Pay and 'Independent' Compensation Consultants," *Journal of Accounting and Economics* 49 (2010): 247–262; Jenny Chu, Jonathan Faasse, and P. Raghavendra Rau, "Do Compensation Consultants Enable Higher CEO Pay? New Evidence from Recent Disclosure Rule Changes," *Social Science Research Network* (2014). Accessed February 19, 2015. See http://ssrn.com/abstract=2500054.

33. Chris S. Armstrong, Christopher D. Ittner, and David F. Larcker (June 2012).

34. Symantec Corp., Form DEF 14A, filed with the Securities and Exchange Commission September 4, 2014.

35. Equilar, Inc., proprietary compensation and equity ownership data for fiscal years from June 2013 to May 2014.

36. David F. Larcker, Allan McCall, and Brian Tayan, "What Does It Mean for an Executive to Make a Million?" Stanford Closer Look Series (December 14, 2011). Accessed May 5, 2015. See http://www.gsb.stanford.edu/faculty-research/centers-initiatives/cgri/research/closer-look.

37. Equilar Inc., "2015 Innovations in CD&A Design: A Proxy Disclosure Analysis" (2015). Accessed April 16, 2015. See www.equilar.com.

38. Xavier Gabaix and Augustin Landier, "Why Has CEO Pay Increased so Much?" *Quarterly Journal of Economics* 123 (2008): 49–100.

39. Steven N. Kaplan and Joshua Rauh, "Wall Street and Main Street: What Contributes to the Rise in the Highest Incomes?" *Review of Financial Studies* 23 (2010): 1004–1050.

40. Companies with weak board oversight are defined as those with dual chairman/CEO, boards with a large number of directors, boards with a large percentage of "gray" directors (directors who are not executives of the company but who have other financial connections to the company or management as a result of serving as a lawyer, banker, consultant, or other provider of services), boards on which a large percentage of outside directors are appointed by the CEO, boards with a large percentage of old directors, and boards with a large percentage of busy directors. See John E. Core, Robert W. Holthausen, and David F. Larcker, "Corporate Governance, Chief Executive Officer Compensation, and Firm Performance," *Journal of Financial Economics* 51 (1999): 371–406.

41. Named executive officer (NEO) is an SEC designation that includes the principal executive officer, the principal financial officer, and the three most highly compensated executive officers. See Securities and Exchange Commission, executive compensation and related person disclosure. Section II.C.6. SEC Release 33-8732A § II.C.3.A. Accessed December 9, 2008. See www.sec.gov/rules/final/2006/33-8732a.pdf.

42. The Office of State Treasurer Denise L. Nappier, Press Release, "Nappier Says Four Companies Agree to Connecticut Pension Fund Resolutions, Setting New Standard for Disclosure of Executive Compensation in 2008 Proxies" (April 16, 2008). Last accessed November 11, 2010. See www.state.ct.us/ott/pressreleases/press2008/pr04162008.pdf.

43. Abercrombie & Fitch Form DEF 14A, filed with the Securities and Exchange Commission May 9, 2008.

44. Equilar, Inc., proprietary compensation and equity ownership data for fiscal years from June 2013 to May 2014.

45. Edward P. Lazear and Sherwin Rosen, "Rank-Order Tournaments as Optimum Labor Contracts," *Journal of Political Economy* 89 (1981): 841–864.

46. Moody's reviews CEO compensation as one factor contributing to a company's credit rating. The rating agency finds that large performance-based compensation packages might be indicative of lax oversight and lead to increased risk taking that ultimately increases the likelihood of corporate default. See Chris Mann, "CEO Compensation and Credit Risk," Moody's Investors Service, Global Credit Research Report No. 93592 (2005). Accessed April 7, 2015. See https://www.moodys.com/researchdocumentcontentpage.aspx?docid=pbc_93592.

47. Jayant R. Kale, Ebru Reis, and Anand Venkateswaran, "Rank-Order Tournaments and Incentive Alignment: The Effect on Firm Performance," *Journal of Finance* 64 (2009): 1479–1512.

48. Lucian A. Bebchuk, K. J. Martijn Cremers, and Urs C. Peyer, "The CEO Pay Slice," *Journal of Financial Economics* 102 (2011): 199–221.

49. Omesh Kini and Ryan Williams, "Tournament Incentives, Firm Risk, and Corporate Policies," *Journal of Financial Economics* 103 (2012): 350–376.

50. Cerner Corporation, Form DEF 14A, filed with the Securities and Exchange Commission April 10, 2014.

51. E.I. du Pont de Nemours and Company, Form DEF 14A, filed with the Securities and Exchange Commission March 14, 2014.

52. Gretchen Morgenson, "Explaining (or Not) Why the Boss Is Paid So Much," *New York Times* (January 25, 2004): BU.1.

53. See Congressional Research Service, cited in Carol Hymowitz, "Pay Gap Fuels Worker Woes," *Wall Street Journal* (April 28, 2008, Eastern edition): B.8. Carola Frydman of Harvard University and Raven Saks of the Federal Reserve, cited in Greg Ip, "Snow Rebuts Critics of Bush's Economic Record; Treasury Chief Says Many Benefit from Expansion; Some Data Show Otherwise," *Wall Street Journal* (March 20, 2006, Eastern edition): A.3. Institute for Policy Studies, cited in Phred Dvorak, "Theory & Practice—Limits on Executive Pay: Easy to Set, Hard to Keep," *Wall Street Journal* (April 9, 2007): B.1. Towers Perrin (now Towers Watson), cited in Gretchen Morgenson AFL-CIO, "Executive Paywatch" (2014). Accessed January 21, 2014. See http://www.aflcio.org/corporate-watch/paywatch-2014.

54. Steve Crawford, Karen K. Nelson, and Brian Rountree, "The CEO–Employee Pay Ratio," *Social Science Research Network* (2014). Accessed February 23, 2015. See http://ssrn.com/abstract=2529112.

55. Whole Foods, Form DEF 14A, filed with the Securities and Exchange Commission January 10, 2014.

56. Kenneth A. Merchant and Jean-Francois Manzoni, "The Achievability of Budget Targets in Profit Centers: A Field Study," *Accounting Review* 64 (1989): 539–558.

57. Raffi J. Indjejikian, Peter Lenk, and Dhananjay Nanda, "Targets, Standards, and Performance Expectations: Evidence from Annual Bonus Plans," *Social Science Research Network* (2000). Accessed October 16, 2008. See http://ssrn.com/abstract=213628.

58. Chen, Cheng, Lo, and Wang (2015) found that contractual protections such as employment and severance agreements can counteract managerial tendencies toward short-termism. See Xia Chen, Qiang Cheng, Alvis K. Lo, and Xin Wang, "CEO Contractual Protection and Managerial Short-Termism," *Accounting Review* (forthcoming September 2015).

59. Paul M. Healy, "The Effect of Bonus Schemes on Accounting Decisions," *Journal of Accounting and Economics* 7 (1985): 85–107. Robert W. Holthausen, David F. Larcker, and Richard G. Sloan, "Annual Bonus Schemes and the Manipulation of Earnings," *Journal of Accounting and Economics* 19 (1995): 29–74.

60. Northrop Grumman, Form DEF 14A, filed with the Securities and Exchange Commission April 4, 2014.

61. Long-term performance plans appear to have a positive impact on managerial behavior and firm performance. For example, Larcker (1983) found that managers are likely to increase long-term capital investment following the adoption of a performance plan. He also found positive stock market response to the adoption of these plans, indicating that shareholders believe that they align managerial and shareholder interests. See David F. Larcker, "The Association between Performance Plan Adoption and Corporate Capital Investment," *Journal of Accounting and Economics* 6 (1983): 3–29.

62. Shivaram Rajgopal and Terry Shevlin, "Empirical Evidence on the Relationship between Stock Option Compensation and Risk Taking," *Journal of Accounting and Economics* 33 (2002): 145–171.

63. W. M. Sanders and Donald C. Hambrick, "Swinging for the Fences: The Effects of CEO Stock Options on Company Risk Taking and Performance," *Academy of Management Journal* 50 (2007): 1055–1078.

64. David de Angelis and Yaniv Grinstein, "Performance Terms in CEO Compensation Contracts," *Review of Finance* (2014): 1–33.

65. Raghuram G. Rajan and Julie Wulf, "Are Perks Purely Managerial Excess?" *Journal of Financial Economics* 79 (2006): 1–33.

66. Rangarajan K. Sundaram and David L. Yermack, "Pay Me Later: Inside Debt and Its Role in Managerial Compensation," *Journal of Finance* 62 (2007): 1551–1588.

67. David Yermack, "Flights of Fancy: Corporate Jets, CEO Perquisites, and Inferior Shareholder Returns," *Journal of Financial Economics* 80 (2006): 211–242.

68. Yaniv Grinstein, David Weinbaum, and Nir Yehuda, "The Economic Consequences of Perk Disclosure," Johnson School Research Paper, Series No. 04-09, AFA 2011 Denver Meetings Paper, *Social Science Research Network* (2010). Accessed October 24, 2010. See http://ssrn.com/abstract=1108707.

69. Erik Beucler and Jack Dolmat-Connell, "Pay Disclosure Rules: Has More Become Less?" *Corporate Board* 28 (2007): 1–5.

70. RR Donnelly, Equilar, and the Rock Center for Corporate Governance at Stanford University, "2015 Investor Survey: Deconstructing Proxies—What Matters to Investors" (2015). Accessed May 5, 2015. See http://www.gsb.stanford.edu/faculty-research/centers-initiatives/cgri/research/surveys.

71. Amgen Inc., Form DEF 14A, filed with the Securities and Exchange Commission April 3, 2014.

72. Amgen, Executive Compensation Survey. Accessed November 11, 2010. See www.amgen.com/executivecompensation/exec_comp_form_survey.jsp.

73. Semler Brossy Consulting Group, LLC., "Year End Say on Pay Report" (2014). Accessed February 24, 2015. See http://www.semlerbrossy.com/sayonpay.

74. Equilar Inc., "CEO Pay Strategies Report" (2014). Accessed February 18, 2015. See www.equilar.com.

75. Yonca Ertimur, Fabrizio Ferri, and Volkan Muslu, "Shareholder Activism and CEO Pay," *Review of Financial Studies* 24 (2011): 535–592.

76. Jie Cai and Ralph A. Walkling, "Shareholders' Say on Pay: Does It Create Value?" *Journal of Financial and Quantitative Analysis* 46 (2011): 299–339.

77. Fabrizio Ferri and D. Maber, "Say on Pay Votes and CEO Compensation: Evidence from the United Kingdom," *Review of Finance* 17 (2013): 527–563.

78. David F. Larcker, Gaizka Ormazabal, and Daniel J. Taylor, "The market reaction to corporate governance regulation," *Journal of Financial Economics* 101 (2011): 431–448.

79. RR Donnelly, Equilar, and the Rock Center for Corporate Governance at Stanford University (2015).

9

Executive Equity Ownership

In this chapter, we examine the relationship between equity ownership and executive behavior. In theory, executives who hold equity in the companies they manage—either directly in the form of stock ownership or indirectly through options, restricted stock, and performance shares—have greater incentive to improve the economic value of the firm. In addition, equity holdings dissuade self-interested behavior, in that any action the executive takes that impairs firm value will inflict corresponding damage to the executive's personal wealth (although not on a "dollar-for-dollar" basis, given that executives are also compensated in forms other than equity). As a result, equity ownership is an important tool that companies use to mitigate agency problems.

At the same time, concern exists that equity ownership might foster undesirable behaviors. Examples include "excessive" risk-taking and the manipulation of earnings, information, or timing of trades to boost the value of the executive's personal equity investment at the expense of shareholders. In this chapter, we examine the potentially positive and negative effects of executive equity ownership.

Equity Ownership and Firm Performance

Executives who have been in their position for a number of years tend to accumulate a substantial investment in their companies by retaining vested equity awards or buying shares.

Based on a sample of the 4,000 largest publicly traded U.S. companies, the median CEO holds an equity position in his or her company with a value of $14.9 million (see Table 9.1). Equity ownership levels vary with company size. Among the largest 100 companies, the median CEO holds equity wealth valued at $104.9 million. Among the smallest 1,000 companies in this sample, median wealth is $3.5 million.

As Table 9.1 also shows, the average value of CEO equity wealth is significantly larger than the average value of annual compensation. This means that for a typical executive, the incentives provided by the equity holdings are at least as important and often dominate the incentives provided by annual compensation. As a result, a typical executive considers how decisions potentially affect *total wealth* and not just one year's pay.[1]

One way to measure the incentive value of wealth is by calculating its sensitivity to changes in stock price. For example, the median CEO in Table 9.1 stands to gain roughly $193,000 in wealth if the stock price increases 1 percent, $9.9 million if the stock price increases 50 percent, and $20.3 million if the stock price doubles. These dollar amounts give considerable incentive to perform.

Table 9.1 CEO Equity Wealth and Sensitivity to Change in Stock Price (Median Values)

Firms (Grouped by Size)	Median Market Cap ($ millions)	Median Total Expected CEO Pay ($)	Total CEO Wealth ($)	Change in Wealth (for % change in stock price)		
				1% Change	50% Change	100% Change
Top 100	$103,493	$12,335,000	$104,912,000	1.53%	79.10%	160.39%
				$1,556,000	$85,535,000	$176,985,000
101 to 500	$18,895	$6,672,000	$59,922,000	1.47%	77.26%	157.12%
				$922,000	$47,470,000	$95,549,000
501 to 1,000	$6,383	$4,132,000	$34,337,000	1.35%	69.85%	1.41%
				$486,000	$25,500,000	$52,131,000
1,001 to 2,000	$2,085	$2,511,000	$22,300,000	1.28%	65.70%	133.33%
				$310,000	$16,645,000	$33,390,000
2,001 to 3,000	$642	$1,542,000	$10,445,000	1.20%	61.77%	125.12%
				$135,000	$6,923,000	$14,235,000
3,001 to 4,000	$161	$828,000	$3,470,000	1.17%	60.03%	122.28%
				$43,000	$2,218,000	$4,534,000
1 to 4,000	$1,070	$1,931,000	$14,946,000	1.25%	64.15%	130.80%
				$193,000	$9,907,000	$20,332,000

Due to missing observations, the samples in Table 8.2 and Table 9.1 differ slightly. Calculations exclude personal wealth outside company stock. Total CEO compensation and total CEO wealth are rounded to the nearest thousand dollars. Total CEO compensation is the sum of salary, annual bonus, expected value of stock options granted, expected value of restricted stock granted, target value of performance plan grants, and other annual compensation. Calculations for compensation exclude changes in pension. Stock options are valued using the Black–Scholes pricing model, with the remaining option term reduced by 30% to compensate for potential early exercise or termination and volatility based on actual results from the previous year.

Source: Equilar, proprietary compensation and equity ownership data for fiscal years from June 2013 to May 2014.

Research generally supports the notion that equity ownership is positively associated with firm performance. Morck, Shleifer, and Vishny (1988) found that equity ownership by the CEO is positively correlated with firm value, measured by market-to-book value ratios. However, the positive correlation only holds in their study at low (less than 5 percent) and high (greater than 25 percent) ownership levels.[2]

McConnell and Servaes (1990) found a positive relationship between equity ownership and firm value across a larger array of ownership levels, up to between 40 and 50 percent.[3]

Elsilä, Kallunki, and Nilsson (2013) measured equity incentives in terms of the personal wealth the executive has in the company (as a percentage of total wealth) rather than in terms of the percentage of the company the executive owns. Using this approach, they found that the ratio of CEO ownership to personal wealth is positively correlated with both firm performance and firm value.[4]

Finally, Lilienfeld-Toal and Ruenzi (2014) found that firms with high CEO ownership levels deliver higher stock market returns than firms with low managerial ownership. They concluded that "owner-CEOs are value increasing [in that] they reduce empire building and run their firms more efficiently."[5]

These studies suggest that managerial incentives are higher and might be more closely aligned with the interests of shareholders when executives have "skin in the game." To encourage these effects, many companies adopt equity ownership guidelines for the senior management team (see the following sidebar).

Target Ownership Plans

A target ownership plan requires that an executive own a minimum amount of company stock. The limit is generally expressed as a multiple of the annual salary and varies among executive officers, depending on their seniority. For example, in 2014, Abbott Laboratories required that CEO Miles White hold stock and options with a value equal to six times his base salary of $1.9 million. Executive and senior vice presidents were required to hold three times base salary, and all other officers two times.[6]

According to Equilar, 89 percent of the largest 100 companies in the United States have executive stock ownership guidelines. Approximately four-fifths of these guidelines are expressed as a multiple of base salary. The remainder are expressed either as a fixed number of shares or as a retention approach, in which executives are required to retain a certain percentage of shares or options as they vest each year.[7]

Researchers find generally positive benefits from the adoption of target ownership plans. For example, Core and Larcker (2002) measured the performance of 195 companies that first adopted target ownership plans. The study found that, before plan adoption, executives in the sample had low levels of direct equity ownership, and the firms had inferior stock price performance relative to peers. Following plan adoption, these companies experienced a significant improvement in subsequent operating performance and stock price performance. The authors cautioned that causality is difficult to determine.[8]

Equity Ownership and Risk

Equity ownership not only provides incentive for performance but also encourages *risk taking*. As we discussed in greater detail in Chapter 6, "Strategy, Performance Measurement, and Risk Management," some degree of risk taking is required for a company to generate returns in excess of its cost of capital. It is the responsibility of the board of directors to determine a company's risk tolerance and establish a compensation program consistent with this view of risk.

The composition of an executive's equity portfolio plays a considerable role in determining his or her appetite for risk. An executive whose wealth consists entirely of direct stock investments—either restricted shares or shares that have vested but not been sold—stands to gain or lose wealth dollar-for-dollar with changes in the stock price. Many boards like this arrangement because it is seen as putting the executive on equal footing with the average investor. However, one important distinction remains: while the average investor holds shares as part of a diversified portfolio, the typical executive has a large, concentrated exposure to a single stock and therefore is exposed to greater personal financial risk. As a result, executives have a tendency to become risk averse, and over time, this can reduce performance. Researchers have shown that some executives decline to pursue new projects that would otherwise be valuable to well-diversified shareholders (that is, projects with positive net present value) because they have more at stake in the event of a loss than those shareholders.[9]

Stock options can be used to counteract risk aversion. The intrinsic value of stock options is a nonlinear function of share price. The value moves dollar-for-dollar with stock price when the option is "in the money" (when the stock price is above the exercise price), but the value is unaffected by stock price when the option is "out of the money" (when the stock price is below the exercise price). This introduces "convexity" into the executive's potential payoff and encourages risk taking (see the following sidebar). As such, stock options are used to encourage managers to become less risk averse by investing in higher-risk, higher-return projects.

Sensitivity of CEO Wealth to Stock Price

Consider the relationship between pay, performance, and risk incentives for a series of direct competitors in 2009:

- **Food companies**—The CEO of General Mills had convexity in his compensation of 2.98, and the CEO of Kraft had convexity of 1.18. However, the CEO of General Mills was newly appointed to the position. Although it can be appropriate to use options to help a CEO build wealth in the company at a faster rate, will a more aggressive compensation structure simultaneously, and perhaps undesirably, impact company strategy and risk (see Figure 9.1)?

- **Pharmaceutical companies**—The CEOs of Johnson & Johnson and Abbott Laboratories had higher convexity in their compensation (2.26 and 2.13, respectively) than the CEOs of Pfizer and Merck (1.78 and 1.67). Does a diversified healthcare model require more risk taking than a pure-play pharmaceutical model (see Figure 9.2)?

- **Regulated utilities**—As shown in Figure 9.3, if the stock price of Southern Company increased by 100 percent, the CEO of the company's Georgia Power division would realize a 235 percent increase in "wealth" (a ratio of 2.35). By comparison, the ratio at Exelon's ComEd division was 1.23. Compensation at Southern Company therefore seemed to encourage more risk taking. Under what circumstances is it appropriate for a public utility to engage in risky activities?

The board should consider the total effects (upside and downside) of investment decisions on the executive's wealth.

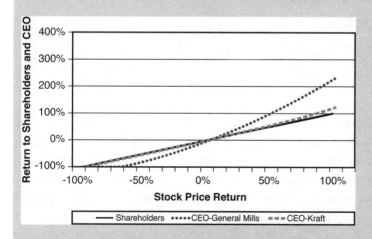

Figure 9.1 Relationship between CEO wealth and stock price: General Mills versus Kraft.

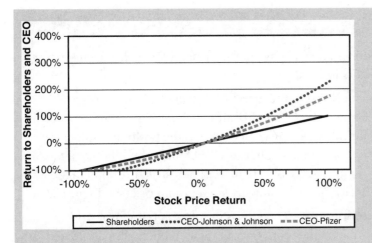

Figure 9.2 Relationship between CEO wealth and stock price: Johnson & Johnson versus Pfizer.

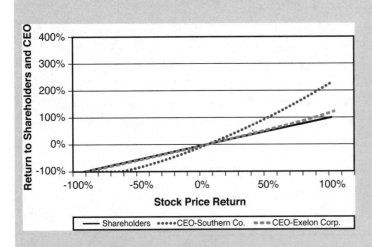

Figure 9.3 Relationship between CEO wealth and stock price: Exelon versus Southern Co.

Research generally shows that executives facing "convex" payoff curves engage in more risk taking. Coles, Daniel, and Naveen (2006) found that executives with large stock option exposure spend more money on research and development, reduce firm diversification, and increase firm leverage—all actions that increase the risk profile of the firm.[10] In the same vein, Gormley, Matsa, and Milbourn (2013) found that a reduction in stock option exposure is associated with a reduction in risk. Managers with less convex payoffs decrease leverage, reduce research and development, hold larger cash balances, and engage in more diversifying acquisitions.[11] Armstrong and Vashishtha (2012) demonstrated that stock options give CEOs incentive to increase systemic risk (which can be hedged through financial instruments) but not idiosyncratic (firm-specific) risk.[12] Kim, Li, and Zhang (2011) found that companies whose chief financial officers have considerable stock option exposure in their equity holdings have a greater risk of a stock price crash (defined as a one-week stock return 3.2 standard deviations below the mean).[13]

The issue of whether stock options might be related to "excessive" risk taking is an important consideration for boards and shareholders when deciding on executive compensation packages. Congress and the media coined the term ***excessive risk taking*** following the financial crisis of 2008. Unfortunately, no standard litmus test exists to distinguish an excessive risk from an acceptable risk. An excessive risk might be one whose downside is so large that the firm cannot financially bear it (see the following sidebar).

Executive Compensation and the Financial Crisis of 2008

Did the structure of executive compensation contracts cause the financial crisis of 2008? Conventional wisdom says yes. For example, a 2009 survey by KPMG found that 52 percent of senior managers at large financial institutions believe that "incentives and remuneration" were most at fault in contributing to the credit crisis.[14] Similarly, a 2008 PricewaterhouseCoopers survey of financial services professionals found that the three most frequently cited factors that created the conditions for the crisis were "culture and excessive risk-taking" (73 percent), "mispricing of risk" (73 percent), and "rewards systems" (70 percent).[15]

This line of reasoning has also been put forth by prominent economists and policymakers. According to former Federal Reserve Chairman Ben Bernanke, "Compensation practices at some banking organizations have led to misaligned incentives and excess risk-taking, contributing to bank losses and financial instability."[16] In Congressional testimony, former Treasury Secretary Timothy Geithner argued, "Although many things caused this crisis, what happened to compensation and incentives in creative risk-taking did contribute in some institutions to the vulnerability that we saw in this financial crisis."[17] Economist and former Federal Reserve Vice Chairman Alan Blinder blamed the crisis on "the perverse incentives built into the compensation plans of many financial firms, incentives that encourage excessive risk-taking with other people's money."[18]

The research evidence is less conclusive. Larcker, Ormazabal, Tayan, and Taylor (2014) demonstrated a significant increase in risk-taking incentives among banks prior to the financial crisis, particularly banks that originated and distributed the securitized assets that were central to the crisis. By 2006, the sensitivity of CEO wealth to stock price volatility at the average securitizing bank was *15-fold* higher than it had been in 1992 and quadruple that of the average nonbank CEO (see Figure 9.4). This suggests that incentives likely played a role in the crisis.[19] DeYoung, Peng, and Yan (2013) found similar results.[20]

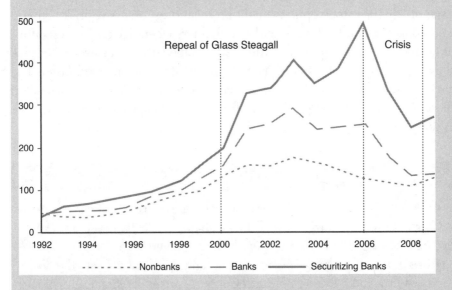

Note: Plot of average portfolio vega by year for all CEOs on ExecuComp with non-missing data. Portfolio vega (in thousands) is calculated as the sensitivity of the CEO's equity portfolio to a 0.01 change in stock volatility and is expressed in units of $1,000. The term "Banks" refers to bank holding companies (132 unique banks), "Securitizing Banks" refers to "Banks" with at least six quarters of nonzero securitized assets (58 unique banks), and "Nonbanks" refers to all other firms (3,232 unique firms). Section 20 of the Glass–Steagall Act was repealed by the Gramm-Leach-Bliley Financial Modernization Act in November 1999; effective March 2000, bank holding companies were allowed to expand the issuance of asset-backed securities.

Source: Larcker, Ormazabal, Tayan, and Taylor (2014).

Figure 9.4   Risk-taking incentives prior to the financial crisis.

Fahlenbrach and Stultz (2011), however, found no evidence that greater sensitivity of bank CEO wealth to stock volatility led to worse performance during the crisis. They posited that "CEOs focused on the interests of their shareholders in the buildup to the crisis and took actions that they believed the market would welcome. Ex post, these actions were costly to their banks and to themselves when the results turned out to be poor."[21]

To temper "excessive" risk-seeking behavior, the compensation committee might alter the mix of stock and options granted to the CEO with the intention of reducing the CEO's personal financial exposure to stock price volatility. However, the board should be mindful that such an approach will also substantially reduce performance incentives. The SEC now requires that companies discuss the relationship between compensation plans and organizational risk in the Compensation Discussion & Analysis section of the annual proxy (see the following sidebar).

Disclosure on Compensation and Risk

Ameriprise Financial

"After discussion with management and the committee's independent compensation consultant, the committee has concluded that our incentive compensation arrangements and practices do not create risks that are reasonably likely to have a material adverse effect on the Company.

"The Committee reached this conclusion after considering a number of features of our incentive compensation structure that are designed to mitigate risk, including but not limited to:

- We use different types of compensation vehicles that provide a balance of long- and short-term incentives and of fixed and variable features, with an emphasis on long-term performance (except for certain sales and sales management positions, whose competitive pay framework is more heavily short-term and where business controls are present to moderate risk);

- We set performance goals that we believe are appropriate in light of past performance and market conditions;

- Our budgeting and internal controls and procedures are sufficient to prevent the manipulation of performance results to enhance payments under incentive compensation arrangements;

- We have stock ownership, retention guidelines and holding periods for all of our senior leaders that call for significant stock ownership and align the interests of our senior leaders with the long-term interests of our shareholders;

- Our executive compensation recovery policy allows the Board of Directors to recoup from any executive officer certain cash or equity incentive compensation in the event of a material restatement of our financial results due to intentional misconduct; and

- Our chief executive officer retains the discretion to adjust plans (other than those for our named executive officers) throughout the year in response to changing business conditions or unexpected events."[22]

Moog

"In formulating and evaluating the Company's executive compensation program, the Executive Compensation Committee considers whether the program promotes excessive risk taking. The Executive Compensation Committee believes the components of the Company's executive compensation program provide an appropriate mix of fixed and variable pay; balance short-term operational performance with long-term increases in shareholder value; reinforce a performance-oriented environment; and encourage recruitment and retention of key executives.

"The Executive Compensation Committee of the Board of Directors has followed consistent practices over the years. Over those years, the members of the Committee have not seen any evidence that our Compensation Programs have had a material adverse effect on our Company. The Company's performance has been consistent, with year over year earnings per share increases of 10% or more in seventeen of the last twenty years. During the last ten years, compound annual growth in earnings per share has been 10.7%. The Directors view this performance as persuasive evidence that the leadership of the Company is not provided with incentives which would result in leadership taking unreasonable risks in order to achieve short term results at the expense of the long term health and welfare of the shareholders' investment."[23]

Equity Ownership and Agency Costs

Equity ownership is intended to provide incentives that motivate managers to improve corporate performance, but it also has the potential to encourage undesirable behaviors. This occurs when an executive seeks to increase the value of equity holdings in ways other than through improvements in operating, financing, and investment decisions. Examples include these:

- Manipulating accounting results to inflate stock price or achieve bonus targets
- Manipulating the timing of option grants to increase their intrinsic value
- Manipulating the release of information to the public to correspond with more favorable grant dates
- Using inside information to gain an advantage in selling or otherwise hedging equity holdings

When these actions occur, they represent the very agency costs that equity ownership is intended to discourage.

Accounting Manipulation

As discussed more completely in the Chapter 10, "Financial Reporting and External Audit," plenty of evidence shows that accounting manipulations occur. Consider these prominent examples:

- Enron, which front-loaded revenues and hid liabilities through off-balance-sheet vehicles
- WorldCom, which capitalized expenses on the balance sheet that should have been treated as operating costs
- Royal Dutch Shell, which inflated the size and value of proved oil reserves

An important question for boards and shareholders is whether such manipulations are *more likely* to occur in companies where executives own a large portion of company stock than in companies where executives own little or no stock. That is, do executives with considerable equity ownership inflate earnings to manipulate the market and produce a higher stock price?

The research evidence on this topic is mixed. For example, Harris and Bromiley (2007) found that financial restatements are more likely to occur at companies where executives are paid a large portion of compensation in the form of options.[24] However, Baber, Kang, Liang, and Zhu (2013) found no such evidence.[25] Johnson, Ryan, and Tian (2009) found that unrestricted equity holdings by executives are associated with a greater incidence of accounting fraud.[26] Erickson, Hanlon, and Maydew (2006) did not find this association.[27] Armstrong, Jagolinzer, and Larcker (2010) also found no evidence that equity incentives are associated with accounting restatements, SEC enforcement actions, or shareholder litigation.[28]

The mixed results are due in part to study design. As noted earlier in this chapter, an executive holding a large equity portfolio has conflicting incentives. Equity holdings encourage an executive to increase value, but they also discourage risk taking. These incentives work at cross-purposes. However, a sudden change in the composition of wealth, such as through a large stock option grant, unambiguously encourages performance and risk. To this end, Armstrong, Larcker, Ormazabal, and Taylor (2013) found strong evidence that an increase in the sensitivity of CEO wealth to stock price volatility is positively associated with financial misreporting. According to the authors, "The results suggest that equity portfolios provide managers with incentives to misreport not because they tie the manager's wealth to equity value but because they tie the manager's wealth to equity risk."[29]

As a result, shareholders and stakeholders should be cognizant of the potential for self-gain that comes through accounting manipulation ("cooking the books"). The potential for this problem seems to be most pronounced when executives have highly convex compensation plans.

Manipulation of Equity Grants

Equity ownership might also encourage executives to manipulate equity grants in order to extract incremental value. This might occur in at least two ways:

- **Manipulating the timing of the grant**—The grant date either is delayed so that it occurs after a stock price decline has already taken place or is brought forward to precede an expected increase in stock price.
- **Manipulating the timing of information released to the public**—The release of favorable information about the company (a new product, a new strategic relationship, stronger-than-expected sales) is delayed so that it occurs after a scheduled grant date; the executive benefits from an immediate increase in value when the favorable information is released. Likewise, unfavorable information is released early, to precede a grant date; the executive benefits by receiving the grant after the unfavorable news has already driven the stock price lower.

In both cases, the executive seeks to maximize the value received from an equity grant by taking actions that are not in the interests of shareholders.

When equity awards are granted on a purely random basis, no discernable pattern emerges in the stock price movement around the grant date. Stock price movements appear random, and the relative favorability of the timing of the grant tends to be unpredictable. Many grants fit this pattern. However, at some companies, stock price movements follow a discernable pattern around the grant date. The grant either coincides with a relative low or immediately precedes a sudden increase in price, resulting in a V-shaped pattern.

Considerable research shows that such patterns occur for a large sample of firms. Yermack (1997) demonstrated a V-shaped pattern around stock option grant dates. Stock prices in that sample mirrored the market before option grant dates, but then exhibited above-market returns in the 50 days following the grant dates. Yermack concluded that some sort of manipulation took place, through either the release of information or the timing of grants, but he was unable to conclusively determine which.[30]

To test the hypothesis that executives might manipulate the release of information, Aboody and Kasznik (2000) examined stock price behavior around *scheduled* option grants. Scheduled option grants include those for which the option grants follow a predetermined schedule (for example, they might be regularly awarded the day after a board meeting). Their findings are similar to those of Yermack (1997). The authors concluded that executives might opportunistically time the release of company information to the market around grant dates.[31]

Lie (2005) tested a hypothesis that executives manipulate the timing of awards in their favor. He divided the sample into companies whose grants were clearly unscheduled (with the grant date made at the discretion of the board) and those whose grants were scheduled. Lie found that the V-shape pattern around *unscheduled* grants was more pronounced (see Figure 9.5). He posited that insiders were retroactively changing the grant date of unscheduled awards to lower the exercise price and increase profits to executives. This practice is now known as **stock option backdating** (see the following sidebar).[32]

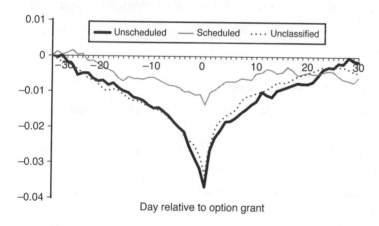

Day relative to option grant

Source: Erik Lie (2005). Reproduced with permission of the Institute for Operations Research and Management Sciences in the format Tradebook via Copyright Clearance Center.

Figure 9.5   Stock price movements around scheduled and unscheduled grant dates.

Stock Option Backdating

The *Wall Street Journal* reported the findings of Lie (2005) in a front-page article. The story soon triggered a wide-ranging investigation by the Securities and Exchange Commission (SEC). The article suggested that dozens of companies might be engaged in backdating.[33] By the end of 2006, more than 120 companies had been implicated.[34] In a separate study, Bebchuk, Grinstein, and Peyer (2010) estimated that the practice was much more prevalent, occurring in approximately 12 percent of companies.[35] Although retroactive manipulation largely stopped with the passage of the Sarbanes–Oxley Act, which required that option grants to executives be reported within two days, alleged abuses have been uncovered stemming back as far as 1981. Still, it has been difficult for U.S. regulators to convict executives who were shown to engage in the practice.

Bernile and Jarrell (2009) found that the cost of backdating (in terms of reduced shareholder value) was well in excess of the associated fines and legal fees. Furthermore, backdating reflected a serious lapse in oversight by boards of directors.[36]

Other Examples of Value Extraction through Timing

Other practices that represent attempts to extract additional value from equity grants include these:

- **Spring-loading**—Awarding options immediately before the release of unexpected positive news that is likely to drive up the price of a stock
- **Bullet-dodging**—Waiting to award options until after the release of unexpected negative news that is likely to drive down the price of a stock
- **Exercise backdating**—Retroactively changing the exercise date of stock options to a date when the market price was lower in order to reduce the reported taxable gain that the option holder would have to pay at an ordinary income tax level[37]

In some instances, these actions result in only marginal increases in value for executives.[38] In others, the dollar amounts can be significant. Regardless, they run counter to the concept of stewardship and demonstrate that some executives will take advantage of weaknesses in oversight for personal gain.[39]

Equity Sales and Insider Trading

Executives can diversify their equity holdings by making open-market sales of company stock or by exercising stock options and selling the acquired shares. However, because executives have access to nonpublic information that could be material to valuing the company's stock, there is always a possibility that executives will use this information to gain an improper trading advantage over public shareholders.

The SEC has established rules that dictate when and how sales by executives may occur. The SEC uses the term **insider** to identify individuals—corporate officers, directors, employees, and certain professional advisors—who have access to material financial and operational information about a company that has not yet been made public. Insiders are restricted in their ability to engage in transactions involving company securities (both purchases and sales) and may trade only when they are not in possession of material nonpublic information. Trades made on the basis of such information are considered illegal **insider trading** and, under various acts passed by Congress, are punishable with jail time and financial penalties (up to three times the profit gained or loss avoided from such activity).[40]

Insider trading lawsuits are prosecuted, in part, under SEC Rule 10b-5, "Employment of Manipulative and Deceptive Devices."[41] Prosecutors argue that the insider has committed fraud on the market by making false statements regarding the prospects of the company or by failing to make appropriate disclosures, thereby maintaining an artificially high share price at the time of sale. For example, in 2007, the SEC charged Joseph Nacchio, former chairman and chief executive officer of Qwest, with insider trading. He was accused of selling more than $100 million of Qwest shares in early 2001 while in possession of material inside information that the company would not meet aggressive financial targets. Qwest shares, which Nacchio sold at approximately $35 per share, subsequently fell below $10. He was sentenced to six years in prison and ordered to pay $19 million in fines and $44.6 million in forfeitures.[42]

To restrict executives from violating insider trading laws, companies typically designate a period of time known as a **blackout period**, in which insiders are restricted from making trades in the company stock. Blackout periods typically occur between the time when material information is known and the time when it is released to the public. Blackout periods are specified in the company's insider trading policy.[43] A typical blackout window has a median length of 50 calendar days.[44] Trades within the blackout period are prohibited, and trades outside the blackout period (during the **trading window**) commonly require approval in advance by the general counsel's office. Jagolinzer, Larcker, and Taylor (2011) found that requiring general counsel approval prior to trading reduces the likelihood that executives gain a trading advantage over public shareholders (see the following sidebar).[45]

Trading Window

Crimson Exploration

"You may not trade in Company securities outside of a trading window. For purposes of this policy, a 'trading window' will commence after the close of trading two full trading days following the Company's widespread public release of quarterly operating results and ending at the close of trading on the last day of the second month of the current fiscal quarter. . . . During a trading window, you may trade in Company securities only after obtaining the approval of the Compliance Officer. If you decide to engage in a transaction involving Company securities during a trading window, you must notify the Compliance Officer in writing of the amount and nature of the proposed trade(s) at least two business days prior to the proposed transaction, and certify in writing that you are not in possession of material nonpublic information concerning the Company. You must not engage in the transaction unless and until the Compliance Officer provides his approval in writing."[46]

Despite these restrictions, extensive evidence indicates that executives rely on nonpublic information to guide their trading. Lakonishok and Lee (2001) found that open-market purchases of company stock by insiders are predictive of future price increases. The effects are particularly pronounced among small-capitalization companies.[47] Seyhun (1986) found both that insider stock purchases tend to precede a period of market outperformance and that sales tend to precede a period of underperformance. Insiders with access to more valuable information about the firm (such as the chairman or the CEO) are found to have a greater trading advantage than other insiders.[48] These and other studies suggest that insiders can earn substantial returns over a period of up to three years.[49]

Rule 10b5-1

The SEC adopted Rule 10b5-1 in 2000 to protect insiders whose position regularly exposes them to important nonpublic information. According to the agency:

As a practical matter, in most situations it is highly doubtful that a person who knows inside information relevant to the value of a security can completely disregard that knowledge when making the decision to purchase or sell that security. In the words of the Second Circuit, "material information cannot lay idle in the human brain." Indeed, even if the trader could put forth purported reasons for trading other than awareness of the inside information, other traders in the market place would clearly perceive him or her to possess an unfair advantage. On the other hand, we recognize that an absolute standard based on knowing possession, or awareness, could be overbroad in some respects. Sometimes a person may reach a decision to make a particular trade without any awareness of material nonpublic information, but then come into possession of such information before the trade actually takes place.[50]

To protect executives in such a situation, the SEC adopted Rule 10b5-1 ("Trading 'on the Basis of' Material Nonpublic Information in Insider Trading Cases"), which outlines a set of procedures that, if followed, provide an "affirmative defense" against alleged violations of insider trading laws.[51]

Under Rule 10b5-1, insiders are allowed to enter into a binding contract that instructs a third-party broker to execute purchase or sales transactions on behalf of the insider (**10b5-1 plans**). The contract can be agreed to only during a period in which the insider does not have knowledge of material nonpublic information (that is, outside the blackout window). The insider is required to specify a program or an algorithm that dictates the conditions under which sales are to be made; such factors might include the number of shares, the interval between transactions, or a share price limit. After the third-party broker receives his or her instructions, the insider is not allowed to exercise any influence over the execution of the plan. From that point forward, the third-party broker has sole discretion, although the executive may amend or terminate the plan at any time (see the following sidebar).[52]

Approximately 80 percent of companies permit executives to trade using 10b5-1 plans.[53] Approval by the general counsel is generally required in advance: Seventy-three percent of companies require such approval to set up a plan, and 59 percent require approval to modify or cancel a plan.[54] Insiders are not required to disclose to the public that they have entered into a 10b5-1 plan (although they are required to disclose each trade on a Form 4).

10b5-1 Disclosures

Datalink Corporation

"On February 13, 2006, our Chairman, Greg R. Meland, established a pre-arranged, personal stock trading plan under SEC Rule 10b5-1 (the 'Plan') to sell a portion of his holdings of our Common Stock. Mr. Meland has advised us that he intends to use proceeds from sales under his Plan to diversify his personal investments. The Plan covers the sale of up to 120,000 shares over a one-year period. Subject to a minimum $3.00 per share price, Mr. Meland's broker will make sales under the Plan of up to 30,000 shares per month. Sales will take place only during the first ten business days of the month. Following completion of the planned sales, and assuming the broker sells all of the shares subject to the Plan, Mr. Meland will continue to own 3,330,690 shares of our Common Stock."[55]

McDATA Corporation

"On May 8, 2002, John A. Kelley, Jr., McDATA's President and COO, entered into a Rule 10b5-1 Stock Purchase Plan with Deutsche Bank Alex Brown to purchase $20,000 worth of McDATA Class B Common Stock on each of the following dates: May 29, 2002; June 26, 2002; July 31, 2002; August 28, 2002; and September 25, 2002, for an aggregate total amount of purchases equal to $100,000."[56]

Research indicates that Rule 10b5-1 might not be achieving the outcome that the SEC envisioned. Jagolinzer (2009) found that insiders who execute sales through 10b5-1 plans outperform the market by an average of 6 percent over the six months following each trade. Moreover, the returns earned by executives using 10b5-1 plans are substantially higher than trades made without such plans. Finally, he found that sales transactions by plan participants systematically precede periods of underperformance by the company's share price and that early terminations of 10b5-1 sales plans systematically precede periods of outperformance.[57]

To minimize insider abuse of 10b5-1 plans, experts recommend that companies adopt strict and transparent procedures to govern their use.

Hedging

An executive might decide to **hedge** the value of his or her equity holdings rather than engage in an outright sale of shares or options. A decision to hedge is often the result of discussion with a personal investment advisor and could be motivated by diversification, tax planning, or a variety of other objectives. Hedging might also allow an executive to avoid the public scrutiny that comes from a substantial sale of company shares.

At the same time, obvious problematic issues are related to executive hedging. First, hedging unwinds equity incentives that the board intended to align the interests of management with those of shareholders. Second, allowing an executive to hedge is costly to the company. Management demands larger compensation for receiving risky equity incentives instead of risk-free cash compensation. Through hedging, however, the executive can translate the value of that premium to cash. This results in a higher compensation bill for the company.[58] Third, explaining to shareholders why it is in their interest to allow executives to hedge is exceedingly difficult. Hedging requires the executive to take a "short" position in the company's shares. Although it is illegal for an executive to short-sell, it is permissible to buy a put option on company stock. For obvious reasons, the compensation committee and the entire board need to discuss and define the circumstances under which hedging is permissible.

According to data from Institutional Shareholder Services (ISS), 54 percent of companies in the Russell 3000 and 84 percent of companies in the S&P 500 have a policy prohibiting executives from hedging.[59] Bettis, Bizjak, and Kalpathy (2013) found hedging transactions by 1,181 executives at 911 firms between 1996 and 2006.[60] The most common techniques for hedging are zero-cost collars and prepaid variable forward contracts (see the following sidebar).[61]

Hedging Examples

Zero-Cost Collar

The executive purchases a put option with an exercise price at or slightly below the current market price of the stock. The executive offsets the cost of the put option by selling a call option, with an exercise price generally 10 to 20 percent above the current market price. The executive has effectively reduced the downside risk and has given up much of the upside gains. In economic substance, the collar is similar to a sale, although taxes are not owed until option expiration and the eventual stock sale. The executive can also take out a loan against the value of the collar and invest the proceeds in a diversified portfolio.

Example

In 2005, Alexander Taylor II, president and COO of Chattem, who beneficially owned approximately 200,000 shares of common stock, arranged a zero-cost collar on 50,000 shares of common stock. The collar comprised the purchase of a put option that gave Taylor the right to sell 50,000 shares at a price of $18.13 and the sale of a call option that gave the purchaser of the call the right to buy 50,000 shares at $34.48. The collar had a two-month term and expired on March 22.[62]

At the time, the company's common stock traded at a price of approximately $34. It had increased almost 80 percent, from $19 one year earlier.

Prepaid-Variable Forward (PVF)

The executive enters into a contract that promises future delivery of shares that he or she owns in company stock in return for an upfront payment of cash. Two aspects of the PVF give it its name. First, the executive prepays for stock that he or she does not have to deliver until the end of the contract (generally two to five years).

Because delivery is deferred, the cash payment is discounted from the current fair value of the stock (say, 15 percent less). The executive can take the cash payment and invest it in a diversified portfolio. As such, the payment is similar to a zero-coupon loan. The executive does not owe capital gains tax on the underlying shares until the end of the contract. Second, the forward contract is variable, in that the number of shares that the executive owes upon delivery is based on a sliding scale. If the price of the stock has fallen below some threshold, the executive is required to deliver all the shares. If the share price has risen, the executive is required to deliver only a fraction of the shares (subject to a minimum percentage defined up front). In some cases, the executive agrees to a cash payment at settlement rather than the delivery of shares. The PVF structure gives the executive full downside protection and allows for partial participation in the upside.

Example

In 2002, David Doyle, president of Quest Software, owned 12.8 million shares of company stock worth approximately $150 million.[63] In November 2002, he entered into a PVF contract with a two-year term. In the deal, he received an upfront cash payment of $9.6 million in exchange for a derivative on 1 million shares (market value $11.9 million). The derivative obligated Doyle to make delivery of shares, with the number of shares dependent upon the stock price, in January 2005:

- If stock price ≤ $10.74 (floor), 1 million shares
- If stock price between floor ($10.74) and cap ($12.88), number of shares = (floor/price) × 1 million shares
- If price > cap ($12.88), number of shares = [(stock price – cap + floor)/stock price] × 1 million shares[64]

If Doyle could earn a total return of 10 percent on the $9.6 million cash payment over two years, the pretax value of the PVF contract to Doyle would be as shown in Figure 9.6.

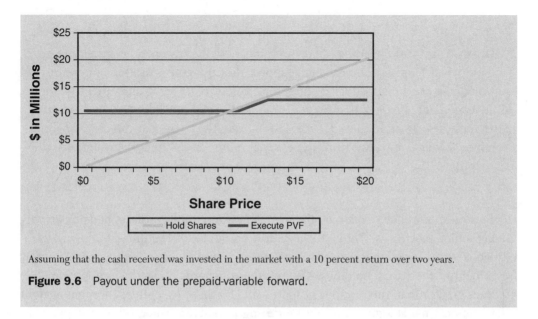

Assuming that the cash received was invested in the market with a 10 percent return over two years.

Figure 9.6 Payout under the prepaid-variable forward.

The Dodd–Frank bill requires companies to disclose whether they allow executives to hedge equity positions. Previously, this disclosure was not required. Guidelines for executive hedging (if they exist) are typically included in the insider trading policy. Companies are not required to make this policy public (see the following sidebar).

Hedging Policies and Disclosure

Delta Airlines

"As part of an update to its insider trading policy in 2012, Delta expanded and clarified prohibitions related to transactions in short-term or highly leveraged transactions. Under the updated policy, Delta prohibits employees from engaging in transactions in Delta securities involving publicly traded options, short sales, and hedging transactions because they may create the appearance of unlawful insider trading and, in certain circumstances, present a conflict of interest. In addition, Delta expanded its insider trading policy to prohibit employees from holding Delta securities in a margin account or otherwise pledging Delta securities as collateral for a loan."[65]

UnitedHealth Group

"In general, SEC rules prohibit uncovered short sales of our common stock by our executive officers, including the named executive officers. Accordingly, our insider trading policy prohibits short sales of our common stock by all employees and directors. Our insider trading policy prohibits hedging transactions by all directors and employees and requires advance approval of the compensation committee of any pledging of common stock by directors, executive officers, and other members of management. Pledges that existed prior to the policy's adoption in November 2012 have been grandfathered. In 2013, no executive officer or director sought or received advance approval from the compensation committee regarding pledging transactions."[66]

Several studies have examined the prevalence and implications of hedging activity among senior executives. Bettis, Bizjak, and Lemmon (2001) studied the use of zero-cost collars and found that executives use these transactions to hedge approximately 36 percent of their total holdings. The number of shares hedged was approximately 10 times greater than the number of shares sold by these executives through outright sales transactions. Hedges were put on during periods in which other insiders were executing a relatively high volume of sales. The authors did not, however, find evidence that executives using these transactions outperformed the market and thus concluded that hedges do not indicate trading on the basis of inside information.[67]

Jagolinzer, Matsunaga, and Yeung (2007) studied the use of prepaid-variable forward transactions. They found that the average PVF transaction hedged 30 percent of the executive's equity position. The number of shares involved in a PVF transaction was approximately 50 times larger than the number of shares sold by these same insiders in outright sales transactions during the preceding year. The authors found that PVF transactions preceded periods of abnormal stock returns and concluded that the hedges were used to protect against anticipated declines in the company stock, generally after a period of strong outperformance.[68]

Bettis, Bizjak, and Kalpathy (2013) found that executives tended to place hedges after the company share price made significant run-ups relative to the market. They also found that zero-cost collar and PVF hedges tended to precede significant declines in the company share price, which might signal that executives were acting on inside information.[69]

Pledging

Instead of selling or hedging, an executive might decide to **pledge** shares as collateral for a loan, with the proceeds used either to purchase a diversified portfolio of assets, to enter new business activities, or for personal spending. As with hedging transactions, pledging might be more tax efficient than an outright sale. The interest rate on collateralized loans might also be relatively low. In addition, the executive does not necessarily have to sell shares to settle the loan and thus may maintain a high level of ownership in the company.

At the same time, the board of directors must understand why the executive wants to pledge shares. If the proceeds of the loans are used for personal consumption (such as paying college tuition or remodeling a home), the board might decide that it has minimal impact on managerial incentives. However, what does it say about the focus and dedication of the executive if the proceeds are used to launch a new business venture or finance risky investments? What would be the impact if these activities failed and the CEO went bankrupt? Is the board willing to offset these losses with additional compensation and equity grants? Clearly, pledging transactions deserve special consideration (see the following sidebar).

Companies are required to disclose whether executives have pledged shares in a brokerage account or used them as collateral for a loan. According to survey data, approximately 20 percent of companies allow their executives to pledge shares.[70] An electronic search of available proxy statements found that 982 executive officers have pledge disclosures. The median percentage of total shares pledged was 44.4 percent. When executives pledge their shares, they tend to do so in an aggressive manner.

Executive Pledges

Chesapeake Energy

In October 2008, Aubrey McClendon, the chairman and CEO of Chesapeake Energy, was forced to sell 31.5 million shares, or 94 percent of his 5.8 percent stake in the company, to meet a margin call. Those shares had been worth $2.2 billion when McClendon bought them on margin just a few months earlier, but he sold them for only $569 million.[71]

Following the sale, the board temporarily suspended the company's stock ownership guidelines (five times annual salary plus cash bonus). The company also signed McClendon to a new five-year contract, even though he had committed to a five-year agreement in 2007. As part of the new agreement, McClendon received a cash bonus of $75 million.[72]

Continental Resources

In March 2013, Harold Hamm, chairman and CEO of Continental Resources, filed for divorce from his wife Sue Ann of 25 years. At the time, Hamm held shares valued at $11 billion, representing 68 percent of the company. As part of the settlement, Sue Ann received $975 million in cash. A few weeks later, Hamm pledged 68.7

million shares (valued at $2.4 billion) as collateral for a personal loan. In a filing with the SEC, the company noted that "the terms of the loan require the pledged shares of Common Stock to meet minimum value requirements in respect of the size of the loan, which could result in additional of Mr. Hamm's shares of Common Stock being pledged if the value of the Common Stock decreases."[73]

Oracle

An interesting example of executive pledging is Larry Ellison, CEO of Oracle, who in 2014 pledged 250,000,000 shares of Oracle common stock, valued at approximately $10 billion. This represented approximately 22 percent of his total investment in the company. It is not clear why an executive would require a loan of this amount. The company only notes in its disclosure that the shares are pledge "to secure certain personal indebtedness" and that they "are not used to shift or hedge any economic risk in owning Oracle common stock."[74]

Repricing and Exchange Offers

A **repricing** or **exchange offer** is a transaction in which employees holding stock options are allowed to exchange those options for either a new option, restricted stock, or (less frequently) cash. A company initiates an exchange offer when the exercise prices of outstanding employee stock options are above the current market price of the stock to such a large extent that it is unlikely that they will become profitable in the near term. The company offers to replace options that have very low market value with more valuable rewards to restore the incentive that employees have to pursue corporate goals.

Management typically initiates the exchange process by evaluating the profile of employee option holdings, the potential incentive and retention effects, shareholder considerations, and the cost of implementation. If shareholder approval is not required under the terms of the equity program, the board can approve and implement an exchange. If shareholder approval is required, the board must seek shareholder approval for the authority (but not the obligation) to implement an exchange. This authority expires after a specified period of time. Proposals are voted on in either the regular annual meeting or a special meeting. If the proposal is approved, the board can then decide to implement an exchange, but if market conditions change between plan inception and shareholder approval, or if there is executive or board turnover, the plan might not be implemented. In addition, employees are not required to accept an exchange offer made by the company; they have the right to retain unexercised options (both vested and unvested) if they choose to do so.

Once approved, the exchange may be made at a premium to fair value, at fair value, or at a discount to fair value (see the next sidebar):

- **Premium to fair value**—This is a straight repricing in which the exercise price of each option is reduced but no other terms of the option (including the number of shares) are changed. Alternatively, a firm may offer restricted shares worth more than the fair value of the underwater options to provide the incentive needed for employees to accept the exchange.

- **Equal to fair value**—New awards are granted so that their value is exactly equal to the fair value of underwater options. When there are multiple outstanding tranches (with varying strike prices and remaining terms), implementing a fair-value program can be difficult. For example, should all the tranches be exchanged, or only tranches that are deeply out of the money?

- **Discount to fair value**—New awards are granted so that their value is less than the fair value of the underwater options.

New awards typically change the vesting terms of the old award, and some firms require additional vesting beyond the term of the forfeited awards to extend the retention period. If fully vested options are being exchanged, a minimum level of vesting (such as six months) typically is attached to the new shares.

Exchange Offer

Citadel Broadcasting

"In the spring of 2002, the Board of Directors granted the 2002 Stock Options to [CEO Farid] Suleman in connection with his agreeing to serve as the Company's chief executive officer. The 2002 Stock Options are nonqualified stock options with a ten-year term. The options vested 25 percent at the date of grant and 25 percent over each of the next three years, and, as of March 16, 2006, the grant was fully vested and unexercised. There are approximately six years remaining on the full option term.

"On March 16, 2006, . . . the compensation committee approved the following:

- The cancellation of the 2002 Options and replacement of them with the Restricted Stock Units (RSUs)

- The cancellation of Mr. Suleman's option to purchase 400,000 shares of common stock of the Company at an exercise price of $16.94 granted to him under the Long-Term Incentive Plan on March 26, 2004

- The modification of the terms of Mr. Suleman's previously granted 1,250,000 time-vesting restricted shares . . .

- The grant to Mr. Suleman of 1,131,994 performance shares under the Long-Term Incentive Plan, which vest in two equal portions annually, beginning on March 16, 2007, and subject to the same vesting requirements as Mr. Suleman's modified restricted share grant."[75]

An exchange offer can effectively restore the incentive value of equity awards that have lost much of their value due to significant stock price declines. This is particularly true when the stock price declines are caused by general market factors (such as a recession or financial crisis) and not events that are specific to the firm (such as underperformance). Exchange offers can reduce voluntary turnover of key employees who might otherwise leave to work at other firms.

On the other hand, exchange offers might signal a culture of entitlement within the company. Frequent repricing encourages the expectation that risky incentives will pay out regardless of company performance. Repricings also put the board in the awkward position of having to explain to investors why employees should be compensated for the reduced value of their holdings when shareholders who have suffered similar losses are not. Some shareholders view exchange offers as a "giveaway" to corporate insiders.

The research results on exchange offers are somewhat mixed. Carter and Lynch (2001) found that firms reprice options as a result of company-specific (not industry-wide) performance problems. Still, they did not find evidence that exchange offers were driven by agency problems; instead, they found that exchanges were made to restore incentive value to employees and prevent turnover.[76] Chidambaran and Prabhala (2003) reached similar conclusions. They found that repricings occurred among companies with abnormally high CEO turnover, suggesting that they were not initiated by entrenched management. Furthermore, more than 40 percent of firms that repriced excluded the CEO in their exchange offers.[77]

Other studies have suggested that repricing might not benefit the firm or its stakeholders. Carter and Lynch (2004) found modest evidence that employee turnover is lower following repricing but that executive turnover is unaffected.[78] Brenner, Sundaram, and Yermack (2000) found that repricing is *negatively* correlated with subsequent firm performance, even adjusting for industry conditions.[79] Chance, Kumar, and Todd (2000) found that firms with greater agency problems, smaller size, and insider-dominated boards are more likely to reprice.[80] Finally, Callaghan, Saly, and Subramaniam (2004) found that repricings tend to precede the release of positive information about the firm or follow the release of negative information, suggesting that repricing events might be opportunistically timed to benefit insiders (similar to the manipulation of the timing of new grants).[81]

Larcker, McCall, and Ormazabal (2013) found that shareholders generally react positively to the announcement of an exchange offer but the structure of these offers are constrained by proxy advisory firms, as we discuss in Chapter 12, "Institutional Shareholders and Activist Investors."[82]

The evidence therefore suggests that exchange offers are not uniformly good or bad and that the benefits to shareholders are somewhat unclear. As such, repricing and exchange offers are controversial decisions for the board and shareholders. Although infrequent, exchange offers are a continuing issue for companies that offer equity-based compensation, particularly during bear markets.

Endnotes

1. Equilar, Inc., proprietary compensation and equity ownership data for fiscal years from June 2013 to May 2014.

2. The authors measured company performance using Tobin's Q, the ratio of market to book value. We discuss this ratio in Chapter 1, "Introduction to Corporate Governance." See Randall Morck, Andrei Shleifer, and Robert W. Vishny, "Management Ownership and Market Valuation: An Empirical Analysis," *Journal of Financial Economics* 20 (1988): 293–315.

3. John J. McConnell and Henri Servaes, "Additional Evidence on Equity Ownership and Corporate Values," *Journal of Financial Economics* 27 (1990): 595–612.

4. Anna Elsilä, Juha-Pekka Kallunki, and Henrik Nilsson, "CEO Personal Wealth, Equity Incentives, and Firm Performance," *An International Review* 21 (2013): 26–41.

5. Ulf von Lilienfeld-Toal and Stefan Ruenzi, "CEO Ownership, Stock Market Performance, and Managerial Discretion," *Journal of Finance* 69 (2014): 1013–1050.

6. Abbott Laboratories, Form DEF 14A, filed with the Securities and Exchange Commission March 14, 2014.

7. Equilar, Inc., "Executive Stock Ownership Guidelines Report" (2013). Accessed March 3, 2015. See www.equilar.com.

8. John E. Core and David F. Larcker, "Performance Consequences of Mandatory Increases in Executive Stock Ownership," *Journal of Financial Economics* 64 (2002): 317–340.

9. See Clifford W. Smith and René M. Stulz, "The Determinants of Firms' Hedging Policies," *Journal of Financial and Quantitative Analysis* 20 (1985): 391–405; Richard A. Lambert, David F. Larcker, and Robert E. Verrecchia, "Portfolio Considerations in Valuing Executive Compensation," *Journal of Accounting Research* 29 (1991): 129–149; and Stephen A. Ross, "Compensation, Incentives, and the Duality of Risk Aversion and Riskiness," *Journal of Finance* 59 (2004): 207–225.

10. Jeff L. Coles, Naveen D. Daniel, and Lalitha Naveen, "Managerial Incentives and Risk-Taking," *Journal of Financial Economics* 79 (2006): 431–468.

11. Todd A. Gormley, David A. Matsa, and Todd Milbourn, "CEO Compensation and Corporate Risk: Evidence from a Natural Experiment," *Journal of Accounting and Economics* 56 (2013): 79–101.

12. Christopher S. Armstrong and Rahul Vashishtha, "Executive Stock Options, Differential Risk-Taking Incentives, and Firm Value," *Journal of Financial Economics* 104 (2012): 70–88.

13. Jeong-Bon Kim, Yinghua Li, and Liandong Zhang, "CFOs versus CEOs: Equity Incentives and Crashes," *Journal of Financial Economics* 10 (2011): 713–730.

14. KPMG, "Never Again? Risk Management in Banking beyond the Credit Crisis" (2009). Accessed August 11, 2014. See https://www.kpmg.com/LU/en/IssuesAndInsights/Articlespublications/Documents/Riskmanagementinbankingbeyondthecreditcrisis.pdf.

15. PricewaterhouseCoopers and Economist Intelligence Unit, "Reward: A New Paradigm?" (September 2008). Accessed August 14, 2015. See http://www.pwc.lu/en_LU/lu/hr/docs/pwc-publ-reward-a-new-paradigm.pdf.

16. Board of Governors of the Federal Reserve System Press Release (October 22, 2009). Accessed April 7, 2014. See http://www.federalreserve.gov/newsevents/press/bcreg/20091022a.htm.

17. Timothy Geithner, "Testimony to Senate Appropriations Subcommittee on the Treasury Department's Budget Request," *Reuters* (June 6, 2009).

18. Edited lightly for clarity. Alan S. Blinder, "Crazy Compensation and the Crisis," *Wall Street Journal* (May 28, 2009, Eastern edition): A.15.

19. David F. Larcker, Gaizka Ormazabal, Brian Tayan, and Daniel J. Taylor, "Follow the Money: Compensation, Risk, and the Financial Crisis," Stanford Closer Look Series (September 8, 2014). Accessed May 5, 2015. See http://www.gsb.stanford.edu/faculty-research/centers-initiatives/cgri/research/closer-look.

20. Robert DeYoung, Emma Y. Peng, and Meng Yan, "Executive Compensation and Business Policy Choices at U.S. Commercial Banks," *Journal of Financial and Quantitative Analysis* 48 (2013): 165–196.

21. Rüdiger Fahlenbrach and René M. Stulz, "Bank CEO Incentives and the Credit Crisis," *Journal of Financial Economics* 99 (2011): 11–26.

22. Ameriprise Financial Inc., Form DEF 14A, filed with the Securities and Exchange Commission March 17, 2014.

23. Moog Inc., Form DEF 14A, filed with the Securities and Exchange Commission December 12, 2014.

24. Jared Harris and Philip Bromiley, "Incentives to Cheat: The Influence of Executive Compensation and Firm Performance on Financial Misrepresentation," *Organization Science* 18 (2007): 350–367.

25. William R. Baber, Sok-Hyon Kang, Lihong Liang, and Zinan Zhu, "External Corporate Governance and Misreporting," *Social Science Research Network* (2013). Accessed November 12, 2010. See http://ssrn.com/abstract=760324.

26. Shane A. Johnson, Harley E. Ryan, Jr., and Yisong S. Tian, "Managerial Incentives and Corporate Fraud: The Sources of Incentives Matter," *Review of Finance* 13 (2009): 115–145.

27. Merle Erickson, Michelle Hanlon, and Edward L. Maydew, "Is There a Link Between Executive Equity Incentives and Accounting Fraud?" *Journal of Accounting Research* 44 (2006): 113–143.

28. Chris S. Armstrong, Alan D. Jagolinzer, and David F. Larcker, "Chief Executive Officer Equity Incentives and Accounting Irregularities," *Journal of Accounting Research* 48 (2010): 225–271.

29. Christopher S. Armstrong, David F. Larcker, Gaizka Ormazabal, and Daniel J. Taylor, "The Relation Between Equity Incentives and Misreporting: The Role of Risk-Taking Incentives," *Journal of Financial Economics* 109 (2013): 327–350.

30. David Yermack, "Good Timing: CEO Stock Option Awards and Company News Announcements," *Journal of Finance* 52 (1997): 449–476.

31. David Aboody and Ron Kasznik, "CEO Stock Option Awards and the Timing of Corporate Voluntary Disclosures," *Journal of Accounting and Economics* 29 (2000): 73–100.

32. Erik Lie, "On the Timing of CEO Stock Option Awards," *Management Science* 51 (2005): 802–812. Reproduced with permission of the Institute for Operations Research and Management Sciences in the format Tradebook via Copyright Clearance Center.

33. Charles Forelle and James Bandler, "The Perfect Payday—Some CEOs Reap Millions by Landing Stock Options When They Are Most Valuable; Luck—or Something Else?" *Wall Street Journal* (March 18, 2006, Eastern edition): A.1.

34. Alan Murray, "The Economy; Business: Will Backdating Scandal Thwart Effort to Roll Back Reforms?" *Wall Street Journal* (December 20, 2006, Eastern edition): A.2. See also "Perfect Payday: Options Scorecard," *Wall Street Journal Online* (2007). Accessed September 4, 2007. See http://online.wsj.com/public/resources/documents/info-optionsscore06-full.html.

35. Lucian A. Bebchuk, Yaniv Grinstein, and Urs C. Peyer, "Lucky CEOs and Lucky Directors," *Journal of Finance* 65 (2010): 2363–2401.

36. The practice of granting in-the-money options to executives is not illegal. Companies may do so with the prior approval of shareholders and as long as the grants are properly reported. Retroactively manipulating a grant date, however, violates Generally Accepted Accounting Principles, IRS tax rules, and SEC regulations. For more on backdating, see Christopher S. Armstrong and David F. Larcker, "Discussion of 'The Impact of the Options Backdating Scandal on Shareholders' and 'Taxes and the Backdating of Stock Option Exercise Dates,'" *Journal of Accounting and Economics* 47 (2009): 50–58.; John Bizjak, Michael Lemmon, and Ryan Whitby, "Option Backdating and Board Interlocks," *Review of Financial Studies* 22 (2009): 4821–4847; Gennaro Bernile and Gregg A. Jarrell, "The Impact of the Options Backdating Scandal on Shareholders," *Journal of Accounting and Economics* 47 (2009): 2–26.

37. Definitions from Mark Maremont and Charles Forelle, "Open Spigot: Bosses' Pay: How Stock Options Became Part of the Problem; Once Seen as a Reform, They Grew into Font of Riches and System to Be Gamed; Reload, Reprice, Backdate," *Wall Street Journal* (December 27, 2006, Eastern edition): A.1. Note that exercise backdating works only for transactions that are executed through the firm, where there is a possibility of getting someone from within the firm to agree to retroactively change the exercise date. Exercise backdating does not work for cashless exercise through a broker.

38. Dhaliwal, Erickson, and Heitzman (2009) found that CEOs who engage in exercise backdating realized average (median) tax savings of $96,000 ($7,000). It is difficult to believe that executives would be motivated by this somewhat trivial magnitude of savings, especially when there is some chance of getting caught by the board of directors or regulators. See Dan Dhaliwal, Merle Erickson, and Shane Heitzman, "Taxes and the Backdating of Stock Option Exercise Dates," *Journal of Accounting and Economics* 47 (2009): 27–49.

39. In 2008, the SEC investigated the stock option grant practices at Analog Devices. At issue was whether the company both backdated and spring-loaded options. Although the company agreed to pay a $3 million fine for backdating, no settlement was sought for spring-loading. An SEC

commissioner indicated that spring-loading was not a form of illegal trading. See Kara Scannell and John Hechinger, "SEC, Analog Settle Case—'Spring-Loading' Options Complaint Isn't Included," *Wall Street Journal* (May 31, 2008, Eastern edition): B.5.

40. For most public purposes, the term *insider trading* refers to illegal activity. The SEC, however, considers all trading by insiders to be insider trading and distinguishes between legal and illegal insider trading. See Securities and Exchange Commission, "Insider Trading" (last modified April 19, 2001). Accessed May 5, 2015. See www.sec.gov/answers/insider.htm.

41. Securities Lawyer's Deskbook, "Rule 10b5: Employment of Manipulative and Deceptive Devices." Accessed May 5, 2015. See https://www.law.cornell.edu/cfr/text/17/240.10b-5.

42. Dionne Searcey, Peter Lattman, Peter Grant, and Amol Sharma, "Qwest's Nacchio Is Found Guilty in Trading Case; Ex-CEO's Conviction on 19 of 42 Counts Adds to Government's Wins," *Wall Street Journal* (April 20, 2007, Eastern edition): A.1. See also, "Judge Cuts Ex-Qwest CEO's Sentence by 2 Months," *Reuters* (June 24, 2010). Accessed November 12, 2010. See http://www.reuters.com/article/2010/06/24/us-nacchio-idustre65n6fe20100624.

43. Recent survey data found that only 30 percent of companies disclose their insider trading policies. See David F. Larcker and Brian Tayan, "Pledge (and Hedge) Allegiance to the Company," Stanford Closer Look Series (October 11, 2010). Accessed May 5, 2015. See http://www.gsb.stanford.edu/faculty-research/centers-initiatives/cgri/research/closer-look.

44. Alan D. Jagolinzer, David F. Larcker, and Daniel J. Taylor, "Corporate Governance and the Information Content of Insider Trades," *Journal of Accounting Research* 49 (2011): 1249–1274.

45. Ibid.

46. Crimson Exploration, Inc., "Crimson Exploration Insider Trading Policy" (2010). Last accessed November 12, 2010. See http://crimsonexploration.com/default/Insider_Trading_Policy_Preclearance_3_1_2010.pdf.

47. Josef Lakonishok and Inmoo Lee, "Are Insider Trades Informative?" *Review of Financial Studies* 14 (2001): 79–111.

48. Nejat H. Seyhun, "Insiders' Profits, Costs of Trading, and Market Efficiency," *Journal of Financial Economics* 16 (1986): 189–212.

49. See also James H. Lorie and Victor Niederhoffer, "Predictive and Statistical Properties of Insider Trading," *Journal of Law and Economics* 11 (1968): 35–53; Jeffrey F. Jaffe, "Special Information and Insider Trading," *Journal of Business* 47 (1974): 410–428; S. P. Pratt and C. W. DeVere, "Relationship between Insider Trading and Rates of Return for NYSE Common Stocks, 1960–1966," in *Modern Developments in Investment Management*, edited by James H. Lorie and Richard Brealey (New York: Praeger, 1970); Joseph E. Finnerty, "Insiders and Market Efficiency," *Journal of Finance* 31 (1976): 1141–1148.

50. Securities and Exchange Commission, "Proposed Rule: Selective Disclosure and Insider Trading" (July 31, 1999; modified January 10, 2000). Accessed May 5, 2015. See www.sec.gov/rules/proposed/34-42259.htm.

51. Securities Lawyer's Deskbook, "Rule 10b5-1: Trading 'on the Basis of' Material Nonpublic Information in Insider Trading Cases." Accessed May 5, 2015. See https://www.law.cornell.edu/cfr/text/17/240.10b5-1.

52. The broker also is not permitted to execute trades under the 10b5-1 plan if he or she comes into possession of material nonpublic information.

53. Larcker and Tayan (2010).

54. Ibid.

55. Datalink Corporation, Form 8-K, filed with the Securities and Exchange Commission February 13, 2006.

56. McDATA Corporation, Form 8-K, filed with the Securities and Exchange Commission May 13, 2002.

57. Alan D. Jagolinzer, "SEC Rule 10b5-1 and Insiders' Strategic Trade," *Management Science* 55 (2009): 224–239.

58. Assume that a CEO requires compensation of $1 million. The board can offer either cash or equity. However, because equity has uncertain value, the executive will require a premium relative to cash (say, $1.2 million in expected value of stock options vs. $1 million riskless cash). Although the CEO might be indifferent between these two forms of payment, if he or she immediately hedges the options, the $1.2 million in risky compensation will be converted to $1.2 million in riskless cash (minus transaction costs). In this case, the board overpaid because it could have satisfied the CEO with $1 million in cash instead of the $1.2 million in equity it gave up.

59. Cited in TheCorproateCounsel.net, "Hedging & Pledging Policies: Possible Approaches & Survey," *TheCorporateCounsel.net Blog* (February 18, 2015). Accessed May 5, 2015. See http://www.thecorporatecounsel.net/blog/2015/02/hedging-pledging-policies-possible-approaches-survey.html.

60. J. Carr Bettis, John M. Bizjak, and Swaminathan L. Kalpathy, "Why Do Insiders Hedge Their Ownership and Options? An Empirical Examination," *Social Science Research Network* (June 18, 2013). Accessed November 12, 2014. See http://ssrn.com/abstract=1364810.

61. Two other (less common) hedging devices are an equity swap and exchange-traded funds. An equity swap is an agreement between two parties to exchange cash flows associated with the performance of their specific holdings. The arrangement allows each party to diversify its income while still holding the original assets. An exchange-traded fund allows an investor to exchange his or her large holding of a single stock for units in a pooled (diversified) portfolio.

62. Chattem Inc., Form 4, filed with the Securities and Exchange Commission January 26, 2005.

63. Quest Software, Form DEF 14A, filed with the Securities and Exchange Commission April 30, 2002.

64. Quest Software, Form 4, filed with the Securities and Exchange Commission November 4, 2002.

65. Delta Air Lines, Form DEF 14A, filed with the Securities and Exchange Commission May 23, 2014.

66. UnitedHealth Group Incorporated, Form DEF 14A, filed with the Securities and Exchange Commission April 23, 2014.

67. J. Carr Bettis, John M. Bizjak, and Michael L. Lemmon, "Managerial Ownership, Incentive Contracting, and the Use of Zero-cost Collars and Equity Swaps by Corporate Insiders," *Journal of Financial and Quantitative Analysis* 36 (2001): 345–370.

68. Alan D. Jagolinzer, Steven R. Matsunaga, and P. Eric Yeung, "An Analysis of Insiders' Use of Prepaid Variable Forward Transactions," *Journal of Accounting Research* 45 (2007): 1055–1079.

69. Bettis, Bizjak, and Kalpathy (2013).

70. An analysis of ISS Governance QuickScore data finds that 54.3% of Russell 3000 companies have a policy prohibiting hedging of company shares by employees, while 84% of large capital S&P 500 companies have such a policy. Executive or director pledging of company shares was prevalent at just 14.2% of Russell 3000 companies, and, notably, 15.8% of S&P 500 companies. TheCorporateCounsel.net (2015). Source for survey data is Larcker and Tayan (2010).

71. Peter Galuszka, "Chesapeake Energy Not Alone in Margin Call Madness," *BNET Energy* (October 13, 2008). Accessed November 17, 2010. See www. bnet.com/blog/energy/chesa-peake-energy-not-alone-in-margin-call-madness/313.

72. Posted by TraderMark on April 3, 2009: "Chesapeake Energy (CHK) CEO Aubrey McClendon with New Shady Compensation Deal; I Was Right in My Prediction." Accessed November 17, 2010. See www.fundmymutualfund.com/ 2009/04/chesapeake-energy-chk-ceo-aubrey.html.

73. Continental Resources, Inc., Schedule 13D, filed with the Securities and Exchange Commission January 13, 2015.

74. Oracle Corp., Form DEF 14A, filed with the Securities and Exchange Commission September 23, 2014.

75. Citadel Broadcasting, Form DEF 14A, filed with the Securities and Exchange Commission April 17, 2006.

76. Mary Ellen Carter and Luann J. Lynch, "An Examination of Executive Stock Option Repricing," *Journal of Financial Economics* 61 (2001): 207–225.

77. N. K. Chidambaran and Nagpurnanand R. Prabhala, "Executive Stock Option Repricing Internal Governance Mechanisms and Management Turnover," *Journal of Financial Economics* 69 (2003): 153–189.

78. Mary Ellen Carter and Luann J. Lynch, "The Effect of Stock Option Repricing on Employee Turnover," *Journal of Accounting and Economics* 37 (2004): 91–112.

79. Menachem Brenner, Rangarajan K. Sundaram, and David Yermack, "Altering the Terms of Executive Stock Options," *Journal of Financial Economics* 57 (2000): 103–128.

80. Don M. Chance, Raman Kumar, and Rebecca B. Todd, "The 'Repricing' of Executive Stock Options," *Journal of Financial Economics* 57 (2000): 129–154.

81. Sandra Renfro Callaghan, P. Jane Saly, and Chandra Subramaniam, "The Timing of Option Repricing," *Journal of Finance* 59 (2004): 1651–1676.

82. David F. Larcker, Allan L. McCall, and Gaizka Ormazabal, "Proxy Advisory Firms and Stock Option Repricing," *Journal of Accounting and Economics* 56 (2013): 149–169.

10

Financial Reporting and External Audit

In this chapter, we examine the process by which the board of directors assesses the integrity of published financial statements. As discussed in previous chapters, the accuracy of financial reporting is important for several reasons. First, this information is critical for the general efficiency of capital markets and the proper valuation of a company's publicly traded securities. Second, an informed evaluation of a company's strategy, business model, and risk level depends on the accurate reporting of financial and operating measures. This is true for both internally and externally reported data. Third, the board of directors awards performance-based compensation to management based on the achievement of predetermined financial targets. Accurate financial reporting is critical to ensuring that results are stated honestly and that management has not manipulated results for personal gain.

The audit committee must ensure that the financial reporting process is carried out appropriately. The committee does so in two ways: first, by working with management to set the parameters for accounting quality, transparency, and internal controls; and, second, by retaining an external auditor to test the financial statements for material misstatement.

In this chapter, we discuss both of these responsibilities. We start by considering the general obligation of the audit committee to oversee the financial reporting and disclosure process. What actions should the committee take to ensure that financial data is reported accurately? How can it decrease the likelihood of material misstatement or manipulation by management? How effective are these efforts?

Next, we evaluate the role of the external auditor. What is the purpose of an external audit? What is it expected to accomplish, and what is it not expected to accomplish? We then consider the impact that various factors have on audit quality, including the structure of the industry itself, the reliance on audit firms for nonaudit-related services, auditor independence, auditor rotation, and the Sarbanes–Oxley Act of 2002.

The Audit Committee

The audit committee has a broad range of responsibilities. These include the responsibility to oversee financial reporting and disclosure, to monitor the choice of accounting principles, to hire and monitor the work of the external auditor, to oversee the internal audit function, to oversee regulatory compliance within the company, and to monitor risk.

Many of these responsibilities are mandated by securities regulation or federal law. For example, the audit committee's oversight of the external audit is required by the Sarbanes–Oxley Act of 2002. Sarbanes–Oxley also mandates that the audit committee establish procedures for receiving and handling complaints about the company's accounting, internal controls, or auditing matters (including anonymous submissions by employees). By contrast, other responsibilities are not mandated by law but instead have evolved from historical practice. For example, the assignment of enterprise risk management to the audit committee is not a legal requirement but is an election that many companies make of their own volition.[1]

To ensure that the work of the committee is carried out free from the influence of management, the audit committee must consist entirely of independent directors. In addition, listing exchanges require that all members of the audit committee be financially literate and that at least one committee member qualify as a **financial expert**. A financial expert is defined as follows:

> [Someone who] has past employment experience in finance or accounting, requisite professional certification in accounting, or any other comparable experience or background which results in the individual's financial sophistication, including being or having been chief executive officer, chief financial officer, or other senior officer with financial oversight responsibilities.[2]

The audit committee can retain external advisors or consultants as it deems necessary to assist in the fulfillment of its duties, with the cost borne by the company.

Accounting Quality, Transparency, and Controls

The work of the audit committee begins with establishing guidelines that dictate the quality of accounting used in the firm. **Accounting quality** is generally defined as the degree to which accounting figures precisely reflect the company's change in financial position, earnings, and cash flow during a reporting period.[3]

An outside observer might think that accounting quality should not be discretionary, but the nature of accounting standards somewhat requires that it be so. This is because oversight bodies—including the Financial Accounting Standards Board (FASB) in the United States and the International Accounting Standards Board

(IASB) abroad—sometimes afford considerable flexibility to companies in the manner in which they interpret and apply accounting standards. They do so to allow for the fact that it is not always clear how transactions should be valued or when the costs and revenues associated with a transaction should be recognized. In many cases, these are subject to interpretation. For example, how should a company allocate the costs associated with completing a multiyear project? Should it be evenly over the life of the project, at the time of delivery, or in some other manner that takes into account the work performed during each reporting period? Correspondingly, should the company be aggressive or conservative in recognition of the associated revenues? The way a company answers these questions has a direct impact on accounting results.

In addition, the audit committee must establish the company's standards for transparency. **Transparency** is the degree to which the company provides details that supplement and explain accounts, items, and events reported in its financial statements and other public filings. Transparency is important for shareholders to properly understand the company's strategy, operations, risk, and performance of management. It is also necessary when shareholders make decisions about the value of company securities. As such, transparent disclosure plays a key role in the efficient functioning of capital markets.

On the other hand, transparency brings risks. When a company is highly transparent, it might inadvertently divulge confidential or proprietary information that puts it at a disadvantage relative to competitors. For example, competitors might be able to use information disclosed about a company's strategy (including the timing of a new product launch, distribution channels, pricing, marketing, and other promotion) to effectively dampen its success. Too much transparency might also weaken the bargaining position of a company. For example, counterparties could use disclosure about a company's potential exposure to litigation to gain leverage and extract additional concessions. For these reasons, the audit committee and the entire board of directors must weigh the costs and benefits of transparency when establishing guidelines for reporting and disclosure.

Finally, the audit committee is responsible for monitoring the internal controls of the corporation. Under Section 404 of the Sarbanes–Oxley Act, management is required to assess the internal controls of the company, and the external auditor is required to attest to management's assessment. **Internal controls** are the processes and procedures that a company puts in place to ensure that account balances are accurately recorded, financial statements reliably produced, and assets adequately protected from loss or theft. Effectively, internal controls act as the "cash register" of the corporation, a system that confirms that the level of assets inside the company is consistent with the level that should be there, given revenue and disbursement data recorded through the accounting system.

The audit committee determines the rigor of controls necessary to ensure the integrity of financial statements. A rigorous system is important for protecting against theft, tampering, and manipulation by management or other employees. It is also important for detecting potential regulatory violations or illegal activity, such as the payment of bribes, which are illegal under the Foreign Corrupt Practices Act of 1977.[4] Rigorous controls help ensure that employees do not make inappropriate adjustments to company accounts to create falsified results. If the company is too zealous in its internal controls, however, the results can be detrimental. Excessive controls can lead to bureaucracy, lost productivity, inefficient decision making, and an inhospitable work environment. As a result, the audit committee must strike a balance between proper controls that prevent inappropriate behavior and excessive controls that impact firm performance.

Survey data suggests that audit committees are confident in their ability to carry out these responsibilities. According to a study conducted by KPMG and the National Association of Corporate Directors (NACD), the vast majority of audit committee members believe they are effective or very effective in overseeing management's use of accounting (90 percent), company disclosure practices (93 percent), and internal controls (87 percent). The majority also believe they are effective in overseeing both the internal and external audit function (89 percent and 94 percent, respectively).[5]

Financial Reporting Quality

Several control mechanisms are in place to assist the audit committee in ensuring the integrity of financial statements. Companies hire an external auditor to test financials for material misstatement based on prevailing accounting rules. The external auditor reports its findings directly to the audit committee to ensure that the audit process has not been compromised by management influence. Companies also employ an internal audit department, which is responsible for separately testing accounting processes and controls. Under Sarbanes–Oxley, management is required to certify that financial reports do not contain misleading information. Companies that violate accounting regulations face the risk of lawsuits from shareholders and regulators. Penalties for violation include fines and, in some cases, bans from serving as an officer of a publicly traded company or even prison time for corporate officers (see the following sidebar).

Whistleblowers

Sarbanes–Oxley requires companies to create a hotline for "whistleblower" employees to confidentially report accounting abuses directly to the audit committee (thereby bypassing management). The Dodd–Frank Act increased the incentives for whistleblowing by providing heightened protections against retaliation and mandating that any employee providing original information on internal fraudulent activity that leads to an enforcement action of $1 million or more be entitled to 10 percent to 30 percent of the proceeds. As of 2014, the largest single payment awarded to an individual whistleblower was $30 million.[6] That same year, four whistleblowers received a combined $170 million for reporting mortgage-related abuses that led to $16.65 billion in penalties against Bank of America.[7]

Audit committee members are confident that accounting controls are effective. According to the KPMG survey cited, 89 percent of audit committee members are confident or very confident that the company's internal audit department would report controversial issues involving senior management. Eighty-six percent are satisfied with the support and expertise they receive from the external auditor.[8]

Still, considerable empirical evidence suggests that accounting controls might not be as effective as audit committee members believe. For example, Dichev, Graham, Harvey, and Rajgopal (2013) conducted a survey of 169 chief financial officers and found that in any given period, about 20 percent of firms manipulate earnings to misrepresent economic performance; the average level of earnings manipulation among these firms is 10 percent. This suggests that management might regularly sidestep internal controls to meet earnings targets.[9] Other studies support this conclusion. For example, Burgstahler and Dichev (1997) found that companies are much less likely to report a small decrease in earnings than a small increase in earnings, even though statistically the distribution between the two should be equal.[10] Carslaw (1988) examined the pattern that occurs in the second-from-left digit of net income figures. He found that zeros are overrepresented and nines are underrepresented, suggesting that companies round up their earnings to convey slightly better results.[11] Similarly, Malenko and Grundfest (2014) examined the pattern that occurs when earnings per share figures are extended by one digit to include tenths of a penny. If no manipulation is occurring, fours should occur in the tenth-of-a-penny digit just as often as other numbers. Instead, the authors found that fours are significantly underrepresented, suggesting that managers manipulate results when possible so that they can report EPS figures that are one penny higher. The authors identified inventory valuation, asset writedowns, accruals, and reserves as areas that are particularly susceptible to manipulation.[12]

Although such behavior might allow management to meet short-term targets, it is generally detrimental to the corporation and provides some insight into the governance quality of the firm. Bhojraj, Hribar, Picconi, and McInnis (2009) found that companies that just beat earnings expectations with low-quality earnings have superior short-term stock price performance compared to companies that just miss earnings expectations with high-quality earnings. However, over the subsequent three-year period, these companies tend to underperform. The authors saw this as evidence that managers make "myopic short-term decisions to beat analysts' earnings forecasts at the expense of long-term performance."[13] Kraft, Vashishtha, and Venkatachalam (2015) found that more frequent financial reporting (quarterly versus annual) is associated with an economically large decline in corporate investment in fixed assets. They also concluded that their results are "suggestive of myopic managerial behavior."[14] Perhaps to discourage myopic behavior among management, some companies have implemented policies that they will not issue quarterly earnings guidance. Examples include AT&T, ExxonMobil, Ford, and Walt Disney.

Financial Restatements

A **financial restatement** occurs when a material error is discovered in a company's previously published financials. When such an error is discovered, the company is required to file a Form 8-K with the Securities and Exchange Commission (SEC) within four days. Form 8-K alerts investors that previously published financials can no longer be relied upon and are under review for restatement. If an error is not material, the financial statements are simply amended.

According to data from the Center for Audit Quality, between 700 and 1,700 restatements occur each year. Of these, approximately 15 percent are issued by foreign companies listed in the United States. In recent years, both the number and percentage of serious restatements (that is, those reported on Form 8-K) has declined. In 2006, approximately half (53 percent) of 1,784 restatements were serious; in 2012, only 35 percent of 738 restatements were serious. Of note, the number of restatements did not increase—and in fact steadily *decreased*—in the five years during and after the financial crisis of 2008. This suggests that, unlike with the accounting scandals in the late 1990s that precipitated the Sarbanes–Oxley Act of 2002, widespread accounting manipulation did not appear to play a significant role in the financial crisis of 2008.[15]

The most frequent causes of a restatement include improper expense recognition relating to accruals and reserve estimates (30 percent), errors related to accounting for debt and equity financing (23 percent), improper revenue recognition

(14 percent), errors related to accounting for fixed assets and intangibles (13 percent), improper expense recognition related to stock-based compensation (13 percent), and tax accounting errors (11 percent). (See Table 10.1.) When a restatement results in a reduction in net income, the median reduction is 15 percent.[16]

Table 10.1   Reasons for Financial Restatement (2003–2012)

Error Category	Description	Frequency
Revenue recognition	Restatements due to improper revenue accounting, including the value and timing of revenues.	14%
Expense recognition	Restatements due to improper expense accounting, including the value and timing of expenses and management estimates of future liabilities. Breakdown includes:	
	Accruals and reserve estimates	30%
	Stock-based compensation	13%
	Depreciation and amortization	10%
	Cost of sales	7%
	Leases	4%
	Contingencies and pensions	3%
Taxes	Restatements due to errors involving tax provisions, improper treatment of tax liabilities, deferred tax assets and liabilities, and tax contingencies.	11%
Investing	Restatements due to misreporting of fixed assets and intangibles, including periodic value assessments and errors in the recognition of gains and losses from sales.	13%
Financing	Restatements due to errors in the accounting for debt and equity, including beneficial conversion features related to warrants and convertible debt; includes derivative accounting.	23%

Total does not equal 100 percent because some restatements are due to more than one reporting issue.

Source: Adapted from Susan Scholz, "Financial Statement Trends in the U.S.: 2003–2012," published by the Center for Audit Quality (2014).

A restatement can be required because of human error, aggressive application of accounting standards, or fraud. The distinctions are important because they have implications on the quality of internal controls and the steps that the company must take to improve oversight. For example, consider three restatements that occurred in the 1990s and 2000s:

- In 1991, Oracle restated second- and third-quarter earnings from the previous year when it was discovered that sales had been recorded prematurely. Investment analysts blamed the incident on management pressure to meet financial targets, which, in turn, caused sales associates to book contracts before they were fully closed. The practice occurred only in these two quarters, and total fiscal year results were unaffected by the timing shift.

- Between 1999 and 2001, Bristol-Myers Squibb used financial incentives to persuade wholesalers to purchase larger quantities of its drugs than needed. The company eventually reduced reported revenues by $2.5 billion because of so-called "channel stuffing" and paid fines.

- Between 1998 and 2000, the CEO and other senior executives of Computer Associates engaged in a systematic process of backdating customer contracts and altering sales documents to move revenue into earlier periods. When questioned about their actions, they lied to internal investigators, the SEC, and the FBI. Those involved went to prison—including the CEO, who was sentenced to a 12-year term.

The actions at Oracle and Bristol-Myers were due to aggressive behavior on the part of management and required a change in incentives and more effective internal controls. The actions at Computer Associates, however, were clearly fraudulent and stemmed from an ethical breakdown that pervaded the entire organization. As a result, it required a much more extensive overhaul of the governance system, including a complete change in senior leadership, dismissal of the external auditor, and fairly substantial turnover among board members.

The evidence indicates that investors differentiate between more and less egregious forms of manipulation. According to the Center for Audit Quality, companies that announce serious restatements exhibit a 2.3 percent decrease in stock price in the two days following the announcement, compared with a 0.6 percent decrease for companies announcing a nonserious restatement. Stock price performance tends to be the worst when the restatement is caused by improper revenue recognition.[17]

Similarly, Palmrose, Richardson, and Scholz (2004) found that companies exhibit a 9 percent average (5 percent median) decrease in stock price in the two days following a restatement announcement. Reaction is more negative when the restatement is due to fraud (–20 percent), was initiated by the external auditor (–18 percent), or reflects a material reduction in the company's previous earnings (–14 percent). The authors hypothesized that "the negative signal associated with fraud and auditor-initiated restatements is associated with an increase in investors' expected monitoring costs, while higher materiality is associated with greater revisions of future performance expectations" (see the following sidebar).[18]

Badertscher, Hribar, and Jenkins (2011) found that the stock price reaction to a restatement is significantly less negative when managers are net purchasers of the stock before the restatement and significantly more negative when managers are net sellers. These results suggest that investors rely on informed insider trading activity as a potential clue to the likely severity of a restatement.[19]

Financial Restatement

Krispy Kreme

In July 2004, Krispy Kreme Doughnuts announced that the Securities and Exchange Commission was conducting an informal inquiry into the company's accounting practices.[20] In October, the status of the investigation was reclassified as formal. On January 4, 2005, Krispy Kreme filed a Form 8-K, alerting investors that it intended to restate its financials, due to errors in the company's accounting for the acquisition of certain franchises:

"The Board of the Directors of the Company has concluded that the Company's previously issued financial statements for the fiscal year ended February 1, 2004, and the last three quarters of such fiscal year should be restated to correct certain errors contained therein, and, accordingly, such financial statements should no longer be relied upon."

When completed, the investigation revealed that the company had engaged in many questionable activities to increase reported income. For example, Krispy Kreme had failed to expense certain items associated with reacquired franchises. Items that should have been treated as operating expenses were instead capitalized on the balance sheet as intangible assets called "reacquired franchise rights." Among the costs capitalized were $4.4 million in compensation paid to the executive of a reacquired franchise, franchise management fees, and other costs. The company also had manipulated revenue accounts. In one transaction, the company had sold equipment to a franchisee immediately before reacquiring it. Krispy Kreme had included the sale of equipment as revenue and then purchased the company for a price that was increased by the cost of the equipment in what is known as a "round-trip transaction." The company had also "sold" equipment to franchises before it was needed. The unused equipment was not shipped for several months and instead was stored in an off-site warehouse. The franchisees did not have to pay for the equipment until delivery.

The company's stock price fell from more than $30 per share before the investigation was initiated to less than $10 by the time it released restated financials in April 2006. Chairman and CEO Scott Lovegood resigned from the company. The company and its officers were named in multiple shareholder-derivative lawsuits, which were settled for $75 million. The cost of the company's external audit increased from $440,000 in fiscal 2004 to $3.5 million in 2006.[21]

Financial restatements tend to have a negative impact on companies well beyond the announcement date. Karpoff, Lee, and Martin (2008) found that companies that issue material restatements continue to trade at lower valuations even after adjusting for reductions in book value and earnings that result from the restatement.[22] Amel-Zadeh and Zhang (2015) found that firms that file a restatement are significantly less likely to become takeover targets and that those that do receive takeover bids take longer to complete or are more likely to have the bids withdrawn. They also found some evidence that deal value multiples are lower for restating firms than for non-restating firms.[23] Research evidence exists that firms that issue a financial restatement are more likely to be sued and suffer other negative repercussions, such as higher management turnover.[24]

Some evidence indicates that financial restatements are correlated with weak governance and regulatory controls. For example, Beasley (1996) found that companies with a lower percentage of outside directors are more likely to be the subject of financial reporting fraud. He also found that other governance features—low director ownership of company stock, low director tenure on the board, and busy board members—are correlated with fraud.[25] Farber (2005) found that firms that are found to have committed fraud have fewer outside directors, fewer audit committee meetings, fewer financial experts on the audit committee, and a higher percentage of CEOs who are also chairman.[26] Correia (2014) found that companies with low accounting quality spend more money on political contributions—particularly to members of Congress with strong ties to the SEC—and that these contributions are correlated with a lower likelihood of SEC enforcement action and lower penalties for firms found guilty of violations. She posited that companies at risk of financial statement fraud might use political contributions to reduce their regulatory exposure.[27]

However, the evidence that financial restatements are correlated with typical governance features is not conclusive. The Committee of Sponsoring Organizations of the Treadway Commission (COSO) reviewed fraud investigations occurring between 1998 and 2007 and found no relation to size of the board, frequency of meetings, or composition and experience of directors.[28]

A behavioral component likely is involved in financial reporting fraud. Magnan, Cormier, and Lapointe-Antunes (2010) argued that an exaggerated sense of self-confidence, encouraged by lavish media attention and praise, might encourage CEOs who are inclined to commit fraud to take increasingly aggressive actions without fear of detection or reproach. As they explained, "Almost all sample firms and/or their CEOs were the objects of positive media or analyst coverage in the period preceding or concurrent to the fraudulent activities. In our view, such coverage translated into a higher sense of self-confidence or invulnerability among the executives, i.e., managerial hubris. Managerial hubris either led guilty executives further down the path of deception and fraud or, alternatively, pulled their supervising executives away from efficient and effective monitoring." They recommend that more attention be paid to behavior cues and that auditors greet the appearances of good governance with skepticism (see the next sidebar).[29] Similarly, Feng, Ge, Luo, and Shevlin (2011) examined why CFOs become involved in material accounting manipulations and concluded that they do so because they succumb to pressure from CEOs rather than because of potential personal financial gain.[30] Conversely, Garrett, Hoitash, and Prawitt (2014) found that organizations with high levels of intraorganizational trust have higher accounting quality, fewer misstatements, and a lower likelihood of material weaknesses in their internal controls.[31]

Dyck, Morse, and Zingales (2010) studied a comprehensive list of fraud cases between 1996 and 2004. They found that legal and regulatory mechanisms (such as the SEC and external auditors) and financial parties (such as equity holders, short sellers, and analysts) were less effective at detecting fraud than uninvolved third parties that are typically seen as less important players in governance systems. Employees, non-financial-market regulators, and the media were credited with uncovering 43 percent of the fraud cases, compared with 38 percent for financial parties and 17 percent for legal and regulatory agents. They offered two explanations for these findings. Employees and nonfinancial regulators might be more effective in discovering fraud because they have greater access to internal information and, therefore, lower costs of monitoring. Journalists might be effective monitors because of reputational gains.[32]

Decentralization and Internal Controls

In 1983, SEC Commissioner James Treadway, Jr., identified a decentralized organizational structure as a common feature among companies involved in financial reporting fraud:

"The single most significant factor to emerge from these cases is the organizational structure of the companies involved. I refer to a decentralized corporate structure, with autonomous divisional management. Such a structure is intended to encourage responsibility, productivity, and therefore profits—all entirely laudable objectives. But the unfortunate corollary has been a lack of accountability."

He identified certain characteristics as being associated with financial fraud:

1. Autonomy among operating divisions
2. Unrealistic profit targets set by corporate headquarters without input from divisions
3. Pressure from headquarters to achieve those targets

4. A sense among divisions that profit targets cannot be achieved without aggressive action

5. Emphasis on sales and marketing by headquarters without concern for internal controls

6. Lack of emphasis on auditing, accounting, and internal controls

7. Limited communication between headquarters and divisions[33]

At the same time, several prominent examples exist of highly successful companies that operate under a decentralized structure. Board members must weigh the risks and benefits of decentralization in determining whether it is appropriate for their companies. Attention should be paid not only to the control mechanisms in place but also to intangible factors such as culture, quality of management and personnel, incentives, reporting and communication structure, and opportunity for misbehavior. As with most other governance systems, these are unique to each organization.

Models to Detect Accounting Manipulations

Researchers and professionals have put extensive effort into developing models to detect the manipulation of reported financial statements. Such tools are useful not only for auditors and the audit committee (and perhaps the board in general) but also for investors, analysts, and others who rely on credible financial reports. These efforts have been met with somewhat limited success, although in certain circumstances they have predictive ability in whether a restatement will occur.

One set of models measures accounting quality in terms of accounting accruals. Accrual accounting is based on the premise that the profitability of a corporation can be measured more accurately by recognizing revenues and expenses in the period in which they are realized than in the period in which cash is received or dispensed. Accrual accounting reduces the variability that is inherent in cash flow accounting and provides a more normalized view of earnings. Because accrual accounting relies more heavily on managerial assumption than cash flow accounting, however, it is more easily subject to manipulation. If management manipulates results over time, reported earnings will steadily diverge from cash flows. The difference between accruals and cash flows (after adjusting for the typical or normal accruals that will occur during the application of the accounting process), known as **abnormal accruals**, might be used as a measure of earnings quality.

Several researchers have developed models that use abnormal accruals to predict financial restatements. One widely used model was developed by Dechow, Sloan, and Sweeney (1995), based on a modification of Jones (1991).[34] Another was developed by Beneish (1999). His model uses the following metrics as inputs:

- The change in accounts receivables as a percent of sales over time
- The change in gross margin over time
- The change in noncurrent assets other than plant and equipment over time
- The change in sales over time
- The change in working capital (minus depreciation) over time, in relation to total assets

Beneish (1999) tested his model against both companies that have restated their earnings and those that have not. He found that excessive changes in these metrics have predictive power in whether a company is likely to restate earnings, and the results were statistically significant.[35] However, accrual-based models such as these tend to have a very modest success rate in predicting future restatements.

GMI Ratings has also developed a model with a slightly higher success rate in predicting financial restatements. The company uses a composite metric that aggregates both accounting and governance data to identify companies at risk of restatement and other negative outcomes such as fraud, debt default, and lawsuits. The company computes Accounting and Governance Risk (AGR) scores on a scale of 0 to 100, with low ratings indicating a higher likelihood of restatement or adverse outcome. GMI Ratings claims that companies that are in the lowest decile according to its model account for 31 percent of all restatements, whereas those in the highest decile account for only 3.1 percent. In addition, it claims that "not only are the high-risk companies substantially more likely to face a restatement than the low-risk firms, but the estimated probabilities neither understate nor overstate the actual likelihood of the restatement."[36]

Independent testing has confirmed that GMI Ratings' models have some predictive power. Price, Sharp, and Wood (2011) found that AGR is more successful in detecting financial misstatements than are standard accrual-based models, such as those discussed earlier.[37] Correia (2014) also found that AGR is slightly more effective (but statistically equivalent) in predicting accounting restatements than accrual-based models. Still, the precision of both models is relatively low—no more than 10 percent.[38]

Finally, evidence indicates that adding linguistic-based analysis can improve the predictive ability of accrual-based models. Larcker and Zakolyukina (2012) studied the Q&A section of quarterly earnings conference calls. They found that certain linguistic tendencies are associated with future restatements:

- CEOs make fewer self-references (that is, they're less likely to use the pronoun *I*).

- They are more likely to use impersonal pronouns (such as *anyone, nobody*, and *everyone*).

- They make more references to general knowledge (such as "you know").

- They express more extreme positive emotions (*fantastic* as opposed to *good*).

- They use fewer extreme negative emotions.

- They express less certainty in their language.

- They are less likely to refer to shareholder value.

The predictive ability of the model using these cues is better than chance and better than the accrual models. The authors conclude that "it is worthwhile for researchers to consider linguistic measures when attempting to measure the quality of reported financial statements."[39] However, this type of research is still in its infancy.

The External Audit

The **external audit** assesses the validity and reliability of publicly reported financial information. Shareholders rely on financial statements to evaluate a company's performance and to determine the fair value of its securities. Because management is responsible for preparing this information, shareholders expect an independent third party to provide assurance that the information they receive is accurate. The external auditor serves this purpose.

The external audit process is broken down as follows:[40]

1. *Audit preparation*—The external audit is tailored to the industry, the nature of operations, and the company's organizational structure and processes. Before the audit takes place, the auditor and the audit committee discuss and determine its scope. The auditor uses professional judgment to determine how best to perform its assessment. This involves identifying areas that require special attention, evaluating conditions under which the company produces accounting data, evaluating the reasonableness of estimates, evaluating the reasonableness of management representations, and making judgments about the appropriateness of the manner in which accounting principles are applied and the adequacy of disclosures.

2. *Review of accounting estimates and disclosures*—The audit is predicated on a sampling of accounts. Highest attention is paid to the accounts that are at the greatest risk of inaccuracy. These generally include the following:

- Revenue recognition
- Restructuring charges
- Impairments of long-lived assets
- Investments
- Goodwill
- Depreciation and amortization
- Loss reserves
- Repurchase obligations
- Inventory reserves
- Allowances for doubtful accounts[41]

In determining the reasonableness of management estimates, the auditor reviews and tests the processes by which estimates are developed, calculates an independent expectation of what the estimates should be and reviews subsequent transactions or events for further comparison. The auditor also evaluates the key factors or assumptions that are significant to the estimate and the factors that are subjective and susceptible to management bias.

3. *Fraud evaluation*—The main objective of the audit is to test for validity and reliability. The auditor does not explicitly focus on whether errors result from inadvertent mistakes or fraudulent action, but public shareholders and many board members expect that auditors will root out fraud if it exists. Auditing standards encourage auditors to use "professional skepticism" to determine whether fraud has occurred.[42] In the scope of the audit, auditors evaluate the incentives and pressures placed on management. They also review the opportunities for fraud to take place. Nevertheless, despite public conception to the contrary, it is not the explicit objective of the audit to identify fraud.[43]

4. *Assessment of internal controls*—Under Section 404 of Sarbanes–Oxley, the external auditor is required to perform an assessment of the company's internal controls.[44] The auditor assesses the design of entity-level controls, controls relating to risk management, significant accounts and their disclosure, the process for developing inputs and assumptions for management estimates, and the use of external specialists who assist in preparing estimates. To identify areas where internal controls can lead to material misstatement, the auditor pays particular attention to significant or unusual transactions, period-ending adjustments, related-party transactions, significant management estimates, and incentives that might create pressure on management to inappropriately manage financial results. In 2010, approximately 2 percent of companies received an adverse opinion from their auditors regarding their internal controls.[45]

5. *Communication with the audit committee*—The external auditor discusses its findings with the audit committee. The auditor's communications with the committee include an assessment of the consistency of the application of accounting principles, the clarity and completeness of the financial statements, and the quality and completeness of disclosures. Particular attention is paid to changes in accounting policies, the appropriateness of estimates, unusual transactions, and the timing of significant items. The auditor reports directly to the audit committee and may also communicate and discuss its findings with the chief financial officer and other employees of the company.

6. *Expressed opinion*—The ultimate objective of the audit is to express an opinion on whether the company's financials adequately comply with regulatory accounting standards. If the auditor finds no reason for concern that the statements are materially misleading, the firm expresses an **unqualified opinion** that accompanies the financial statements in the annual report. (Alternatively, the auditor issues a **qualified opinion** and explains the reason for concern.) The unqualified opinion generally states that "the financial statements present fairly the financial condition, the results of operations, and the cash flows of the company [for specific years], in accordance with accounting principles generally accepted in the United States of America." The auditor also specifies whether the company can continue to operate profitably as a **going concern**. Qualified, adverse, or no opinions occur very infrequently (see Table 10.2).[46]

In summary, the external auditor is not responsible for the presentation or accuracy of financial statements but instead reduces the risk that statements are misleading by performing a check on management and its financial reporting procedures. The board of directors and company shareholders may expect the auditor to find all material errors and instances of fraud, but given the process of the audit, that is an unrealistic expectation (see the following sidebar).

According to data from Audit Analytics, companies in the Russell 3000 spend approximately 0.1 percent of revenue on audit fees.[47] Audit fees are only a portion of the total cost of ensuring the integrity of financial reporting and controls. A complete assessment would include the incremental cost of the audit committee, the internal audit department, and the fraction of time spent by the finance, accounting, and legal departments on reporting-related issues.

Table 10.2 Auditor Opinions (2008–2013)

Year	Unqualified	Qualified	No Opinion	Additional Language	Adverse Opinion	Total
2008	5,085	2	2	2,674	2	7,915
2009	5,611	2	2	3,023	2	8,640
2010	6,322	0	2	2,258	2	8,584

2011	6,567	1	0	2,007	2	8,577
2012	6,905	2	2	2,199	2	9,110
2013	6,807	1	2	2,127	2	8,939

Additional language might be used in an unqualified opinion to indicate an inconsistency in the application of an accounting principle, to emphasize a matter of importance, or to express concern about the company's ability to remain a going concern. An adverse opinion means that the company's financial statements are misstated. No opinion (or a disclaimer of opinion) means that the auditor could not complete the scope of the audit.

Source: Computed from Standard & Poor's Compustat.

Fraud and the External Auditor

HealthSouth

In Chapter 1, "Introduction to Corporate Governance," we told the story of HealthSouth, whose CEO, Richard Scrushy, and other corporate officers were accused of overstating earnings by at least $1.4 billion between 1999 and 2002. When their scheme unraveled in 2003, outside observers expressed outrage that Ernst & Young, the company's external auditor for more than a decade, had failed to detect the fraud. A committee member investigating the incident on behalf of the U.S. Congress declared that it "raises serious questions about the extent to which Ernst & Young was diligently performing its auditing duties."[48]

Ernst & Young defended its actions, stating, "When individuals are determined to commit a crime . . . a financial audit cannot be expected to detect that crime. . . . The level of fraud and financial deception that took place at HealthSouth is a blatant violation of investor trust and Ernst & Young is as outraged as the investing public."[49] Knowing that the auditors were looking for material errors to their accounts, HealthSouth executives perpetrated fraud by making adjustments to small-dollar accounts that the auditors were less likely to examine: revenue accounts for clients reporting $5,000 or less in annual billings. Although each entry was not material, the accumulation of the adjustments created a significant misstatement of earnings. To meet quarterly earnings targets, executives had to make 120,000 fraudulent entries each quarter.[50] According to Ernst & Young, "[HealthSouth's] accounting personnel designed the false journal entries to the income statement and balance sheet accounts in a manner calculated to avoid detection by the outside auditors."[51] The firm claimed that its auditors followed appropriate procedures but were "provided fraudulent information as part of the criminal conspiracy specifically designed to defeat the audit process."[52]

Still, HealthSouth shareholders sued Ernst & Young, alleging that the firm had knowingly acquiesced to management and allowed for the improper booking of certain revenues, to secure additional nonaudit-related contracts.[53] Ernst & Young eventually settled the charges for $109 million.[54]

Audit Quality

Given the importance of the external audit, much attention has been paid to factors that might impact audit quality. These include consolidation among the major audit firms, whether conflicts exist when the auditor also provides nonaudit-related services to the client, whether conflicts exist when a member of the audit firm is hired into a senior finance role at the client, and how auditor rotations impact audit quality. We discuss these in the remainder of this chapter.

Structure of Audit Industry

The audit industry is characterized by extreme concentration among four main firms: Deloitte & Touche, Ernst & Young, KPMG, and PricewaterhouseCoopers. Together, these firms are known as the **Big Four**. The Big Four handle approximately 98 percent of the audits of large U.S. companies and earn 94 percent of total industry revenue for audit and audit-related services.[55] The rest of the industry is characterized by several midsize firms, such as Grant Thornton and BDO Seidman, and thousands of boutique firms that cater primarily to local businesses.

As recently as the late 1980s, there were eight major accounting firms, but in the ensuing years, the industry has consolidated (see Figure 10.1).

Several factors have contributed to concentration in the audit industry. First, scale among accounting firms is required to match the scale of international corporations. As companies expand around the globe, they require larger and more sophisticated accounting firms to resolve complex issues. These same firms are equipped to handle the complexity of an international audit. Scale is also important for the significant investment in information technology systems that are required to support a global audit. Second, because audit firms have deep expertise about their clients' accounting systems, their clients historically have hired them for nonaudit-related services, including tax, advisory, information technology systems, and consulting services. This has contributed to the global size and reach of the largest firms. Third, auditors are subject to intense legal scrutiny. Large firms are capable of surviving large legal penalties that would bankrupt smaller competitors. For example, between 1992 and 2014, the Big Four paid a combined total of $6.2 billion in legal settlements.[56]

Significant Mergers of the 1980s and 1990s

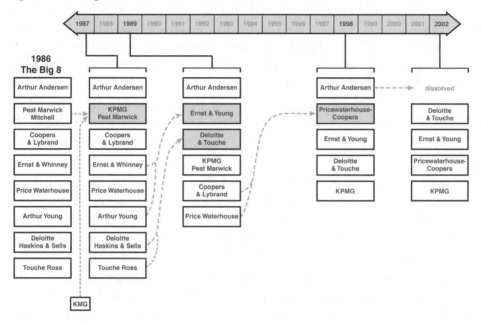

In 2002, the Department of Justice indicted Arthur Andersen on obstruction of justice charges for destroying documents relating to its audit of Enron. The firm was found guilty, lost its SEC license, and was forced to dissolve. In 2005, the U.S. Supreme Court overturned the verdict on procedural grounds. Nevertheless, it was too late to salvage the company.

Source: U.S. Government Accountability Office, "Audits of Public Companies: Continued Concentration in Audit Market for Large Public Companies Does Not Call for Immediate Action," GAO-08-163.

Figure 10.1 Consolidation among large accounting firms.

Most countries require that audit firms be owned and managed by locally licensed auditors. As a result, the Big Four are not organized as a single corporation managed by a CEO and overseen by a board of directors. Instead, the Big Four consist of a collection of affiliated firms, each of which is locally owned and operated.[57] These firms benefit from the reputation and global resources of the Big Four but have the expertise of understanding country-specific regulations, accounting standards, and business practices. This structure allows them to cater to the local offices of multinational corporations and still maintain the economies of scale to make them globally competitive. It also means that, for the most part, when a Big Four firm is subject to shareholder or regulatory litigation, only the local office is named in the lawsuit.[58]

Much debate circulates over whether the concentration of market share among the Big Four has led to a decrease in competition and reduction in audit quality. In 2008, the GAO examined this issue and was unable to find a clear link between industry concentration and anticompetitive behavior. Still, 60 percent of the large companies that the GAO surveyed believed they did not have an adequate number of firms from which to choose their auditor. Smaller companies saw no such problem; 75 percent of them believed that the number of audit firms available to them was sufficient. Respondents also indicated that, although audit and audit-related fees have increased significantly in recent years, they did not believe that the increase in cost was due to anticompetitive behavior. Instead, they believed that it reflected the cost of compliance with stricter regulatory oversight (including Sarbanes–Oxley); the greater scope of the audit; and the cost of hiring, training, and retaining qualified professionals.

The GAO (2008) also examined the possibility of requiring the Big Four to split into smaller firms to increase competition and selection. Executives from large companies expressed concern that forced divestiture by the Big Four would reduce their expertise and decrease audit quality, although they agreed that further concentration among the Big Four might lead to insufficient choice.[59]

Research evidence on whether Big Four auditors provide higher-quality audits than non–Big Four auditors among similar types of firms is inconclusive. Palmrose (1988) and Khurana and Raman (2004) found positive evidence that this is the case, based on lower litigation risk.[60] However, Lawrence, Minutti-Meza, and Zhang (2011) found no significant difference between Big Four and non–Big Four auditors in terms of the accounting quality and cost of equity capital of their clients.[61] One limitation that researchers face in assessing the audit quality of Big Four firms is that comparisons can only be made among smaller and mid-sized companies that can reasonably be audited by either Big Four and non–Big Four firms. Comparisons cannot be made among large companies that, because of their size and complexity, can only reasonably be audited by very large audit firms.

Impact of Sarbanes–Oxley

The audit industry in the United States has historically been self-regulated. For many years, auditing standards were developed by the American Institute of Certified Public Accountants (AICPA), a national association of accountants. These standards, known as Generally Accepted Auditing Standards (GAAS), set professional and ethical guidelines for auditors. Following the scandals of Enron, WorldCom, and others in 2001 and 2002, congressional leaders made efforts to formalize auditor oversight as a step toward improving investor confidence in published financial statements.

Therefore, the U.S. government passed the Sarbanes–Oxley Act of 2002 (SOX). Among its provisions, Sarbanes–Oxley established the Public Company Accounting Oversight Board (PCAOB) to regulate the audit industry. Prior to Sarbanes–Oxley, audit firms were subject to a peer review every three years, in which outside accountants tested the firm's compliance with quality-control systems for both accounting and audit. The peer review system was seen as deficient because it relied on industry self-policing and because the review was limited to testing control systems and did not examine the full scope of the audit firm's activities.[62] This system was replaced by one in which auditors are required to register with a public regulator (PCAOB), which inspects large audit firms every year and small audit firms every three years. PCAOB inspections differ from the peer review process in that they:

- Are structured around a risk-based inspection (the audits subject to review are those seen as having the highest likelihood of a material omission or misstatement)

- Are given broad latitude to inspect any audit firm activity that might violate auditing standards or SOX

- Examine the "tone from the top" (attitude of the firm's management toward regulatory compliance)[63]

The PCAOB has the power to impose disciplinary measures when violations are detected. In addition to its inspection and enforcement powers, the PCAOB proposes auditing standards. Following passage of SOX, the PCAOB adopted the auditing standards of the AICPA while it drafted its own standards.[64]

Sarbanes–Oxley also enacted measures to reduce potential conflicts of interest between auditors and their clients. Section 201 of the law prohibits auditors from performing certain nonaudit services for their audit clients, including bookkeeping, financial information system design, fairness opinions, and other appraisal and actuarial work. These measures are intended to increase the independence of the external auditor by encouraging the auditor to stand up to management without fear of recourse that would result from losing a lucrative consulting relationship.

A number of studies have examined the impact of Sarbanes–Oxley or features restricted by SOX on audit quality. Interestingly, most of the research suggests that SOX restrictions on nonaudit-related service are not shown to improve audit quality. Romano (2005) provided a comprehensive review of the research literature and came to this conclusion. In the studies she reviewed, audit quality was measured in a variety of ways, including abnormal accruals, earnings conservatism, failure to issue qualified opinions, and financial restatements. She interpreted these results as indicating that marketplace factors (such as concern for reputation and competition for clients) deterred auditors from abusing their position to gain auxiliary revenue from nonaudit services.[65]

Romano (2005) also found that the U.S. Congress, in debating Section 201 of SOX, had ignored most of the research literature. Only one study was cited in congressional debate, and it was one that had already been largely disproven at the time.[66] None of the contravening evidence was considered, even though it was well understood by academics and professionals. Romano blamed this willful ignorance on a rush to respond to the collapse of Enron, a declining stock market, and upcoming midterm elections that compelled politicians to pass an important piece of legislation without "the healthy ventilation of issues that occurs in the usual give-and-take negotiations." She concluded that because the evidence does not support their effectiveness, the "corporate governance provisions of SOX should be stripped of their mandatory force and rendered optional for registrants."[67]

This is not to say that Sarbanes–Oxley has been negative. In many ways, the legislation has focused the efforts of many constituents—including external auditors, internal auditors, audit committee members, managers, and shareholders—on practical methods to improve financial statement quality.

Still, these changes have come at a considerable cost. According to Audit Analytics, audit costs almost doubled among the 3,000 companies that came into compliance with SOX in the two years following enactment.[68] Furthermore, the amount of the increase was substantially higher than expected. Maher and Weiss (2010) found that the median cost of compliance with new provisions of SOX was between $1.3 million and $3.0 million annually in the four years following enactment. This compares with an original estimate of $91,000 by the SEC.[69] The largest increase in audit costs has been incurred by financial institutions, due to the complexity of their audits and internal controls. In addition, smaller companies have incurred higher costs (relative to revenues) than larger companies because of the considerable fixed-cost portion of an external audit. A survey by Grant Thornton found that the increased cost of regulatory compliance is a top concern among internal audit departments.[70]

More than a decade after the enactment of Sarbanes–Oxley, its cost–benefit implications remain unclear. Based on a survey of 2,901 corporate insiders, Alexander, Bauguess, Bernile, Lee, and Marietta-Westberg (2013) found that 80 percent of respondents ascribe some benefits to the Act. These benefits include positive impact on firms' internal controls (73 percent), audit committee confidence in internal controls (71 percent), improved financial reporting quality (48 percent), and ability to prevent and detect fraud (47 percent). Still, the majority of companies believe that the benefits do not outweigh the costs of compliance.[71]

Coates and Srinivasan (2014) conducted a comprehensive review of the research on the Act's impact. They found that the quality of financial reporting improved following enactment and that the cost of compliance has steadily decreased following an initial spike; however, they found that the direct costs continue to fall disproportionately on small firms. They also noted several indirect costs, such as decreased listings of small firms in public equity markets and a decline in corporate investment, but they could not accurately measure the size of these costs or induce causality from Sarbanes–Oxley. They concluded that the cost–benefit trade-off is unclear.[72]

External Auditor as CFO

A company might find it beneficial to offer a job to a member of the external auditing team, in either the finance, treasury, internal audit, or risk management departments. Hiring a former auditor has several advantages. These individuals are familiar with the company's business, internal practices, and procedures. They know (and presumably have good working relations with) other members of the staff. The company has had the opportunity to witness their working style, knowledge, and expertise firsthand. Therefore, hiring a former auditor allows a company to benefit from lower training costs and more reliable cultural fit.

Hiring a former auditor also has potential drawbacks. These individuals might feel an allegiance to their former employer and, therefore, be less willing to challenge their work. In addition, a former auditor has intimate knowledge of the company's internal control procedures and would be more adept at maneuvering around them without detection. As such, the company might find itself more greatly exposed to fraud. To address these concerns, Sarbanes–Oxley requires that former auditors undergo a one-year "cooling-off" period before they can accept an offer to work for a former client.

Some research evidence shows that audit quality suffers when a company hires a former auditor. Dowdell and Krishnan (2004) found that companies that hire a former auditor as their new CFO tend to exhibit a decrease in earnings quality. In addition, the authors found that a cooling-off period did not improve earnings quality. Observed decreases in earnings quality were not materially different whether the employee was hired more than or less than one year after leaving the audit firm.[73]

Other studies did not find significant evidence that hiring a former audit team member leads to a decrease in earnings quality. Geiger, North, and O'Connell (2005) examined a sample of more than 1,100 executives who were hired into a financial reporting position (CFO, controller, vice president of finance, or chief accounting officer) between 1989 and 1999. Of this group, 10 percent were hired from the company's current external audit firm. The authors compared the earnings quality of this group against three control groups: (1) executives who had not worked as an auditor immediately before being hired by the company, (2) executives who had worked for an audit firm that was not the company's current auditor prior to being hired, and (3) companies that had not made a new hire and instead retained their existing financial executives. They found no evidence that the source of hire had an impact on earnings quality. The authors concluded that even though "several recent highly publicized company failures have involved [so-called] 'revolving door' hires . . . there does not appear to be a pervasive problem regarding excessive earnings management associated with this hiring practice."[74]

That is, even though hiring a former auditor as a financial officer might carry potential risks (as at HealthSouth), the evidence is weak that such a practice routinely compromises audit quality.

Auditor Rotation

Proposals have also been made that companies be required to rotate the external auditor periodically to ensure its independence and decrease the risk of fraud. Advocates of this approach argue that, over time, audit firms grow stale in their review of the same accounts and that a new audit firm brings fresh perspective to company procedures. Furthermore, they argue that members of the audit team develop personal relationships with company employees, further reducing their independence. Rotating the audit firm or the lead engagement partner is intended to counteract these tendencies. Critics of auditor rotation contend that it is overly costly to change audit firms or lead engagement partners because the new audit team must learn company policies and procedures from scratch. This can be time-consuming and can reduce audit quality while the new firm is going up the learning curve.

Regulators in many countries tend to view auditor rotation favorably. For example, Sarbanes–Oxley requires that audit firms rotate the lead engagement partner on all public company audits every five years.[75] The law stopped short of requiring that companies rotate their audit firm on a fixed schedule. Other countries have such regulations, however. For example, Italy, Brazil, and South Korea require audit firm rotation for all publicly traded companies. In India and Singapore, mandatory rotation is required only for domestic banks and certain insurance companies. Australia, Spain, and Canada previously required audit rotation but ultimately dropped the requirement.

The empirical evidence indicates that auditor rotation most likely does not improve audit quality. Cameran, Merlotti, and Di Vincenzo (2005) reviewed 26 regulatory reports and 25 empirically based academic studies on auditor rotation.[76] Only 4 of the regulatory reports concluded that auditor rotation is favorable; the rest determined that the costs of rotation outweighed its benefits. For example, the Association of British Insurers (ABI), American Institute of Certified Public Accountants (AICPA), European Federation of Accountants and Auditors (EFAA), Fédération des Experts Comptables Européens (FEE), Institut der Wirtschaftsprüfer (IDW), and U.S.

General Accounting Office (GAO) all found that mandatory auditor rotation is not cost-effective. Similarly, 19 of the 25 empirically based academic studies did not support mandatory rotation.[77]

Of course, some companies change auditors through the normal course of business.[78] The company might have grown to such a size or level of sophistication that it requires an auditor with greater expertise or geographical reach. The company might also simply be dissatisfied with the auditor's services or fees. When the company decides to replace its auditor, it is known as a **dismissal**. Dismissals can be concerning to investors because they might indicate that the company is seeking more lenient treatment of its accounting and controls procedures (**opinion shopping**). Alternatively, the auditor can resign from a client account. In this case, it is considered a **resignation**. Auditor resignations are potentially more troublesome for investors than dismissals in that they are more likely to indicate a disagreement over the application of accounting principles, company disclosure, or material weaknesses in the company's internal controls. Given the auditor's exposure to potential liability from a financial misstatement or fraud, the auditor might decide that it is easier to resign from an account than to continue to negotiate with management over accounting changes. Still, both a dismissal and a resignation can indicate deterioration in governance oversight.

Auditor changes must be disclosed to investors through a Form 8-K filing with the SEC. In the filing, the company outlines that a change in auditor has taken place and the reason for that change. The audit firm is required to report whether it agrees or disagrees with the company's explanation. The auditor must also report any concern about the reliability of the company's internal controls or financial statements.[79]

As we might expect, the market reacts negatively to auditor resignations. Shu (2000) found that a company's stock price significantly underperforms the market around the announcement of an auditor resignation but does not underperform following dismissals. She interpreted these results as indicating that investors react negatively to audit resignations because of their implication for future earnings or financial restatement risk.[80] Whisenant, Sankaraguruswamy, and Raghunandan (2003) reported similar findings. They found that the market reacts negatively when the auditor's resignation calls into question the reliability of financial statements but not when it suggests that the company might have insufficient internal controls. They speculated that auditor resignations due to a disagreement over the reliability of financial statements signals an "early warning" of accounting trouble to market participants, whereas a disagreement over insufficient internal controls is too imprecise for the market to react to.[81]

Endnotes

1. Under Sarbanes–Oxley, the audit committee is required to oversee the risks associated with internal controls and the preparation of financial statements but not to oversee enterprise risk management, as defined in Chapter 6, "Strategy, Performance Measurement, and Risk Management."

2. NASDAQ, "NASDAQ Rule Filings: Listed Companies—2002, SR NASD 2002 141." Accessed April 20, 2015. See http://www.nasdaq.com/about/RuleFilingsListings/Filings_Listing.stm.

3. Considerable disagreement exists among academics regarding how to measure accounting quality. Dechow and Schrand (2004) measured earnings quality in terms of the precision with which business operating performance is reported. This approach is consistent with a view that large noncash accruals denote low-quality earnings, in that earnings diverge from reported cash flows. Francis, Schipper, and Vincent (2003) measured earnings quality in terms of the precision with which the change in corporate value is reported. This view prescribes that the earnings should reflect the change in the market value of the balance sheet during a reporting period. The American Accounting Association (2002) takes a holistic assessment of earnings quality, including operating results; balance sheet valuation; earnings management; and the perspectives of external auditors, analysts, and international organizations. See Patricia M. Dechow and Catherine M. Schrand, "Earnings Quality," Research Foundation of CFA Institute (2004); Jennifer Francis, Katherine Schipper, and Linda Vincent, "The Relative and Incremental Explanatory Power of Earnings and Alternative (to Earnings) Performance Measures for Returns," *Contemporary Accounting Research* 20 (2003): 121–164; *The Accounting Review* Conference (January 24–26, 2002); and a special issue of *The Accounting Review* (Volume 77, Supplement 2002), edited by Katherine Schipper.

4. See David F. Larcker and Brian Tayan, "Baker Hughes: Foreign Corrupt Practices Act," Stanford GSB Case No. CG-18 (August 31, 2010).

5. Audit Committee Institute, "The Audit Committee Journey. Recalibrating for the New Normal. 2009 Public Company Audit Committee Member Survey," KPMG (2009). Accessed November 11, 2010. See www.kpmginstitutes.com/insights/2009/highlights-5th-annual-issues-conference. aspx.

6. U.S. Securities and Exchange Commission, "2014 Annual Report to Congress on the Dodd–Frank Whistleblower Program" (November 17, 2014). Accessed April 17, 2015. See http://www. sec.gov/about/offices/owb/annual-report-2014.pdf.

7. Christina Rexrode and Timothy W. Martin, "Whistleblowers Score a Big Payday," *Wall Street Journal Online* (December 19, 2014). Accessed April 17, 2015. See http://www.wsj.com/articles/ third-whistleblower-to-collect-reward-related-to-bank-of-america-settlement-1419014474.

8. Audit Committee Institute (2009).

9. Ilia D. Dichev, John R. Graham, Campbell R. Harvey, and Shivaram Rajgopal, "Earnings Quality: Evidence from the Field," *Journal of Accounting and Economics* 56 (2013): 1–33.

10. David Burgstahler and Ilia Dichev, "Earnings Management to Avoid Earnings Decreases and Losses," *Journal of Accounting and Economics* 24 (1997): 99–126.

11. Charles A. P. N. Carslaw, "Anomalies in Income Numbers: Evidence of Goal-Oriented Behavior," *The Accounting Review* 63 (1988): 321–327.

12. Nadya Malenko and Joseph Grundfest, "Quadrophobia: Strategic Rounding of EPS Data," Rock Center for Corporate Governance at Stanford University Working Paper No. 65; Stanford Law and Economics Olin Working Paper No. 388, *Social Science Research Network* (July 2014). Accessed May 5, 2015. See http://ssrn.com/abstract=1474668.

13. Sanjeev Bhojraj, Paul Hribar, Marc Picconi, and John McInnis, "Making Sense of Cents: An Examination of Firms That Marginally Miss or Beat Analyst Forecasts," *Journal of Finance* 64 (2009): 2361–2388.

14. Arthur G. Kraft, Rahul Vashishtha, and Mohan Venkatachalam, "Real Effects of Frequent Financial Reporting," *Social Science Research Network* (January 8, 2015). Accessed May 5, 2015. See http://ssrn.com/abstract=2456765.

15. Susan Scholz, "Financial Statement Trends in the U.S.: 2003–2012," Center for Audit Quality (2014).

16. Ibid.

17. Ibid.

18. Zoe-Vonna Palmrose, Vernon J. Richardson, and Susan Scholz, "Determinants of Market Reactions to Restatement Announcements," *Journal of Accounting and Economics* 37 (2004): 59.

19. Brad A. Badertscher. Paul Hribar, and Nicole Thorne Jenkins, "Informed Trading and the Market Reaction to Accounting Restatements," *Accounting Review* 86 (2011): 1519–1547.

20. The information in this sidebar is adapted with permission from Madhav Rajan and Brian Tayan, "Financial Restatements: Methods Companies Use to Distort Financial Performance," Stanford GSB Case No. A-198 (June 10, 2008). See Krispy Kreme Doughnuts, Forms 8-K, filed with the Securities and Exchange Commission July 30, 2004; October 10, 2004; January 4, 2005; and August 10, 2005.

21. Krispy Kreme Doughnuts, Form 10-K, filed with the Securities and Exchange Commission October 31, 2006; and Form DEF 14A, filed April 14, 2004, and April 28, 2006.

22. Jonathan M. Karpoff, D. Scott Lee, and Gerald S, Martin, "The Cost to Firms of Cooking the Books," *Journal of Financial and Quantitative Analysis* 43 (2008): 581–611.

23. Amir Amel-Zadeh and Yuan Zhang, "The Economic Consequences of Financial Restatements: Evidence from the Market for Corporate Control," *Accounting Review* 90 (2015): 1–29.

24. Daniel Bradley, Brandon N. Cline, and Qin Lian, "Class Action Lawsuits and Executive Stock Option Exercise," Journal of Corporate Finance 27 (2014): 157–172; also see Hemang Desai, Chris E. Hogan, and Michael S. Wilkins, "The Reputational Penalty for Aggressive Accounting: Earnings Restatements and Management Turnover," *The Accounting Review* 81 (2006): 83–112.

25. Mark S. Beasley, "An Empirical Analysis of the Relation between the Board of Director Composition and Financial Statement Fraud," *Accounting Review* 7 (1996): 443–465.

26. David B. Farber, "Restoring Trust after Fraud: Does Corporate Governance Matter?" *Accounting Review* 80 (2005): 539–561.

27. Maria M. Correia, "Political Connections and SEC Enforcement," *Journal of Accounting and Economics* 57 (2014): 241–262.

28. Mark S. Beasley, Joseph V. Carcello, Dana R. Hermanson, and Terry L. Neal, "Fraudulent Financial Reporting 1998–2007: An Analysis of U.S. Public Companies," Committee of Sponsoring Organizations of the Treadway Commissions (May 2010). Accessed November 13, 2010. See www.coso.org/documents/cosofraudstudy2010.pdf.

29. Michel Magnan, Denis Cormier, and Pascale Lapointe-Antunes, "Like Moths Attracted to Flames: Managerial Hubris and Financial Reporting Fraud," CAAA Annual Conference 2010, *Social Science Research Network* (2010). Accessed May 5, 2015. See http://ssrn.com/abstract=1531786.

30. Mei Feng, Weili Ge, Shuqing Luo, and Terry Shevlin, "Why Do CFOs Become Involved in Material Accounting Manipulations?" *Journal of Accounting and Economics* 51 (2011): 21–36.

31. Jace Garrett, Rani Hoitash, and Douglas F. Prawitt, "Trust and Financial Reporting Quality," *Journal of Accounting Research* 52 (2014): 1087–1125.

32. Alexander Dyck, Adair Morse, and Luigi Zingales, "Who Blows the Whistle on Corporate Fraud?" *Journal of Finance* 65 (2010): 2213–2253.

33. Paraphrased SEC Commissioner James C. Treadway remarks made to the American Society of Corporate Secretaries, Inc., in Cleveland, Ohio, on April 13, 1983, titled "Are 'Cooked Books' a Failure of Corporate Governance?"

34. Patricia M. Dechow, Richard G. Sloan, and Amy P. Sweeney, "Detecting Earnings Management," *Accounting Review* 70 (1995): 193–225. Also see Jennifer J. Jones, "Earnings Management during Import Relief Investigations," *Journal of Accounting Research* 29 (1991): 193–228.

35. Other ratios in the analysis were not shown to have predictive power. These included leverage growth, the rate of change in depreciation, and changes in SG&A as a percent of sales. See Messod D. Beneish, "The Detection of Earnings Manipulation," *Financial Analysts Journal* 55 (1999): 24–36.

36. GMI Ratings, "The GMI Ratings AGR Model: Measuring Accounting and Governance Risk in Public Corporations" (2013). Accessed February 26, 2015. See http://www3.gmiratings.com.

37. Richard A. Price, Nathan Y. Sharp, and David A. Wood, "Detecting and Predicting Accounting Irregularities: A Comparison of Commercial and Academic Risk Measures," *Accounting Horizons* 25 (2011): 755–780.

38. Correia (2014).

39. David F. Larcker and Anastasia A. Zakolyukina, "Detecting Deceptive Discussions in Conference Calls," *Journal of Accounting Research* 50 (2012): 495–540.

40. Public Company Accounting Oversight Board, "PCAOB Staff Audit Practice Alert No. 3, Audit Considerations in the Current Economic Environment" (December 5, 2008). Accessed March 5, 2009. See http://pcaobus.org/Standards/QandA/12-05-2008_APA_3.pdf.

41. American Institute of Certified Public Accountants (AICPA), Overview of Summary Fraud Conference "Fraud . . . Can Audit Committees Really Make a Difference?" (New York, 2006).

42. American Institute of Certified Public Accountants (AICPA), Statements on Auditing Standards: SAS No. 99, AU §316.02 Consideration of Fraud in a Financial Statement Audit. (New York).

43. Still, many feel that the auditor should have greater accountability for rooting out fraud, and shareholder groups continue to press for liability. See Ian Fraser, "Holding the Auditors Accountable for Missing Corporate Fraud," QFinance blog (September 22, 2010). Accessed November 13, 2010. See www.qfinance.com/blogs/ian-fraser/2010/09/22/holding-the-auditors-accountable-for-missing-corporate-fraud-auditor-liability.

44. Management, too, is required to produce an "internal controls report," which establishes that adequate internal controls are in place.

45. Audit Analytics, "404 Dashboard: Year 6 Update, October" (2010). Accessed March 23, 2015. See http://www.auditanalytics.com/0002/view-custom-reports.php?report=cb248e6c34bc3e56c5 1aad7fb8e50c99.

46. Standard & Poor's Compustat data for fiscal years ending May 2009 to May 2014.

47. Audit Analytics, "Analysis of Audit Fees by Industry Sector" (January 7, 2014). Accessed April 17, 2015. See http://www.auditanalytics.com/blog/analysis-of-audit-fees-by-industry-sector/.

48. Jonathan Weil, "HealthSouth Becomes Subject of a Congressional Probe," *Wall Street Journal* (April 23, 2003, Eastern edition): C.1.

49. Jonathan Weil and Cassell Bryan-Low, "Questioning the Books: Audit Committee Met Only Once During 2001," *Wall Street Journal* (March 21, 2003, Eastern edition): A.2.

50. Aaron Beam and Chris Warner, *HealthSouth: The Wagon to Disaster* (Fairhope, Ala.: Wagon Publishing, 2009).

51. Jonathan Weil, "Accounting Scheme Was Straightforward but Hard to Detect," *Wall Street Journal* (March 20, 2003, Eastern edition): C.1.

52. Carrick Mollenkamp, "HealthSouth Figure Avoids Prison," *Wall Street Journal* (June 2, 2004, Eastern edition): A.2.

53. Carrick Mollenkamp and Ann Davis, "HealthSouth Ex-CFO Helps Suit," *Wall Street Journal* (July 26, 2004, Eastern edition): C.1.

54. SCAC, "HealthSouth Corporation: Stockholder and Bondholder Litigation," Stanford Law School, Securities Class Action Clearinghouse in cooperation with Cornerstone Research. Accessed April 14, 2015. See http://securities.stanford.edu/filings-case.html?id=100835.

55. U.S. Government Accountability Office (GAO), "Audits of Public Companies: Continued Concentration in Audit Market for Large Public Companies Does Not Call for Immediate Action: Report to Congressional Addressees," Report no. GAO-08-163 (January 2008). Accessed May 20, 2010. See www.gao.gov/new.items/d08163.pdf.

56. These break down as follows: Deloitte ($1.1 billion), Ernst & Young ($2.6 billion), KPMG ($1.5 billion), and PricewaterhouseCoopers ($1.0 billion). In addition, Arthur Andersen paid settlements of $0.7 billion before ultimately dissolving following the Enron scandal. See Mark Cheffers and Robert Kueppers, "Audit Analytics: Accountants Professional Liability Scorecards and Commentary," paper presented at the ALI CLE Accountants' Liability Conference (September 11–12, 2014).

57. In the United States, each of the Big Four is organized as a partnership, owned by the partners who run the firm. Each partnership is overseen by a governing board, which numbers approximately 20 directors, the majority of whom are certified public accountants.

58. However, plaintiffs' lawyers have attempted to name the international office in liability lawsuits. In 2004, Parmalat shareholders named Deloitte Touche Tohmatsu (the international associa- tion) along with Deloitte's Italian office, in a lawsuit alleging that the auditors were liable for failing to detect or report management fraud. Deloitte Touche Tohmatsu asked a U.S. District Court judge to remove its name from the case, claiming that it is a legally separate entity and provides no services to the local office. In a 2009 ruling, the judge ruled that the international association should remain defendants. He cited the marketing, financial, and quality control ties that the international association provided to the local office as evidence that a substantial connection exists between the entities. According to Stanford Law School professor and former SEC commissioner Joseph A. Grundfest: "All of them have structures designed to build fire walls [between the local office and the international association]. The question is, will the dikes hold when you have this kind of a flood?" See Nanette Byrnes, "Audit Firms' Global Ambitions Come Home to Roost," *BusinessWeek Online* (February 3, 2009). Accessed November 13, 2010. See http://search.ebscohost. com/login.aspx?direct=true&db=bth&AN=36427167&si te=ehost-live&scope=site. Also see Securities Class Action Clearinghouse, "Case Summary Parmalat Finanziaria, SpA. Securities Litigation," Rock Center for Corporate Governance and Cornerstone Research. Accessed April 10, 2015. See http://securities.stanford.edu/filings-case. html?id=102961.

59. U.S. Government Accountability Office (2008).

60. Zoe-Vonna Palmrose, "An Analysis of Auditor Litigation and Audit Service Quality," *The Accounting Review* 63 (1988): 55–73; and Inder K. Khurana and K. K. Raman, "Litigation Risk and the Financial Reporting Credibility of Big 4 versus Non-Big 4 Audits: Evidence from Anglo-American Countries," Accounting Review 79 (2004): 473–495.

61. Alastair Lawrence, Miguel Minutti-Meza, and Ping Zhang, "Can Big 4 versus Non-Big 4 Differences in Audit-Quality Proxies Be Attributed to Client Characteristics?" Accounting Review 86 (2011): 259–286.

62. Public Oversight Board, "The Road to Reform—A White Paper from the Public Oversight Board on Legislation to Create a New Private-Sector Regulatory Structure for the Accounting Profession" (March 19, 2002). Accessed November 13, 2010. See www.publicoversightboard. org/White_Pa.pdf.

63. Jerry Wegman, "Government Regulation of Accountants: The PCAOB Enforcement Process," *Journal of Legal, Ethical, and Regulatory Issues* 11 (2008): 75–94.

64. Louis Grumet, "Standards Setting at the Crossroads," *The CPA Journal* (July 1, 2003). Accessed November 13, 2010. See www.nysscpa.org/cpajournal/2003/0703/nv/nv2.htm.

65. Larcker and Richardson (2004) found that, for the subset of firms that have apparent account- ing deficiencies, the problem is weak governance systems (such as low institutional holdings and higher insider holdings) rather than payments made to the auditor for nonaudit ser- vices. See Roberta Romano, "The Sarbanes–Oxley Act and the Making of Quack Corporate Governance," *Yale Law Review* 114 (2005): 1521–1612. Also see David F. Larcker and Scott A. Richardson, "Fees Paid to Audit Firms, Accrual Choices, and Corporate Governance," *Journal of Accounting Research* 42 (2004): 625–658.

66. That study is Richard M. Frankel, Marilyn F. Johnson, and Karen K. Nelson, "The Relation between Auditors' Fee for Nonaudit Services and Earnings Management," *Accounting Review* 77 (2002): 71–105.

67. Romano (2005) is referring to restrictions including audit committee independence, limits on corporate loans to executives, and executive certification of the financial statements.

68. Mark Cheffers and Don Whalen, "Audit Fees and Nonaudit Fees: A Seven-Year Trend," *Audit Analytics* (March 2010): 1–12.

69. Michael W. Maher and Dan Weiss, "Costs of Complying with SOX—Measurement, Variation, and Investors' Anticipation," *Social Science Research Network* (October 29, 2010). Accessed May 5, 2015. See http://ssrn.com/abstract=1699828.

70. Grant Thornton LLP, "Chief Audit Executive Survey 2014: Adding Internal Audit Value, Strategically Leveraging Compliance Activities" (2014). Accessed February 26, 2015. See https://www.grantthornton.com/~/media/content-page-files/advisory/pdfs/2014/bas-cae-survey-final.ashx.

71. Cindy R. Alexander, Scott W. Bauguess, Gennaro Bernile, Yoon-Ho Alex Lee, and Jennifer Marietta-Westberg, "Economic Effects of SOX Section 404 Compliance: A Corporate Insider Perspective," *Journal of Accounting and Economics* 56 (2013): 267–290.

72. John C. Coates and Suraj Srinivasan, "SOX after Ten Years: A Multidisciplinary Review," *Accounting Horizons* 28 (2014): 627–671.

73. Measured in terms of abnormal accruals. See Thomas D. Dowdell and Jagan Krishnan, "Former Audit Firm Personnel as CFOs: Effect on Earnings Management," *Canadian Accounting Perspectives* 3 (2004): 117–142. Beasley, Carcello, and Hermanson (2000) found that 11 percent of financial restatements due to fraud involved a CFO who had previously been employed at the company's audit firm. However, the authors do not provide descriptive statistics to determine whether this represents an above-average incidence rate. See Mark S. Beasley, Joseph Y. Carcello, and Dana R. Hermanson, "Should You Offer a Job to Your External Auditor?" *Journal of Corporate Accounting and Finance* 11 (2000): 35–42.

74. Marshall A. Geiger, David S. North, and Brendan T. O'Connell, "The Auditor-to-Client Revolving Door and Earnings Management," *Journal of Accounting, Auditing and Finance* 20 (2005): 1–26.

75. The SEC audit review partner (or "concurring reviewer") also rotates every five years.

76. Mara Cameran, Emilia Merlotti, and Dino Di Vincenzo, "The Audit Firm Rotation Rule: A Review of the Literature," SDA Bocconi research paper, *Social Science Research Network* (September 2005). Accessed February 20, 2009. See http://ssrn.com/abstract=825404.

77. The authors reviewed 34 "academic" studies, 25 of which were based on empirical data and 9 of which were opinion based. Although the authors considered all 34 to be academic studies, we refer only to the 25 empirical studies here because the others did not test their conclusions against observable evidence. Interestingly, the authors noted that although 76 percent of the empirical studies concluded against mandatory auditor rotation, only 56 percent of the opinion-based reports opposed the practice. This is consistent with a general bias among thought leaders who advocate a best practice without regard to rigorous evidence.

78. For example, in 2008, there were approximately 50 audit firm changes among companies that use Big Four or other national accounting firms. Among all publicly traded companies, there are approximately 1,000 auditor changes each year. Audit Analytics, "Where the Audit Gains & Losses Came From: January 1, 2008–December 31, 2008" (2009). Accessed May 5, 2015. See http://www.auditanalytics.com/doc/CY_2008_WhereTheyWent_1-12-09.pdf. Also see Lynn E. Turner, Jason P. Williams, and Thomas R. Weirich, "An Inside Look at Auditor Changes," *The CPA Journal* (2005): 12–21.

79. "Standard Instructions for Filing Forms under the Securities Act of 1933, Securities Exchange Act of 1934, and Energy Policy and Conservation Act of 1975 Regulation S-K," Cornell University Law School. Accessed April 10, 2015. https://www.law.cornell.edu/cfr/text/17/part-229.

80. Susan Zhan Shu, "Auditor Resignations: Clientele Effects and Legal Liability," *Journal of Accounting and Economics* 29 (2000): 173–205.

81. J. Scott Whisenant, Srinivasan Sankaraguruswamy, and K. Raghunandan, "Market Reactions to Disclosure of Reportable Events," *Auditing* 22 (2003): 181–194.

11

The Market for Corporate Control

A well-functioning governance system consists of more than a board of directors to provide oversight for the corporation and an external auditor to ensure the integrity of financial reporting. It includes all disciplining mechanisms—legal, regulatory, and market driven—that influence management to act in the interest of shareholders. For example, in Chapter 7, "Labor Market for Executives and CEO Succession Planning," we examined how a competitive labor market for CEOs puts pressure on management to perform or risk being replaced by another executive, either from within or outside the company, who can deliver better corporate results.

Instead of removing an executive, the board of directors (or in some cases shareholders directly) can decide to transfer ownership of the firm to new owners who will manage its assets more profitably. A change in control involves not only replacing management but also possibly making substantial changes to firm strategy, cost structure, and capital structure. In theory, a change of control makes economic sense only when the value of the firm to new owners, minus transaction costs associated with the deal, is greater than the value of the firm to current owners.[1] When this scenario occurs, the acquirer will attempt to purchase the target and capture the resulting economic gains. This general idea is called the **market for corporate control**.

Of course, the preceding discussion is somewhat simplistic. Clearly, acquisitions also occur for nonstrategic reasons. For example, management might want to increase the scope of operations simply for the sake of managing a larger operation. When this occurs, the acquiring company might receive less in value than it gives up. The management of the acquiring firm might be better off, but the economic impact on shareholders would be considerably less positive. Similarly, the management of the target firm might seek to impede a takeover—even one that makes economic sense— to protect their present jobs. If successful, these actions can lead to inefficiencies in the market for corporate control and can weaken the disciplining effects on managerial performance.

In this chapter, we start by examining the market for corporate control. In general, how beneficial are acquisitions? Do they create or destroy value? Then we examine the steps companies take to protect themselves from unsolicited acquisitions. When is it appropriate for the firm to adopt antitakeover protections? Do they lead to enhanced shareholder value, or are they a source of value-destroying friction?

The Market for Corporate Control

The concept of a market for corporate control was succinctly described by Henry Manne: "The lower the stock price, relative to what it could be with more efficient management, the more attractive the takeover becomes to those who believe that they can manage the company more efficiently."[2] Manne's thesis was that the price of a company's stock partly reflects management performance. A low stock price indicates poor management of company assets and provides incentive to outside investors to find alternative sources of capital to acquire the company, replace its management, and maximize its resources for their own gain.

Today we think of the market for corporate control as consisting of all mergers, acquisitions, and reorganizations, including those by a competitive firm, by a conglomerate buyer, or through a leveraged buyout (LBO), management buyout (MBO), or private equity firm. The company that makes the offer is known as the **acquirer** (or **bidder**). The company that is the subject of the offer is the **target**.

An acquisition attempt can either be friendly or hostile. **Friendly acquisitions** are those in which the target is open to receiving an offer from the acquiring firm. An acquisition might still be considered friendly if the target rejects the initial bid as inadequate but signals that it is willing to negotiate a higher takeover price. **Hostile takeovers** are those in which the target resists attempts to be acquired at any reasonable price. Management of the target firm might adopt a defense mechanism to protect itself from a takeover, or more likely, it might already have such a mechanism in place that management declines to remove. These are known as **antitakeover protections**, or **antitakeover defenses**.

Takeover offers can be structured in three basic forms. A **merger** occurs when two companies directly negotiate a takeover. Mergers tend to be friendly. A merger is complete when it has been approved by both companies' boards and shareholders. A **tender offer** occurs when the acquirer makes a public offer to acquire the shares of the target at a stated price. Tender offers tend to be hostile. In the absence of antitakeover defenses, a tender offer allows a hostile bidder to bypass the target's board of directors and seek approval directly from shareholders. When antitakeover defenses are in place, a tender offer is combined with a **proxy contest**. In the proxy contest, the acquirer asks the target shareholders to elect a board proposed by the acquirer to replace the incumbent board. If elected, the new board will disable the antitakeover defenses and allow the acquisition to go forward.[3]

Acquisitions occur for many reasons. The most frequently cited reason is that the acquiring firm believes it can enhance the profitability of the target company in a manner that the company could not achieve in its existing ownership structure. In this way, the firm's assets might be worth more to an acquirer than the company as a free-standing entity.[4] Examples include these:

- **Financial synergies**—An acquiring firm believes that it can increase profits through revenue improvements, cost reductions, or vertical integration that comes from combining the two companies' business lines.

- **Diversification**—Two companies whose earnings are uncorrelated (for example, because they are in unrelated or countercyclical industries) might benefit by merging because the capital generated when one business is thriving can help the other when it is under pressure. This is the logic behind the conglomerate structure. Conglomerates can also transfer noncash resources, such as management, among divisions.[5]

- **Change in ownership**—A new ownership group might be able to improve the profitability of the target through its access to capital, managerial expertise, and other business resources. For example, private equity firms dramatically change the capital structure and incentive plans in the target firm after acquisition (see the following sidebar).

Eckbo (2013) provided an extensive review of the research literature on corporate mergers. He showed that takeover activity enhances production efficiency along the supply chain through consolidation, increased buying power, plant eliminations, more efficient plant operations, and other restructuring activities. He found evidence that large corporations that engage in acquisitions subsequently reduce innovation (investment in research and development); conversely, he found that an active market for corporate control encourages small firms to innovate to increase the probability of becoming takeover candidates. Approximately half of takeovers involving public corporations are initiated by the seller and not by the buyer.[6]

Private Equity

Private equity firms are active participants in the market for corporate control. Private equity firms are privately held investment firms that acquire companies for the benefit of retail and institutional investors. A private equity investor commits to invest in a fund managed by the firm for a finite period (10 to 12 years, on average); the fund in turn invests this money by acquiring companies for an average duration of 4 to 5 years, after which the investment is sold and the invested capital returned.[7] Because private equity firms acquire companies on behalf of institutional investors, they are referred to as "financial buyers," in contrast to corporate acquirers, which are known as "strategic buyers." Private equity firms are also known for the aggressive use to leverage to amplify returns over the 4- to 5-year investment period.

Mixed evidence has emerged over whether private equity firms generate superior, risk-adjusted returns. Guo, Hotchkiss, and Song (2011) found that private equity companies generate large, positive returns; however, gains in operating performance post-buyout are either comparable to or only slightly higher than those for benchmark firms. They find that cash flow gains are greater for firms with greater leverage and that the tax benefits of debt explain a large portion of realized returns.[8] Kaplan and Schoar (2005) found that median private equity returns are 5 to 10 percent *below* the S&P 500 Index. However, large firms that have been in business for an extended time period have outperformed the index by 60 to 80 percent over a 17-year period.[9] We discuss the governance of private equity–backed companies in greater detail in Chapter 14, "Alternative Models of Governance."

Companies can also merge for nonstrategic reasons, such as for empire building, management hubris, herding behavior, and compensation incentives. **Empire building** describes a situation in which the acquiring company's management seeks to acquire another company primarily for the sake of managing a larger enterprise. **Hubris** represents overconfidence on the part of management that it can more efficiently utilize the assets of a target to achieve greater revenues or cost savings than current owners can.[10] **Herding behavior** occurs when the senior management team of one company pursues acquisitions because its competitors have recently completed acquisitions.[11] **Compensation incentives** might encourage management to pursue deals that are not in the best interest of shareholders. Management of the acquiring company might pursue a deal because the executives will receive greater compensation for managing a larger enterprise.[12] Management of the target company might want to accept a takeover bid because the executives stand to receive large severance or change-in-control payments. According to a study by Equilar, the average CEO stands to receive $29 million in cash and accelerated equity grants following a change in control (see the following sidebar).[13]

The Personalities behind Mergers

Empire Building

Empire building might have been the driving factor behind the series of acquisitions led by former Citigroup CEO Sandy Weill.[14] Weill, who took over as CEO of little-known Commercial Credit, aggressively expanded by purchasing Primerica (parent of the prestigious brokerage firm Smith Barney), Travelers Insurance, Salomon Brothers, and Citicorp to create Citigroup—at one time, the largest financial institution in the world. Although improved service was often the stated motivation behind each acquisition, the emphasis was also on size. For example, upon announcing the Citicorp/Travelers merger, Weill asserted:

"Citicorp and Travelers Group bring together some of the best people in the financial services business, creating a resource for customers like no other—a diversified global consumer financial services company, a premier global bank, a leading global asset management company, a pre-eminent global investment banking and trading firm, and a broad-based insurance capability. Our ability to serve consumers, corporations, institutions, and government agencies, domestic and foreign, will be without parallel. This is a combination whose time has come."[15]

Hubris

Hubris might have driven AT&T CEO Michael Armstrong in his bold acquisition strategy in the late 1990s.[16] Armstrong joined the company in 1997, following an accomplished career at IBM and then serving as CEO of Hughes Electronics. In the next few years, he moved aggressively to accumulate a significant collection of telecommunication assets; he spent more than $100 billion on cable companies TCI and MediaOne. Armstrong believed that by managing a diverse set of telecommunication assets under one roof, AT&T would be positioned to capitalize on a convergence between voice, data, and Internet technologies. However, the strategy largely failed: AT&T was unable to realize revenue and profit objectives, and the company struggled under significant debt. AT&T was steadily dismantled, and the company was sold to SBC in 2005.

Herding Behavior

After pharmaceutical giant Pfizer agreed to acquire Wyeth in 2009 and Merck announced that it was merging with Schering Plough, the *Wall Street Journal* predicted that a "wave of acquisitions is likely as companies worry about their drug pipelines."[17] Senior management teams might justify copy-cat moves in economic terms (such as a "change in the competitive landscape"), but herding behavior is likely also driven by psychological tendencies, including envy, social proof, a desire for media attention, and reputational factors. Investment bankers also might exploit these tendencies to encourage deal making.

Compensation Incentives

In 2005, Gillette Company agreed to sell itself to Procter & Gamble in a deal valued at $57 billion. Following the deal, Gillette CEO James Kilts received $185 million in severance and other benefits. Critics of the deal alleged that Kilts had put his own financial consideration above that of the company by agreeing to the acquisition. According to NYU Professor David Yermack, "Many [CEOs] really dip in and take an extra bonus, an extra augmentation of their contract at the eleventh hour, when there's very little ability of the shareholders or even their own directors to do anything about it." Kilts defended the deal by claiming that it was not done to "aggrandize management or myself, but to do what is right for shareholders and employees."[18] He pointed out that much of the gain was from appreciated equity compensation that he had accepted in lieu of cash during his tenure.

Stock Market Assessment of Acquiring and Target Firms

A vast research literature has examined the market for corporate control and the impact of the acquisitions on corporate performance. Here we summarize some of the basic results.

Who Gets Acquired?

Many researchers have attempted to develop models that predict which companies are likely to become acquisition targets, based on financial and stock price performance.[19] Palepu (1986) found some evidence that firms with poor performance, small size, and a need for resources for growth are most likely to be takeover targets. Still, he cautions that it is difficult to predict takeover targets with accuracy.[20]

Professional studies have also identified attributes that might be common across takeover targets:

- **Fundamentally weak performance**—The company can be purchased at a low price (relative to assets) and performance can be subsequently improved through managerial changes or capital infusions.

- **Companies in an industry with heightened merger activity**—Industry groups tend to experience merger activity in waves. An example is the casino industry in the 2000s. A merger wave might be caused by a shift in the marketplace that makes these firms more attractive or encourages consolidation. It might also be driven by psychological factors, such as the herding behavior discussed earlier.

- **Low debt levels**—Companies with low debt levels have greater financial flexibility. The acquirer can increase the debt levels of the target as part of the financial strategy.

- **Strong cash flows**—Companies with strong cash flows have greater financial flexibility. Strategic buyers can use internally generated cash flow to fund expansion; private equity buyers can rely on cash flow to support a higher debt burden.

- **Valuable assets**—The target's assets might be underutilized, they might be complementary to those of the acquirer, or they might have value that is not readily apparent to public shareholders (such as land, intellectual property, or patents that are not carried on the balance sheet at fair value).[21]

As mentioned earlier, it is necessary to offer a premium relative to the current stock price in order to convince the target company to accept a deal. As we discussed in Chapter 3, "Board of Directors: Duties and Liability," the board of directors must evaluate the premium offered in relation to the standalone, long-term value of the company and make a decision that the board members believe is in the interest of shareholders. Eckbo (2009) calculated that the average takeover premium between 1973 and 2002 was about 45 percent (see Figure 11.1).[22] Eckbo (2013) found that initial and final takeover premiums are unaffected by whether the target is hostile to the initial bid, the liquidity of the target company's stock, whether multiple bidders are involved, or whether the takeover is by an acquirer in the same industry or a conglomerate buyer.[23]

Sample	Number of cases	Deal value ($ million)		% of contests where the winner is:			Average offer premium (%)	
		Mean	Median	Initial bidder	Rival	No bidder wins	Initial bid	Final bid
All contests	10,806	715	89	66.6	3.7	29.7	44.5	46.1
1973–1989	3,730	312	60	58.7	5.2	36.1	45.0	48.5
1990–2002	7,076	903	108	70.7	3.0	26.4	44.2	45.0
Merger bid	7,750	827	92	63.5	3.3	33.2	43.6	44.5
Tender offer	3,056	433	78	74.8	4.8	20.4	46.5	50.2
Acquirer public	6,726	902	112	75.6	3.2	21.3	46.1	47.5
Acquirer private	4,080	285	52	51.7	4.6	43.7	40.1	42.6
Single bidder	9,944	693	88	70.5	0.0	29.5	44.8	45.4
Multiple bidders	862	989	101	20.6	47.8	31.7	41.1	53.2
Target friendly	10,295	688	85	68.0	3.2	28.8	44.1	45.1
Target hostile	511	1,204	183	34.4	16.3	49.2	49.0	60.9
All cash	4,185	320	66	69.1	4.0	27.0	44.1	46.6
Stock/mixed	6,621	1,048	119	65.0	3.6	31.4	44.7	45.8

Source: Eckbo (2009).

Figure 11.1   Initial and final offer premiums (1973–2002).

Researchers have also studied the practice of awarding change-of-control payments (**golden parachutes**) for their implications on takeover activity. Lambert and Larcker (1985) found that the stock market reacts positively to the adoption of a golden parachute provision in the executive employment contract. They suggested that shareholders might view such provisions favorably if they believe it means that a takeover is more likely or that management has greater incentive to negotiate a larger premium in a prospective deal.[24] Fich, Tran, and Walkling (2013) studied 851 acquisitions between 1999 and 2007 and found that golden parachutes significantly increase the probability of deal completion; however, they also found that golden parachutes are associated with lower takeover premiums.[25] By contrast, Machlin, Choe, and Miles (1993) found that golden parachute provisions significantly increase the likelihood of a takeover and that the size of the payment positively influences the magnitude of the takeover premium. They saw no evidence that such payments are made as a form of rent extraction (that is, if they are awarded only after a deal is already pending) but instead concluded that "golden parachutes encourage managers to pursue shareholder interests."[26]

To reduce the likelihood that management pursues a deal simply to realize an accelerated payment, most companies require a "double trigger" before the golden parachute becomes payable: The corporation must undergo a change in control *and* the executive must be terminated without cause in connection with the deal. According to Equilar, 98 percent of companies that offer cash payments upon a change in control require a double trigger.[27]

Finally, even successfully negotiated takeovers are often subject to litigation from plaintiffs' attorneys representing shareholder groups alleging that they did not receive adequate compensation for their shares. These lawsuits typically allege that the target company's board conducted a flawed sales process that failed to maximize shareholder value. Allegations might include that the process was not sufficiently competitive, that antitakeover protections reduced the deal price, that management or members of the board that negotiated the deal were conflicted (say, due to potential compensation), or that disclosure was inadequate. According to Cornerstone Research, 93 percent of M&A deals valued over $100 million were litigated in 2014. The average number of lawsuits per deal was 4.5. Fifty-nine percent were resolved before the deal closed, and only one went to trial, resulting in $76 million in damages. Eighty percent of settlements required only additional disclosure. Only six involved payments to shareholders.[28]

Who Gets the Value in a Takeover?

The benefits of a change in ownership are not evenly shared between the acquirer and the target. Research studies routinely have found that the incremental value anticipated by a merger tends to flow predominantly to the target, in the form of a large premium relative to past stock price. Jensen and Ruback (1983) reviewed 12 studies on successful tender offers and acquisitions. They found that target companies exhibit double-digit excess stock price returns between the announcement and consummation of a merger.[29] The amount of outperformance varies by the nature of the deal. For example, Servaes (1991) found that companies that are the target of a hostile bid outperform the market by 32 percentage points in the month following the takeover announcement, while companies that agree to a friendly merger outperform by 22 percent.[30] Gains also vary by the structure of the deal. Andrade, Mitchell, and Stafford (2001) found that mergers funded with equity result in lower excess returns for target companies than all-cash offers.[31]

At the same time, the benefits of a change in ownership are decidedly less favorable for the acquirer. Martynova and Renneboog (2008) found that the acquiring firm's shareholders enjoy no bump up in share price following the announcement of a takeover. Instead, the stock price returns of the acquirer are indistinguishable from those of the general market.[32] Studies also show that relative performance depends on the nature of the bid. Goergen and Renneboog (2004) found that hostile takeovers result in worse stock price performance for the acquirer than friendly deals.[33] Mergers financed with equity destroy more value for the acquiring firm than mergers financed with cash.[34]

However, these studies focus on the market's expectations for the merger based on stock price changes around the announcement date. But what does the evidence say about the long-term economics of deals? The evidence is fairly negative. Studies that measure long-term operating performance (such as earnings-per-share growth or cash flows over a one- to three-year period) largely find that firms tend to underperform their peers following an acquisition.[35] In particular, mergers initiated during a wave of activity exhibit below-average long-term performance.[36] One obvious explanation is that the acquisition is simply a bad investment in which revenue and cost synergies do not meet expectations. If a target has multiple bids, the acquirer might experience the "winner's curse," in which the final bid is actually too high. Acquirers sometimes cut back on investment in working capital and capital expenditures following a deal, actions that can improve cash flow but destroy value. Furthermore, companies that acquire targets within the same industry enjoy no performance advantage over companies that acquire targets from an unrelated industry. Still, some evidence indicates that acquisitions financed with cash perform better than acquisitions financed with equity.[37]

Although much attention is paid to the economics of a merger, the merger process itself is equally important. Proposed mergers can be highly disruptive to both the target and the acquirer. This is particularly true of hostile takeover attempts, in which considerable resources are expended to mount or defend an unsolicited bid.

The bidder must acquire a list of shareholders, contact major shareholders to assess their willingness to sell, and mail proxy materials to all parties. For its part, the target must contact shareholders and convince them not to sell. If the target believes that the threat is credible, it might engage in value-destroying behaviors to thwart the acquisition. All these actions detract from a focus on running day-to-day operations, and boards need to be especially diligent during these activities (see the following sidebar).

The Struggles of a Hostile Takeover

Allergan

In April 2014, Canada-based drug maker Valeant Pharmaceuticals International made an unsolicited offer to acquire Allergan (maker of Botox) for $46 billion, for a mix of cash and stock. At $153 per share, the offer represented a 30 percent premium over the current share price. In making its bid, Valeant partnered with activist investor William Ackman and his hedge fund Pershing Square. Earlier in the month, Pershing Square had disclosed a 9.7 percent stake in Allergan. Allergan's board rejected the offer as substantially undervaluing the company. Allergan CEO David Pyott questioned Valeant's plans to significantly reduce Allergan's cost structure by slashing its research-and-development and marketing budgets: "We question how Valeant could maintain Allergan's sales growth, especially considering the significant cost reductions Valeant is proposing."[38]

Valeant subsequently raised its bid to $166 per share. One week later, it raised it again, to $179. Allergan's board rejected both offers. Valeant announced a tender offer to acquire shares directly from Allergan investors and use the tendered shares to call a special meeting to replace Allergan's board with a new slate of directors that would approve the deal.

In response, Allergan filed a federal lawsuit, alleging that Valeant's joint bid with Pershing Square violated insider trading laws because Pershing Square knew of the bid before it was made public. The company also approached Salix Pharmaceuticals about a potential tie-up to thwart Valeant's bid. Valeant raised its offer again, to $186. In November, Allergan agreed to be purchased by Ireland-based Actavis in a deal valued at $66 billion, or $219 per share. Valeant CEO Michael Pearson walked away, saying that "Valeant cannot justify to its own shareholders paying a price of $219 or more."[39] In February 2015, Valeant agreed to purchase Salix for $11 billion in cash.

Even successful deals result in considerable turmoil for the acquirer. For example, takeovers commonly lead to layoffs as acquirers seek to capture operating efficiencies by reducing labor expenses. Takeovers also lead to executive turnover as management teams are integrated. Krug and Shill (2008) found that executive turnover rates double following an acquisition and that executive turnover remains elevated for 10 years. The authors noted that "long-term leadership instability . . . should be viewed as potentially harmful to integration and long-term performance."[40] Other studies have suggested that how well a company manages the integration process is a key determinant of whether a merger will ultimately generate economic benefits to the acquirer.[41]

Based on the evidence, considerable debate arises over whether acquisitions are a good idea for the acquiring firm. Consensus seems to have formed that the value of deals generally flows to shareholders of the target firm. Furthermore, experience shows that the surviving firm often fails to realize economic value. As a result, the board should carefully consider whether to allow management to complete large acquisitions. Although in some examples such deals lead to substantial value creation, the average results (discussed earlier) are considerably less compelling for shareholders.

On the other hand, target companies often go through considerable effort to protect themselves from being acquired. Why this is so, given the potential economic returns that target shareholders stand to receive, remains a question. In the second half of this chapter, we consider the actions that targets take to defend themselves from an unsolicited offer and the impact of these actions on shareholder value.

Antitakeover Protections

A company that does not want to become the target of an unsolicited takeover can adopt defense mechanisms that discourage or dissuade potential bidders from making a formal offer. Several important economic reasons justify doing so:

- **Preservation of long-term value**—A company with attractive future growth prospects that is selling at a depressed market price might want to prevent another company from making a bid at artificially low prices. For example, the firm might have developed a new technology but has chosen not to disclose this information to the public for competitive reasons. The current stock price will not reflect the value of this innovation. By remaining independent, the company will have time to commercialize this technology and deliver long-term value to current shareholders.

- **Acquirer myopia**—A company that is protected from unsolicited takeovers has greater flexibility to pursue risky, long-term projects that offer attractive future gains. Management is able to make investments with positive net present value that depress current earnings, without having to worry about being taken over before those investments have had time to pay off.

- **Enhanced bargaining power**—When a company implements antitakeover protections, a potential acquirer is more likely to be compelled to engage management rather than make a hostile bid. This increases management's negotiating leverage and offers the target the opportunity to secure a higher deal price.

However, antitakeover provisions can also be a manifestation of agency problems, such as **management entrenchment**. An entrenched management is one that erects barriers to retain its position of power and insulate itself from market forces. An entrenched management is able to extract rents from the company (through continued employment or excessive compensation and perquisites) when these are not merited based on performance.

The board must determine whether antitakeover provisions are truly in the interest of shareholders. Even with antitakeover protections in place, the board of directors has a fiduciary obligation to weigh all offers—both friendly and hostile.

Antitakeover Actions

The most common antitakeover defense is the **poison pill**—also known as a **shareholder's rights plan**. Many companies have this defense in place on an ongoing basis, but even those that do not can adopt one at any time without delay and without shareholder approval.[42] When triggered, poison pills have the potential to grant holders of the company's shares the right to acquire additional shares at a deep discount to fair market value (such as $0.01 per share). The poison pill is triggered if a shareholder or shareholder group accumulates an ownership position above a threshold level (typically 15 to 20 percent of shares outstanding). Once this threshold is exceeded, the market is flooded with new shares that dilute the would-be acquirer's shareholdings and make it prohibitively expensive for the acquirer to take control of the firm through open market purchases or a tender offer. The effect is so severe that no acquirer will trigger the pill; instead, it will pressure the target board to disable the pill and allow the acquisition to go forward. At the same time, the acquirer will launch a proxy contest to replace the incumbent board with a board that is friendly to the deal and will disable the pill.[43]

A second layer of antitakeover defenses include those that prevent a hostile acquirer from replacing the incumbent board. The strongest protection is dual-class stock, which gives a controlling shareholder or management enough votes to control board elections. As explained in Chapter 3, a company with **dual-class shares** has more than one class of common stock. Each class is afforded a different set of voting rights even though they are otherwise economically equivalent. For example, Class A shareholders might have 10 times as many votes per share as Class B shareholders. The class of shares with more generous voting rights typically is not publicly traded, but is held by an insider, the founding family, or another shareholder that is friendly to management. A dual-class share structure means that a corporate raider can accumulate a majority economic stake in a company but still not have majority voting control to replace the board.

A company might also restrict the ability of shareholders to replace the incumbent board by adopting a **staggered board**, or **classified board**. As discussed in Chapter 3, with a staggered board, directors typically are grouped into three classes, each of which is elected to a three-year term. Only one class of directors stands for reelection in a given year. A staggered board structure prevents a corporate raider from gaining majority control of a board in a single year. Any proxy contest to have board members removed must be waged over at least a two-year period. The coupling of a poison pill with a staggered board is a very formidable antitakeover defense.

A company with an annually elected board might protect itself by restricting the ability of shareholders to replace the incumbent board between annual meetings. This is achieved through charter provisions that both restrict shareholder rights to call a special meeting (in which the vote would occur) and prohibit shareholders from voting by written consent (in which shareholders who are unable to meet physically can still vote on a matter). If either of these avenues is available to the target's shareholders, it can be used to hold an election in which the incumbent board is replaced. Still, these defenses are weaker than those described earlier because they only protect the incumbent board until the next annual meeting.

Finally, the state of a target's incorporation might provide takeover defenses by statute. However, as discussed in Chapter 3, expanded constituency provisions are limited in the protections they afford.

The vast majority of U.S. corporations have adopted some level of protection. Among companies in the Russell 2000, 53 percent have a staggered board, 10 percent have multiple classes of shares with unequal voting rights, and 9 percent have a poison pill protection in place. Seventy-three percent do not allow shareholder action by written consent, and 46 percent have limited shareholder rights to call a special meeting (see Table 11.1).[44]

The question for the board is, should the company implement antitakeover protections? In the following sections, we examine the research on four common defense mechanisms: poison pills, staggered boards, state of incorporation, and dual-class shares. We consider whether these protections are successful in deterring takeovers and what impact they have on governance quality.

Table 11.1 Antitakeover Protections

	Companies (%)
Poison pills (in force)	8.6%
Dual-class shares	9.9%
Staggered (classified) board	52.6%
No cumulative voting	95.0%
Shareholders have limited rights to call special meeting	46.4%
Shareholders cannot act by written consent	73.0%
Supermajority vote required for mergers	17.2%
Supermajority vote required to remove directors	34.0%
Directors removed for cause only	52.6%
Board fills vacant director seats	80.5%
Blank check preferred stock	94.1%
Expanded constituency provision in bylaws or charter	9.2%

Source: Computed using 2014 data for 1,871 companies in the Russell 2000 Index covered by SharkRepellent, FactSet Research Systems, Inc.

Poison Pills

As explained earlier, poison pills are very effective at stopping a hostile takeover (particularly when they are combined with a staggered board). The poison pill defense was first used in 1982 by General American Oil to prevent a hostile takeover by T. Boone Pickens. The defense was ruled legal in 1985 by the Delaware Supreme Court and subsequently has been imitated by numerous other firms.[45] A poison pill might also be adopted to delay a takeover bid and give additional companies time to come forward with a competing bid. In rare cases, a poison pill can be adopted to limit the ownership stake and influence of an activist investor that might agitate for a sale of the company. For example, in 2013, Sotheby's adopted a unique poison pill that limited passive investors such as mutual funds to a 20 percent ownership level and activist shareholders to a 10 percent level.[46]

In recent years, many companies in the United States have dropped their poison pills. According to data from SharkRepellent, the number of companies that had a poison pill fell by 85 percent between 2004 and 2014 (see Figure 11.2).[47] But as explained earlier in this chapter, a firm can adopt a poison pill quickly after a takeover attempt has become known. To this end, some companies that have eliminated their poison pills have expressly reserved the right to adopt a plan in the future. Some shareholder groups, however, have moved to limit this right by requiring that any new plan be subject to shareholder approval.[48]

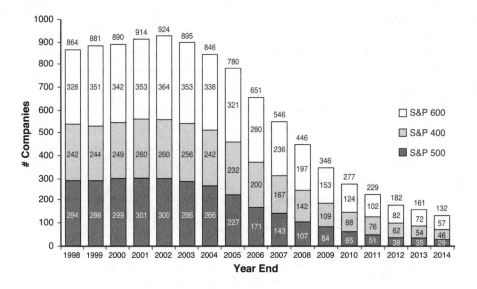

Source: Adapted from SharkRepellent, FactSet Research Systems, Inc.

Figure 11.2   S&P 1500 poison pills in force at year end (including non-U.S. incorporated companies).

Institutional investors take a mixed view on poison pills. The AFL-CIO supports "the legitimate use of shareholder plans," with the stipulation that its support applies only as long as "shareholders [are] given the opportunity to vote on these plans."[49] Morgan Stanley Investment Management votes "case-by-case on whether the company has demonstrated a need for the defense in the context of promoting long-term shareholder value; whether provisions of defense are in line with generally accepted governance principles [. . .]; and specific context if the proposal is made in the midst of a takeover bid or contest for control."[50] By renewing poison pills with a periodic vote, shareholders are able to cast their opinion on whether the provision provides legitimate economic protection or acts as management entrenchment.

Cremers and Ferrell (2014) found that poison pills have a negative relationship with firm value, as measured by market-to-book value ratios. They estimated that firm value decreases by 5 percent upon the adoption of a pill.[51]

Brickley, Coles, and Terry (1994) found that the market reacts positively to the adoption of a poison pill if the company's board has a majority of outside directors and negatively if the board does not have a majority of outside directors. They concluded that shareholders view poison pills as protecting their economic interests if the board is independent and that they view poison pills as entrenching management when insiders control the board.[52] Ryngaert (1988) reached a similar conclusion. He found no statistically significant reaction to the adoption of a poison pill across a broad sample of firms. However, among firms perceived to be takeover targets, he found a significant negative reaction. He also found that stock prices fall an average 2.2 percent when the plan is upheld in court and rise 3.4 percent when the plan is ruled invalid.[53]

Poison pills are generally effective in preventing unsolicited takeovers. Ryngaert (1988) found that companies that implement a poison pill are twice as likely to defeat an unsolicited offer as companies without a poison pill.[54] Furthermore, companies with a poison pill in place ultimately agree to takeover premiums that are roughly 5 to 10 percent higher.[55] These statistics are somewhat misleading, however, because they fail to take into account the decline in stock price that takes place when a company successfully uses a poison pill to defeat an unsolicited takeover. Ryngaert (1988) found that companies that defeat an offer experience market-adjusted declines of 14 percent.[56] That is, poison pills tend to reward shareholders if the bid is successful, but not if it fails.

Poison pills have extensive history in the United States but are less common in other countries. For example, in Japan, unsolicited takeovers have generally not occurred, and so Japanese companies have not had to adopt poison pills. In recent years, however, with the growth of global capital markets, international investors have pressured Japanese managers to take aggressive actions to improve performance. This has encouraged the adoption of poison pills among Japanese companies to preserve their autonomy. It also reflects the tensions that can occur when Western styles of capitalism are applied to countries with different societal values (see the following sidebar).

Poison Pills in Japan

Bull-Dog Sauce

In 2007, U.S.-based hedge fund Steel Partners made a tender offer to acquire Bull-Dog Sauce, a Japanese-based food manufacturer, for ¥1,700 per share. The price represented a 27 percent premium over the company's 30-day average closing price. At the time, Steel Partners owned 10 percent of Bull-Dog's shares, which it had accumulated through open-market purchases. Steel Partners believed that the company's value could be improved through better management and more aggressive international distribution.

To block Steel Partners's efforts, Bull-Dog adopted a poison pill. The poison pill granted shareholders (including Steel Partners) three equity warrants for each Bull-Dog share. However, the plan barred Steel Partners from exercising its warrants for shares and instead required that they be converted into cash at ¥396 ($3.33) a share (¥2.3 billion, or $19.3 million total). The plan was approved by a shareholder vote, with 80 percent in favor.[57]

Steel Partners sued the company, alleging that the poison pill was discriminatory and violated Japanese law. A district court found in favor of Bull-Dog. It ruled that the plan was not discriminatory because shareholders had approved it. The Japanese Supreme Court upheld the decision, labeling Steel Partners "an abusive acquirer."[58]

Bull-Dog shareholders exercised their warrants and Steel Partners' ownership position was diluted to 3 percent (it did receive cash in compensation for its warrants). The hedge fund later sold its entire position.

Staggered Board

Staggered boards pose an obstacle to hostile takeover attempts, in that a corporate raider cannot gain control of the board in a single year through a proxy contest. Instead, the raider must win at least two elections, one year apart from each other, to gain majority representation. Although it is not impossible, winning two consecutive elections is significantly more costly and less likely to succeed (the corporation has the opportunity to quell shareholder dissatisfaction in the intervening year).[59] In recent years, the use of staggered boards has dramatically decreased. In 2004, approximately 900 of the S&P 1500 had a staggered board; by 2014, this figure had decreased to 477 (see Figure 11.3).[60]

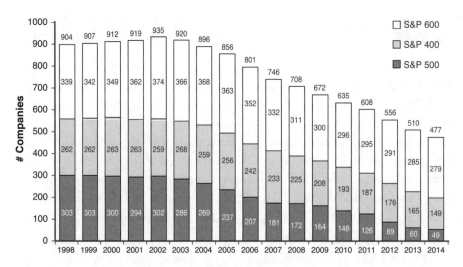

Source: Adapted from SharkRepellent, FactSet Research Systems, Inc.

Figure 11.3 S&P 1500 staggered (classified) boards (including non-U.S. incorporated companies).

Board classification is a significant deterrent to unsolicited takeovers. Bebchuk, Coates, and Subramanian (2002) examined merger activity between 1996 and 2000 and found no instances of a corporate raider gaining control of a staggered board through a proxy contest. Furthermore, they found that companies with a staggered board are significantly more likely to defeat an unsolicited bid and remain independent (61 percent versus 34 percent of companies with a single-class board). At the same time, companies with a staggered board that do get acquired receive a premium that is fairly similar to those with a single-class board (54 percent versus 50 percent). The authors concluded that the staggered board structure does not "provide sufficiently large countervailing benefits to shareholders of hostile bid targets, in the form of higher deal premiums, to offset the substantially lower likelihood of being acquired."[61]

Pound (1987) reached similar conclusions. He examined a sample of 100 companies with staggered boards and supermajority provisions (companies with supermajority provisions require that mergers be approved by more than half of shareholders, typically 66 percent to 80 percent). He found that 28 percent of companies with these protections receive takeover bids, compared with 38 percent for a control sample without these protections. He also found that companies with these provisions that ultimately accept the bid do not receive a significantly higher premium to compensate for the lower likelihood of acquisition (51 percent vs. 49 percent). He, too, concluded that "these amendments increase the bargaining power of management . . . to the detriment of shareholder wealth."[62]

Guo, Kruse, and Nohel (2008) found that the announcement to destagger is associated with about a 1 percent increase in stock price. They also found that firms that are considered to have good governance are more inclined to drop the staggered structure.[63] Faleye (2007) found that staggered boards are associated with lower CEO turnover, less CEO pay-performance sensitivity, and lower likelihood of proxy contests or shareholder proposals.[64]

Research evidence, however, is not uniformly negative. Cremers, Litov, and Sepe (2014) examined the effect of staggering and destaggering boards using a time series analysis rather than cross-section analysis, over the time period 1978 to 2011. They found that the adoption of a staggered board is associated with a subsequent increase in firm market-to-book value and destaggering is associated with a decrease in value.[65] Ge, Tanlu, and Zhang (2014) examined destaggering transactions in recent years, motivated by activist shareholders, and found that they do not lead to improved performance and might lead to worse outcomes.[66] Consistent with these findings, Larcker, Ormazabal, and Taylor (2011) examined the market reaction to proposed regulations that would bar staggered boards and found that firms with staggered boards suffered a negative market response to these proposals.[67]

Staggered boards therefore are likely to have positive as well as negative implications for shareholders, depending on the situation. Staggered boards afford greater independence to outside directors who can take a long-term perspective without pressure from management or shareholders. For this reason, staggered boards remain a prominent feature of innovative and fast-growing companies, including newly issued IPO companies. At the same time, a clear risk exists that board classification insulates directors from shareholder pressure and reduces director accountability by reducing the frequency of elections. For this reason, many institutional shareholders oppose staggered boards. For example, in 2013, shareholder-sponsored proposals to destagger boards were voted on for 29 companies; 26 of these passed, and average support was 80 percent.[68]

State of Incorporation

Approximately 60 percent of publicly traded companies in the United States are incorporated in the state of Delaware.[69] The rest are predominantly incorporated in the state in which they were founded or are headquartered. The state of incorporation is important because state law dictates most corporate governing rights. A company that faces the threat of a hostile bid can reincorporate in a state with more protective antitakeover laws. For example, Barzuza (2009) provided a review of state antitakeover laws and found that, whereas Delaware tends to have laws that protect shareholder value, at least some states have entered into a "race to the bottom" by allowing very restrictive protections.[70]

Most institutional investors oppose reincorporation for the purpose of protecting the firm from an unsolicited bid. They view this as an attempt to expand the powers of the board at the expense of shareholders, whose rights are curtailed. To this end, activist investor Carl Icahn has proposed that shareholders be given greater say over the matter with "a federal law that allows shareholders to vote by simple majority to move their company's incorporation to another state."[71]

State law can have an important impact on governance quality. Shareholders view restrictive state laws as negative. For example, Szewczyk and Tsetsekos (1992) measured the impact of the Pennsylvania Senate Bill (PA-SB 1310), which added significant new protections for Pennsylvania-based firms. Under PA-SB 1310, the following holds:

- Directors can consider the short-term and long-term impact *on all stakeholders* in their assessment of a takeover proposal. This provides considerably more flexibility than a focus on maximization of shareholder value, which is primarily achieved through takeover premium.

- Voting rights of shareholders who control 20 percent or more of the stock are removed until a majority of disinterested shareholders vote to restore their votes. As a result, a corporate raider who accumulates a significant position is not allowed to vote on his or her own takeover proposal unless other shareholders allow this.

- Profits realized by a control group from the disposition of equity within 18 months of obtaining control status are disgorged. This prohibits a raider from driving up the price of a stock and then dumping shares for a short-term gain.

- Severance (up to 26 weeks) must be provided to any employee terminated within 24 months after a change in control.

- An acquirer cannot terminate existing labor contracts after a change in control.

- However, firms can opt out of some or all of these provisions.

Szewczyk and Tsetsekos (1992) tracked the share price performance of a sample of Pennsylvania-based firms from the day PA-SB 1310 was first introduced in the state senate until it was signed into law six months later. They found that these firms performed significantly worse than a comparable sample of firms incorporated outside Pennsylvania. Based on the abnormal change in stock prices over the measurement period, the sample of Pennsylvania firms lost nearly $4 billion in market value through the enactment of the law. Furthermore, companies that subsequently chose to opt out of some or all of the provisions of PA-SB 1310 experienced significant positive stock price returns on the day of the announcement. The authors attributed "this favorable share price response to the firms' reaffirmation of the fiduciary responsibility of their directors to shareholders."[72]

Similarly, Subramanian (2003) examined whether companies are compensated for restrictive antitakeover laws through higher buyout premiums if the bid is ultimately successful. He found that companies incorporated in states with high takeover protections do not receive premiums that are significantly higher than companies incorporated in states with low takeover protections. He concluded that restrictive state laws do not increase the bargaining power of management relative to potential bidders.[73]

Dual-Class Shares

A company with dual-class shares has more than one class of common stock. In general, each class has proportional ownership interests in the company but disproportionate voting rights. The difference between the economic interest and voting interest of the classes is known as the **wedge.** (For example, if Class A has 10 percent economic interest and 30 percent voting interest, the wedge is 20 percent.)

The class with favorable voting rights typically does not trade in the public market but is instead held by an insider, the founding family, or another shareholder that is friendly to management.

In a dual-class share structure, a corporate raider can accumulate a majority economic stake in a company but still not have majority voting control. For example, prior to its sale to News Corp., the Dow Jones Company had two classes of stock: Class A shares, which were publicly traded, and Class B shares, which were privately held by the Bancroft family. Shareholders of Class A and Class B were afforded equal ownership interests in terms of their rights to profits, dividends, and a claim on company assets. However, Class B shareholders were granted ten times as many votes per share as Class A shareholders. This meant that even though the Bancrofts had less than a 10 percent ownership interest, they still controlled 64 percent of the votes (a wedge of 54 percent). The only way for News Corp. to succeed with its unsolicited offer was to convince members of the Bancroft family to vote in favor of the deal.[74]

Most institutional investors oppose dual-class shares. Morgan Stanley Investment Management proxy guidelines state that it "generally supports management and shareholder proposals aimed at eliminating unequal voting rights, assuming fair economic treatment of classes of shares held."[75] Likewise, proxy advisory firm Institutional Shareholder Services votes "against proposals to create a new class of common stock with superior voting rights" and "votes against proposals at companies with dual-class capital structures to increase the number of authorized shares of the class of stock that has superior voting rights."[76] These positions are understandable, in light of the fact that institutional owners generally own the shares with inferior voting rights.

In some circumstances, it might make sense to create dual-class stock. For example, a high-growth firm might want to raise capital to pursue a promising new project but might not want to issue straight common stock for fear of giving up too much voting control (that is, the firm does not mind giving up a substantial economic interest to invest in the project but is concerned about losing control over the project to new investors). As a result, the company might decide to issue new stock in a separate class of shares with inferior voting rights. Companies might also opt for a dual-class structure to preserve the independence of management and the board. This is particularly the case when the company's founder retains a considerable ownership stake in the company. For example, several prominent technology companies with large founder ownership such as Alibaba, Facebook, and Google all elected to have more than one share class following their initial public offerings (see the following sidebar).

Controlled Corporations

A "controlled company" is a publicly listed company of which more than 50 percent of the voting power for the election of directors is held by an individual or a group. A company might be "controlled" either through a dual-class structure or because a single shareholder or shareholder group owns more than 50 percent of the voting rights in a single-class structure. Controlled corporations are exempt from certain corporate governance listing standards by the New York Stock Exchange, including the requirements for a majority of independent directors, an independent compensation committee, and an independent nominating and governance committee. In 2014, approximately 200 companies were "controlled companies."[77]

Shareholders that invest in controlled corporations have much more limited rights to influence corporate matters than investors of single-class corporations. For example, Oil-Dri Corporation advises shareholders that they "may not have the same benefits and information available to stockholders of [listed companies] that are subject to all of the NYSE corporate governance requirements."[78] Similarly, the prospectus for Alibaba's 2014 initial public offering warns that, as controlling owners of the corporation, "the Alibaba Partnership or its director nominees may make decisions with which you disagree, including decisions on important topics such as compensation, management succession, acquisition strategy and our business and financial strategy."[79]

Little research exists that specifically examines the governance of controlled corporations. Still, the research on dual-class shares cited in this chapter and the research on outside directors cited in Chapter 5, "Board of Directors: Structure and Consequences," suggest that controlled corporations are likely subject to the same risk of abuse by inside owners.

The evidence suggests that companies with dual-class shares tend to have lower governance quality. Masulis, Wang, and Xie (2009) examined the relationship between dual-class share structure and shareholder response to company behavior in terms of acquisitions, CEO compensation, cash levels, and capital expenditures. On average, insiders at the companies in the study held 67.4 percent of the voting rights, compared with only 40.8 percent of the economic rights (the wedge was 26.6 percent). The authors found that public shareholders respond negatively and are skeptical about the economic merits of an acquisition announcement. Furthermore, the authors found that as the size of the wedge increases, CEO compensation is higher, shareholders believe that large cash holdings are more likely to be put to uneconomic use, and shareholders place less value on large capital expenditures. The authors concluded that the evidence was "consistent with the hypothesis that insiders holding more voting rights relative to cash flow rights extract more private benefits at the expense of outside shareholders." That is, companies with dual-class shares are more likely to have agency problems than those with a single share class.[80] Gompers, Ishii, and Metrick (2010) reached a similar conclusion.[81]

Warding Off Unwanted Acquirers

Research demonstrates that antitakeover protections generally reduce governance quality and shareholder value. They do so by increasing the transaction costs associated with a successful acquisition and by shielding management from the disciplining mechanism of otherwise efficient capital markets. However, as we have seen, some evidence also shows appropriate uses for antitakeover provisions.

Daines and Klausner (2001) provided a useful summary that ranks antitakeover protections by their level of protectiveness (from most difficult to least difficult to acquire):

1. Companies that have either dual-class shares or staggered boards and prohibitions on shareholder rights to call special meetings or act by written consent

2. Companies with staggered boards but no limitations on shareholder rights to call special meetings or act by written consent

3. Companies with annually elected boards but prohibitions on shareholder rights to call special meetings or act by written consent

4. Companies with annually elected boards and full shareholder rights to call a special meeting or act by written consent

5. Companies with no antitakeover provisions[82]

Similarly, Klausner (2013) reviewed the empirical evidence on antitakeover protections in IPO charters and concluded that "the idea that more takeover defenses means greater insulation against the takeover threat [. . .] is not true. Once a company has a staggered board, additional defenses provide no protection at the margin, and even in companies without staggered boards multiple defenses are generally redundant."[83]

The key issue for the board is to determine whether maintaining control over the corporation or fighting a takeover attempt is in the best interest of shareholders. Unfortunately, the research literature on this topic is mixed. Atanassov (2013) found that antitakeover provisions lead to management entrenchment and less pressure on companies to innovate: Stronger antitakeover protections are associated with a decline in patent filings and citations.[84] Bhojraj, Sengupta, and Zhang (2014), however, found the opposite to be true: Innovative companies with strong protections are less likely to engage in myopic activities such as reducing research and development expenditures and filing fewer patents. They concluded that "In contrast to prior research that predominantly documents evidence of harmful effects of antitakeover provisions (ATPs) on average, we show that ATPs can provide benefits to a subset of firms."[85]

Similarly, the research on whether a company benefits by resisting a hostile takeover is fairly inconclusive. Bradley, Desai, and Kim (1983) found that companies that reject a takeover offer and are not subsequently taken over lose all the stock price gains earned prior to the announcement.[86] Similarly, Safieddine and Titman (1999) found that firms rejecting a takeover on the basis that the offer "is insufficient" experience a 3.4 percent stock price decline on the announcement date.[87] Nevertheless, if the target company is truly committed to increasing shareholder value, evidence shows that they can successfully do so. Safieddine and Titman (1999) find that target firms that increase their leverage after rejecting a bid outperform similar firms by about 40 percent over the following five years, whereas firms that do not increase their leverage underperform similar firms by about 25 percent over this time period. That is, the greater debt load gives management incentive (and demonstrates management's commitment) to increasing cash flow and shareholder value.[88] Thus, important contextual elements seem to contribute to whether stock prices rise or decline after a rejected takeover. Nevertheless, boards should consider the very real possibility that the stock price for their firm might never recover following a successful takeover defense (see the following sidebar).

Yahoo! versus Microsoft

In January 2008, Microsoft made an unsolicited offer to acquire Yahoo! for $44.6 billion ($31 per share) in cash and stock. The bid represented a 62 percent premium over Yahoo!'s previous stock price of $19.[89] In pursuing Yahoo!, Microsoft sought to increase market share in online advertising and better position itself to compete against industry leader Google.

Yahoo! rejected the offer as "undervalued." In an effort to ward off Microsoft, the company pursued strategic alternatives with AOL, Google, and others. In a move that received less attention, Yahoo! implemented what is known as a **tin parachute**: a provision that allowed every employee in the company who was terminated without cause during the two years following a change in control to receive both their annual salary over a designated number of months and immediate vesting of all unvested stock options and restricted shares.[90] The move was designed to make a deal prohibitively expensive to Microsoft. Microsoft responded by withdrawing its bid. The stock price retreated to the mid-$20s, as some investors held out hope that some sort of deal would materialize.

In May, activist investor Carl Icahn purchased 50 million shares (through a combination of stock and options) and launched a proxy contest to replace Yahoo!'s 10-member board. In an interview, Icahn stated, "I am amazed at the lengths that [founder and CEO] Jerry Yang and the board went to entrench themselves in this situation." If the proxy contest was successful, Icahn would use the position to resume merger talks with Microsoft.[91]

At the company's annual meeting, Yahoo!'s directors were reelected, but with low support. CEO Jerry Yang received only 66 percent support and Chairman Roy Bostock 60 percent.[92] Following the vote, Yang resigned, and Yahoo! invited two Icahn nominees to the board. Still, Yahoo! and Microsoft could not agree to a merger, ultimately agreeing instead to a much smaller advertising deal. Yahoo!'s stock price fell into the low teens, where it remained for the next few years and performed significantly worse than the general market.

In evaluating antitakeover protections, shareholders and board members might consider several issues. First, how important is the market for corporate control as a disciplining mechanism in the firm-specific governance structure? Perhaps other features of the corporate governance system are sufficient to mitigate agency problems. Second, what are the motives of potential acquirers? Are these motives consistent with the long-term shareholder or stakeholder objectives of the company? Finally, are the antitakeover provisions truly adopted to protect shareholder interests, or are they a manifestation of "entrenched management"?

Endnotes

1. Transaction costs can be substantial. The various parties bidding for RJR Nabisco racked up $203 million in investment banking fees before KKR ultimately emerged as the winner, taking the firm private in 1988.

2. H.G. Manne, "Mergers and the Market for Corporate Control," *Journal of Political Economy* 73 (1965): 110–120.

3. On average, 60 proxy contests were initiated at U.S. public companies each year for the period 2001–2005 and 112 for the period 2006–2010. See Warren S. De Wied, "Proxy Contests," *Practical Law: The Journal* (November 2010).

4. Note that this is not inconsistent with efficient markets. The market price of the firm can be correct as a free-standing entity, even though the sale of the firm to a different owner can still merit a substantial premium because it can more effectively use the assets.

5. Many researchers question the logic behind this argument. They argue that if shareholders value diversification, they can achieve it on their own through a diversified stock portfolio. To this end, the research literature has shown that companies organized in a conglomerate structure trade at a discount to a portfolio of similar monoline companies that exist as standalone entities.

6. B. Espen Eckbo, "Corporate Takeovers and Economic Efficiency," ECGI Finance Working Paper No. 391/2013; Tuck School of Business Working Paper No. 2013-122, *Social Science Research Network*, (October 15, 2013). Accessed May 5, 2015. See http://ssrn.com/abstract=2340754.

7. Steven N. Kaplan and Antoinette Schoar, "Private Equity Performance: Returns, Persistence, and Capital Flows," *Journal of Finance* 60 (2005): 1791–1823.

8. Shourun Guo, Edith S. Hotchkiss, and Weihong Song, "Do Buyouts (Still) Create Value?" *Journal of Finance* 66 (2011): 479–517.

9. Kaplan and Schoar (2005).

10. Jeffrey Pfeffer, "Curbing the Urge to Merge," *Business 2.0* (2003): 58.

11. Researchers have long noted that acquisitions occur in waves. See Michael Gort, "An Economic Disturbance Theory of Mergers," *Quarterly Journal of Economics* 83 (1969): 624–642.

12. As we saw in Chapter 8, "Executive Compensation and Incentives," the size of compensation packages tends to be correlated with company size. It is commonly alleged that this correlation encourages managers to seek growth via acquisitions. Lambert and Larcker (1987) and Avery, Chevalier, and Schaefer (1998) did not find this simple relationship to be true. By contrast, Fich, Starks, and Yore (2014) found that CEO compensation is positively related to deal activity. See Richard A. Lambert and David F. Larcker, "Executive Compensation Effects of Large Corporate Acquisitions," *Journal of Accounting and Public Policy* 6 (1987): 231–243; Christopher Avery, Judith A. Chevalier, and Scott Schaefer, "Why Do Managers Undertake Acquisitions?" An Analysis of Internal and External Rewards for Acquisitiveness." *Journal of Law, Economics, & Organization* 14 (1998): 24–43; and Eliezer M. Fich, Laura T. Starks, and Adam S. Yore, "CEO Deal-Making Activities and Compensation," *Journal of Financial Economics* 3 (2014): 471–492.

13. Equilar Insight, "Executive Compensation Trends—June: CEO Exit Packages, Fortune 200 CEO Severance & Change-in-Control Packages" (2007).

14. Carol Loomis, "Sandy Weill's Monster," *Fortune* (April 16, 2001).

15. "Mega-Merger Mania Strikes U.S. Banks," *The Banker* (May 1, 1998).

16. Janice Revell, "Should You Bet on the CEO?" *Fortune* 146 (November 18, 2002): 189–191.

17. Avery Johnson and Ron Winslow, "Drug Industry Shakeout Hits Small Firms Hard," *Wall Street Journal* (March 10, 2009, Eastern edition): A.12.

18. Mark Maremont, "No Razor Here: Gillette Chief to Get a Giant Payday," *Wall Street Journal* (January 31, 2005, Eastern edition): A.1.

19. Michael A. Simkowitz and Robert J. Monroe, "A Discriminant Analysis Function for Conglomerate Targets," *Southern Journal of Business* (November 1971): l–16. Donald L. Stevens, "Financial Characteristics of Merged Firms: A Multivariate Analysis," *Journal of Financial and Quantitative Analysis* 8 (1973): 149–158. A. D. Castagna and Z. P. Matolcsy, "Financial Ratios as Predictors of Company Acquisitions," *Journal of the Securities Institute*

of Australia (1976): 6–10. Ahmed Belkaoui, "Financial Ratios as Predictors of Canadian Takeovers," *Journal of Business Finance and Accounting* 5 (1978): 93–108. J. Kimball Dietrich and Eric Sorensen, "An Application of Logit Analysis to Prediction of Merger Targets," *Journal of Business Research* 12 (1984): 393–402.

20. Krishna G. Palepu, "Predicting Takeover Targets: A Methodological and Empirical Analysis," *Journal of Accounting and Economics* 8 (1986): 3–35.

21. Paul Tracy, "How to Find Probable Takeover Targets," *StreetAuthority Market Advisor* (February 1, 2007). Accessed November 14, 2010. See http://web.streetauthority.com/cmnts/pt/2007/02-01-takeover-candidates.asp.

22. B. Espen Eckbo, "Bidding Strategies and Takeover Premiums: A Review," *Journal of Corporate Finance* 15 (2009): 149–178.

23. Eckbo (2013).

24. Richard A. Lambert and David F. Larcker, "Golden Parachutes, Executive Decision Making, and Shareholder Wealth," *Journal of Accounting and Economics* 7 (1985): 179–203.

25. Eliezer M. Fich, Anh L. Tran, and Ralph A. Walkling, "On the Importance of Golden Parachutes," *Journal of Financial and Quantitative Analysis* 48 (2013): 1717–1753.

26. Judith C. Machlin, Hyuk Choe, and James A. Miles, "The Effects of Golden Parachutes on Takeover Activity," *Journal of Law and Economics* 36 (1993): 861–876.

27. Equilar, "Equilar Study: Change-in-Control Cash Severance Analysis Findings from a Study of Change-in-Control Payments at Fortune 100 Companies" (2011). Accessed May 5, 2015. See http://www.globalequity.org/geo/node/3231.

28. Cornerstone Research, "Shareholder Litigation Involving Acquisitions of Public Companies: Review of 2014 M&A Litigation" (2015). Accessed April 1, 2015. See https://www.cornerstone.com/GetAttachment/897c61ef-bfde-46e6-a2b8-5f94906c6ee2/Shareholder-Litigation-Involving-Acquisitions-2014-Review.pdf.

29. Michael C. Jensen and Richard S. Ruback, "The Market for Corporate Control: The Scientific Evidence," *Journal of Financial Economics* 11 (1983): 5–50.

30. Two explanations for this exist. In a hostile takeover, the acquirer is required to offer a more attractive price to overcome the target's objections to the merger and to persuade shareholders to accept the offer. Hostile bids are also likely to trigger a bidding war if the target seeks a friendly merger partner or more attractive terms. See Henri Servaes, "Tobin's Q and Gains from Takeovers," *Journal of Finance* 46 (1991): 409–419.

31. Gregor Andrade, Mark Mitchell, and Erik Stafford, "New Evidence and Perspectives on Mergers," *Journal of Economic Perspectives* 15 (2001): 103–120.

32. Marina Martynova and Luc Renneboog, "A Century of Corporate Takeovers: What Have We Learned and Where Do We Stand?" *Journal of Banking and Finance* 32 (2008): 2148–2177.

33. Mark Goergen and Luc Renneboog, "Shareholder Wealth Effects of European Domestic and Cross-border Takeover Bids," *European Financial Management* 10 (2004): 9–45.

34. Martynova and Renneboog (2008).

35. Ibid.

36. Ran Duchin and Breno Schmidt, "Riding the Merger Wave: Uncertainty, Reduced Monitoring, and Bad Acquisitions," *Journal of Financial Economics* 107 (2013): 69–88.

37. Aloke Ghosh, "Does Operating Performance Really Improve Following Corporate Acquisitions?" *Journal of Corporate Finance* 7 (2001): 151–178.

38. Joseph Walker, Michael Calia, and David Benoit, "Allergan Rejects Valeant Takeover Bid," *Wall Street Journal* (May 13, 2014, Eastern edition): B.3.

39. Jonathan D. Rockoff, Liz Hoffman, and David Benoit, "Actavis Offers $66 Billion for Allergan: Secret Talks, Aliases, Ski Cap as Disguise," Wall Street Journal (November 18, 2014, Eastern edition): B.1–B.5.

40. Jeffrey A. Krug and Walt Shill, "The Big Exit: Executive Churn in the Wake of M&As," *Journal of Business Strategy* 29 (2008): 15–21.

41. "Executive Agenda: Not So Fast," *A.T. Kearney* 8 (2005): 1–13. Accessed April 11, 2015. See http://gillisjonk.com/wp-content/uploads/2013/11/EA2005Not_So_Fast.pdf.

42. It is easiest for a company to adopt a poison pill if its charter authorizes blank check preferred stock. Preferred stock is a class of stock that is senior to common stock shareholders in terms of credit and capital. A target can protect itself from a corporate raider by issuing preferred stock with special voting rights to a friendly company or investor (white knight). The authorization of preferred stock has a similar effect as issuing dual-class shares. Blank check preferred stock is a class of unissued preferred stock that is provided for in the articles of incorporation and that the company can issue when threatened by a corporate raider.

43. Cross-holdings can also be an effective deterrent to a takeover. Cross-holdings generally occur between companies that have close interrelation along the supply chain. This practice protects firms by having a friendly, passive shareholder that is sympathetic to present management. Cross-holdings are prevalent in several countries, such as the *keiretsu* of Japan (see Chapter 2, "International Corporate Governance").

44. Antitakeover protections computed using 2014 data for 1,871 companies in the Russell 2000 Index, SharkRepellent, FactSet Research Systems, Inc.

45. Money-Zine, "Poison Pill Defense" (2009). Accessed November 14, 2010. See www.money-zine.com/Investing/Stocks/Poison-Pill-Defense/.

46. Sotheby's, Form 8-K, filed with the Securities and Exchange Commission October 4, 2013.

47. SharkRepellent, "S&P 1500 Poison Pills in Force at Year End 1998–2014," SharkRepellent, FactSet Research Systems, Inc. (2015.). Accessed March 26, 2015. See www.sharkrepellent.net.

48. Robert Schreck, "Inside M&A: Poison Pill Redux—Now More Than Ever," *McDermott Will & Emery* (May/June 2008). Accessed April 12, 2015. See http://www.mwe.com/publications/uniEntity.aspx?xpST=PublicationDetail&pub=4777&PublicationTypes=d9093adb-e95d-4f19-819a-f0bb5170ab6d.

49. AFL-CIO, "Exercising Authority, Restoring Accountability: AFL-CIO Proxy Voting Guidelines" (2012). Accessed April 3, 2015. See http://www.aflcio.org/content/download/12631/154821/proxy_voting_2012.pdf.

50. Morgan Stanley, "2013 Investment Management Proxy Voting Policy And Procedures" (October 3, 2013). Accessed April 3, 2015. See https://materials.proxyvote.com/Approved/99999Z/20140812/other_217038.pdf.

51. Martijn Cremers and Allen Ferrell, "Thirty Years of Shareholder Rights and Firm Value," *Journal of Finance* 69 (2014): 1167–1196.

52. James A. Brickley, Jeffrey L. Coles, and Rory L. Terry, "Outside Directors and the Adoption of Poison Pills," *Journal of Financial Economics* 35 (1994): 371–390.

53. Michael Ryngaert, "The Effect of Poison Pill Securities on Shareholder Wealth," *Journal of Financial Economics* 20 (1988): 377–417.

54. Ibid.

55. John Laide, "Poison Pill M&A Premiums," SharkRepellent, FactSet Research Systems, Inc. (2005). Accessed March 21, 2009. See www.sharkrepellent.net/pub/rs_20050830.html.

56. Ryngaert (1988).

57. Hiroyuki Kachi and Jamie Miyazaki, "In Japan, Activists May Find Poison," *Wall Street Journal* (August 8, 2007, Eastern edition): C.2.

58. Andrew Morse and Sebastian Moffett, "Japan's Companies Gird for Attack; Fearing Takeovers, They Rebuild Walls; Rise of Poison Pills," *Wall Street Journal* (April 30, 2008, Eastern edition): A.1.

59. Air Products and Chemicals attempted to circumvent this obstacle in its purchase attempt of competitor Airgas. In 2010, Air Products made an unsolicited offer to purchase Airgas for $5.5 billion. Airgas rejected the offer. Air Products waged a proxy contest and successfully gained three board seats on Airgas's board at the annual meeting held September 2010. At that same meeting, shareholders approved a bylaw amendment that brought forward the next annual meeting to January 2011, thereby allowing Air Products to run three more board candidates just 4 months later. Airgas sued, claiming that a 12-month wait was required between meetings. While a Delaware Chancery Court upheld the bylaw amendment, the Delaware Supreme Court reversed the lower court's decision, ruling instead that directors had been elected under the company's charter to serve three-year terms and that changing the meeting date improperly shortened their terms. When a separate challenge to the company's poison pill was rejected by the courts, Air Products gave up its attempt to acquire Airgas. See Jef Feeley, "Airgas Trial on Air Products Bid to Focus on Meeting," *Bloomberg* (October 1, 2010). Accessed June 30, 2014. See http://www.bloomberg.com/news/articles/2010-10-01/airgas-trial-over-air-products-bid-to-focus-on-challenge-of-meeting-date. Davis Polk, "Delaware Court Permits Stockholders to Shorten Term of Airgas Staggered Board," *Client Newsflash* (October 11, 2010). Accessed November 14, 2010. See http://www.davispolk.com/Delaware-Court-Permits-Stockholders-to-Shorten-Term-of-Airgas-Staggered-Board-10-11-2010/. Jef Feeley and Sophia Pearson, "Airgas Wins Ruling Invalidating Annual-Meeting Bylaw," *Bloomberg Businessweek* (November 23, 2010). Accessed February 2, 2011. See http://www.bloomberg.com/news/articles/2010-11-23/airgas-wins-ruling-on-annual-meeting-date-in-bid-to-fend-off-air-products.

60. SharkRepellent, "S&P 1500 staggered (Classified) Board Trend Analysis 1999–Present," SharkRepellent, FactSet Research Systems, Inc. (2015). Accessed March 26, 2015. See www.sharkrepellent.net.

61. Lucian Arye Bebchuk, John C. Coates IV, and Guhan Subramanian, "The Powerful Antitakeover Force of Staggered Boards: Theory, Evidence, and Policy," *Stanford Law Review* 54 (2002): 887–951.

62. John Pound, "The Effects of Antitakeover Amendments on Takeover Activity: Some Direct Evidence," *Journal of Law and Economics* 30 (1987): 353–367.

63. Re-Jin Guo, Timothy A. Kruse, and Tom Nohel, "Undoing the Powerful Antitakeover Force of Staggered Boards," *Journal of Corporate Finance* 14 (2008): 274–288.

64. Olubunmi Faleye, "Classified Boards, Firm Value, and Managerial Entrenchment," *Journal of Financial Economics* 83 (2007): 501–529.

65. Martijn Cremers, Lubomir P. Litov, and Simone M. Sepe, "Staggered Boards and Firm Value, Revisited," *Social Science Research Network* (July 14, 2014). Accessed May 5, 2015. See http://ssrn.com/abstract=2364165.

66. Weili Ge, Lloyd Tanlu, and Jenny Li Zhang, "Board Destaggering: Corporate Governance Out of Focus?" AAA 2014 Management Accounting Section (MAS) Meeting Paper, *Social Science Research Network* (January 29, 2014). Accessed May 5, 2015. See http://ssrn.com/abstract=2312565.

67. David F. Larcker, Gaizka Ormazabal, and Daniel J. Taylor, "The Market Reaction to Corporate Governance Regulation," *Journal of Financial Economics* 101 (2011): 431–448.

68. ISS, "2013 Proxy Season Review: United States" (August 22, 2013). Accessed April 7, 2015. See http://www.issgovernance.com/library/united-states-2013-proxy-season-review/.

69. SharkRepellent (2015).

70. Michal Barzuza, "The State of State Antitakeover Law," *Virginia Law Review* 95 (2009): 1973–2052.

71. Carl C. Icahn, "Capitalism Should Return to Its Roots," *Wall Street Journal Online* (February 7, 2009). Accessed November 14, 2010. See http://online.wsj.com/article/SB123396742337359087.html.

72. Samuel H. Szewczyk and George P. Tsetsekos, "State Intervention in the Market for Corporate Control: The Case of Pennsylvania Senate Bill 1310," *Journal of Financial Economics* 31 (1992): 3–23.

73. Guhan Subramanian, "Bargaining in the Shadow of Takeover Defenses," *Yale Law Journal* 113 (2003): 621–686.

74. The Bancroft family held 83 percent of Class B shares. See Matthew Karnitschnig, "News Corp., Dow Jones Talks Move Forward," *Wall Street Journal* (June 27, 2007, Eastern edition): A.3.

75. Morgan Stanley Investment Management, "Proxy Voting: Policy Statement (October 3, 2013)." Accessed April 3, 2015. See https://materials.proxyvote.com/approved/99999Z/20140812/other_217038.pdf.

76. ISS policy gateway, "United States Concise Proxy Voting Guidelines 2015 Benchmark Policy Recommendations" (January 7, 2015). Accessed March 9, 2015. See http://www.issgovernance.com/policy-gateway/policy-outreach/.

77. Calculation by the authors.

78. Oil-Dri Corporation of America, Form 10-K, filed with the Securities and Exchange Commission November 10, 2014.

79. Alibaba Group Holding Limited, Form F-1/A, filed with the Securities and Exchange Commission September 15, 2014.

80. Ronald W. Masulis, Cong Wang, and Fei Xie, "Agency Problems at Dual-Class Companies," *Journal of Finance* 64 (2009): 1697–1727.

81. Paul A. Gompers, Joy Ishii, and Andrew Metrick, "Extreme Governance: An Analysis of Dual-Class Firms in the United States," *Review of Financial Studies* 23 (2010): 1051–1088.

82. Robert Daines and Michael Klausner, "Do IPO Charters Maximize Firm Value? Antitakeover Protection in IPOs," *Journal of Law Economics and Organization* 17 (2001): 83–120.

83. Michael Klausner, "Fact and Fiction in Corporate Law and Governance," *Stanford Law Review* 65; Stanford Law and Economics Olin Working Paper No. 449. *Social Science Research Network* (July 23, 2013). Accessed May 5, 2015. See http://ssrn.com/abstract=2297640.

84. Julian Atanassov, "Do Hostile Takeovers Stifle Innovation? Evidence from Antitakeover Legislation and Corporate Patenting," *Journal of Finance* 68 (2013): 1097–1131.

85. Sanjeev Bhojraj, Partha Sengupta, and Suning Zhang, "Takeover Defenses: Entrenchment and Efficiency," *Social Science Research Network* (July 31, 2014). Accessed May 5, 2015. See http://ssrn.com/abstract=2474612.

86. Michael Bradley, Anand Desai, and E. Han Kim, "The Rationale behind Interfirm Tender Offers: Information or Synergy?" *Journal of Financial Economics* 11 (1983): 183–206.

87. Assem Safieddine and Sheridan Titman, "Leverage and Corporate Performance: Evidence from Unsuccessful Takeovers," *Journal of Finance* 54 (1999): 547–580.

88. Ibid. This is consistent with target management committing itself to value-enhancing investments (similar to the disciplining role of debt suggested by Jensen [1986]). See Michael Jensen, "Agency Costs of Free Cash Flow, Corporate Finance, and Takeover," *American Economic Review* 76 (1986): 323–339.

89. Kevin J. Delaney, Robert A. Guth, and Matthew Karnitschnig, "Microsoft Makes Grab for Yahoo!" *Wall Street Journal* (February 2, 2008, Eastern edition): A.1.

90. Steven M. Davidoff, "Dealbook Extra," *New York Times* (June 6, 2008): 6.

91. Gregory Zuckerman and Jessica E. Vascellaro, "Corporate News: Icahn Aims to Oust Yahoo! CEO Yang if Bid for Board Control Succeeds," *Wall Street Journal* (June 4, 2008, Eastern edition): B.3.

92. Jessica E. Vascellaro, "Yahoo! Vote-Counting Error Overstated Support for Yang," *Wall Street Journal* (August 6, 2008, Eastern edition): B.6.

12

Institutional Shareholders and Activist Investors

Despite their ownership positions, institutional investors have only indirect influence on company affairs. The majority of their influence must be exerted through the board of directors, whom they elect to govern on their behalf. However, institutional shareholders can still be powerful: They can communicate their opinions directly to management and the board. If the response they receive is not satisfactory, they can seek to have directors removed, vote against proxy proposals sponsored by management, put forth their own proxy measures, or express their dissatisfaction by selling their shares ("voting with their feet").

In this chapter, we review these points in detail. We examine the broad universe of institutional investors to understand their objectives and the methods they use to gain influence. We consider the role that proxy advisory firms play in influencing the annual voting process. In addition, we consider the impact of recent and potential regulatory changes, including the trend toward "shareholder democracy" and corporate engagement.

The Role of Shareholders

As discussed in Chapter 1, "Introduction to Corporate Governance," the **shareholder perspective** of the corporation states that the primary purpose of the corporation is to maximize wealth for owners. This implies that the question of effective governance, from the standpoint of shareholders, is quite simple: Governance practices should seek to create better alignment between management and shareholder interests, thereby reducing agency costs and increasing shareholder value. Therefore, effective governance focuses on the best way to create this alignment and increase shareholder value.

However, this is an oversimplification of the problem. Disagreements arise among shareholders about the best way to structure a firm's governance because shareholders themselves are not a homogeneous group.[1] They differ in terms of several important attributes. For example, shareholders do not have a single, common *investment horizon*. Long-term investors might tolerate significant swings in quarterly earnings and share price if they believe that the decisions management is making will ultimately yield a higher level of profitability. Investors with a shorter investment horizon might prefer that management focus on maximizing near-term earnings and stock price.

Shareholders also have different *objectives*. A large mutual fund institution might only care about the economic results of the corporation. An institutional investor that represents a specific constituent—such as a union pension fund or socially responsible investment fund—might focus on how economic results are achieved and the impact on various stakeholders.

Furthermore, not all shareholders exhibit the same *activity level*. On one end of the spectrum are **passive investors**, such as index funds.[2] These investors attempt to generate returns that mirror the returns of a predetermined market index. They might be less attentive to firm-specific performance and governance matters. On the other end of the spectrum are **active investors**. These investors are active in the trading of company securities and care greatly about individual firm outcomes. They might also try to influence corporate affairs (by meeting with management, lobbying to have board members removed, voicing concern about compensation practices, and advancing policy measures through the company proxy).[3] Investors who try to influence governance-related matters within the corporation are referred to as **activist investors**.

Finally, shareholders vary by *size*. In contrast to small funds, large institutional investors tend to have significant financial resources that they can dedicate to governance matters. For example, BlackRock, with $4.7 trillion in assets under management, has about 20 people in a group that directs proxy voting. These individuals—based in the United States, Europe, Japan, Hong Kong, and Australia—coordinate voting policies and activities across 85 national markets and the 14,000 companies in which BlackRock invests.[4]

The heterogeneity of shareholder groups creates a coordination problem. Differences in investment horizon, investment objective, activity level, and size make it difficult for shareholders to coordinate efforts to influence management and the board toward a common goal. In some cases, shareholders can work at cross-purposes to one another, even though they share an objective of improving corporate performance.

Coordination is further complicated by the well-known **free rider problem**. Shareholder actions—such as proxy contests and shareholder-sponsored proxy proposals—require the expenditure of resources. While one institutional investor bears the cost of these efforts, the benefits are enjoyed broadly by all shareholders (who are said to enjoy a "free ride"). For example, an activist institutional fund might lead a successful campaign to destagger a company board or remove economically harmful antitakeover protections. Although all shareholders enjoy the outcome of this effort, the activist investor alone incurs the costs. The asymmetry of cost and payout creates a disincentive for any one firm to take action and can result in underinvestment by institutional investors to improve corporate governance.

Shareholders suffer from having only **indirect influence** over the corporation (see the following sidebar). They must rely principally on the board of directors to exert direct influence. The board hires and fires the CEO, sets compensation, oversees firm strategy and risk management, oversees the work of the external auditor, writes company bylaws, and negotiates for a change of control. If shareholders do not believe that the board is sufficiently representing their interests in these matters, they must either persuade them to change policies or seek to have them removed. As we saw in Chapter 11, "The Market for Corporate Control," removing the board is a cumbersome and costly process.

Does the Composition of a Company's Shareholder Base Matter?

Because of their potential influence on corporate policy and board-related matters, corporations dedicate significant time and attention to managing their shareholder base. A 2014 survey by the National Investor Relations Institute (NIRI) and the Rock Center for Corporate Governance at Stanford University found that 91 percent of companies discuss shareholder composition at the senior-executive level, and 75 percent discuss it at the board level. CEOs spend 4.2 days per quarter managing their shareholder base, and CFOs spend 6.4 days—considerable figures given the managerial responsibilities of senior leaders. Most companies (80 percent) believe that their stock would trade at a higher price if they could attract their "ideal" shareholder base. On average, companies estimate that their stock would rise 15 percent and that share price volatility would decrease 20 percent over a two- to three-year period if they had the right shareholders.[5]

Furthermore, companies overwhelmingly prefer "long-term shareholders" to "short-term shareholders." Ninety-two percent of companies in the NIRI/Rock Center study describe their ideal shareholder as having a "long-term investment horizon"—the most highly rated among all attributes surveyed. They describe long-term shareholders as having an investment horizon of at least 2.8 years. Respondents believe that investors with a short-term perspective distract from strategic decision making (65 percent) and focus on cost reduction (51 percent). A majority (57 percent) believes that a company whose shareholder base is dominated by short-term investors will have reduced market growth and/or reduced long-term growth.[6]

Still, little research evidence demonstrates that the composition of a company's shareholder base directly impacts corporate decision making, operating performance, or value creation. Furthermore, it is not clear that companies whose shareholder base has a "short-term" investment horizon perform differently than companies whose shareholder base has a "long-term" investment horizon. Bushee (2004) found some evidence that companies with a high percentage of "transient" (short-term) investors have incrementally higher stock price volatility, while those with a high percentage of "quasi-index" (long-term) investors have lower volatility. However, he did not examine whether shareholder groups with differing time horizons have any impact on valuation or long-term operating performance.[7] It remains an open question as to whether substantial changes in the composition of the shareholder base increase shareholder value.

Blockholders and Institutional Investors

A **blockholder** is an investor with a significant ownership position in a company's common stock. No regulatory statute classifies an investor as a blockholder, although researchers generally define a blockholder as any shareholder with at least a 1 to 5 percent stake. A blockholder can be an executive, a director, an individual shareholder, another corporation, a foreign government, or an institutional investor (see the next sidebar). Institutional investors include mutual funds, pension funds, endowments, hedge funds, and other investment groups. For the purposes of this chapter, we limit our discussion to nonexecutive and institutional blockholders. (Chapter 9, "Executive Equity Ownership," discusses executive blockholders and Chapter 14, "Alternative Models of Governance," discusses family-controlled businesses.)

U.S. regulations require that corporations disclose major shareholders to the public. According to Thomson Reuters, 95 percent of publicly listed companies have an institutional shareholder with at least a 1 percent ownership position, 85 percent with at least a 3 percent position, and 74 percent with at least a 5 percent position (see Table 12.1).[8] Furthermore, the data suggests that blockholders tend to retain their ownership position over time. Barclay and Holderness (1989) found that firms that have a blockholder at one point in time are likely to continue to have a blockholder five years later. They also found that the ownership position of the largest blockholder tends to increase over time.[9]

Table 12.1   Blockholders among U.S. Corporations

Firms (Grouped by Size)	Market Value ($ Millions)	Average Number of Institutional Holders	Average Number of Holders		
			1%	3%	5%
Top 1,000	$9,296.0	350	14	4	2
1,001 to 2,000	$1,984.9	151	16	5	2
2,001 to 3,000	$690.8	93	12	4	2
3,001 to 4,000	$261.1	49	8	3	1
4,001 to 5,000	$75.7	19	4	2	1
All firms	$582.4	79	10	3	2

Median values. Sample includes 5,347 firms during 2013.
Source: Thomson Reuters Institutional Holdings (13F) Database.

Blockholders are predominantly institutions rather than individuals. Among a sample of randomly selected manufacturing firms with blockholders, Mehran (1995) found that 23 percent are individuals, and 77 percent are corporate and institutional blockholders.[10] Approximately 70 percent of the shares of publicly traded corporations are held by institutional investors.[11]

If they decide to act, institutional investors and blockholders are in a position to impose governance reforms on corporations. Their significant voting stakes can determine the outcome of a contested director election or proxy proposal. They can change the outcome of a heated takeover battle or prod a company to put itself up for sale or change strategy. If they hold a large enough position, they can gain board representation and directly influence strategy, risk management, executive compensation, and succession planning.

However, the blockholders' influence likely depends on the nature of the investment, the nature of the investor, and the relationship between the investor and the corporation. For example, Toyota likely has a different relationship with the auto suppliers it invests in than does a large institutional owner or an activist hedge fund. As we saw in Chapter 9 when we examined managerial equity ownership, block ownership has the potential to either improve or impair firm performance, depending on whether the blockholder treats ownership as an incentive to better the business or uses the position of influence for private gain.

The research literature has examined the impact of block ownership on firm performance. Barclay and Holderness (1989) found that large blocks of shares (at least 5 percent of a company's stock) trade at a 16 percent premium to open-market prices.[12] This indicates that block ownership is perceived to have value either because the acquirer believes it will provide the influence needed either to monitor and improve firm outcomes or to extract some type of private gain from the corporation.

The research does not, however, demonstrate that block ownership actually translates to superior performance. McConnell and Servaes (1990) found no relationship between block ownership by an outside investor and a company's market-to-book value.[13] Mehran (1995) also did not find a relationship between block ownership and market value or between block ownership and firm performance.[14] This suggests that the presence of outside blockholders is not associated with improvements in firm performance. In aggregate, however, the research is inconclusive on this point.[15]

Researchers have also studied the relationship between block ownership and governance quality. Core, Holthausen, and Larcker (1999) found that CEO compensation is lower among firms in which an external shareholder owns at least 5 percent of the company shares.[16] Similarly, Bertrand and Mullainathan (2000) examined the relationship between representation by a blockholder on the board of directors and "pay for luck." They found that companies with blockholder directors are less likely to give pay increases for profit improvements that result from industry conditions outside the executive's control (such as changes in commodity prices).[17] Aggarwal, Erel, Ferreira, and Matos (2011) found that increases in institutional ownership positively improve firm-level governance and shareholder protections in international markets. They also found that firms with higher levels of institutional ownership are more likely to terminate a poorly performing CEO and exhibit improvements in valuation over time. These results suggest that active shareholder monitoring can compel a company to adopt better governance standards.[18]

Furthermore, Mikkelson and Partch (1989) found that companies with an external blockholder on the board of directors are more likely to be the target of a successful acquisition.[19] At the same time, they found that if the external blockholder is not on the board, the company is no more likely to receive an acquisition offer or to accept the offer. This suggests that a *combination* of concentrated ownership and board representation might be effective in decreasing management entrenchment.

Sovereign Wealth Funds

Sovereign wealth funds are investment vehicles established by foreign governments to invest the surplus funds of those nations. In 2015, the largest sovereign wealth funds were administered by the nations of Norway, the United Arab Emirates, Saudi Arabia, China, Kuwait, and Singapore. The Norway Government Pension Fund was the largest single fund, with $863 billion in assets; however, 4 of the 10 largest funds held assets worth $1.9 trillion on behalf of various agencies from China and Hong Kong.[20]

Sovereign wealth funds typically have long-term investment horizons, with the primary objectives of stable returns and preservation of wealth. They usually adopt a passive approach to investing in order to avoid the claim that a foreign government is seeking to influence the industry and management of other countries. Still, in some cases, sovereign wealth funds use the size of their holdings to influence corporate policy. For example, the Norway Government Pension Fund has adopted "active ownership" priorities to advocate on behalf of social and environmental priorities such as children's rights, climate change, and water management. The fund advances these priorities by voting and sponsoring resolutions at annual meetings and by engaging with the management of corporations in which the fund has its largest investments.[21] In 2012, the Qatar Investment Authority used its 12 percent ownership stake in mining company Xstrata to demand a higher takeover premium from Glencore; Glencore originally offered 2.8 shares for every Xstrata share but increased the ratio to 3.05 after the Qatar fund went public with its opposition to the terms.[22]

Institutional Investors and Proxy Voting

Publicly traded corporations are required by state law to hold an annual meeting of shareholders to elect the board of directors and transact other business that requires shareholder approval. In the U.S., shareholders are provided advance notice of the annual meeting through a written **proxy statement**, and they vote their shares on ballot items in person or by proxy over the Internet, via the phone, or by mail.

Because of their size, institutional investors are in a better position than individuals to impose governance changes through the proxy voting process. They might exercise this influence by voting against management recommendations on company-sponsored proxy matters, such as director elections, auditor ratification, equity-based compensation plans, and proposed bylaw amendments. Furthermore, they might sponsor or vote in favor of shareholder resolutions that recommend or require bylaw amendments or policy changes not sought by the corporation. (We discuss shareholder-sponsored resolutions in the next section.)

In 2003, the SEC began to require that registered institutional investors develop and disclose proxy voting policies and disclose their votes on *all* shareholder ballot items.[23] The voting records of registered institutions are available to their beneficial owners through Form N-PX. If shareholders believe the institution is overly supportive of management, they can put pressure on it to take a tougher stance or shift their investment to another fund. (Hedge funds are not registered with the SEC and are exempt from these regulations.)

According to data from Institutional Investor Services (ISS), institutional investors vote in line with management recommendations about 95 percent of the time when management is seeking a vote "for" a proposal and 56 percent of the time when management is seeking a vote "against" a proposal. Among the 10 institutional investors with the largest number of votes, Rydex votes with management the most (100 percent when management recommends both in favor of and against an issue), Charles Schwab votes with management the least when management is in favor of a proposal (89 percent), and ProFund Advisors votes with management the least when management is against a proposal (27 percent).[24] (See Table 12.2.)

Table 12.2   Institutional Investor Voting Record (Voting with Management)

Institution	Number of Votes	With Management "For"	With Management "Against"
BlackRock Advisors	407,235	96%	83%
Vanguard Group	319,419	96%	88%
Fidelity Management & Research	312,302	95%	74%
Dimensional Fund Advisers	211,439	92%	48%
TIAA-CREF Asset Management	205,519	96%	66%
EQ Advisors Trust	180,155	95%	66%
Rydex Investments	144,909	100%	100%
Charles Schwab Investment Management	137,142	89%	62%
ProFund Advisors	135,435	95%	27%
ProShare Advisors	133,383	93%	28%

Includes the 10 institutional investors with the largest number of votes, based on Form N-PX 2013 filings.
   Source: Data from ISS Voting Analytics (2013). Calculation by the authors.

It is not clear whether these levels of support are appropriate. On one hand, many proxy proposals are routine, including most director elections, ratification of the external auditor, and the approval of various noncontroversial bylaw amendments.

In these cases, no significant governance impact might occur from regularly voting in favor of these matters. On the other hand, it is plausible that routinely voting in accordance with management recommendations is not consistent with fiduciary oversight on behalf of institutional shareholders. Beneficial owners are ultimately responsible for determining whether fund managers vote in their best interest.

Activist Investors

Loosely speaking, an **activist investor** is a shareholder who uses an ownership position to actively pursue governance changes at a corporation. Any investor can employ an activist strategy, including a union-backed pension fund; an institutional investor with an environmental, religious, or social mission; a hedge fund; or an individual investor with outspoken beliefs. Activists use lobbying efforts to increase leverage and influence corporate governance outcomes beyond what can be achieved by simply voting shares in the proportion of their ownership position. Although activists might have a stated objective of improving shareholder value, they also might have secondary motives that are not value enhancing for shareholders over the long term.

Activists use a variety of mechanisms to influence corporate policy, including sponsoring proposals on the proxy, proxy contests (threatened or actual), pressure through the media and other public forums, and direct engagement.

Under SEC Rule 14a-8, a shareholder owning at least $2,000 or 1 percent in market value of a company's securities for at least one year is eligible to submit a **shareholder proposal**. The shareholder must continue to hold the shares through the annual meeting and present the proposal in person at the meeting. Shareholders are limited to submitting one proposal at a time, which is due by a company-specified deadline, generally 120 days before the annual meeting. The company is entitled to exclude shareholder proposals that violate certain restrictions. These include proposals that would violate federal or state law or that deal with functions under the purview of management, the election of directors, the payment of dividends, or other substantive matters. Furthermore, the company can reject a proposal if it relates to a "personal grievance [or] special interest . . . which is not shared by the other shareholders at large." Also, the company is entitled to exclude proposals that deal with "substantially the same subject matter" as another proposal on the proxy in the preceding five calendar years that received only nominal support.[25]

In recent years, shareholder proposals have focused primarily on board structure and antitakeover protections (39 percent), social policy issues (39 percent), and executive compensation (22 percent). Individual activists are the most active sponsor of shareholder resolutions, filing 40 percent of the total between 2006 and 2014, followed by labor-affiliated groups (32 percent), religious and other social responsibility investors (27 percent), and other institutional investors (1 percent).[26]

Shareholders have mixed results gaining majority approval for their proxy proposals. According to Institutional Shareholder Services, shareholder-sponsored proposals that garnered majority support on average in 2013 included proposals to destagger the board of directors (80 percent support), to end or reduce supermajority requirements (72 percent), and to adopt majority voting requirements (58 percent). Shareholder-sponsored proposals that did not receive majority support on average included proposals to give shareholders the right to call special meetings (42 percent), to act by written consent (41 percent), and to nominate directors for election to the board ("proxy access," 32 percent). Proposals to require a separation between the chairman and CEO also did not receive majority support (31 percent).[27]

Shareholders can also influence corporate policy through a proxy contest. In a proxy contest, an activist shareholder nominates its own slate of directors to the company's board (known as a **dissident slate**). The proxy contest represents a direct attempt to gain control of the board and alter corporate policy, and it is usually attempted in conjunction with a hostile takeover. As we discussed in Chapter 11, proxy contests require significant out-of-pocket expense by the activist shareholder, including purchasing the list of shareholders, preparing and distributing proxy materials, and soliciting a favorable response from key institutional investors. The cost and risk of failure substantially limit the frequency of proxy contests.[28] Still, many contests that make it to a vote are successful. According to Institutional Shareholder Services, among 23 proxy contests in 2013, the dissident slate won seats 13 times, lost 7 times, and settled with management 3 times.[29]

Shareholder activism remains a highly controversial topic. Proponents of activism argue that companies with an engaged shareholder base are more likely to be successful in the long term. Active shareholders reduce agency problems, limit management entrenchment, and combat complacency by pressuring corporate officials to put the interests of shareholders first. Under this argument, activists are a necessary element of the market for corporate control. Opponents argue that shareholder activism is a guise for disruptive behavior that takes managerial and board attention away from substantive corporate matters and the pursuit of long-term value enhancement. In its extreme form, opponents liken activism to extortion that weakens corporations through reckless changes to strategy, capital structure, and asset mix in order to boost stock prices in the short term.

With these competing narratives in mind, we discuss various forms of shareholder activism, including activism by pension funds, socially responsible investment funds, and hedge funds.

Pension Funds

Public pension funds manage retirement assets on behalf of state, county, and municipal governments. Examples include the California Public Employees' Retirement System (CalPERS), New York State and Local Retirement System, and California State Teachers' Retirement System (CalSTRS). **Private pension funds** manage retirement assets on behalf of trade union members. The largest trade union is the American Federation of Labor and Congress of Industrial Organizations (AFL-CIO), comprising more than 50 national unions and 12 million workers. Other trade unions include the International Brotherhood of Teamsters, the Service Employees International Union, and the United Brotherhood of Carpenters and Joiners of America. Pension assets are held in trust, and the management of these funds is overseen by a board of trustees whose sole purpose is to meet the financial obligations to trust beneficiaries.

Pension fund administrators are active participants in the proxy voting process. As noted earlier, more than 40 percent of shareholder proxy proposals are sponsored by a union-backed or public pension fund. However, pension activism is not limited to proxy items that the organization has sponsored. Funds also take vocal positions on proposals that other institutions have sponsored. For example, the AFL-CIO keeps a scorecard of what it considers "key votes." The 2014 scorecard recommended an affirmative vote on 25 proxy measures, including requirements for an independent chairman, proxy access, lobbying disclosure, and other policy reform (see Table 12.3).

Table 12.3　AFL-CIO Key Vote Scorecard (2014)

Company	Proposal Subject
Abercrombie & Fitch	Proxy access
Bank of America	Lobbying disclosure
Boston Properties	Proxy access
Cablevision	1 share, 1 vote recapitalization
Charles Schwab	Equal employment opportunity
Chevron	Country selection guidelines
Crown Holdings	Executive retirement benefits
Equity Lifestyle Properties	Lobbying disclosure
Exxon	Lobbying disclosure
Facebook	Sustainability report
FirstEnergy	Executive retirement benefits
Google	Tax policy principles
Healthcare Services Group	Independent chair
Kellogg	Human rights report

Company	Proposal Subject
Leggett & Platt	Equal employment opportunity
Nabors Industries	Pay for performance standards
Reynolds American	Lobbying disclosure
SLM	Lobbying disclosure
Superior Energy	Human rights report
Swift Transportation	1 share, 1 vote recapitalization
T-Mobile US	Human rights report
Urban Outfitters	Board diversity
Vornado	Independent chair
Wal-Mart	Pay clawback disclosure policy
Wells Fargo	Mortgage servicing operations

Shareholder proposals "for" are consistent with the AFL-CIO Proxy Voting Guidelines.

Source: AFL-CIO, "Key Votes Survey," (2014). Accessed May 5, 2015. See http://www.aflcio.org/content/download/65871/1747351/2013+AFL-CIO+Key+Votes+Survey.pdf.

Some research suggests that union pension funds might not place a priority on maximizing financial returns for their beneficiaries but instead use their ownership position to support union- and labor-related causes. In a highly controversial study, Agrawal (2012) examined the voting record of the AFL-CIO between 2003 and 2006. He found that the AFL-CIO is significantly more likely to vote against directors at companies that are in the middle of a labor dispute, particularly when the AFL-CIO represents the workers. He concluded that "union pension funds cast proxy votes in part as a means of pursuing union labor objectives, rather than maximizing shareholder value alone."[30]

The evidence also suggests that pension fund activism has only a moderate impact on long-term corporate performance. Barber (2007) examined whether CalPERS activism increased shareholder value. His sample included all companies that made the pension fund's annual "focus list" from 1992 to 2005. Companies on the focus list included those that CalPERS believed exhibited especially poor corporate performance and governance quality (see Figure 12.1). He found only marginal increases in shareholder value on the day CalPERS announced that a company was on the list, indicating that the market expected only a moderate impact from CalPERS intervention. Over the long term, Barber (2007) found practically no excess positive returns. He commented that "long-run returns are simply too volatile to conclude that the long-run performance of focus-list firms is unusual." This suggests either that CalPERS did not select the right targets for its activism, that it did not have the ability to influence the governance choices at these firms, or that CalPERS's alternative governance features were no better than the existing governance structure.[31] As a result, the influence of public pension funds, although visible, is not well established.

(In 2010, CalPERS discontinued the practice of using a public focus list, choosing instead to pursue direct communication with companies.)[32]

Market Capitalization: $1.5 Billion

CalPERS' Holdings: $6.0 Million

Total Return Returns Ending 02/29/2008

TSR Ending 2/29/2008	Cheesecake Factory Inc (CAKE)	Russell 3000 Index	Relative Return Russell 3000 Index	Restaurants Russell Industry Peer Index	Relative Return Russell Peer Index
5 years	6.00%	79.70%	-73.70%	146.52%	-140.5%
3 years	-38.55%	18.13%	-56.69%	25.51%	-64.06%
1 year	-23.38%	-4.52%	-18.86%	-2.19%	-21.19%

CalPERS' Concerns:

• Cheesecake Factory's stock has severely underperformed relative to the Russell 3000 index and its industry peer index over the 1, 3, and 5 year time periods ending February 29th.

• Deterioration in annual business fundamentals such as same store sales, operating margin, return on assets, and return on equity.

• Lack of board accountability—The company would not agree to seek shareowner approval to remove the company's 80% supermajority voting requirements in the articles and bylaws. Only a small minority of companies in the Russell 3000 have voting thresholds of this magnitude.

• Concern over shareowner rights—The company would not agree to grant shareowners the right to act by written consent.

• Board Entrenchment Concern—Uncontested director elections are currently conducted using a plurality vote standard.

• The company does not currently disclose a policy for recapturing executive compensation ("Clawback Policy") in the event of executive fraud or misconduct.

Source: CalPERS.

Figure 12.1 CalPERS 2008 focus list company at-a-glance: Cheesecake Factory.

Social Responsibility and Other Stakeholder Funds

Social responsibility and other stakeholder funds cater to investors who value specific social objectives and want to invest only in companies whose practices are consistent with those objectives. Examples of social responsibility include fair labor practices, environmental sustainability, and the promotion of religious or moral values. By one estimate, more than 150 socially responsible mutual funds exist, totaling more than $300 billion in assets.[33]

Socially responsible funds vary in the extent to which they engage in activism to achieve their objectives. Some funds limit their activism to abstaining from investments in companies that violate their social values. Other funds actively attempt to change corporate practices. For example, Walden Asset Management claims on its Web site, "We do not subscribe to the simplistic view that some companies are 'socially responsible' while others are not. Instead, Walden seeks to build portfolios that not only adhere to a client's risk/return objectives, but are also comprised of companies that best reflect their environmental, social and governance (ESG) priorities. Going further, Walden engages in shareholder advocacy on behalf of our clients to strengthen corporate responsibility and accountability."[34]

According to Proxy Monitor, shareholders submitted 136 resolutions related to social and environmental objectives at Fortune 250 companies in 2014. Of these, 135 were defeated, and 1 was approved with the support of the board. On average, social and environmental proposals receive low levels of support (between 5 and 20 percent).[35]

The low approval rate of resolutions related to social causes suggests that these investors do not hold considerable influence over the proxy voting process. Nevertheless, even failed shareholder initiatives can still be an effective tool for influencing governance outcomes if they are coupled with other public and behind-the-scenes efforts to compel policy change (see the following sidebar).

Shareholder Influence Outside the Proxy Voting Process

Nike

In 1996, the General Board of Pension and Health Benefits of the United Methodist Church (owning 61,700 Class B shares) submitted a proposal that would require Nike to perform a summary review of labor conditions in the factories of certain suppliers in Indonesia. Among other things, Nike would be required to work with Indonesian-based nongovernmental organizations to "establish independent monitoring and enforcement mechanisms," "strengthen internal monitoring procedures," and "utilize positive influence to encourage suppliers to adhere to Nike standards of conduct."[36] The proxy proposal was just one tactic that activists employed to coerce Nike to improve labor conditions in supplier factories. Even though the proxy proposal was rejected by a wide margin (3.6 million votes in favor, 111.2 million opposed, 5.8 million abstained), the company ultimately enacted a series of reforms consistent with the spirit of the proposal, including establishing a minimum age for employment, stricter clean air regulations in supplier factories, and training and monitoring programs.[37]

The research literature is inconclusive regarding whether socially responsible investment funds achieve their dual objectives of advocating a social mission and generating financial returns on behalf of shareholders. Geczy, Stambaugh, and Levin (2005) found that socially responsible mutual funds significantly underperform comparable indices. However, the authors acknowledged that their model did not take into account the "nonfinancial utility of 'doing good.'" That is, the social benefit that restricting investment might have on corporate behavior was not included.[38] Similarly, Renneboog, Ter Horst, and Zhang (2008) found that socially responsible mutual funds in the United States, the United Kingdom, and many European and Asian countries underperform their respective benchmarks by 2.2 percent to 6.6 percent per year. However, they found that risk-adjusted returns are not significantly different from comparable mutual funds (that is, the difference in performance might be driven by the cost of active management instead of the social constraints).[39]

Activist Hedge Funds

Hedge funds are private pools of capital that engage in a variety of strategies— long–short, global macro, merger arbitrage, distressed debt, and so on—in an attempt to earn above-average returns in the capital markets. More than 1,000 hedge funds exist in the United States, managing between $2 trillion and $2.5 trillion in assets.[40] Because they limit their investor pool to **accredited investors** (those with at least $1 million in investable assets or $200,000 in annual income), many hedge funds are exempt from the Investment Company Act of 1940. Following the Dodd–Frank Act, hedge funds with more than $150 million in assets under management are required to register with the SEC.

Hedge funds are notable among institutional investors in the fee structure that they charge clients. The typical hedge fund charges both a management fee, which is a fixed percentage of assets (typically 1 to 2 percent) and a performance-based fee (typically 20 percent) known as the **carry**, which is a percentage of the annual return or increase in the value of the investor's portfolio. The fee structure charged by the industry necessitates superior financial performance. The magnitude of the fees is a considerable hurdle for the fund manager to overcome to simply match an index return.

Pressure to perform might shorten the investment time horizon of hedge funds. The importance of short-term performance presents a challenge because the prices of common stocks are subject to market forces that are outside the control of any one investor. Even a security that is deemed to be "undervalued" does not necessarily revert to "fair value" simply because it has been identified as such. As a result, some hedge funds decide to engage in activism to compel the price of the stock to converge upon its estimated fair value. Notable activist hedge funds include Icahn Capital Management, Pershing Square, Third Point, and Trian Partners. Brav, Jiang, Thomas, and Partnoy (2008) provided a detailed analysis of hedge fund activism. They found that activist hedge funds resemble value investors. Target companies have relatively high profitability in terms of return on assets and cash flow (relative to matched peers) but sell in the market at lower price-to-book ratios. They tend to have underperformed the market in the period preceding the hedge fund's investment. They have more leverage and a lower dividend payout ratio, and are slightly more diversified in terms of operating businesses. Finally, they tend to be small in terms of market valuation, although their shares trade with more liquidity and are followed by a higher number of investment analysts.[41] Of note, they do not tend to suffer from noticeable firm-specific operating deficiencies.[42]

On average, activist hedge funds accumulate an initial position representing 6.3 percent of the company's shares (median average). In 16 percent of the cases, the funds also disclose derivative positions or securities with embedded options, such as convertible debt or convertible preferred stock. (This figure likely understates the true derivative exposure because disclosure of derivative investments is not required under SEC regulations.) Hedge funds are likely to coordinate their efforts with other funds to gain leverage. The study found that, in 22 percent of the cases, multiple hedge funds reported as one group in their regulatory filings with the SEC. (This figure likely understates coordination because funds employing a **wolf pack strategy,** and those that "pile on," are not required to report a coordinated relationship.)[43] Multiple hedge funds reporting as a single group take a 14 percent position, on average.

Institutional investors that acquire material ownership in a company are required to disclose the nature of their investment with the SEC.[44] Approximately half of the funds in this study cited "undervaluation" as the reason for their investment. The rest stated that they intended to compel the company to make some sort of business or structural change—such as a change in strategy, capital structure, or governance system—or to pursue a sale of the company. These funds also used aggressive tactics to achieve their objectives, including regular and direct communication with the board or management (48 percent), shareholder-sponsored proposals and public criticism (32 percent), and full-fledged proxy contests to seize control of the board (13 percent).

The market reacts positively to news of initial investment by an activist hedge fund. On the announcement day, target stock prices generate abnormal returns of approximately 2.0 percent. During the next 20 days, the stock price continues to trend higher, with cumulative abnormal returns of 7.2 percent. However, the extent to which piling on by other hedge funds and institutional investors contributes to these short-term abnormal returns is unclear.

Klein and Zur (2009) studied the long-term success of activist hedge funds. Using a sample of 151 funds between 2003 and 2005, they found that hedge funds achieved a 60 percent success rate in meeting their stated objectives. Almost three-quarters (73 percent) of the funds that pursued board representation were successful. All hedge funds (100 percent) that wanted the target company to repurchase stock, replace the CEO, or initiate a cash dividend were successful. And half (50 percent) were able to compel the company to alter its strategy, terminate a pending acquisition, or agree to a proposed merger. These findings indicate that activist hedge funds are influential as a disciplining mechanism on the corporation.[45]

However, the evidence for their impact on long-term financial performance is mixed. Klein and Zur (2009) found that target companies exhibit abnormal returns around the announcement day of the investment but no subsequent improvement in operating performance. Instead, they reported a modest decline in return on assets and cash from operations. They also reported a decline in cash levels (consistent with increased stock buybacks and dividend payouts) and an increase in long-term debt. Bratton (2006) found some evidence that hedge funds are able to beat a benchmark portfolio in terms of shareholder value creation. However, these computations are quite sensitive to assumptions regarding risk adjustment and choice of the firms selected for the benchmark portfolio. Bebchuk, Brav, and Jiang (2015) studied 2,000 activist hedge fund interventions between 1994 and 2007 and found positive long-term improvements in operating performance, measured by return on assets.[46] However, much of this improvement seems to be due to the natural tendency of poor operating performance to be followed by good performance (that is, "regression toward the mean"). deHaan, Larcker, and McClure (2015) found no statistical difference in operating performance among activist targets after controlling for regression tendencies. In fact, the only firms that earned excess stock price returns were those that were ultimately acquired. Activists appear to be good value investors that use the market for corporate control to fairly quickly generate value improvements for shareholders of target firms. Activists do not appear to improve strategy or operations for target companies that continue to be going concerns.[47]

Gantchev (2013) examined whether proxy contests waged by activist hedge funds result in net positive returns, taking into account the full cost of their efforts, including demand negotiations, board representation, and the contest itself. He calculated that a campaign for control costs on average $10.7 million and that estimated monitoring costs reduce activist returns by more than two-thirds. He found that the mean net activist return is close to zero, but the top quartile of activists earns higher returns on their activist holdings than on their non-activist investments.[48]

Shareholder Democracy and Corporate Engagement

In recent years, we have seen a considerable push by Congress, the SEC, and governance experts to increase the influence that shareholders have over corporate governance systems. These efforts are broadly labeled **shareholder democracy** because they are intended to give shareholders a greater say in corporate matters. Advocates of shareholder democracy believe that it will make board members more accountable to shareholder (and possibly stakeholder) objectives.

Elements of shareholder democracy include majority voting in uncontested director elections, proxy access, say-on-pay, and other voting-related issues. Closely related to shareholder democracy is the issue of direct engagement between shareholders and the board of directors. See Chapter 8, "Executive Compensation and Incentives," for a discussion of say-on-pay. We discuss the other elements of shareholder democracy and corporate engagement next.

Majority Voting in Uncontested Director Elections

Companies have a choice of method for conducting director elections. Under plurality voting, directors who receive the most votes are elected, regardless of whether they receive a majority of votes. In an uncontested election, a director is elected as long as he or she receives at least one vote.

Many shareholder advocates believe that plurality voting reduces governance quality by insulating directors from shareholder pressure. They therefore recommend that companies adopt majority voting procedures in which a director must receive at least 50 percent of the votes (even in an uncontested election) to be elected. A director who receives less than a majority must tender a resignation to the board. The board can either accept the resignation or, upon unanimous consent, reject the resignation and provide an explanation for its conclusion. (Mandatory resignation and acceptance by the board if a director running unopposed fails to get a majority of votes was part of the original the Dodd–Frank Act but was ultimately dropped from the final version of the legislation.)

Majority voting in director elections has been widely adopted by large corporations, with 86 percent of companies in the S&P 500 Index adopting some variant of majority voting. However, it remains less common among small companies. Only 30 percent of the S&P SmallCap 600 Index have adopted majority voting.[49]

It is not clear whether majority voting improves governance quality. Dissenting votes are often issue driven and not personal to the director. For example, an institutional investor might withhold votes to reelect members of the compensation committee if it believes the company's compensation practices are excessive. This might inadvertently work to remove a director who brings important strategic, operational, or risk-management qualifications to the board. As we saw in Chapter 4, "Board of Directors: Selection, Compensation, and Removal," the vast majority of directors receive greater than 50 percent support from shareholders; in 2013, only 44 directors (less than 0.1 percent) failed to receive majority approval.[50]

Proxy Access

Historically, the board of directors has had sole authority to nominate candidates whose names appear on the company proxy. In 2010, the Dodd–Frank Act instructed the SEC to amend Rule 14a-8 to allow shareholder-designated nominees to be included on the proxy, alongside the nominations set forth by the company. This rule was vacated by a U.S. Court of Appeals in 2011.[51] However, shareholder groups subsequently have sponsored resolutions that would grant qualifying investor groups the right to nominate directors on the company's proxy ("proxy access").

Under a typical proxy access proposal, shareholders or coalitions of shareholders who hold 3 percent or more of the company's shares and who have held their positions continuously for at least three years would be eligible to nominate up to 25 percent of the board. Some proxy access proposals have lower thresholds.

According to data from Sullivan & Cromwell, 10 proposals for proxy access were voted on in 2014. Of these, 3 passed and 7 failed; average support was 34 percent.[52] The following year, a much greater effort to promote proxy access was under way. The comptroller of the City of New York, overseeing pension funds with a combined $160 billion in assets, submitted proxy access proposals at 75 public companies, including ExxonMobil, Staples, and Abercrombie & Fitch. The outcome of this is not yet known, nor is the impact that proxy access will have on director elections or governance quality known. Few, if any, traditional institutional investors that own block positions are likely to run a dissident slate of directors. It is more likely that activist investors will do so.

Recent research suggests that shareholder democracy initiatives reduce shareholder value. A study by Larcker, Ormazabal, and Taylor (2011) found that the market reacts negatively to potential say-on-pay regulation and proxy access and that the reaction is more negative among companies that are most likely to be affected. They concluded that "the market perceives that the regulation of executive compensation will ultimately result in less efficient contracts and potentially decrease the supply of high-quality executives to public firms." They also concluded that "blockholders . . . may use the new privileges afforded them by proxy access regulation to manipulate the governance process to make themselves better off at the expense of other shareholders."[53]

Proxy Voting

The SEC has been examining the proxy voting process to determine whether rules should be implemented to increase voting participation, efficiency, and transparency. At issue is whether third-party agents have inappropriate influence on the voting process to the detriment of shareholder value. One such party is broker-dealers who act as a fiduciary for beneficial shareholders. Another is vote tabulators (such as Broadridge), intermediaries, and proxy service providers who have access to vote data and might influence votes. A third is institutional investors who lend their securities and might not recall their shares in time to vote on certain matters. The SEC is examining whether the voting process should be changed or disclosure increased to improve decision making. The SEC is also examining ways to increase voting participation by individual shareholders.[54] According to data from Broadridge and PricewaterhouseCoopers, retail investors vote only 30 percent of their shares, compared with 95 percent of shares held by institutional investors.[55]

As Figure 12.2 illustrates, the proxy voting process is extremely complicated and, in some cases, not well understood.

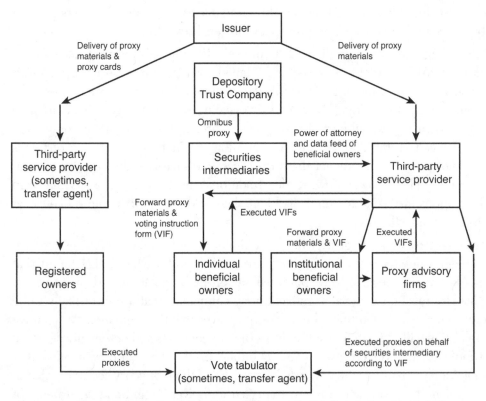

Source: Securities and Exchange Commission: Concept Release on the U.S. Proxy System. July 14, 2010.

Figure 12.2   Proxy voting procedures: a complex process.

A 2015 survey by RR Donnelley, Equilar, and the Rock Center for Corporate Governance at Stanford University underscores the frustration that many investors feel about the proxy voting process. The survey found that 55 percent of institutional investors believe that the typical proxy statement is too long. Forty-eight percent believe it is difficult to read and understand. Investors claim to read only 32 percent of a typical proxy, on average. They report that the ideal length of a proxy is 25 pages, compared with an actual average of 80 pages among companies in the Russell 3000.

The survey also found that while investors believe the proxy voting process to be a valuable exercise, portfolio managers are only moderately involved in voting decisions. Among large institutional investors with assets under management greater than $100 billion, portfolio managers are involved in only 10 percent of decisions. Only 59 percent of institutional investors use information in the proxy for investment decisions.[56] These data reinforce problems with the current voting system. They also suggest that investors might make more informed decisions if the quality of disclosure were improved.

Corporate Engagement

Finally, institutional investors influence corporate matters not only through the proxy voting process but also through direct engagement with corporations. These efforts are not always visible to the individual shareholder but can have a tangible effect on corporate policy. For example, in 2014 Vanguard sent a letter to approximately 350 companies in which the fund invested to encourage them to declassify their boards, adopt majority voting for directors, and provide shareholders the right to call a special meeting. Vanguard dubbed the effort "quiet diplomacy" and explained that it sent letters "to share our views about corporate governance practices that create the best opportunity for both long-term business success and superior investment returns."[57] That same year, the CEO of BlackRock wrote to companies in the S&P 500 Index to express concern that corporations were being too "short-term" in perspective by favoring dividends and share repurchases over capital expenditures and that these decisions might "jeopardize a company's ability to generate sustainable long-term returns."[58]

Still, direct dialogue between institutional investors and a company's board of directors is relatively infrequent in the United States. According to the survey by RR Donnelley referenced in the previous section, institutional investors engage with only 9 percent on average of the companies they invest in.[59] A PricewaterhouseCoopers survey found that 54 percent of directors believe that it is not appropriate for the board to engage in direct discussion with investors about earnings results, 44 percent believe it is not appropriate to discuss strategy or management performance, and 38 percent that it is in not appropriate to discuss financial oversight or risk management. When asked to elaborate, 94 percent claim that direct communication with shareholders creates too great a risk of mixed messages and 89 percent believe it is not appropriate because investors who seek direct communication with the board often have a special agenda.[60]

In Europe, direct engagement between shareholders and corporations is more common. For example, the United Kingdom Corporate Governance Code states that "the board as a whole has a responsibility for ensuring that a satisfactory dialogue with shareholders takes place." It also recommends that "the board should keep in touch with shareholder opinion in whatever ways are most practical and efficient."[61]

Proxy Advisory Firms

Many institutional investors rely on a **proxy advisory firm** to assist them in voting the company proxy and fulfilling the fiduciary responsibility to vote the shares on behalf of clients. The largest proxy advisory firms are Institutional Shareholder Services (ISS) and Glass Lewis & Co., whose clients manage $25 trillion and $15 trillion in assets, respectively.

For a variety of reasons, proxy advisory firms are highly influential in the voting process. First, institutional investors have little economic incentive to incur the research costs necessary to develop proprietary voting policies. Proxy research suffers from the same free rider problem common to many voting situations and discussed at the beginning of this chapter. The average institutional investor has little incentive to bear the cost of researching proxy issues relating to individual firms across a diversified portfolio when it only stands to receive a small fraction of the benefit. Proxy advisory firms can satisfy this need by researching the same set of issues across multiple firms and selling their research to multiple investors. Second, in 2003, the SEC began to require that registered institutional investors develop and disclose their proxy voting policies, and disclose their votes on all shareholder ballot items. The rule was intended to create greater transparency into the voting process and to ensure that institutional investors act without conflict of interest. At the same time, the SEC clarified that the use of voting policies developed by an independent, third-party agency (such as a proxy advisor) would be viewed as being non-conflicted.[62] As a result, the proxy voting guidelines of third-party firms have become a cost-effective means of satisfying fiduciary and regulatory voting obligations for institutional investors.

However, several potential drawbacks can occur from relying on the advice of a proxy advisory firm. First, proxy advisory firms take a somewhat inflexible approach toward certain governance matters and do not always properly consider the unique company situation (see the following sidebar). As a result, the recommendations of these firms might reflect a one-size-fits-all approach to governance and the propagation of "best practices" that the research literature has not supported. Second, these firms might not have sufficient staff or adequate expertise to evaluate the items subject to shareholder approval, particularly complicated issues such as the approval of equity-based compensation plans or proposed acquisitions.[63] Third, some of these firms have potential conflicts of interest because they provide consulting services to the companies whose proxies they evaluate (see Chapter 13, "Corporate Governance Ratings," for a discussion). Finally, the complete reliance on proxy advisory firms might constitute an abdication of fiduciary responsibility. Institutional investors are ultimately responsible for ensuring that their votes are in the best interest of their shareholders.[64]

The Reelection of Warren Buffett

The Coca-Cola Company

In 2004, ISS opposed the reelection of Warren Buffett to the board of the Coca-Cola Company. At the time, Buffett served on Coke's audit committee. ISS recommended that shareholders withhold their vote for his reelection because Buffett's company, Berkshire Hathaway, distributed Coca-Cola products in two of its subsidiaries. The proxy advisory firm believed this business relationship compromised his independence. It did not make an exception for the fact that Berkshire was the largest shareholder in the company or that Coca-Cola was Berkshire's largest equity investment, valued at $10 billion.[65]

ISS explained its opposition by stating: "It's not that we distrust Buffett. We want him on the board. But when you're talking about the external market in the current environment, we think it's the best thing for the company to literally have a zero tolerance policy when it comes to directors having ties and serving on the audit committee." It also stated, "It's a very slippery slope you start down when you start making exceptions for individuals."

The Coca-Cola Company responded to this position by stating, "Mr. Buffett's independence is consistent with the standards set by the New York Stock Exchange (NYSE). . . . Mr. Buffett is a man with an eminent reputation for integrity and his effectiveness as an audit committee member is widely regarded. Given his substantial ownership in our Company, there are few people more closely aligned with the interests of our shareowners."

Buffett was ultimately reelected to the board with 84 percent of the vote. He commented, "I think it's absolutely silly. . . . Checklists are no substitute for thinking. We've encouraged the idea of shareholders behaving like owners. The question is: Can they behave like intelligent owners?"[66]

Considerable evidence documents the influence that proxy advisory firms have over voting matters. Several institutional investors vote in near-perfect lockstep with the recommendations of proxy advisory firms across all proxy resolutions (see Table 12.4).[67]

Table 12.4 Institutional Investor Voting Record (Voting with ISS)

Institution	Number of Votes	With ISS "For"	With ISS "Against"
BlackRock Advisors	407,059	97%	28%
Vanguard Group	319,265	98%	37%
Fidelity Management & Research	312,203	98%	57%
Dimensional Fund Advisers	211,362	100%	99%
TIAA-CREF Asset Management	205,442	98%	26%
EQ Advisors Trust	180,078	97%	41%
Rydex Investments	144,832	100%	0%
Charles Schwab Investment Management	137,065	91%	44%
ProFund Advisors	135,358	100%	100%
ProShare Advisors	133,317	100%	100%

Includes the 10 institutional investors with the largest number of votes based on Form N-PX 2013 filings.
Source: Data from ISS Voting Analytics (2013). Calculation by the authors.

Bethel and Gillan (2002) found that an unfavorable recommendation from ISS can reduce shareholder support on proxy items by 13.6 to 20.6 percent, depending on the matter of the proposal.[68] Cai, Garner, and Walkling (2009) found that directors who receive a negative recommendation from ISS receive 19 percent fewer votes.[69] Morgan, Paulson, and Wolf (2006) found that an unfavorable recommendation from ISS reduces shareholder support by 20 percent on compensation-related issues.[70] Ertimur, Ferri, and Oesch (2013) had similar findings.[71]

In response to this and other empirical evidence, an SEC commissioner has expressed concern that "it is important to ensure that advisers to institutional investors . . . are not over-relying on analyses by proxy advisory firms" and that institutional investors should not "be able to outsource their fiduciary duties."[72]

A growing body of evidence also suggests that proxy advisory firms have influence over corporate decisions on compensation design. A 2012 survey found that more than 70 percent of companies report that their executive compensation programs are influenced by the policies and guidelines of proxy advisory firms.[73] Furthermore, an analysis by Gow, Larcker, McCall, and Tayan (2013) indicated that companies adjust the size of their equity compensation programs to meet ISS maximum thresholds. Among a sample of 4,230 company observations between 2004 and 2010, 34 percent of proposed equity plans would put the company within 1 percent of the ISS cap. By a greater than 20-to-1 margin, companies request equity that would put them 1 percent below the cap rather than 1 percent above the cap. These results are highly improbable based on chance alone and suggest that many companies acquire information on ISS thresholds and design their equity plans to fall just below this number (see Figure 12.3).[74] The proxy statements of companies such as Chesapeake Energy and United Online explicitly reference ISS thresholds in justifying the size of their equity compensation programs.[75]

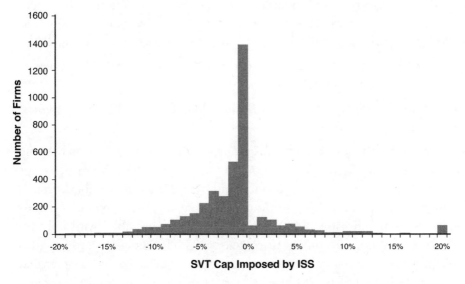

Source: ISS Proxy Recommendation Reports (2004–2010). Calculations by Gow, Larcker, McCall, and Tayan (2013).

Figure 12.3   Relation between company equity plan requests and ISS caps.

Finally, research studies suggest that the recommendations of proxy advisory firms are not value increasing and might be value decreasing for shareholders. Larcker, McCall, and Ormazabal (2013) found that many corporations constrain stock option repricing programs to meet the guidelines of proxy advisory firms and that those that do exhibit statistically lower market reactions to the repricing, lower operating performance, and higher employee turnover.[76] In a separate study, Larcker, McCall, and Ormazabal (2015) found that a substantial number of firms change their compensation programs to garner a favorable say-on-pay recommendation from proxy advisory firms, and that these changes are also value decreasing to shareholders.[77] These results call into question the quality of proxy advisory recommendations (see the following sidebar).

How Do Proxy Advisory Firms Develop Policy Guidelines?

Glass Lewis provides little information to the general public on the development of their voting policies. According to a Glass Lewis discussion paper:

"Glass Lewis' policies, tailored for each market, are formulated via a bottoms-up approach that involves discussions with a wide range of market participants, including investor clients, corporate issuers, academics, corporate directors and other subject matter experts, among others. The process takes into consideration relevant corporate governance standards, company, local regulations and market trends. Policy changes and report enhancements are driven by such discussions, as well as through consultations with the Glass Lewis Research Advisory Council."[78]

Moreover, the firm does not explain how general corporate governance concepts and standards translate into codified policy.

ISS discloses more extensive information about the firm's policy development process:

"ISS is committed to openness and transparency in formulating its proxy voting policies and in applying these policies to more than 40,000 shareholder meetings each year. . . . Our bottom-up policy formulation process collects feedback from a diverse range of market participants through multiple channels: an annual Policy Survey of institutional investors and corporate issuers, roundtables with industry groups, and ongoing feedback during proxy season. The ISS Policy Board uses this input to develop its draft policy updates on emerging governance issues each year. Before finalizing these updates, we publish draft updates for an open review and comment period."[79]

However, several aspects of ISS's approach raise questions about the accuracy of its recommendations. First, the ISS policy survey collects data from a small number of participants—only 97 institutional investors for fiscal 2013. Second, it does not disclose detailed information on the composition of the respondent pool to demonstrate that they are representative of investors broadly. Third, the survey contains biases in language that affect the framing of questions and steer respondents toward specific response choices (for example, a question on executive compensation practices falls under the title "pay for failure" and asks about "problematic" pay practices). Fourth, the survey does not seek to quantify thresholds but instead uses qualifying language (that is, a question on "overboarded" directors that serve on an "excessive" number of boards does not quantify these terms). Fifth, ISS is not clear about how it incorporates feedback during the open comment period to finalize voting policies. Finally, the linkage between the opinions that ISS collects through the solicitation process and the policies ultimately enacted are not clear. The ISS survey does not ask for feedback on specific policies but instead asks for general sentiment about broad issues and translates these into codified policies.[80]

Most importantly, neither ISS nor Glass Lewis demonstrates that it engages in testing to ensure that its final policies are accurate. Ultimately, the accuracy of the recommendation models should be determined by rigorous statistical analysis showing the positive impact of their policies on shareholder value. This could be accomplished through back-testing and independent analysis by third-party researchers.

Endnotes

1. The investor relations consulting industry attempts to understand the various roles played by different types of institutional investors and to move the shareholder base to investor types that are perceived as more desirable by management. See David F. Larcker and Brian Tayan, "Sharks in the Water: Battling an Activist Investor for Corporate Control," Stanford GSB Case No. CG–20 (February 2, 2010).

2. The role of passive index funds in the governance debate is somewhat problematic. If the fund holds roughly the same stocks as the index, it is not clear whether passive funds will be an active change agent for better corporate governance. Still, many people believe that given their sizable ownership position, index funds should use their position to advocate responsible governance reforms when appropriate.

3. Regulation FD (fair disclosure) has greatly limited the extent to which company management meets with individual investor groups. The SEC adopted Regulation FD in October 2000 to limit the selective disclosure of material nonpublic information to investors who might gain an advantage by trading on such information. The rule provides that when an issuer, or person acting on the issuer's behalf, unintentionally discloses such information, it has an obligation to promptly disclose the same information to the public. Since the adoption of Regulation FD, companies have been less likely to meet with individual investor groups.

4. BlackRock, "2013 Corporate Governance & Responsible Investment Report: Taking the Long View" (2014). Accessed April 4, 2015. See http://www.blackrock.com/corporate/en-us/about-us/responsible-investment/responsible-investment-reports.

5. National Investor Relations Institute and the Rock Center for Corporate Governance at Stanford University, "2014 Study on How Investment Horizon and Expectations of Shareholder Base Impact Corporate Decision-Making" (2014). Accessed May 6, 2015. See http://www.gsb.stanford.edu/faculty-research/centers-initiatives/cgri/research/surveys.

6. Ibid.

7. Brian Bushee, "Identifying and Attracting the 'Right' Investors: Evidence on the Behavior of Institutional Investors," *Journal of Applied Corporate Finance* 16 (2004): 28–35.

8. Thomson Reuters on WRDS, 13F Institutional Holdings (CDA/Spectrum).

9. Michael J. Barclay and Clifford G. Holderness, "Private Benefits from Control of Public Corporations," *Journal of Financial Economics* 25 (1989): 371–395.

10. Hamid Mehran, "Executive Compensation Structure, Ownership, and Firm Performance," *Journal of Financial Economics* 38 (1995): 163–184.

11. Stuart Gillan and Laura Starks, "The Evolution of Shareholder Activism in the United States," *Journal of Applied Corporate Finance* 19 (2007): 55–73.

12. Barclay and Holderness (1989).

13. John L. McConnell and Henri Servaes, "Additional Evidence on Equity Ownership and Corporate Value," *Journal of Financial Economics* 27 (1990): 595–612.

14. Mehran (1995).

15. Clifford G. Holderness, "A Survey of Blockholders and Corporate Control," *Economic Policy Review—Federal Reserve Bank of New York* 9 (2003): 51–63.

16. John E. Core, Robert W. Holthausen, and David F. Larcker, "Corporate Governance, Chief Executive Officer Compensation, and Firm Performance," *Journal of Financial Economics* 51 (1999): 371–406.

17. Marianne Bertrand and Sendhil Mullainathan, "Do CEOs Set Their Own Pay? The Ones without Principals Do," NBER working paper Series w7604, *Social Science Research Network* (2000). Accessed May 6, 2015. See http://ssrn.com/abstract=228095.

18. Reena Aggarwal, Isil Erel, Miguel Ferreira, and Pedro Matos, "Does Governance Travel around the World? Evidence from Institutional Investors," *Journal of Financial Economics* 100 (2011): 154–181.

19. Wayne H. Mikkelson and Megan Partch, "Managers' Voting Rights and Corporate Control," *Journal of Financial Economics* 25 (1989): 263–290.

20. Sovereign Wealth Fund Institute, "Sovereign Wealth Fund Rankings," Data as of April 6, 2015. Accessed May 6, 2015. See http://www.swfinstitute.org/fund-rankings/.

21. Norway Ministry of Finance, "The Management of the Government Pension Fund in 2013" (April 4, 2014.) Accessed April 6, 2015. See http://www.nbim.no/globalassets/documents/governance/stortingsmeldinger/report-to-the-storting-no-19-on-the-management-of-the-government-pension-fund-global.pdf?ID=5229.

22. Mark Scott, "Qatar Wealth Fund Backs Glencore's Bid for Xstrata," *New York Times* (November 16, 2012).

23. Securities Exchange Commission, "Disclosure of Proxy Voting Policies and Proxy Voting Records by Registered Management Investment Companies," Release No. 25922 (January 31, 2003). Accessed October 8, 2013. See www.sec.gov/rules/final/33-8188.htm.

24. ISS Voting Analytics data for fiscal years from June 2013 to May 2014.

25. Securities Lawyer's Deskbook, "Rule 14a8: Proposals of Security Holders." Accessed May 5, 2015. See https://www.law.cornell.edu/cfr/text/17/240.14a-8.

26. Proxy Monitor, "A Report on Corporate Governance and Shareholder Activism," Manhattan Institute (2014). Accessed April 7, 2015 See http://www.proxymonitor.org/Forms/pmr_09.aspx.

27. ISS, "2013 Proxy Season Review: United States" (August 22, 2013). Accessed April 7, 2015. See http://www.issgovernance.com/library/united-states-2013-proxy-season-review/.

28. See Chapter 11, endnote 3. Warren S. De Wied, "Proxy Contests," *Practical Law: The Journal* (November 2010). Accessed November 13, 2010. See http://us.practicallaw.com/.

29. ISS, "2013 Proxy Season Review: United States" (August 22, 2013).

30. Ashwini K. Agrawal, "Corporate Governance Objectives of Labor Union Shareholders: Evidence from Proxy Voting," *Review of Financial Studies* 25 (2012): 187–226.

31. Brad Barber, "Monitoring the Monitor: Evaluating CalPERS' Activism," *Journal of Investing* 16 (2007): 66–80.

32. Marc Lifsher, "CalPERS Changes Tactics on Poor Performers," *Los Angeles Times blogs online* (November 15, 2010). Accessed November 25, 2010. See http://latimesblogs.latimes.com/money_co/2010/11/calpers-company-focus-list.html.

33. Social Investment Forum, "Socially Responsible Mutual Funds Chart: Financial Performance. Information Current as of September 30, 2010." Accessed November 15, 2010. See www.social-invest.org/resources/mfpc/.

34. Walden Asset Management, "Advocating for Social Change" (2010). Accessed November 15, 2010. See www.waldenassetmgmt.com/social.html.

35. Proxy Monitor (2014).

36. Nike Corp., Form DEF 14A, filed with the Securities and Exchange Commission August 12, 1996.

37. Voting results from Nike Corp., Form 10-Q for the quarter ending August 31, 1996, filed with the Securities and Exchange Commission October 15, 1996. Corporate reforms from Debora L. Spar and Lane T. La Mure, "The Power of Activism: Assessing the Impact of NGOs on Global Business," *California Management Review* 45 (2003): 78–101.

38. Christopher Charles Geczy, Robert F. Stambaugh, and David Levin, "Investing in Socially Responsible Mutual Funds," *Social Science Research Network* (October 2005). Accessed June 2, 2014. See http://ssrn.com/abstract=416380.

39. Luc Renneboog, Jenke Ter Horst, and Chendi Zhang, "The Price of Ethics and Stakeholder Governance: The Performance of Socially Responsible Mutual Funds," *Journal of Corporate Finance* 14 (2008): 302–322.

40. Wikipedia, "Hedge Funds." Accessed May 5, 2015. See http://en.wikipedia.org/wiki/Hedge_fund.

41. Small, liquid targets enable the activist hedge fund to accumulate a sizable position with relative speed and without running up the price of the stock. Presumably, it also enables the firm to eventually exit the position quickly and without depressing the stock.

42. Alon Brav, Wei Jiang, Frank Partnoy, and Randall Thomas, "Hedge Fund Activism, Corporate Governance, and Firm Performance," *Journal of Finance* 63 (2008): 1729–1775.

43. In a wolf pack strategy, multiple hedge funds work together to force change on a target company. *Piling on* refers to unaffiliated hedge funds accumulating a position in a stock when they learn that an activist has taken a significant position. Hedge funds that pile on to a target are not activists themselves. However, these hedge funds are likely to support the recommendations of the activist.

44. SEC rules require that an investor who holds more than 5 percent of a company's stock disclose its position. Disclosure on Form 13G indicates that the investor intends to hold the position as a passive investment (that is, the investor does not intend to become active with management or to seek a change in control). Disclosure on Form 13D indicates a possible active holding.

45. April Klein and Emanuel Zur, "Entrepreneurial Shareholder Activism: Hedge Funds and Other Private Investors," *Journal of Finance* 64 (2009): 187–229.

46. Lucian A. Bebchuk, Alon Brav, and Wei Jiang, "The Long-Term Effects of Hedge Fund Activism," *Columbia Law Review* (forthcoming, June 2015).

47. Ed deHaan, David F. Larcker, and Charles McClure, "Activists as Value Investors," unpublished working paper (2015).

48. Nickolay Gantchev, "The Costs of Shareholder Activism: Evidence from a Sequential Decision Model," *Journal of Financial Economics* 107 (2013): 610–631.

49. SharkRepellent, "Takeover Defenses Trend Analysis, 2014," SharkRepellent, FactSet Research Systems, Inc. (2015). Accessed March 26, 2015. See www.sharkrepellent.net.

50. ISS, "2013 Proxy Season Review: United States" (August 22, 2013).

51. The Court's decision was in response to a September 2010 lawsuit filed by the Chamber of Commerce and Business Roundtable against the SEC that claimed "the rule is arbitrary and capricious [and] violates the Administrative Procedure Act, and . . . the SEC failed to properly assess the rule's effects on 'efficiency, competition, and capital formation' as required by law." See U.S. Chamber of Commerce press release, "U.S. Chamber Joins Business Roundtable in Lawsuit Challenging Securities and Exchange Commission" (September 29, 2010). The Business Roundtable and U.S. Chamber of Commerce Petition for Review filed in the United States Court of Appeals for the District of Columbia Circuit (September 29, 2010). Accessed May 5, 2015. See www.uschamber.com/sites/default/files/files/1009uscc_sec.pdf.

52. Sullivan & Cromwell, "2014 Proxy Season Review" (June 25, 2014). Accessed April 8, 2015. See http://www.sullcrom.com/siteFiles/Publications/SC_Publication_2014_Proxy_Season_Review.pdf.

53. David F. Larcker, Gaizka Ormazabal, and Daniel J. Taylor, "The Market Reaction to Corporate Governance Regulation," *Journal of Financial Economics* 101 (2011): 431–448.

54. See Securities and Exchange Commission, "Securities and Exchange Commission Proxy Roundtable" (February 19, 2015). Accessed May 5, 2015. See http://www.sec.gov/news/statement/ensuring-shareholders-have-meaningful-effective-vote.html. Also see "Securities and Exchange Commission: Concept Release on the U.S. Proxy System" (July 14, 2010). Accessed May 6, 2015. http://www.sec.gov/rules/concept/2010/34-62495.pdf.

55. Broadridge and PricewaterhouseCoopers, "Directors and Investors: Are They on the Same Page? Insights from the 2014 Proxy Season and Recent Governance Surveys" (October 2014). Accessed May 6, 2015. See http://www.pwc.com/en_US/us/corporate-governance/publications/assets/proxypulse-3rd-edition-october-2014-pwc.pdf.

56. RR Donnelly, Equilar, and the Rock Center for Corporate Governance at Stanford University, "2015 Investor Survey: Deconstructing Proxies—What Matters to Investors" (2015). Accessed May 6, 2015. See http://www.gsb.stanford.edu/faculty-research/publications/2015-investor-survey-deconstructing-proxy-statements-what-matters.

57. According to Vanguard, "We sent formal written communications to the chairpersons and CEOs of nearly 1,000 of our largest holdings. We customized our communications based on specific changes we wanted to see. Nearly 350 of these communications committed requests for companies to remove problematic governance structures (such as classes of stock that disproportionally give one class more votes, or staggered director elections) or to revisit compensation policies. To date, nearly one-half of the companies followed up and more than 80 have also made, or committed to try to make, at least one of the changes. We are still receiving responses as companies address our requests at board and shareholder meetings." See Vanguard, "Our Proxy Voting and Engagement Efforts: An Update." Accessed April 13, 2015. See https://about.vanguard.com/vanguard-proxy-voting/update-on-voting/.

58. Text of letter sent by Larry Fink, BlackRock's Chairman and CEO, encouraging a focus on long-term growth strategies, *Wall Street Journal online*. Accessed April 4, 2015. See http://online.wsj.com/public/resources/documents/LDF_letter_to_corporates_2014_public.pdf.

59. RR Donnelly, Equilar, and the Rock Center for Corporate Governance at Stanford University (2015).

60. PricewaterhouseCoopers LLC, "PWC's 2014 Annual Corporate Directors Survey: Trends Shaping Governance and the Board of the Future: Executive Compensation and Director Communications" (2014). Accessed April 7, 2015. See http://www.pwc.com/us/en/corporate-governance/annual-corporate-directors-survey/assets/annual-corporate-directors-survey-full-report-pwc.pdf.

61. Financial Reporting Council, "The UK Corporate Governance Code" (September 2012). Accessed April 7, 2015. See https://www.frc.org.uk/Our-Work/Publications/Corporate-Governance/UK-Corporate-Governance-Code-September-2012.aspx.

62. According to the SEC, "An independent [investment] adviser that votes client proxies in accordance with a pre-determined policy based on the recommendations of an independent third party will not necessarily breach its fiduciary duty of loyalty to its clients even though the recommendations may be consistent with the adviser's own interest. In essence, the recommendations of a third party that is in fact independent of an investment adviser may cleanse the vote of the adviser's conflict." U.S. Securities and Exchange Commission, "Egan-Jones Proxy Services: No-Action letter dated May 27, 2004" (2004). Accessed October 8, 2013. See www.sec.gov/divisions/investment/noaction/egan052704.htm.

63. Institutional Shareholder Services has approximately 800 employees. Not all 800 employees are "governance analysts." Some employees are involved in tedious data collection and other administrative tasks. See ISS, "The Leader in Corporate Governance." Accessed March 9, 2013. See http://www.issgovernance.com/about/about-iss/.

64. The Department of Labor has proposed broadening the definition of a *fiduciary* to any entity that provides investment advice to employee benefit plans. If enacted, this would include proxy advisory firms. Marc Hogan, "DOL Proposal Could Threaten ISS," *Agenda* (November 8, 2010). Also see Melissa J. Anderson, "SEC to Examine Proxy Advisors for Conflicts of Interest," *Agenda* (January 16, 2015). Accessed March 9, 2015. See http://agendaweek.com/pc/1046003/107713.

65. Berkshire Hathaway, "2003 Annual Report." Accessed August 27, 2007. See www.berkshirehathaway.com/2003ar/2003ar.pdf.

66. Philip Klein, "Reformers' Proxy Votes Polarize Governance Debate," *Reuters News* (April 18, 2004). Andrew Countryman, "Coke Can Go Better with Icon Buffett," *Courier-Mail* (April 12, 2004): 18. The Coca-Cola Company, Form DEF 14A, filed with the Securities and Exchange Commission April 9, 2004. Margery Beck, "Buffett Calls Effort to Make Him Leave Coca-Cola Board 'Absolutely Silly,'" *Associated Press Newswires* (May 2, 2004).

67. ISS Voting Analytics data for fiscal years from June 2013 to May 2014.

68. Jennifer E. Bethel and Stuart L. Gillan, "The Impact of Institutional and Regulatory Environment on Shareholder Voting," *Financial Management* (2002): 29–54.

69. Jie Cai, Jacqueline L. Garner, and Ralph A. Walking, "Electing Directors," *Journal of Finance* 64 (2009): 2389–2421.

70. Angela Morgan, Annette Paulson, and Jack Wolf, "The Evolution of Shareholder Voting for Executive Compensation Schemes," Journal of *Corporate Finance* 12 (2006): 715–737.

71. Yonca Ertimur, Fabrizio Ferri, and David Oesch, "Shareholder Votes and Proxy Advisors: Evidence from Say on Pay," *Journal of Accounting Research* 51 (2013): 951–996.

72. Daniel M. Gallagher, "Gallagher on the Roles of State and Federal Law in Corporate Governance," Columbia Law School's Blog on Corporations and the Capital Markets (June 18, 2013). Accessed April 9, 2015. See http://clsbluesky.law.columbia.edu/2013/06/18/gallagher-on-the-roles-of-state-and-federal-law-in-corporate-governance/.

73. The Conference Board, NASDAQ, and the Rock Center for Corporate Governance at Stanford University, "The Influence of Proxy Advisory Firm Voting Recommendations on Say-on-Pay Votes and Executive Compensation Decisions" (2012). Accessed May 6, 2015. See http://www.gsb.stanford.edu/faculty-research/publications/2012-proxy-advisory-survey.

74. David F. Larcker, Ian D. Gow, Allan McCall, and Brian Tayan, "Sneak Preview: How ISS Dictates Equity Plan Design," Stanford Closer Look Series (October 23, 2013). Accessed May 6, 2015. See http://www.gsb.stanford.edu/faculty-research/centers-initiatives/cgri/research/closer-look.

75. See Chesapeake Energy Corp., Form DEF 14A, filed with the Securities and Exchange Commission April 30, 2014; and United Online Inc., Form DEF 14A, filed with the Securities and Exchange Commission April 30, 2013.

76. David F. Larcker, Allan L. McCall, and Gaizka Ormazabal, "Proxy Advisory Firms and Stock Option Repricing," *Journal of Accounting and Economics* 56 (2013): 149–169.

77. David F. Larcker, Allan L. McCall, and Gaizka Ormazabal, "Outsourcing Shareholder Voting to Proxy Advisory Firms," *Journal of Law and Economics* (forthcoming 2015).

78. Glass Lewis & Co., "Discussion Paper—An Overview of the Proxy Advisory Industry. Considerations on Possible Policy Options" (June 25, 2012). Accessed March 9, 2015. See http://www.glasslewis.com/assets/uploads/2012/12/062512_glass_lewis_comment_esma_discussion_paper_vf.pdf.

79. ISS, "Policy Formulation and Application" (2015). Accessed March 9, 2015. See http://www.issgovernance.com/policy-gateway/policy-formulation-application/.

80. David F. Larcker, Allan McCall, and Brian Tayan, "And Then a Miracle Happens," Stanford Closer Look Series (February 25, 2013). Accessed May 6, 2015. See http://www.gsb.stanford.edu/faculty-research/centers-initiatives/cgri/research/closer-look.

13

Corporate Governance Ratings

Governance ratings is a relatively new industry in which consulting companies develop quantitative metrics to measure the effectiveness of a company's governance system. The inputs in these models are based on governance attributes that we have discussed throughout this book, including the structure of the board, elements of the executive compensation plan, antitakeover provisions, and other features. Researchers have also developed indices that rely on similar inputs. The question remains whether governance ratings and indices accurately measure governance quality and predict the likelihood of negative outcomes.

In this chapter, we discuss the methodology used to develop governance ratings and evaluate their accuracy. We begin by reviewing the ratings developed by Institutional Shareholder Services and GMI Ratings. We then examine the models of governance quality that have been developed by researchers.

Third-Party Ratings

Ratings by knowledgeable independent third parties are common and can be useful to consumers in assessing the quality of products or services. Ratings are particularly important in markets where consumers do not have complete information about the items they are evaluating or when product or service quality is not easily observable. For example, restaurant customers can rely on Michelin Guide or Zagat ratings to select a restaurant in a new city, auto customers can review J.D. Power and Associates or Consumer Reports rankings to assess customer satisfaction with various models, and prospective undergraduate and graduate students can read the rankings of *U.S. News & World Report* to determine the prestige of a particular educational institution.

For ratings to be useful, they must provide credible information. Three factors are particularly critical in establishing credibility. First, ratings must be objective, in that they are based on data that an outside observer would similarly evaluate. Second, the ratings provider must be free from conflicts of interest that would compromise the judgment of the provider. Third, the ratings provider must be able to demonstrate the **predictive ability** of its ratings. That is, the ratings must not simply describe past outcomes but must be correlated with future outcomes of interest to the users. This last point is critical. For example, if a traveler finds that the ratings of Zagat are not consistent with her own experience at the same restaurants, she will cease to rely on them when making decisions about where to eat. The Zagat system then would lose its relevance. Market pressure creates an incentive for Zagat to maintain the integrity of its ratings system.

Ratings are also important not only for their role in shaping consumer behavior but also for their impact on the company whose products and services are being rated. The very presence of J.D. Power in the market puts pressure on car manufacturers to maintain and improve the quality standards of each successive model. Because of their perceived expertise, ratings firms can serve as a disciplining mechanism on product or service providers. Given this position of influence, it is particularly important that the ratings system maintain integrity. The ratings industry can provide important information to consumers and firms that ultimately leads to more efficient decision making and resource allocation.

Credit Ratings

Perhaps the most prominent providers of financial ratings in the marketplace are **credit-rating agencies**. The largest three credit-rating agencies are Moody's Investor Services, Standard & Poor's, and Fitch Ratings. These institutions provide ratings on corporations based on their expected ability to repay debt obligations, or their **creditworthiness**. Creditworthiness is determined based on a combination of quantitative and qualitative factors, including availability of collateral, leverage ratios, interest coverage, and diversity and stability of revenue streams, among other factors. Institutional investors that invest in corporate debt use credit ratings to determine the likelihood that they will be paid the full principal and interest owed to them over the life of the bond. In some cases, investors such as money market funds are only allowed to invest in debt with a sufficiently high rating. Companies with higher credit ratings are generally rewarded in the market with lower interest rates on their borrowings, while companies with lower credit ratings are generally charged higher interest rates in an effort to compensate for the inherent risk.

The relative success of the credit rating system can be demonstrated by its predictive ability over time. For example, Moody's keeps detailed statistics on default frequency by ratings category. Through this data, the company can demonstrate that higher-rated institutions have a lower likelihood of default than lower-rated institutions.

For example, corporations that received Moody's highest rating (Aaa) between 1970 and 2013 defaulted at a rate of 0.1 percent over the 10 years following the receipt of that rating. By contrast, corporations that received a speculative-grade rating (Ba or lower) defaulted on their debt obligations 33 percent of the time during the 10 years following that rating.[1] As a result, Moody's can point to historical correlations, supported by a deep sample of data, to demonstrate that its corporate credit ratings are predictive in nature (see Figure 13.1).

As with other ratings systems, credit ratings fail when they are based on faulty assumptions or omit critical input data. Recent failures by the credit rating industry illustrate these risks. For example, in 2001, Moody's came under considerable criticism for maintaining an investment-grade rating on Enron (Baa1) just weeks before the company collapsed into bankruptcy. Although the default of an investment-grade rated company is not a failure in a statistical sense, in the case of Enron, it was a failure in a methodological sense. Moody's rating model failed to incorporate significant off-balance-sheet obligations that Enron had committed to through special-purpose vehicles. By failing to count these toward the total indebtedness of the company, Moody's did not properly measure the riskiness of Enron's capital structure. As a result, Enron's creditworthiness was not consistent with the Baa1 rating assigned to it by Moody's.

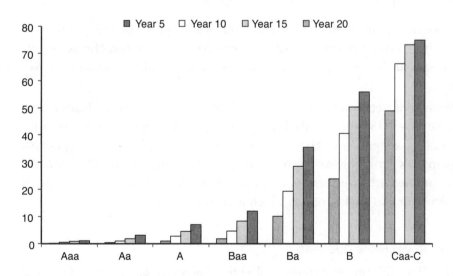

Source: Ou, Chiu, Zeng, and Metz (2014).

Figure 13.1 Cumulative corporate default rates by ratings categories.

A similar methodological breakdown occurred in the rating of various asset-backed securities backed by U.S. subprime residential home mortgages between 2006 and 2008. Moody's and the other two major rating agencies made assumptions about future home price appreciation, default frequency at the individual borrower level, and the correlation of default across geographical markets that proved to be highly erroneous. As a result, there was a systemic failure in securities backed by these mortgages, which spread to affect derivative investments that were tied to those securities as well. This failure contributed to the collapse of the credit markets in 2008.

The success and failure of credit ratings can serve as an example as we turn to the topic of corporate governance ratings. As we examine models developed by commercial providers and academics, we ask first and foremost whether they pass the test of predictive ability. Are positive corporate governance ratings correlated with positive corporate outcomes? Are the relative ratings assigned by each provider consistent with the relative outcomes of the entities being rated? Are methodological shortcomings compromising the integrity of these ratings systems? After all, if market participants are expected to make investment and financial decisions in part based on corporate governance ratings, they should have some assurance that these ratings are accurate. To make that assessment, the ratings must stand up to rigorous, objective testing.

Commercial Corporate Governance Ratings

Governance ratings firms rate companies on the overall quality of their governance system, taking into account structural factors. Some governance ratings firms include subratings on specific areas, such as audit quality, compensation, and antitakeover protections.

Two prominent corporate governance ratings firms exist: Institutional Shareholder Services (ISS) and GMI Ratings. ISS has developed three successive governance ratings systems over the past 15 years. ISS ratings are sold separately from the company's proxy advisory services discussed in Chapter 12, "Institutional Shareholders and Activist Investors." GMI Ratings has acquired three ratings systems through predecessor companies, one of which is currently in use.

ISS: Corporate Governance Quotient

One of the first ISS ratings systems, called the Corporate Governance Quotient (CGQ), was developed in 2002. The CGQ model included 65 variables in eight categories: the board of directors, audit, charter and bylaw provisions, state of incorporation, executive and director compensation, qualitative factors, equity ownership by board members and executives, and director education (see Table 13.1).

Table 13.1   Selected Ratings Variables: CGQ (2007)

Ratings Factors	
Board	**Executive and Director Compensation**
Board composition	Cost of option plans
Board size	Option repricing permitted in plan
Cumulative voting	Director compensation
Boards served on	Option burn rate
Former CEOs	Performance-based compensation
Chairman/CEO separation	
Board attendance	
Related party transactions	
Majority voting	
Audit	**Qualitative Factors**
Audit committee	Board performance reviews
Audit committee, financial experts	Individual director performance reviews
Audit fees	CEO succession plan
Auditor ratification	Directors resign upon job change
Restatements	
Charter/Bylaws	**Ownership**
Poison pill adoption	Executive stock ownership guidelines
Vote requirements, charter/bylaw amendments	Director stock ownership guidelines
Vote requirements, approval of mergers	Mandatory holding period for equity grants
Written consent	**Director Education**
State of incorporation	Director education
Special meetings	
Capital structure, dual class	

Source: Institutional Shareholder Services, "U.S. Corporate Governance Quotient Criteria."

Companies were assigned a numeric score on a scale of 0 (unfavorable) to 100 (favorable), based on their performance across these variables. Ratings were then distributed along a forced curve to reflect relative rather than absolute levels of corporate governance risk. Each company received two CGQ scores: The first measured its governance quality relative to its market index and the second relative to its industry.

ISS did not disclose technical details of how it developed CGQ. The ratings agency generally stated that it gathered a list of best practices—as reflected in rigorous research and in consultation with professionals and institutional money managers—and performed statistical analysis to determine correlations of each metric with performance and to assign weightings.[2] ISS claimed that CGQ was a reliable tool for "identifying portfolio risk related to governance" and "leveraging governance to drive increased shareholder value."[3]

ISS: Governance Risk Indicators

The second ISS ratings system, called Governance Risk Indicators (GRId), was introduced in 2010 to replace CGQ.[4] The GRId model included a maximum of 166 data inputs in four "subsections": audit, board structure, shareholder rights, and compensation. Selected inputs included these:

- The percentage of nonaudit fees as a percentage of total fees
- Whether the company had been subjected to an enforcement action in the previous two years
- The percentage of independent directors
- Independent or dual chairman/CEO
- Single or dual class of shares
- Poison pill that shareholders did not approve
- The percentage of the chairman's compensation that is performance-based

The actual number of variables included in a company's rating varied based on country of origin. The rating of a U.S. company was based on 63 variables. Variables mandated by law (such as independence standards of the compensation committee) and variables based on governance features that were not applicable (such as composition of the supervisory board) were not included. Each variable was then weighted. The weightings themselves also varied based on country of origin. For example, annual director elections were more heavily weighted in Canada than in the U.S. "to reflect geographical differences."[5]

Companies received a composite GRId score to demonstrate overall governance quality and a GRId score for each subsection. Scores were distributed across a 10-point scale, +5 to –5, with zero representing neutral. Positive scores indicated "low concern" for a company's governance and were awarded to companies that "exceed local best practice guidelines." Neutral scores indicated "medium concern," and negative scores indicated "high concern."

According to ISS, GRId ratings were not intended to predict future operating performance or shareholder returns but to "help institutions and other financial market participants measure and flag investment risk."[6]

ISS: QuickScore

ISS released its third ratings system, QuickScore, in 2013 to replace GRId. QuickScore rates companies on 200 governance factors categorized under four "pillars": board structure, shareholder rights and takeover defenses, compensation, and audit and risk oversight. The factors are similar to those used in GRId, with additional factors such as these:

- The percentage of nonexecutive directors with lengthy tenure
- Whether the board recently took action that materially reduced shareholder rights
- The number and percentage of women on the board
- Whether the most recent say-on-pay proposal received shareholder support below 70 percent
- Whether the board failed to implement a majority-supported shareholder proposal

QuickScore includes other methodological features that are similar to GRId. For example, corporate ratings are assigned on a scale of 1 to 10, with 10 representing "high concern level." Companies are also assigned pillar-level scores on this scale. QuickScores are given relative to the market index and on a geographic basis. ISS claims that its ratings "help institutional investors identify and monitor potential governance risk in their portfolios, and help companies identify possible investor concerns based on signals of governance risk."[7]

GMI Ratings

GMI Ratings is owned by MSCI and represents the consolidation of three previous ratings companies that merged in 2010: GovernanceMetrics International, The Corporate Library, and Audit Analytics. (Prior to the acquisition of GMI Ratings, MSCI owned ISS from 2010 to 2014. In addition to GMI Ratings, MSCI owns firms that provide ratings and analysis of companies' environmental, social, and governance-related business practices.)

The GMI Ratings system in place today is based on the methodology developed by Audit Integrity. The ratings agency assigns companies an Accounting and Governance Risk. (AGR) score based on data inputs that capture both accounting and governance risk factors.[8] That is, unlike the ISS model, AGR takes into account detailed financial reporting metrics, such as abnormal accruals and variability in accounts. The AGR model also relies on time-series data to track the change in variables over time. Based on the output of this analysis, companies are forced into percentiles that reflect their aggregate level of accounting and governance risk and are categorized as follows:

- **Very Aggressive**—highest-risk companies, top 10 percent of the total universe
- **Aggressive**—high-risk companies, next 25 percent
- **Average**—moderate-risk companies, next 50 percent
- **Conservative**—low-risk companies, bottom 15 percent

GMI Ratings claims that the purpose of the AGR system is "to use publicly available data to discriminate between fraudulent and nonfraudulent companies."[9]

Testing the Predictability of Corporate Governance Ratings

Ultimately, the usefulness of a governance rating is contingent upon its predictive nature. It is not sufficient for a governance ratings firm to articulate and defend the rationale behind its methodology. It needs to demonstrate that its ratings are correlated with outcomes that investors care about, such as operating performance, stock price performance, or the avoidance of bankruptcy, accounting restatements, and litigation (see the following sidebar).

Ratings Miss: One-Time Error or Methodological Flaw?

American International Group (AIG)

In 2004, ISS assigned AIG a CGQ index rating of 88.3 and an industry rating of 92. Among the positive attributes supporting the rating were the facts that the full board was elected annually, the company had a board-approved CEO succession plan in place, all directors with more than one year of service owned stock, and fees paid to the company's accounting firm for nonaudit services were less than those paid for audit services. Among the negative attributes were lack of disclosure about a mandatory retirement age or term limits for directors, lack of disclosure about equity ownership guidelines for executives or directors, and the fact that no directors had participated in an "ISS accredited" director education program.[10]

At the time, Hank Greenberg was chairman and CEO of the company. Less than six months later, the New York State attorney general and the Department of Justice launched inquiries into certain business practices of the company, including allegations that it had participated in "bid rigging" (issuing false and artificially high insurance bids to create the appearance of a competitive bidding process) and had used retroactive insurance policies to smooth earnings.[11] Greenberg was forced to step down from the company he had led for more than 40 years.

Three years later, the company again ran into trouble following disclosure that it had suffered severe financial losses from derivative contracts tied to the value of mortgage securities. After a series of CEO resignations, the company sought a bailout from the U.S. government. Its collapse, along with that of Lehman Brothers, was widely seen as triggering the financial crisis of 2008.[12]

An ISS executive admitted that the company's ratings were not foolproof: "If we had a perfect solution, I'd be a billionaire running a hedge fund."[13]

The research evidence suggests that ISS ratings do not have predictive ability. Daines, Gow, and Larcker (2010) found that ISS ratings (CGQ) were not correlated with future accounting restatements, class-action lawsuits, accounting operating performance (return on assets), market-to-book ratio, and stock price performance. They also found little correlation between the CGQ ratings assigned by ISS and its proxy recommendations. The authors concluded that "substantial measurement error [exists] in commercial corporate governance ratings" and that "boards of directors should not implement governance changes solely for the purpose of increasing their ranking."[14]

Rigorous research on subsequent ISS ratings systems—GRId and QuickScore—has not been performed, but there is little reason to believe that these ratings, which are similar in structure to CGQ, can accurately measure governance quality.

Research suggests that the GMI Ratings system has somewhat higher predictive ability. As discussed in Chapter 10, "Financial Reporting and External Audit," Price, Sharp, and Wood (2011) and Correia (2014) both found that AGR scores are correlated with financial misstatements.[15] Daines, Gow, and Larcker (2010) found that AGR has some ability to predict future restatements, class-action lawsuits, and operating and stock price performance. The authors noted that the success of the model might be due to the inclusion of financial statement data rather than a pure reliance on "observable corporate governance mechanisms, such as board structure."[16] To our knowledge, there are no commercial governance ratings that are highly correlated with future outcomes likely to be associated with poor corporate governance.

Governance Rating Systems by Academic Researchers

Academic researchers have also put considerable effort toward the development of models to measure governance quality. The typical model takes the form of a **corporate governance index** that aggregates several input variables into a single metric. To construct an index, the researcher selects governance features that are deemed to be important, such as board structure, antitakeover provisions, and bylaw restrictions. These variables are quantified (usually through the assignment of binary numerical values, 0 or 1) and compiled into a single index that is said to reflect overall governance quality. A company's governance score can be readily compared against those of others to gauge its relative effectiveness.

Gompers, Ishii, and Metrick (2003) developed one of the first firm-specific corporate governance indices.[17] They included in their study 1,500 publicly traded U.S. corporations (primarily those in the S&P 500 Index and other major indices) between 1990 and 1999. To construct the index, they relied on corporate governance features tracked by the Investor Responsibility Research Center (IRRC). IRRC collects data on 28 variables, 22 of which are related to governing documents and 6 of which are related to antitakeover protections (reduced by the authors to 24 after taking into account overlaps—see Figure 13.2).

	Percentage of firms with governance provisions in			
	1990	1993	1995	1998
Delay				
Blank Check	76.4	80.0	85.7	87.9
Classified Board	59.0	60.4	61.7	59.4
Special Meeting	24.5	29.9	31.9	34.5
Written Consent	24.4	29.2	32.0	33.1
Protection				
Compensation Plans	44.7	65.8	72.5	62.4
Contracts	16.4	15.2	12.7	11.7
Golden Parachutes	53.1	55.5	55.1	56.6
Indemnification	40.9	39.6	38.7	24.4
Liability	72.3	69.1	65.6	46.8
Severance	13.4	5.5	10.3	11.7
Voting				
Bylaws	14.4	16.1	16.0	18.1
Charter	3.2	3.4	3.1	3.0
Cumulative Voting	18.5	16.5	14.9	12.2
Secret Ballot	2.9	9.5	12.2	9.4
Supermajority	38.8	39.6	38.5	34.1
Unequal Voting	2.4	2.0	1.9	1.9
Other				
Antigreenmail	6.1	6.9	6.4	5.6
Directors' Duties	6.5	7.4	7.2	6.7
Fair Price	33.5	35.2	33.6	27.8
Pension Parachutes	3.9	5.2	3.9	2.2
Poison Pill	53.9	57.4	56.6	55.3
Silver Parachutes	4.1	4.8	3.5	2.3
State				
Antigreenmail Law	17.2	17.6	17.0	14.1
Business Combination Law	84.3	88.5	88.9	89.9
Cash-Out Law	4.2	3.9	3.9	3.5
Directors' Duties Law	5.2	5.0	5.0	4.4
Fair Price Law	35.7	36.9	35.9	31.6
Control Share Acquisition Law	29.6	29.9	29.4	26.4
Number of Firms	1357	1343	1373	1708

Source: Gompers, Ishii, and Metrick (2003). Copyright by the President and Fellows of Harvard College and the Massachusetts Institute of Technology.

Figure 13.2   Governance features included in G-Index.

As we can see from the list, the input variables are heavily weighted toward antitakeover measures, which was the main focus of IRRC during this time. Each company was assigned one point for each provision that is viewed as negatively impacting shareholder rights and zero for each provision that favors shareholder rights. These values were then totaled to create a governance index (or G-Index), which, according to the authors, served as a "proxy for the balance of power between shareholders and managers."

To test their model, the authors grouped companies with similar G-Index scores into buckets. Those with a low G-Index score (less than or equal to five) were deemed to be shareholder friendly. These companies were given the label "democratic" companies. Those with a high G-Index (greater than or equal to 14) were deemed to restrict shareholder rights and were labeled "dictator" companies. The results of the study are striking. An investment strategy that involves simultaneously buying the democratic portfolio and shorting the dictator portfolio earned abnormal returns of 0.71 percent per month (8.5 percent annually) over the measurement period (September 1, 1990, to December 31, 1999). Furthermore, the authors found that a one-point increase in the G-Index was correlated with an 11.4 percent reduction in market-to-book value over the measurement period. That is, the companies with more favorable shareholder rights exhibited higher stock price returns and higher market valuations than companies with worse shareholder protections.

These returns are extremely impressive. In fact, they are so impressive that they merit closer scrutiny. Is it possible for a collection of publicly available, plain-vanilla governance features to produce this level of excess stock returns? Is the stock market this inefficient in processing information on corporate governance?

Several researchers have reexamined the findings. Core, Guay, and Rusticus (2006) found that the G-Index investment strategy lost the ability to generate substantial excess returns when the time period in the analysis was extended to include 2000–2003.[18] Whereas the democratic portfolio of Gompers, Ishii, and Metrick (2003) outperformed the dictatorship portfolio between 1990 and 1999 (23.3 percent versus 14.1 percent), it substantially underperformed between 2000 and 2003 (–5.8 percent versus 4.3 percent). That is, after the crash of the technology sector, there were no statistical differences between the returns to dictator and democracy firms (see Figure 13.3).

Does Weak Governance Cause Weak Stock Returns?

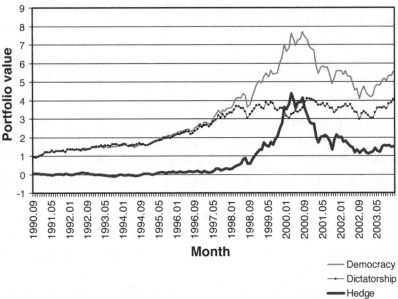

Source: Core, Guay, and Rusticus (2006).

Figure 13.3 Performance of G-Index before and after 2000.

More recently, Bebchuk, Cohen, and Ferrell (2009) attempted to refine the G-Index to improve its predictive ability. The authors posited that one of the shortcomings of the G-Index could be that its inputs were not selected based on a preexisting and proven correlation to corporate performance. Instead, they were chosen based on the simple fact that IRRC tracked them. Therefore, several could potentially be irrelevant or redundant. The authors therefore selected a subset of the IRRC inputs that they believed had the strongest relationship to corporate performance. These included staggered boards, limitations on shareholder ability to amend the company bylaws, limitations on shareholder ability to amend the company charter, the requirement of a supermajority to approve a merger, the use of golden parachutes, and the use of a poison pill. The authors explained that they selected the first four of these because they limited "the extent to which a majority of shareholders can impose their will on management." They selected the last two because they are "the most well-known and salient measures taken in preparation for a hostile offer."[19]

Companies were assigned a 1 for the enactment of each provision that restricted shareholder rights and a 0 for the absence of such provisions. Total values therefore ranged from 6 to 0, with a 6 indicating poor corporate governance and a 0 indicating good corporate governance. The authors named their index the E-Index because it was intended to measure management entrenchment. Most firms scored between 1 and 4, indicating moderately low levels of management entrenchment. The measurement period included 1990–2003, thereby taking into account both favorable and adverse stock market conditions.

The authors then applied a similar "long–short" strategy, whereby companies with low E-Index scores were purchased and companies with high E-Index scores were shorted. They found that such a strategy would have yielded average abnormal returns of nearly 7 percent per year over the measurement period. Furthermore, they found that a long–short strategy that pitted the very best E-Index companies (long = 0) against the very worst (short = 5–6) was superior to one that pitted several rankings of the best scores (long = 0–2) against several rankings of the worst (short 3–6) (see Figure 13.4).

The results of Bebchuk, Cohen, and Ferrell (2009) are also striking, and research efforts to assess their validity are mixed. Johnson, Moorman, and Sorescu (2009) argued that excess returns in the portfolio were driven by different industry composition in the long and short portfolios and not by differences in governance features. Using better-specified tests for computing excess returns that adjust for industry differences, they concluded that neither the Gompers, Ishii, and Metrick (2003) trading strategy nor the Bebchuk, Cohen, and Ferrell (2009) trading strategy produced excess returns.[20] Lewellen and Metric (2010) showed that although the trading returns vary depending on industry adjustment, the original G-Index and E-Index results remain intact.[21]

Cremers and Ferrell (2014) found mixed evidence that the G-Index and E-Index are associated with future abnormal stock returns.[22] Their results varied depending on time period considered and the specific computation used to calculate returns.

Finally, Larcker, Reiss, and Xiao (2015) found coding errors in the underlying IRRC data and definitions used to produce E-Index and G-Index scores (such as the definition of golden parachutes and the method for measuring supermajority requirements for changing corporate bylaws and charters). After correcting errors and refining the variable definitions to conform to contemporary legal thinking, the trading strategy returns reported by Bebchuk, Cohen, and Ferrell (2009) are substantially reduced and in many cases no longer statistically significant.[23]

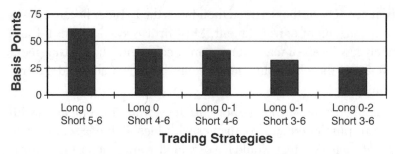

Monthly abnormal returns: baseline model, equally weighted portfolios.

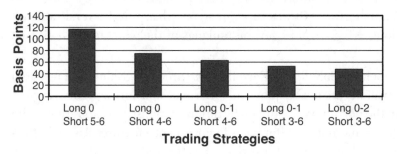

Monthly abnormal returns: baseline model, value-weighted portfolios.

Source: Bebchuk, Cohen, and Ferrell (2009).

Figure 13.4   E-Index.

All in all, definitive conclusions have not been reached about the predictive ability of an index composed of mostly antitakeover provisions on future firm performance.

The Viability of Governance Ratings

Holding aside the mixed empirical research described in this chapter, a fundamental conceptual flaw arises with the idea of developing governance indices and ratings. Throughout this book, we have seen that although elements such as board independence, compensation structure, audit quality, and antitakeover provisions are important to governance quality, few obvious and uniform standards exist to aid in measuring these elements.[24] In certain corporate situations, one structure might be effective in decreasing agency costs, while in other situations, that same structure might impose inefficient costs that actually impair corporate performance. A ratings model built on the assumption that a single governance structure can be built as a "best practice" and then uniformly applied across firms seems likely to fail.

Instead, governance quality should be assessed on a case-by-case basis, using independent judgment and a critical understanding of how various governance structures interact to improve or detract from corporate performance. One example of how this might work is seen in the method by which Fitch Ratings incorporates governance data into its credit analysis. The firm is cognizant of the fact that corporate governance can have an important influence on the likelihood of corporate default, so it incorporates an assessment of governance quality into its credit ratings. Although the firm reviews statistical data to uncover differences between companies and flags those with potentially outsized risk, Fitch makes its ultimate evaluation using what it calls a "contextual review." This includes a "review [of] governance practices that require more qualitative analysis and cannot be readily measured in a data set (including the interplay of different practices)." Areas of particular focus are "board quality (independence and effectiveness), related party transactions, reasonableness of management compensation, integrity of audit process, executive and director stock ownership, and shareholder rights/takeover defenses." Companies with "exceptionally weak or deficient governance practices" face the risk of downgrade.[25]

That is, Fitch aims to evaluate many of the governance functions that we have discussed throughout this book, but it does so through independent analysis, not under a check-the-box methodology. The firm clearly believes that this leads to richer, more thoughtful conclusions. Investors, regulators, and other constituents with a vested interest in corporate success might benefit by adopting a similar approach.

Endnotes

1. Sharon Ou, David Chiu, Zhi Zeng, and Albert Metz, "Special Comment: Corporate Default and Recovery Rates, 1920–2013," Moody's Investors Service (February 28, 2014). Accessed April 9, 2015. See https://www.moodys.com.

2. In its marketing materials, ISS claimed that CGQ was "a reliable tool for 1) identifying portfolio risk related to governance and 2) leveraging governance to drive increased shareholder value." It also claimed, "There is no doubt that CGQ ratings could have helped some investment manager avoid the gigantic losses experienced during the corporate scandal era defined by the meltdowns at Enron, Global Crossing, and WorldCom." See Institutional Shareholder Services, "U.S. Corporate Governance Quotient Criteria." Accessed August 27, 2007. See www.issproxy. com/esg/uscgqcriteria.html. Also see Robert Daines, Ian D. Gow, and David F. Larcker, "Rating the Ratings: How Good Are Commercial Governance Ratings?" *Journal of Financial Economics* 98 (2010): 439–461.

3. Institutional Shareholder Services, "Corporate Governance Quotient." Accessed August 27, 2007. See www.issproxy.com/esg/cgq.

4. Subodh Mishra, "Governance Risk Indicators: A New Measure of Governance-Related Risk," Governance Institute and ISS (March 10, 2010). Accessed October 18, 2010. See www. riskmetrics.com/sites/default/files/ISS_GRId_Tech_Doc_20100310.pdf.

5. RiskMetrics/ISS explains: "[T]he weighting is higher in Canada (50 percent, compared with 33.3 percent for U.S. companies, of the takeover defenses subsection), reflecting the sharpened focus on Canadian issuers who elect their board through bundled or slated elections." See ibid.

6. These claims are self-contradictory. Risk and performance are related. If you can predict "investment risk," this necessarily translates into better risk-adjusted performance. See ibid.

7. ISS, "ISS Governance QuickScore: Overview," (January 2013). Accessed May 5, 2015. See http://www.issgovernance.com/governance-solutions/investment-tools-data/quickscore/.

8. GMI Ratings, "The GMI Ratings AGR Model: Measuring Accounting and Governance Risk in Public Corporations" (2013). Accessed April 10, 2015. See http://www3.gmiratings.com/wp-content/uploads/2013/11/GMIRatings_AGR3.0Whitepaper_102013.pdf.

9. Ibid.

10. Institutional Shareholder Services, American International Group, Inc. CGQ Governance Profile, shareholder meeting date May 19, 2004; most recent CGQ profile update April 30, 2004.

11. Ian McDonald and John Hechinger, "Uneasy Sits the Greenbergs' Insurance Crown: Marsh Faces Hurdles to Regain Investor Trust as It Confronts yet Another Batch of Allegations," *Wall Street Journal* (October 18, 2004, Eastern edition): C1. Theo Francis and Jonathan Weil, "AIG Could Face Criminal Charges," *Wall Street Journal* (October 22, 2004, Eastern edition): C.1.

12. Matthew Karnitschnig, Deborah Solomon, Liam Pleven, and Jon E. Hilsenrath, "U.S. to Take Over AIG in $85 Billion Bailout: Central Banks Inject Cash as Credit Dries Up; Emergency Loan Effectively Gives Government Control of Insurer; Historic Move Would Cap 10 Days That Reshaped U.S. Finance," *Wall Street Journal* (September 17, 2008, Eastern edition): A.1.

13. Stephen Taub, "Did Governance Raters Foresee Marsh, AIG?" *Compliance Week* (October 26, 2004). Accessed November 12, 2010. See https://www.complianceweek.com/news/news-article/did-governance-raters-foresee-marsh-aig.

14. As cited in Daines, Gow, Larcker (2010).

15. Richard A. Price, Nathan Y. Sharp, and David A. Wood, "Detecting and Predicting Accounting Irregularities: A Comparison of Commercial and Academic Risk Measures," *Accounting Horizons* 25 (2011): 755–780. Also see Maria M. Correia, "Political Connections and SEC Enforcement," *Journal of Accounting and Economics* 57 (2014): 241–262.

16. Daines, Gow, Larcker (2010).

17. Paul Gompers, Joy Ishii, and Andrew Metrick, "Corporate Governance and Equity Prices," *Quarterly Journal of Economics* 118 (2003): 107–155.

18. John E. Core, Wayne R. Guay, and Tjomme O. Rusticus, "Does Weak Governance Cause Weak Stock Returns? An Examination of Firm Operating Performance and Investors' Expectations," *Journal of Finance* 61 (2006): 655–687.

19. Lucian Bebchuk, Alma Cohen, and Allen Ferrell, "What Matters in Corporate Governance?" *Review of Financial Studies* 22 (2009): 783–827.

20. Shane A. Johnson, Theodore C. Moorman, and Sorin Sorescu, "A Reexamination of Corporate Governance and Equity Prices," *Review of Financial Studies* 22 (2009): 4753–4786.

21. Stefan Lewellen and Andrew Metrick, "Corporate Governance and Equity Prices: Are Results Robust to Industry Adjustments?" Unpublished working paper, Yale University (2010).

22. Martijn Cremers and Allen Ferrell. "Thirty Years of Shareholder Rights and Firm Value," *Journal of Finance* 69 (2014): 1167–1196.

23. David F. Larcker, Peter C. Reiss, and Youfei Xiao, "The Entrenchment Index and the Value of 'Corporate Governance.'" Unpublished working paper (2015).

24. Larcker, Richardson, and Tuna (2007) tested a comprehensive list of governance attributes and found no statistical relation to corporate outcomes. See David F. Larcker, Scott A. Richardson, and İrem Tuna, "Corporate Governance, Accounting Outcomes, and Organizational Performance," Accounting Review 82 (2007): 963–1008.

25. Kim Olson, "Corporate Governance from the Bondholder's Perspective: Measurement and Analytical Considerations," *Fitch Ratings* (February 9, 2005).

14 ———————————————————

Alternative Models of Governance

In this book, we have primarily limited ourselves to an examination of the governance practices of publicly traded corporations. Many features of this system are imposed on the firm either by legislative, regulatory, and listing requirements or by market pressures exerted by public shareholders and other providers of capital.

In this chapter, we consider four alternative models of governance: those adopted by family-controlled businesses, venture-backed companies, private equity–owned companies, and nonprofit organizations. Each of these types of organizations must deal with its own set of challenges related to ownership, control, and purpose. As a result, the solutions they elect are somewhat different from those discussed throughout this book and provide a useful contrast for stakeholders in public and private organizations alike.

Family-Controlled Corporations

Family-controlled corporations are those in which a founder or founding-family member maintains a presence in the firm as a shareholder, director, or manager. The level of control that the founder or family exerts varies based on ownership level, voting rights, and personal involvement at the managerial or board levels.

According to research by McKinsey & Co., family-controlled businesses account for a large portion of global economic production, approximately 70 to 90 percent of gross domestic product. While the majority of family-controlled businesses are private, several publicly traded corporations exist. Approximately one-third of the Fortune Global 500 companies are founder- or family-controlled. Family control among large corporations is highest in emerging markets (60 percent). However, even in developed economies such as Europe, family control over large corporations remains high (40 percent).[1]

In the United States, family control is lower, although still significant. Founding families are present at the management or board level in approximately one-third of

S&P 500 companies and hold 18 percent of outstanding equity.[2] The largest family-controlled corporations by revenue—both public and private firms—include Wal-Mart, Ford Motor Company, Cargill, and Koch Industries (see Table 14.1).[3]

Table 14.1 Largest Family Businesses in the United States

Company	Industry	Public/Private	Revenue	Controlling Family
Wal-Mart	Retail	Public	$421.9 billion	Walton
Ford Motor	Automotive	Public	$129.0 billion	Ford
Cargill	Commodities	Private	$107.9 billion	Cargill/MacMillan
Koch Industries	Diversified	Private	$100 billion	Koch
Carlson Companies	Hospitality	Private	$38 billion	Carlson
Comcast	Media	Public	$37.9 billion	Roberts
News Corp	Media	Public	$33.4 billion	Murdoch
HCA Holdings	Hospital management	Public	$31.5 billion	Frist
Bechtel Group	Engineering and construction	Private	$30.8 billion	Bechtel
Mars	Food	Private	$30 billion	Mars

Source: Karlee Weinmann and Aimee Groth, "The 10 Largest Family Businesses in the U.S," Business Insider (November 17, 2011).

Several reasons exist why family-controlled businesses might have lower agency problems than a typical public corporation. Founders and founding-family members tend to have a large financial stake, lessening the divide between ownership and control that is central to agency risks. In addition, they tend to have a personal stake in the company (some see it as their "legacy") and are concerned with its performance beyond their tenure. As such, founders and founding-family members might exert more vigilant oversight over management, strategy, and risk; design more rational compensation packages; and encourage a focus on long-term performance.

On the other hand, family ownership can be negative if family members use the corporation to extract private benefits or seek to influence outcomes beyond their legal voting rights. We saw evidence that this occurs in some large, family-controlled pyramidal business groups in emerging economies, particularly those where capital markets are underdeveloped (see Chapter 2, "International Corporate Governance"). Furthermore, the concentration of family wealth in one company might make controlling members risk-averse and therefore less willing to pursue promising but risky investment that can contribute to long-term value creation.

Research evidence illustrates both positive and negative aspects of family control. Anderson and Reeb (2003) found that family firms perform better than nonfamily firms and that performance improves further when the family member serves as CEO.

They attributed the results in part to family members viewing themselves as "stewards of the firm." They concluded that "in well-regulated and transparent markets, family ownership in public firms reduces agency problems without leading to severe loss in decision-making efficiency."[4] Fahlenbrach (2009) found that companies controlled by a founder-CEO invest more in research and development, have higher capital expenditures, and make more focused mergers and acquisitions. He also found that they exhibit superior long-term stock price performance.[5]

Villalonga and Amit (2006) found that the presence of the founding family has a positive impact on firm value when the *founder* serves as chairman or CEO but a negative impact when a *descendent* of the founder serves in one of these roles. That is, the nature of the agency problem might depend on the relationship between the family member and the firm.[6]

Research by McKinsey & Co. suggests that family ownership contributes positively to firm culture. They found that 90 percent of nonfamily managers report that family values are present in the organization, and 70 percent believe these values are part of day-to-day operations. Among family businesses, top management rate their personal sense of "emotional ownership" of the company 4.1 on a scale of 1 to 5. McKinsey found that family firms also rank highly on worker motivation and leadership.[7] Consistent with this, Mueller and Philippon (2011) found that family-controlled businesses have better labor relations, in part because management is in a position to make credible long-term promises.[8]

Somewhat surprisingly, evidence suggests that family-controlled businesses are not well prepared for management succession. PricewaterhouseCoopers (2014) found that 44 percent of private family businesses have no succession plan in place. Among those that do, only 30 percent report that their succession plan is robust and well-documented.[9] Pérez-González (2006) found that family businesses make worse succession decisions and that firms where the incoming CEO is related to the founder or to a large shareholder by blood or by marriage exhibit worse future operating performance.[10]

Finally, the research evidence on financial reporting quality and transparency among family-controlled businesses is mixed. Ali, Chen, and Radhakrishnan (2007) found that family-controlled firms report higher-quality earnings and are more likely to warn about an earnings downturn. They concluded that this is "consistent with the notion that, compared to nonfamily firms, family firms face less severe agency problems, leading to less opportunistic behavior in terms of withholding bad news."[11] Wang (2006) also found that family ownership is associated with higher earnings quality.[12] By contrast, Anderson, Duru, and Reeb (2009) found that family-controlled companies have less transparent disclosure and exploit this opacity to extract private benefits at the expense of minority shareholders.[13] Similarly, Anderson, Reeb, and

Zhao (2012) found that inside executives within family-controlled firms are more likely to take advantage of private information and sell shares prior to the announcement of negative news than those within nonfamily firms.[14] To this same end, Lins, Volpin, and Wagner (2013) found that family firms responded to the financial crisis of 2008–2009 by taking actions to preserve family control over the organization, even though these moves were detrimental to minority shareholders.[15]

Given the inconsistent evidence, it might be the case that the personal attributes of family members determine whether they are more or less likely to engage in self-interested behavior that is harmful to outside shareholders.

Venture-Backed Companies

Venture-backed companies are small, high-growth companies that rely on venture capital firms for initial and early-stage equity financing. Venture-backed companies tend to cluster in rapidly changing industries—such as technology, life sciences, and alternative energy—where potential returns and the likelihood of failure are high. Because of their risk, venture-backed companies in their early stages lack access to common sources of financing—such as bank loans and other public or private debt and equity—and instead turn to venture capital firms that specialize in high-risk investing. The venture capital firm reduces its own risk exposure by investing in a diversified portfolio of such companies with the expectation that a few highly successful investments will offset losses in other parts of its portfolio and result in an appropriate risk-adjusted return.

Venture capital firms receive their capital from institutional and retail investors. The venture capital firm establishes a limited partnership, with its investors as limited partners and the firm itself as general partner. A venture capital firm typically manages multiple funds (or portfolios) simultaneously, each with a 10-year average life. Investments are made in the first few years following the establishment of the fund, and capital is returned to the investor when portfolio companies are acquired or go public in an initial public offering (IPO). The venture capital firm receives in compensation a percentage of the profits generated (typically 20 percent), known as "carried interest."

According to the National Venture Capital Association (NVCA), more than 800 venture capital firms operated in 2013, up from 370 two decades prior. Venture capital firms managed a combined $193 billion, and the average fund size was $110 million (see Table 14.2).[16]

Table 14.2 Venture Capital Summary Statistics

	1993	2003	2013
Number of VC firms	370	951	874
Number of VC funds raising money this year	93	160	187
VC capital raised this year ($ billions)	4.5	9.1	16.8
VC capital under management ($ billions)	29.3	263.9	192.9
Average VC fund size to date ($ millions)	40.2	94.4	110.3
VC investments by stage (based on capital invested)			
Seed	17.2%	1.9%	3.3%
Early stage	15.7%	18.3%	33.5%
Expansion	51.0%	49.7%	33.2%
Later stage	16.1%	30.1%	30.0%
Percentage of IPOs that are VC-backed	N/A	37.1%	47.9%

Source: Thomson Reuters, "2014 National Venture Capital Association Yearbook," National Venture Capital Association (March 2014).

Data demonstrates the high-risk nature of venture capital investing. According to the NVCA, only 14 percent of nearly 11,700 venture-backed companies first funded between 1991 and 2000 eventually went public, 33 percent were acquired, 18 percent are known to have failed, and 35 percent are still private or of unknown status.[17]

The unique nature of venture capital investing influences the governance choices of venture-backed firms. Venture-backed firms tend to be tightly controlled by their funders. A typical venture-backed company has a median board size of four, two of whom are members of the venture capital firm. Only 15 percent of the time does the CEO also serve as chairman.[18]

The boards of venture-backed companies are less independent than is the board of a typical publicly traded corporation. Immediately prior to IPO, only 56 percent of venture-backed company directors are independent. Many venture-backed companies do not convene formal audit, compensation, or nominating and governance committees until the period leading up to an IPO. Even then, when these committees are first established, they generally are not fully or majority independent.[19] (We expect this because they are privately held, and all major shareholders have board representation.)

Compensation among venture-backed companies is heavily weighted toward equity-based awards. According to Compensia, 97 percent of high-growth technology companies award their executives and employees stock options, and 85 percent offer restricted stock. On average, 21 percent of shares are available for future award under equity-based compensation plans, representing a considerable level of dilution ("stock overhang").[20] Immediately prior to IPO, the venture capital firm owns 54 percent of the total equity outstanding, the CEO 15 percent, the top five managers 26 percent, and total directors and officers 63 percent.[21]

Finally, venture-backed companies remain tightly "controlled" even following an IPO. Venture capital–backed firms are characterized by a high number of antitakeover protections. A 2015 study by law firm Proskauer found that 77 percent of newly issued IPO companies have a staggered board, 15 percent have multiple classes of stock, 66 percent restrict shareholder access by written consent, 69 percent restrict shareholder rights to call a special meeting, and 72 percent have supermajority voting requirements.[22] This raises questions about potential agency conflicts between equity holders and managers in newly listed venture-backed firms.

Research suggests that venture capital firms generally have a positive influence on the governance choices of their portfolio companies. Hellman and Puri (2002) found that venture capital companies contribute to the professionalization of startup companies. Venture-backed companies are more likely to replace the founder with an outside CEO. They are also more likely to introduce employee stock option plans and influence human resource policies, including recruitment and selection practices.[23] Celikyurt, Sevilir, and Shivdasani (2014) found that companies that retain members of the venture capitalist firm on the board post-IPO are characterized by higher levels of research and development investment, innovation, and deal activity. They concluded that venture capitalists "play a significant role in mature public firms and have a broad influence in promoting innovation."[24] Hochberg (2012) found that venture-backed firms have lower levels of earnings management.[25] Despite the prevalence of antitakeover protections among venture-backed companies, Daines and Klausner (2001) found no evidence that these protections are adopted to entrench management. Instead, they are most commonly adopted among companies "where the firm's investments are relatively transparent, information asymmetries less likely, and where bidder competition is most likely to provide a target with bargaining power."[26] It might be that antitakeover protections are adopted at IPO to preserve preexisting commitments and long-term business relationships.[27]

Furthermore, research indicates that governance quality and company performance are positively associated with the reputation of the firm that provides venture funding. In an examination of startup companies that received first-round funding, Wongsunwai (2007) found that companies backed by top-quartile venture capital firms subsequently had larger, more independent boards and greater venture capital firm involvement at the board level. Among a subset of companies that reached IPO, those backed by top-quartile venture capitalists had higher earnings quality, as measured by abnormal accruals and future restatements.[28] Similarly, Krishnan, Ivanov, Masulis, and Singh (2011) found that companies backed by high-quality venture capitalists demonstrate superior long-term operating and stock-price performance. They found that venture capitalists with the highest reputation tend to stay on the board and hold their shares longer post-IPO and that their continued involvement with the company positively influences performance.[29]

Private Equity-Owned Companies

Private equity firms are privately held investment companies that invest in businesses for the benefit of retail and institutional investors. The structure of private equity is similar to that of venture capital: The firm itself is organized as a limited liability company, while its investment capital is deployed through limited partnerships with the private equity firm acting as general partner.[30] This structure allows the private equity firm to manage multiple funds, each with its own portfolio of assets. It also allows the firm to avoid liability to creditors if an investment in one of the funds fails.

Private equity firms invest in publicly traded businesses, privately held firms, and subsidiaries spun off from larger corporations. Their targets are generally mature companies that generate substantial free cash flow to support a leveraged capital structure. After they are acquired, portfolio companies can undergo a complete change in management, board of directors, operating strategy, and capital structure. If successful, the private equity firm sells the company, either back into the public markets through an IPO or to a strategic buyer that is interested in the improved operations. The private equity firm retains a percentage of the profit in carried interest (typically 20 percent) and returns the remaining proceeds to investors.

Private equity has seen considerable growth as an asset class since the 1980s. According to data from *Private Equity Analyst*, over $1.2 trillion in capital was committed to private equity between 2000 and 2008, compared with $233 billion between 1990 and 1999 and only $48 billion between 1984 and 1989.[31]

Tables 14.3 and 14.4 provide summary statistics of private equity transactions over time. Approximately 17,000 private equity–sponsored corporate buyouts occurred globally between 1985 and 2007. Twenty-seven percent of acquisition targets are publicly traded companies, 23 percent are independent private companies, 30 percent divisions of corporations, and 20 percent secondary purchases from other private equity companies.[32]

Private equity firms invest in a company for an average of six years, at the end of which they are either sold to a strategic buyer (38 percent), financial buyer (24 percent), other private equity company (5 percent), or management (1 percent); go public (14 percent); or file for bankruptcy (6 percent).[33]

Table 14.3 Private Equity Summary Statistics

	1985–1989	1990–1994	1995–1999	2000–2004	2005–2007	1970–2007
Combined enterprise value ($ billions)	$257.2	$148.6	$553.9	$1,055.1	$1,563.3	$3,616.8
Number of transactions	642	1,123	4,348	5,673	5,188	17,171
LBOs by type:						
Public to private	49%	9%	15%	18%	34%	27%
Independent private	31%	54%	44%	19%	14%	23%
Divisional	17%	31%	27%	41%	25%	30%
Secondary	2%	6%	13%	20%	26%	20%
Distressed	0%	1%	1%	2%	1%	1%
LBOs by target location:						
United States and Canada	87%	72%	60%	44%	47%	52%
United Kingdom	7%	13%	16%	17%	15%	15%
Western Europe	3%	13%	20%	32%	30%	26%
Asia and Australia	3%	1%	2%	4%	6%	4%
Rest of the world	0%	2%	2%	3%	3%	3%

Data for 2007 represents a partial year (through June 30). LBOs by type and location calculated as a percent of combined enterprise value.

Source: Kaplan and Strömberg (2008).

Table 14.4 Exit Characteristics of Leveraged Buyouts

	1985–1989	1990–1994	1995–1999	2000–2002	2003–2004	2004–2006	1970–2007
Type of exit:							
Bankruptcy	6%	5%	8%	6%	3%	3%	6%
IPO	25%	23%	11%	9%	11%	1%	14%
Sold to strategic buyer	35%	38%	40%	37%	40%	34%	38%
Sold to financial buyer	13%	17%	23%	31%	31%	17%	24%
Sold to LBO-backed firm	3%	3%	5%	6%	7%	19%	5%
Sold to management	1%	1%	2%	2%	1%	1%	1%
Other or unknown	18%	12%	11%	10%	7%	24%	11%
% of deals exited within:							
2 years	12%	14%	13%	9%	13%		12%
5 years	40%	53%	41%	40%			42%
6 years	48%	63%	49%	49%			51%
7 years	58%	70%	56%	55%			58%
10 years	75%	82%	73%				76%

Data for 2007 represents a partial year (through June 30).

Source: Kaplan and Strömberg (2008).

Private equity deals are known for their leverage. Leverage is used to increase returns on invested capital and reduce taxes. (For this reason, some critics of private equity refer to their activities as "financial engineering.") Based on a sample of buyouts of previously publicly traded companies, Guo, Hotchkiss, and Song (2011) calculated that the average debt-to-capital ratio of a target company nearly triples post-acquisition, from 25 percent to 71 percent. Leverage is achieved through a mix of public, private, and bank debt.[34]

Because private equity–backed companies are not publicly traded, they are not required to adopt the governance standards of the New York Stock Exchange. As a result, their governance structure tends to be very different from that of a publicly traded corporation. The board of directors is relatively small (five to seven individuals). The composition of the board is heavily represented by insiders (executives of the portfolio company and members of the private equity firm) that own a majority of the firm. The private equity partners are closely involved in strategic and operating matters, and the focus of board meetings is on business, financial, and risk-management issues more than compliance and regulatory issues.

Survey data suggests that a directorship at a private equity–owned portfolio company requires a significantly greater time commitment than at a publicly owned corporation. According to one report, the average private equity director spends nearly three times the number of hours in his or her role as a public company director—54 days versus 19 days per year, on average.[35] A private equity director also potentially adds more value. Acharya, Kehoe, and Reyner (2008) surveyed a small sample of individuals who served concurrently on the boards of a large U.K.-based corporation (in the FTSE 100 or FTSE 250 Index) and a private equity–owned company. Three-quarters believed that private equity boards added more value; none reported that public boards did. On average, they rated private equity boards more effective at strategic leadership, performance management, and stakeholder management; they rated public boards more effective in succession planning and governance (audit, compliance, and risk management).[36]

Executive compensation in private equity is also larger and more heavily weighted toward equity incentives. Leslie and Oyer (2009) found that the CEOs of private equity–owned companies receive almost twice the equity, 10 percent lower salary, but more cash compensation, including bonus, than their counterparts at comparable public corporations.[37] Cronqvist and Fahlenbrach (2013) examined how CEO compensation changes among a sample of companies that transition from public to private ownership. They found that base salary and annual cash bonus increase and that the CEO's equity stake in the company approximately doubles. Performance targets are redesigned away from qualitative and nonfinancial performance measures to profitability measures.[38]

A survey of mid-sized private equity–owned companies also illustrates the heavy use of equity compensation. PricewaterhouseCoopers (2013) found that a typical portfolio company CEO holds approximately 2 percent of the company's equity on a fully diluted basis. The next four most highly compensated executives hold an additional 2.9 percent combined. Twenty-one percent of shares are kept in reserve for future grant. Equity grants comprise a mix of performance and time-vested awards—typically in a ratio of two-to-one. Performance awards are contingent upon exit multiples, internal rates of return upon exit, and financial targets.[39]

Research demonstrates that private equity companies are successful in generating large returns. However, it is not clear the extent to which returns are driven by operating improvements rather than leverage and tax reduction, nor is it clear how private and public equity returns compare on a risk-adjusted basis.

Phalippou and Gottschalg (2009) calculated that private equity investments produce a risk-adjusted return net-of-fees 6 percent per year below that of the S&P 500.[40] By contrast, Harris, Jenkinson, and Kaplan (2014) found that private equity funds outperform the S&P 500 by 3 percent annually.[41]

Guo, Hotchkiss, and Song (2011) found that leverage accounts for a significant portion of private equity returns.[42] Acharya, Gottschalg, Hahn, and Kehoe (2013) found that private equity investments outperform public benchmarks even after controlling for leverage and that private equity–owned companies exhibit better sales growth and margin expansion than publicly traded peers. They also found some evidence that the nature of improvement is related to the skills and background of the lead deal partner.[43] Davis, Haltiwanger, Handley, Jarmin, Lerner, and Miranda (2014) found that in the manufacturing sector, private equity owners more aggressively redirect investment from less-productive to more-productive plants. They calculated that while legacy plants exhibit a higher rate of job loss than peers, private equity owners invest more aggressively in new operations and that, in aggregate, they create more jobs than they eliminate. The authors concluded that they see "private equity as agents of change in the sense that buyouts accelerate retrenchments at some target firms, while accelerating expansion at others."[44] Still, the research on private equity remains mixed.

Nonprofit Organizations

A nonprofit organization is an organization that is tax-exempt under rule 501(c) of the Internal Revenue Code. Approximately 1.5 million nonprofits operate today in a wide range of activities that include education, social and legal services, arts and culture, health services, civic and fraternal organizations, and religious organizations; labor unions; and business and professional associations. In 2012, nonprofit organizations reported aggregate revenues of $1.6 trillion and assets of $4.8 trillion (see Table 14.5). Charities related to health, education, and human services (for example, those that provide food, shelter, and assistance) are the most numerous and largest by revenues and assets; religious and educational institutions receive the largest share of total donations (see Table 14.6).[45]

Table 14.5   Nonprofit Organizations in the U.S.

	2002	**2012**
Number of registered nonprofits	1.32 million	1.44 million
Financial information:		
Revenues	$1.24 trillion	$2.16 trillion
Expenses	$1.22 trillion	$2.03 trillion
Assets	$3.12 trillion	$4.84 trillion
Number of public charities, 501(c)(3)	0.7 million	1.0 million
Financial information:		
Revenues	$0.91 trillion	$1.65 trillion
Expenses	$0.88 trillion	$1.56 trillion
Assets	$1.64 trillion	$2.99 trillion

Does not include organizations that are not registered with the Internal Revenue Service, such as religious congregations and nonprofits with annual revenue less than $5,000. Financial data is provided for nonprofits required to file Form-990 with the IRS, approximately 35 percent of registered organizations.

Source: McKeever and Pettijohn (October 2014).

Table 14.6   Nonprofit Organizations by Count and Activity

	By Count	**By Revenues**	**By Assets**	**By Contributions**
Breakdown of public charities				
Arts, culture, and humanities	9.9%	1.9%	3.5%	5.0%
Education	17.1%	17.2%	30.3%	15.5%
Environment and animals	4.5%	0.9%	1.3%	2.9%
Health	13.0%	59.3%	42.8%	9.5%
Human services	35.5%	12.5%	10.5%	12.4%
International and foreign affairs	2.1%	1.8%	1.0%	4.5%
Public and social benefit	11.6%	5.6%	9.5%	7.1%
Religion-related	6.1%	0.8%	1.1%	31.5%
Foundations and other	°	°	°	11.8%

Data for 2012 except charitable contributions, which are for 2013. Foundations are not reported as a separate category in columns labeled with an (*).

Source: McKeever and Pettijohn (2014).

Nonprofits are granted tax-exempt status by the U.S. government to encourage the pursuit of charitable and social activities unrelated to commerce.[46] As such, they have a stakeholder—rather than shareholder—orientation, and this influences their governance system.

The board of directors (or board of trustees) is responsible for oversight of the organization, including reviewing strategy, finances, and performance; hiring and firing the CEO; and setting compensation. They are also subject to the same duties of care and loyalty that govern public company boards. Because nonprofits are stakeholder oriented, the board must establish the metrics by which organizational success is measured. While financial measures play a role in organizational success, the board must determine nonfinancial and qualitative measures to assess whether the organization is meeting its mission.

The board tends to be larger than the average for-profit board: approximately 16 members compared with 12. Board members meet 7 times per year. Nonprofit boards have greater female representation but not a considerably different racial mix. The CEO rarely serves as dual chairman, doing so only 3 percent of the time. The CEO sits on the board only 54 percent of the time, often as a nonvoting member. Most directors are not compensated for their service. Most nonprofits require that board members make personal donations, and a significant number (42 percent) require that directors personally solicit funds on behalf of the organization. The policy of requiring directors to donate or raise money is known as a "give or get" policy.[47] (See Table 14.7 for summary statistics on nonprofit boards. We provided comparable data for for-profit boards in Chapter 5, "Board of Directors: Structure and Consequences.")

Considerable board work takes place at the committee level. The average board maintains between five and six standing committees, and these may include an executive committee (which generally meets prior to full board meetings to review major issues and make preliminary decisions); a fundraising committee; a finance and/or audit committee; a governance/nominating committee; and committees for programs, marketing, and strategy. Of note, nonprofit boards typically do not have a compensation committee.

Table 14.7 Nonprofit Board Structure and Practices

Board Structure Attribute	2012
Number of voting members	16.2
Meetings per year	7.1
Gender breakdown:	
Male	55%
Female	45%

Racial composition:	
African American	8%
Asian American	3%
Caucasian	82%
Hispanic	3%
Other or mix	5%
Average number of committees	5.5
Committees:	
Executive committee	79%
Fundraising/development	46%
Finance/audit	
Combined finance/audit	46%
Audit standalone	26%
Finance standalone	37%
Governance/nominating	
Combined governance/nominating	38%
Nominating standalone	29%
Program	27%
Marketing/communications	23%
Planning/strategy	23%
Board compensation:	
Fee or honorarium	3%
Reimburse for travel and expenses	26%
Board requires personal donation	75%
Board requires directors to solicit donations	42%
CEO role on board:	
Chairman	3%
Voting member	14%
Nonvoting member	40%
Not on board	46%

Sample includes organizations with a median operating budget in excess of $1 million.

Source: BoardSource (September 2012).

Executive compensation among nonprofit organizations is significantly lower than among for-profit companies. According to a survey of approximately 4,000 mid-sized and large charities, the CEO earned median compensation of $130,400 in 2012. The maximum compensation awarded among the sample that year was $3.7 million. Compensation is highest among nonprofits involved in arts, culture, and education and lowest among religious-based organizations.[48]

Nonprofits are not subject to the audit and internal control requirements of the Sarbanes–Oxley Act. As such, the board of directors must determine whether to conduct an audit and the level of internal controls required to safeguard funds. In some cases, external stakeholders—such as a government agency providing grant money—require audited financials.

Survey data suggest that nonprofits face several governance-related challenges. A survey by BoardSource (2012) found that most nonprofits operate with a board of directors that is not fully staffed: 46 percent of respondents report that they are currently recruiting between one and three members, 26 percent between four and six members, and 5 percent more than six members; only 23 percent report being fully staffed. A significant minority (47 percent) report that it is difficult to recruit new members.[49]

A survey by the Rock Center for Corporate Governance at Stanford University, BoardSource, and GuideStar (2015) found that many board members do not fully understand their obligations as directors. [50] Directors place considerable emphasis on their fundraising obligations and significant minorities do not fully understand the strategy, mission, or performance of their organization. For this reason, some experts recommend that nonprofits adopt a bifurcated board structure, in which fiduciary oversight and fundraising obligations are separated.[51] The survey also found that many nonprofits lack formal governance processes. Forty-two percent do not have an audit committee, 69 percent do not have a succession plan in place for the current CEO, and 36 percent never perform board evaluations.

Research demonstrates that governance quality varies across organizations. Aggarwal, Evans, and Nanda (2012) found that board size is positively associated with the complexity of the organization and the number of programs it pursues. Furthermore, they found that increasing complexity is associated with worse CEO pay-for-performance sensitivity and, in some areas, worse organizational performance.[52] O'Regan and Oster (2005) found that board size and executive director control (indicated by the power to nominate board members) are positively associated with organizational performance. Long-tenured directors and directors on multiple boards are also associated with positive performance. These suggest informational benefits of greater board experience.[53]

Baber, Daniel, and Roberts (2002) found that managerial compensation among nonprofits is positively associated with total revenues and program spending, indicating that boards give management incentive to grow the size of the organization.[54] Frumkin and Keating (2010) found no association between compensation and donation revenue but did find a negative association between compensation and the administrative expense ratio, suggesting that nonprofit executives are given incentives to reduce administrative costs.[55] Little research exists to explain whether or how nonprofits rely on nonfinancial performance metrics to set compensation or monitor performance. Given the paucity of information on nonfinancial performance metrics among nonprofits, it is unlikely that they are widely used to evaluate the executive director; if they are used, it is likely that they are used informally.

Finally, research suggests that nonprofits with weaker controls and governance mechanisms are more likely to exhibit agency problems. Core, Guay, and Verdi (2006) found that nonprofits holding "excess" endowment funds (funds larger than are necessary to finance current and future expenses) are subject to greater agency problems; they spend a lower percentage of funds on direct program costs and pay higher compensation to the CEO, officers, and board members.[56] Krishnan, Yetman, and Yetman (2006) found that many nonprofits systematically understate fundraising costs and that in cases where this occurs, management incentives encourage understatement. They found that the use of an outside accountant reduces the likelihood of misreporting.[57] Similarly, Krishnan and Yetman (2011) found that nonprofit hospitals that receive higher donations revenue are more likely to shift costs away from administrative categories in order to appear more efficient.[58]

Petrovits, Shakespeare, and Shih (2011) found that nonprofits with weak internal controls receive lower future support from donors.[59] Yermack (2015) found that donors react to weak governance oversight by adding restrictions to gifts.[60] Harris, Petrovits, and Yetman (2015) found that donation revenue and government grants are positively associated with visible indicators of governance quality, including formal written policies such as a conflict-of-interest policy, independent audits and an audit committee, an independent board, and accessible financial information. They comment that "mandatory disclosure of governance policies of nonprofit organizations provides an interesting contrast to mandatory adoption of governance policies for publicly traded companies."[61]

Endnotes

1. McKinsey & Company, "Perspectives on Founder- and Family-Owned Businesses" (October 2014). Accessed April 11, 2015. See Perspectives_on_founder_and_family-owned_businesses. pdf.

2. Ashiq Ali, Tai-Yuan Chen, and Suresh Radhakrishnan, "Corporate Disclosures by Family Firms," *Journal of Accounting and Economics* 44 (2007): 238–286. Also see Ronald C. Anderson and David M. Reeb, "Founding-Family Ownership and Firm Performance: Evidence from the S&P 500," *The Journal of Finance* 58 (2003): 1301–1328.

3. Karlee Weinmann and Aimee Groth, "The 10 Largest Family Businesses in the U.S.," *Business Insider* (November 17, 2011).

4. Anderson and Reeb (2003).

5. Rüdiger Fahlenbrach, "Founder-CEOs, Investment Decisions, and Stock Market Performance," *Journal of Financial and Quantitative Analysis* 44 (2009): 439–466.

6. Belen Villalonga and Raphael Amit, "How Do Family Ownership, Control, and Management Affect Firm Value?" *Journal of Financial Economics* 80 (2006): 385–417.

7. McKinsey & Company (2014). Also see "Business in the Blood," *The Economist* 413 (November 2014): 59–63.

8. Holger M. Mueller and Thomas Philippon, "Family Firms and Labor Relations," *American Economic Journal: Macroeconomics* 3 (2011): 218–245.

9. PricewaterhouseCoopers LLC, "Up Close and Professional: The Family Factor Global Family Business Survey (2014). Accessed October 30, 2014. See www.pwc.com/familybusinesssurvey.

10. Francisco Pérez-González, "Inherited Control and Firm Performance," *American Economic Review* 96 (2006): 1559–1588.

11. Ali, Chen, and Radhakrishnan (2007).

12. Dechun Wang, "Founding Family Ownership and Earnings Quality," *Journal of Accounting Research* 44 (2006): 619–656.

13. Ronald C. Anderson, Augustine Duru, David M. Reeb, "Founders, Heirs, and Corporate Opacity in the United States," *Journal of Financial Economics* 92 (2009): 205–222.

14. Ronald C. Anderson, David M. Reeb, and Wanli Zhao, "Family-Controlled Firms and Informed Trading: Evidence from Short Sales," *Journal of Finance* 67 (2012): 351–386.

15. Karl V. Lins, Paolo Volpin, and Hannes F. Wagner, "Does Family Control Matter? International Evidence from the 2008–2009 Financial Crisis," *Review of Financial Studies* 26 (2013): 2583–2619.

16. Thomson Reuters, "2014 National Venture Capital Association Yearbook," NVCA (March 2014). Accessed April 12, 2015. See http://nvca.org/research/stats-studies/.

17. Ibid.

18. Wan Wongsunwai, "Does Venture Capitalist Quality Affect Corporate Governance?" Working paper (February 4, 2007). Accessed April 12, 2015. See http://www.gsb.stanford.edu/sites/default/files/documents/WanWongsunwai_VCqualityandCG_Feb2007.pdf.

19. PricewaterhouseCoopers LLC, "Governance for Companies Going Public What Works Best" (2013). Accessed April 12, 2015. See http://www.pwc.com/us/en/transaction-services/publications/companies-going-public.jhtml.

20. Compensia, "Bay Area 150: Equity Compensation Practices" (October 2009). Accessed April 12, 2015. See http://www.compensia.com/surveys/BayArea150_Equity_1009.pdf.

21. Robert Daines and Michael Klausner, "Do IPO Charters Maximize Firm Value? Antitakeover Protection in IPOs," *Journal of Law, Economics, and Organization* 17 (2001): 83–120.

22. Proskauer LLP, "2015 IPO Study" (March 17, 2015). Accessed April 13, 2015. See http://www.proskauer.com/publications/special-report/proskauers-exclusive-study-analyzes-2014-ipos-03-17-2015/.

23. Thomas Hellmann and Manju Puri, "Venture Capital and the Professionalization of Start-Up Firms: Empirical Evidence," *Journal of Finance* 57 (2002): 169–197.

24. Ugur Elikyurt, Merih Sevilir, and Anil Shivdasani, "Venture Capitalists on Boards of Mature Public Firms," *Review of Financial Studies* 27 (2014): 56–101.

25. Yael V. Hochberg, "Venture Capital and Corporate Governance in the Newly Public Firm," *Review of Finance* 16 (2012): 429–480.

26. Daines and Klausner (2001).

27. Michael Klausner, "Fact and Fiction in Corporate Law and Governance," *Stanford Law Review* 65 (2013). Accessed May 6, 2015. See http://ssrn.com/abstract=2297640. Also see William C. Johnson, Jonathan M. Karpoff, and Sangho Yi, "The Bonding Hypothesis of Takeover Defenses: Evidence from IPO Firms," *Journal of Financial Economics* (2015). Accessed May 6, 2015. See http://ssrn.com/abstract=1923667.

28. Wongsunwai (2007).

29. C. N. V. Krishnan, Vladimir I. Ivanov, Ronald W. Masulis, and Ajai K. Singh, "Venture Capital Reputation, Post-IPO Performance, and Corporate Governance," *Journal of Financial and Quantitative Analysis* 46 (2011): 1295–1333.

30. Two exceptions are Blackstone and KKR, which are publicly traded; their investments are still made through limited partnerships.

31. Private Equity Analyst data. See http://dowjones.com/privateequityventurecapital/product-pea.asp. As cited in Robert S. Harris, Tim Jenkinson, and Steven N. Kaplan, "Private Equity Performance: What Do We Know?" *Journal of Finance* 69 (2014): 1851–1882.

32. Steven N. Kaplan and Per Strömberg, "Leveraged Buyouts and Private Equity," *Journal of Economic Perspectives* 22 (2008): 1–27.

33. Ibid.

34. Shourun Guo, Edith S. Hotchkiss, and Weihong Song, "Do Buyouts (Still) Create Value?" *Journal of Finance* 66 (2011): 479–517.

35. Viral Acharya, Conor Kehoe, and Michael Reyner, "Governance and Value Creation: Evidence from Private Equity," McKinsey & Company (January 2, 2009). As cited in Fir M. Geenen and Sohail Malad, "Corporate Governance and Value Creation: Private Equity Style," Harlingwood Equity Partners (November 2009). Accessed April 13, 2015. See http://www.harlingwood.com/docs/corporate_governance and_value_ceation.pdf.

36. Viral Acharya, Conor Kehoe, and Michael Reyner, "The Voice of Experience: Public versus Private Equity," *The McKinsey Quarterly* (December 2008). Accessed April 13, 2015. See http://www.mckinsey.com/insights/corporate_finance/the_voice_of_experience_public_versus_private_equity.

37. Phillip Leslie and Paul Oyer, "Managerial Incentives and Value Creation: Evidence from Private Equity," EFA 2009 Bergen Meetings Paper, *Social Science Research Network* (January 27, 2009). Accessed May 6, 2015. See http://ssrn.com/abstract=1341889.

38. Henrik Cronqvist and Rudiger Fahlenbrach, "CEO Contract Design: How Do Strong Principals Do It?" *Journal of Financial Economics* 108 (2013): 659–674.

39. PricewaterhouseCoopers LLC, "2013 Private Equity Portfolio Company Stock Compensation Survey: Driving Portfolio Company Performance in a Changing Private Equity Environment" (2013). Accessed April 12, 2015. See http://www.pwc.com/us/en/private-equity/publications/private-equity-stock-compensation-survey.jhtml.

40. Ludovic Phalippou and Oliver Gottschalg, "The Performance of Private Equity Funds," *Review of Financial Studies* 22 (2009): 1747–1776.

41. Harris, Jenkinson, and Kaplan (2014).

42. Guo, Hotchkiss, and Song (2011).

43. Viral V. Acharya, Oliver F. Gottschalg, Moritz Hahn, and Conor Kehoe, "Corporate Governance and Value Creation: Evidence from Private Equity," *Review of Financial Studies* 26 (2013): 368–402.

44. Steven J. Davis, John Haltiwanger, Kyle Handley, Ron Jarmin, Josh Lerner, and Javier Miranda, "Private Equity, Jobs, and Productivity," *American Economic Review* 104 (2014): 3956–3990.

45. Brice S. McKeever and Sarah L. Pettijohn, "The Nonprofit Sector in Brief 2014," The Urban Institute (October 2014). Accessed April 14, 2015. See http://www.urban.org/research/publication/nonprofit-sector-brief-public-charities-giving-and-volunteering-2014.

46. Nonprofit organizations are required to pay taxes on profit earned through business activities unrelated to their basic purpose (known as "unrelated business income," or UBI). They are also required to pay sales tax on applicable purchases.

47. These figures are for nonprofit organizations with a median annual operating budget of $1 million and therefore can be thought of as representative of a typical "large" organization. See BoardSource, "Nonprofit Governance Index 2012: Data Report 1, CEO Survey of BoardSource Members" (September 2012). Accessed August 18, 2014. See https://www.boardsource.org.

48. Charity Navigator, "2014 CEO Compensation Study" (October 2014). Accessed April 14, 2015. See http://www.charitynavigator.org/index.cfm?bay=studies.ceo#.VS7OGF3F-EI.

49. BoardSource (2012).

50. Stanford Graduate School of Business, Rock Center for Corporate Governance at Stanford University, BoardSource, and GuideStar, "2015 Survey on Board of Directors of Nonprofit Organizations" (April 2015). Accessed May 6, 2015. See http://www.gsb.stanford.edu/faculty-research/centers-initiatives/cgri/research/surveys.

51. Michael Klausner and Jonathan Small, "Failing to Govern?" *Stanford Social Innovation Review* 3 (2005): 42–49.

52. Rajesh K. Aggarwal, Mark E. Evans, and Dhananjay Nanda, "Nonprofit Boards: Size, Performance and Managerial Incentives," *Journal of Accounting and Economics* 53 (2012): 466–487.

53. Katherine O'Regan and Sharon M. Oster, "Does the Structure and Composition of the Board Matter? The Case of Nonprofit Organizations," *Journal of Law, Economics, and Organization* 21 (2005): 205–227.

54. William R. Baber, Patricia L. Daniel, and Andrea A. Roberts, "Compensation to Managers of Charitable Organizations: An Empirical Study of the Role of Accounting Measures of Program Activities," *Accounting Review* 77 (2002): 679–693.

55. Peter Frumkin and Elizabeth K. Keating, "The Price of Doing Good: Executive Compensation in Nonprofit Organizations," *Policy and Society* 29 (2010): 269–282.

56. John E. Core, Wayne R. Guay, and Rodrigo S. Verdi, "Agency Problems of Excess Endowment Holdings in Not-for-Profit Firms," *Journal of Accounting and Economics* 41 (2006) 307–333.

57. Ranjani Krishnan, Michelle H. Yetman, and Robert J. Yetman, "Expense Misreporting in Nonprofit Organizations," *Accounting Review* 81 (2006): 399–420.

58. Ranjani Krishnan and Michelle H. Yetman, "Institutional Drivers of Reporting Decisions in Nonprofit Hospitals," *Journal of Accounting Research* 49 (2011): 1001–1039.

59. Christine Petrovits, Catherine Shakespeare, and Aimee Shih, "The Causes and Consequences of Internal Control Problems in Nonprofit Organizations," *Accounting Review* 86 (2011): 325–357.

60. David Yermack, "Donor Governance and Financial Management in Prominent U.S. Art Museums," *Social Science Research Network* (March 28, 2015). Accessed May 6, 2015. See http://ssrn.com/abstract=2586622.

61. Erica Harris, Christine M. Petrovits, and Michelle H. Yetman, "The Effect of Nonprofit Governance on Donations: Evidence from the Revised Form 990," *Accounting Review* 90 (2015): 579–610.

15

Summary and Conclusions

In this book, we have taken a thorough and critical look at corporate governance from an organizational perspective. We started by reviewing the environment in which the organization competes to understand how legal, social, and market forces influence the control mechanisms it adopts to prevent or discourage self-interested behavior by management. Next, we introduced the board of directors and examined the structure, processes, and operations of the board. We emphasized that the qualifications and engagement of these individuals are likely the most important determinants of their ability to advise and monitor the organization.

We then explored the functional responsibilities of the board, including strategic oversight and risk management, CEO succession planning, executive compensation, accounting quality and audit, and the consideration of mergers and acquisitions. In later chapters, we examined the role of the institutional investor to understand how diverse shareholder groups and third-party proxy advisory firms influence governance choices. We ended with an assessment of commercial and academic governance ratings systems and a discussion of alternative models of governance employed by family-controlled businesses, venture-backed and private equity-owned firms, and nonprofit organizations. Throughout this book, we have attempted to discuss each topic through the lens of rigorous statistical and research analysis, supplemented by real-life examples, to arrive at informed conclusions. We hope that we have met this objective. Furthermore, we hope that, in reading this book, you have a more thorough understanding of the governance choices an organization has and the consequences of those choices for future performance and oversight.

Many of the conclusions of this book are phrased in the negative. For example, we have seen that many of the structural features of the board, such as the percentage of independent directors, have little or no relation to governance quality or firm performance. We have seen that most auditor restrictions have no impact on financial statement quality, that commercial and academic governance ratings systems largely lack predictive ability, and that regulatory requirements for many mandated governance practices have neutral or negative impacts on corporate outcomes and shareholder value.

While the lack of positive correlations may disappoint you, this has important implications for the current debate on governance and your evaluation of the types of governance systems that organizations might require. The central lessons of the book follow.

Testing Remains Insufficient

First, the lack of positive correlations suggests that most of the best practices—either those recommended by blue-ribbon commissions and high-profile experts or those required by regulators—have likely not been tested, or important influencers have not properly understood the results of those tests. We saw this clearly in the passage of both Sarbanes–Oxley and the Dodd–Frank Act, in which considerable disconfirming evidence was not considered when restrictions were placed on nonaudit services provided by the auditor (see Chapter 10, "Financial Reporting and External Audit") and greater shareholder democracy was required (see Chapter 12, "Institutional Shareholders and Activist Investors").

Instead, we share the sentiments of Myron Steel, chief justice of the Delaware Supreme Court, who wrote:

> Until I personally see empirical data that supports in a particular business sector, or for a particular corporation, that separating the chairman and CEO, majority voting, elimination of staggered boards, proxy access with limits, holding periods, and percentage of shares—until something demonstrates that one or more of those will effectively alter the quality of corporate governance in a given situation, then it's difficult to say that all, much less each, of these proposed changes are truly reform. Reform implies to me something better than you have now. Prove it, establish it, and then it may well be accepted by all of us.[1]

This standard should be a precondition to all governance changes, both those mandated by law and those voluntarily adopted. Governance changes are costly, and failed governance changes especially so. They are costly to the firm in terms of reduced decision-making quality and inefficient capital allocation, and they are costly to society in terms of reduced economic growth and value destruction for both shareholders and stakeholders. We believe that careful theoretical and empirical work can go a long way toward better understanding what works and does not work so that changes can be made in a cost-effective manner. There is no question to us that "governance matters." The fundamental challenge is to understand *when* and *how* it matters.[2]

The Current Focus Is Misdirected

Second, the lack of positive correlation signals that much of the discussion focuses on the wrong issues. As such, efforts to improve governance systems (and the regulations that tend to come with them) are likely misdirected. Instead of focusing on *features* of governance, more attention should be paid to the *functions* of governance, such as the process for identifying qualified directors and executives, strategy development, business model analysis and testing, and risk management. To illustrate this point, consider the following sets of questions:

CEO Succession

1. Does the company have a CEO succession plan in place?
2. Is the CEO succession plan operational? Have qualified internal and external candidates been identified? Does the company engage in ongoing talent development to support long-term succession needs?

Risk Management

1. Is risk management a responsibility of the full board of directors, the audit committee, or a dedicated risk committee?
2. Do the board and management understand how the various operational and financial activities of the firm work together to achieve the corporate strategy? Have they determined what events might cause one or more of these activities to fail? Have these risks been properly mitigated?

Executive Compensation

1. What is the total compensation paid to the CEO? How does this compare to the compensation paid to other named executive officers?
2. How is the compensation package expected to attract, retain, and motivate qualified executive talent? Does it provide appropriate incentive to achieve the goals set forth in the business model? What is the relationship between large changes in the company stock price and the overall wealth of the CEO? Does this properly encourage short- and long-term performance without excessive risk?

In each of these sets, the first question asks about a governance feature and the second about a governance function. A focus on the latter will almost certainly yield significantly more benefit to the organization and its stakeholders.

A mistake that many experts make is to assume that the presence of a feature necessarily implies that the function is performed properly. That is, if a succession plan is in place, the assumption is that it is a good one; if there is a risk committee, the company takes risk management seriously; if compensation is not excessive, it encourages performance. Throughout this book, we have seen clear evidence that this is not always the case. If experts and proxy advisory firms are to add any value, they should shift from a service that verifies that features are in place to one that evaluates the success of various functions. This no doubt would require a substantial increase in analytical skills and processes, but it is a shift that markets would likely value.

Important Variables Are Clearly Missing

Third, the lack of positive correlation suggests that important variables that impact governance quality have been inappropriately omitted or underemphasized in the discipline. After all, governance is an *organizational* discipline. As such, the analysis should incorporate organizational issues—such as personal and interpersonal dynamics and models of behavior, leadership, cooperation, and decision making. Without offering a comprehensive list, we believe the following elements are central to understanding how a governance system should be structured and when and where it is likely to fail:

- **Organizational design**—Is the company decentralized or centralized in structure? Have internal processes been rigorously developed, or did they evolve from historical practice?

- **Organizational culture**—Does the culture encourage individual performance or cooperation? How are successes and failures treated? Is risk-taking encouraged, tolerated, or discouraged?

- **The personality of the CEO**—Who is the CEO, and what motivates this individual? What is his or her leadership style? What are the individual's ethical standards?

- **The quality of the board**—What are the qualifications of these individuals? Why and how were they selected? Are they engaged in their responsibility, or do they approach it with a compliance-based mindset? What is their character?

As evidence, we saw throughout this book that some of these aspects appear in the literature but often peripherally and without thorough consideration. For example, an analysis of the linguistic patterns of the CEO and CFO is shown to have some relation to the probability that the company will have to restate earnings in the future (see Chapter 10). Strong leadership, clear access to information, and parameters around corporate risk taking are important in ensuring that the company develops an appropriate risk culture (see Chapter 6, "Strategy, Performance Measurement, and Risk Management"). Directors with extensive personal and professional networks facilitate the flow of information between companies. This can lead to improved decision making by both allowing for the transfer of best practices and acting as a source of important business relationships (see Chapter 5, "Board of Directors: Structure and Consequences").

We believe that these types of analyses should be pursued further and with greater rigor. Doing so will require tools and techniques across disciplines. It is a mistake to think that corporate governance can be adequately understood from a strict economic, legal, or behavioral (psychological and sociological) perspective. All of these views are necessary to understanding complex organizational systems.

Furthermore, this necessarily implies that the optimal governance system of an organization will be firm-specific and take into account its unique culture and attributes. Adopting "best practices" will likely fail because that approach attempts to reduce a complex human system into a standardized framework that does not do justice to the factors that make it successful in the first place. This explains why two companies can both succeed under very different governance structures.

Context Is Important

Finally, governance systems cannot be completely standardized because their design depends on the setting. For example, governance systems differ depending on whether you take a shareholder perspective or a stakeholder perspective of the firm, as well as the efficiency of local capital markets, quality of the legal system, and labor markets. They also differ depending on your view of the prevalence of self-interest among executives.

Consider, for example, John Bogle, founder of Vanguard, who has written about self-interested behavior among executives:

> Self-interest got out of hand. It created a bottom-line society in which success is measured in monetary terms. Dollars became the coin of the new realm. Unchecked market forces overwhelmed traditional standards of professional conduct, developed over centuries. The result is a shift from moral absolutism to moral relativism. We've moved from a society in which "there are some things that one simply does not do" to one in which "if everyone else is doing it, I can, too."[3]

The extent to which you believe this is the norm in society will have a direct impact on the extent to which you believe control mechanisms should be in place to prevent the occurrence of self-interested behavior and the rigor of those controls. Nevertheless, in the end, a balance must be struck. Excessive controls will lead to economic loss by retarding the rate of corporate activity and decision making. Lenient controls will lead to economic loss through agency costs and managerial rent extraction.

As this book demonstrates, context is critical to designing an effective corporate governance system.

Endnotes

1. Myron Steele, "Verbatim: 'Common Law Should Shape Governance,'" *NACD Directorship* (February 15, 2010). Accessed November 16, 2010. See https://www.nacdonline.org/Magazine/author.cfm?ItemNumber=9159.

2. To this end, some rules required by the Dodd–Frank Act, such as proxy access, were tossed out by U.S. courts because the SEC could not demonstrate that they were accretive to shareholders. Accessed May 5, 2015. See http://www.gelaw.com/wp-content/uploads/2011/08/Shareholder-Rights-and-Corporate-Governance-in-the-Dodd-Frank-Act.pdf.

3. John C. Bogle, "A Crisis of Ethic Proportions," *Wall Street Journal* (April 21, 2009, Eastern edition): A.19.

Index

A

AAER (Accounting and Auditing Enforcement Releases), 16

Abbott Laboratories, 249, 251

Abercrombie & Fitch, 225

abnormal accruals, 290

abnormal returns, 14

academic researchers, rating systems by, 383-388

accounting

accounting manipulation, executive equity ownership and, 257-258

AGR (Accounting and Governance Risk) scores, 291, 381

models to detect accounting manipulations, 290-292

quality, 280-282, 304

standards

GAAP (Generally Accepted Accounting Principles), 24

IASB (International Accounting Standards Board), 24-25

importance of reliable accounting standards, 25

international corporate governance, 23-26

International Financial Reporting Standard (IFRS), 24

principles-based accounting systems, 24

rules-based accounting systems, 24

Accounting and Auditing Enforcement Releases (AAER), 16

Accounting and Governance Risk (AGR) scores, 291, 381

accredited investors, 357

Ackman, William, 321

acquirers, 312

acquisitions

acquirers, 312

antitakeover protections

dual-class shares, 331-334

evaluating, 334-336

overview, 323-325

poison pills, 325-328

reasons for, 322-323

staggered boards, 328-330

state of incorporation, 330-331

attributes of acquisition targets, 316-319

friendly acquisitions, 312

hostile takeovers, 312, 321

initial and final offer premiums, 318

mergers, 312

personalities behind mergers, 315-316

private equity firms, 313-314

proxy contest, 312

reasons for, 313-314

tender offer, 312

value in acquisitions, 319-322

active advisors (outgoing CEOs), 198

active CEOs on board of directors, 82-83

active investors, 344

activist investors, 11

activist hedge funds, 357-359

defined, 344

overview, 351-352